LAWYER'S DESK BOOK

ELEVENTH EDITION

by Dana Shilling

2002 SUPPLEMENT

PRENTICE HALL

Library of Congress Cataloging-in-Publication Data

Shilling, Dana.
    Lawyer's desk book / c Dana Shilling.—11th ed.
      p. cm.
    Includes index.
    ISBN 0-13-011077-9   ISBN 0-13-042371-8 (supplement)
    1. Law—United States. 2. Practice of law—United States.

  KF386.L39 2000
  349.73—dc21   99-055711

©2002 by Prentice Hall

All rights reserved. No part of this book may be reproduced in any form or by any means, without permission in writing from the publisher.

This publication is designed to provide accurate and authoritative information in regard to the subject matter covered. It is sold with the understanding that the publisher is not engaged in rendering legal, accounting, or other professional service. If legal advice or other expert assistance is required, the services of a competent professional person should be sought.
—From the Declaration of Principles jointly adopted by a Committee of the American Bar Association and a Committee of Publishers and Associations

Printed in the United States of America

10 9 8 7 6 5 4 3 2 1

ISBN 0-13-042371-8

ATTENTION: CORPORATIONS AND SCHOOLS
Prentice Hall books are available at quantity discounts with bulk purchase for educational, business, or sales promotional use. For information, please write to: Prentice Hall Special Sales, 240 Frisch Court, Paramus, New Jersey 07652. Please supply: title of book, ISBN, quantity, how the book will be used, date needed.

PRENTICE HALL
Paramus, NJ 07652

On the World Wide Web at http://www.phdirect.com

CONTENTS

Note: Secions labeled ¶xx01 are introductions.

INTRODUCTION

This is the second Supplement to the Eleventh Edition of the *Lawyer's Desk Book*. The Eleventh Edition represents a complete rewrite and re-ordering of the material in earlier editions, in order to respond to the changes in the legal system and the practice of law.

The place of computers and the Internet in the legal system continues to grow larger in many ways: a growing role in the law office and court system, as well as an increasing domination of intellectual property issues such as copyrights (some commentators even argue that, by making access to all kinds of digital files so easy, the Internet makes copyright obsolete), trademarks (especially when used as URLs to identify Web sites), and patents (especially for business methods used online).

From now on, Supplements will cover approximately one year's developments, roughly from the end of one Supreme Court term to the end of the next.

The year 2000, after unusually exciting developments in the usually placid realm of election law, marked a transition from a Democratic to a Republican administration.

In the courts, trends included greater latitude for searches and smaller scope for class actions. The Bush administration's priorities included appointing new judges, a tax cut to stimulate the economy, and pro-business measures.

The tax cut arrived in May, 2001, in the form of EGTRA, the Economic Growth Tax Reform and Reconciliation Act of 2001. Although the bill was passed by Congress in an unusual Saturday session just before the Memorial Day recess, it was not signed by President Bush until June 6, as P.L. 107-16. This is a long, complex statute made even harder to understand by its numerous provisions for phasing in the effectiveness of changes—and phasing them out again (the entire statute sunsets on December 31, 2010, returning the Internal Revenue Code and other laws to their pre-EGTRA status quo—unless Congress adopts further tax provisions in the interim).

EGTRA contains major provisions in three areas:

- A significant tax cut (including a sure-to-be-popular "advance credit" check issued in 2001) in the form of lower tax brackets and marriage penalty relief.

- Retirement plan changes, particularly with respect to much higher amounts that can be contributed to IRAs and qualified plans; numerous provisions about 401(k) plans; enhanced options for portability between plans.
- Cuts in estate tax rates, increases in the amount exempt from estate taxation, and major changes in the way inheritors will calculate the basis of inherited assets. These changes are phased in gradually, until the estate tax itself is repealed in 2010—but only for one year, because of the sunset date of the entire EGTRA statute.

In this Supplement, there are new sections covering the major EGTRA areas. However, because it takes many years for our legal system to handle issues and controversies, there are also sections about recent developments in pre-EGTRA law. Such cases and rulings will continue for several years, overlapping with cases and rulings interpreting EGTRA.

LATE-BREAKING NEWS

The following highly significant decisions were announced after the initial copy deadline for this book. They are summarized here for your reference and will be incorporated and discussed in more detail in the next Supplement.

¶300 Employer–Employee Relations

¶310 Labor Law

The Supreme Court reversed the NLRB. The court determined that registered nurses who direct the work of non-R.N. health care employees are supervisors who exercise independent judgment. Therefore, they cannot be organized in the same bargaining unit as the non-R.N.s: *N.L.R.B. v. Kentucky River Community Care Inc.*, #99-1815, 121 S.Ct. 1861 (5/29/01).

¶355 Litigation Issues

Front pay ordered as a remedy in a discrimination suit does not fall into the category of "compensatory damages," and therefore it is not subject to the Civil Rights Act of 1991 "cap" on damages: *Pollard v. duPont*, #00-763, 121 S.Ct. 1483 (6/4/01).

¶400 Business Taxes

¶450 Corporate Tax

The product liability loss of an affiliated group of corporations must be determined as if the group were a single entity, and not on a member-by-member basis: *United Dominion Industries Inc. v. U.S.*, #00-157, 121 S.Ct. 1934 (6/4/01).

¶800 Antitrust

¶810 The Sherman Act

The D.C. Circuit upheld the finding that Microsoft engaged in monopolistic conduct—but vacated the order to break up the company. The

D.C. Circuit found that the divestiture remedy was not supported by sufficient evidence: *U.S. v. Microsoft*, 70 LW 1003 (D.C. Cir. 6/28/01).

¶1300 Intellectual Property

¶1310.11 Technology and Copyright

The Supreme Court struck down publishers' contention that articles in a collective work (e.g., a newspaper or magazine) can be placed on an online database without consent of the authors (or prior grant of electronic reproduction rights). The court did not accept the theory that inclusion in the database is merely a permissible revision of the collective work: *New York Times Co. v. Tasini*, #00-201, 69 LW 4567 (6/25/01).

¶3300 Immigration

¶3310 Visa Categories

The Supreme Court upheld 8 USC §1409(a), which makes it easier for a child born outside the United States to unmarried parents to obtain U.S. citizenship when the U.S. citizen parent is the mother rather than the father. In this reading, Equal Protection is not violated, because paternity is more difficult to prove than maternity: *Nguyen v. INS*, #99-2071, 69 LW 4438 (6/11/01).

¶3370 Removal

Although the INA allows detention of removable aliens after the 90-day statutory removal period has elapsed, indefinite detention is not permitted merely because the home country refuses to allow removal of the alien to the home country. *Zadvydas v. Davis*, #99-7791, 69 LW 4626 (6/28/01) holds that detention cannot exceed six months unless the Attorney General can rebut the alien's showing that removal is not likely within the foreseeable future.

¶3370.1 Discretionary Relief

AEDPA and IIRIRA did not completely repeal habeas jurisdiction pursuant to 28 USC §2241. Therefore, a habeas petition can be heard in a case seeking discretionary relief from deportation under INA §212(c): *I.N.S. v. St. Cyr*, #00-767, 69 LW 4510 (6/25/01) and *Calcano-Martinez v. I.N.S.*, #00-1011, 69 LW 4526 (6/26/01).

¶5000 Federal Civil Procedure

¶5600 Appeals

When a Court of Appeals reviews a District Court as to whether the lower court's punitive damage award was constitutional, the standard of review is de novo, not whether the lower court abused its discretion: *Cooper Industries Inc. v. Leatherman Tool Group Inc.*, #99-2035, 121 S.Ct. 1678 (5/14/01).

¶6000 Criminal Law

¶6002 Substantive Criminal Law

The Supreme Court rejected a "medical necessity" defense to the Federal Controlled Substances Act, 21 USC §841(a)(1). The court found that Congress has determined that marijuana does not offer medical benefits: *U.S. v. Oakland Cannabis Buyers' Cooperative*, #00-151, 121 S.Ct. 1711 (5/14/01).

¶6005 Defenses

It is permissible, and not a denial of due process, to give retroactive application to a state's abolition of a common-law rule (making it possible to convict a defendant of murder even though the victim did not die within one year of the attack): *Rogers v. Tennessee*, #99-6218, 121 S.Ct. 1693 (5/14/01).

¶6020.10 RICO

A sole owner can be held liable under RICO (as a separate "person") for unlawful conduct of corporate affairs, as can an employee acting in the scope of employment: *Cedric Kushner Promotions Ltd. v. King*, #00-549, 121 S.Ct. 2087 (6/11/01).

¶6030.4 What is a Search?

Thermal heat scanning of a home (to determine if marijuana is being grown inside) constitutes a "search," and therefore is presumed unreasonable without a warrant: *Kyllo v. U.S.*, #99-8508, 121 S.Ct. 2038 (6/11/01).

¶6085 Capital Punishment

Jury instructions at the penalty phase of a capital trial must provide a vehicle for considering and giving effect to mitigating factors such as retardation and child abuse: *Penry v. Johnson*, #00-6677, 121 S.Ct. 1910 (6/4/01).

¶6087 Post-Conviction Remedies

The provisions of 28 USC §§2254 and 2255 (dealing with habeas and related relief) cannot be used to challenge prior convictions that are being used to enhance the current sentence: *Daniels v. U.S.*, #99-9136, 121 S.Ct. 1578 (4/25/01) and *Lackawanna County District Attorney v. Coss*, #99-1884, 121 S.Ct. 1567 (4/25/01).

A new rule of constitutional law is retroactive under the AEDPA (and therefore can be used to justify a second or subsequent habeas petition) only if the Supreme Court explicitly designated the rule as retroactive, or if the rule is necessarily interpreted as retroactive when reading together multiple Supreme Court rulings: *Tyler v. Cain*, #00-5961, 69 LW 4620 (6/28/01).

¶6090 Prison Litigation

The Prison Litigation Reform Act's requirement of exhaustion of remedies (42 USC §1997e(a)) prior to instituting a federal suit applies even if the remedies sought by the potential plaintiff (e.g., money damages) are not available under the administrative process: *Booth v. Churner*, #99-1964, 121 S.Ct. 1819 (5/29/01).

Regulation of the Practice of Law

¶7060.1 Prevailing Party

Despite rulings to the contrary by nine Circuits, the Supreme Court held that, to receive a fee award under federal fee-shifting statutes that refer to the "prevailing party," a plaintiff must obtain a court-ordered consent decree or a judgment on the merits. It is not sufficient to assert a "catalyst theory" under which the plaintiff achieved a beneficial result by inducing the defendant to make voluntary changes in its practices: *Buckhannon Board and Care Home Inc. v. West Virginia Dep't of Health and Human Services*, #99-1848, 121 S.Ct. 1835 (5/29/01).

¶200

Commercial Transactions

[¶205] Sale of Goods

Getting a release from liability with respect to a contract for the sale of goods is not covered by the Texas UCC's duty of good faith and fair dealing.[1] (In the merchant context, good faith is defined as honesty in fact and observance of reasonable commercial standards of fair dealing in the trade.)

The obligation of good faith applies to enforcement, performance, or modification—but not the formation—of a contract for the sale of goods. A final release is merely a contract expressing the parties' agreement that no duties remain under the contract for the sale of goods.

This case involved a take-or-pay contract for natural gas, which became uneconomical when prices dropped. In 1988, the seller got the buyer to sign a final termination of the agreement, and mutual releases of liability were granted. In 1992, the seller, claiming that the release was obtained in bad faith and therefore was invalid, sued to enforce the take-or-pay provision.

UCC 2-207 doesn't presume that buyers who are silent object in advance to terms on seller invoices that contradict the gap-filler terms prescribed by the UCC. In this case, the invoice said that no claim of any kind can be asserted that is greater than purchase price of the materials.

The First Circuit had to decide if the damage cap was part of the contract.[2] UCC 2-207 is supposed to eliminate the common-law mirror image rule, which makes terms that are materially different from buyer's offer a mere counter-offer, with no contract formed until there has been express or implied acceptance of the terms.

But 2-207 says that any definite expression of acceptance is an acceptance, and so is a written confirmation sent within a reasonable time, even if it has additional or different terms—unless the acceptance is expressly conditioned on taking the new terms as well. The additional terms are proposed additions to the contract, and become part of the contract between merchants unless the offer says it can only be accepted on its own terms, or unless objections are raised with reasonable promptness.

An earlier First Circuit case[3] rejects the mirror image rule in favor of the UCC provision. *Ionics* doesn't automatically give a silent buyer protection under 2-207, but neither silent nor non-silent buyers are subject to the mirror image rule. Silence doesn't necessarily mean the buyer prefers the UCC gap fillers to the contract terms. Comment 5 gives, as an example of an immaterial alteration, a clause that places a reasonable limitation on remedies. The First Circuit decided that a silent buyer must show that it would have rejected the damage limitation as a material alteration.

[¶220.4] Checks

In a case of first impression decided by the Colorado Court of Appeals in September, 1999[4] the plaintiff got a cashier's check from a bank in exchange for a previously dishonored check. Just after issuing the cashier's check, the bank found that there was a stop payment order on the dishonored check. It told the plaintiff that it would not honor the cashier's check, and asked that the check be returned. The plaintiff refused. He deposited the cashier's check in his own bank and withdrew the amount immediately.

The issuing bank refused to honor the check, and the plaintiff's bank debited his account accordingly. He brought suit against the issuing bank for wrongful or negligent dishonor of a cashier's check. The bank got summary judgment at the trial court level.

Before 1990, most banks treated cashier's checks as cash-equivalent, so it was impossible for an issuing bank to refuse payment. But a minority of courts did allow dishonor in limited circumstances, analyzing cashier's checks as more like promissory notes.

The 1990 NCCUSL amendments, which were adopted by Colorado in 1994, define a cashier's check as a draft with a single bank as drawer and drawee. An Official Comment to 4-412 makes it clear that the issuer is obligated as the maker of a note, not the drawer of a draft. Therefore, the obligor on a note retains defenses that can be asserted against the holder (or whoever else can enforce the instrument). An obligor's defenses against a holder in due course (HDC) are limited to defenses involving validity of instrument at its inception, but defenses against a non-HDC include simple contract defenses and recoupment.

The UCC allows an obligated bank to assert the defense of lack of consideration or mistake against a non-HDC of an issued cashier's check that it refuses to pay, because Articles 3 and 4 were amended to expand the bank's defenses.

[¶240] [NEW] Article 4A: Funds Transfers

When a wire transfer is sent to the right account number but the wrong beneficiary, the bank accepting the wire is only liable if it had actual knowledge of the discrepancy when the payment was made. "Payment" means that the accepting bank credits the beneficiary's account and the beneficiary has access to the funds.[5]

[¶280.3] Perfecting a Security Interest

A security interest in a patent is perfected by UCC filing, not federal filing[6]—even though federal filing is required to perfect a security interest in a copyright.[7] Although Patent Act §261 provides a system of federal registration, that covers patent assignments (conveyance of legal title to the patent), whereas Article 9 envisions a single form of security interest that is not title-based. For UCC purposes, a patent is considered a "general intangible," so that determines the office where filing must be made to perfect the security interest.

[¶290] [NEW] e-Sign

The Electronic Records and Signatures in Global and National Commerce Act (nicknamed e-Sign), P.L. 106-229, was passed on June 30, 2000, enacted at 15 USC §7001 et. seq. Its basic rule is that, in all transactions in interstate and foreign commerce, contract signatures in electronic form must be given the same legal effect and be just as enforceable as if they were in conventional written form. (But that means that wholly intrastate transactions are not covered.)

An electronic signature is any electronic sound, symbol, or process attached to or associated with a document, and used with the intention of signing the record. Notarization, authorization, etc. can also be done through the use of electronic signatures. However, e-Sign does not apply to court orders, notices, or briefs, pleadings, and other writings that must be executed in connection with litigation.

After e-Sign, the basic contract principles remain in force, and private parties (as distinct from government agencies) cannot be forced to agree to, use, or accept electronic records. Only part of the UCC (1-107, 1-206, Article 2, and Article 2A) is subject to e-Sign—which means that Article 9 is conspicuous by its absence.

E-Sign does not apply to the execution of wills, codicils, or testamentary trusts, or to state family law statutes.

Disclosure and other "writing" requirements for consumer contracts can be satisfied by electronic documents—but only if the consumer gives informed consent in advance to receiving the disclosures or other information in electronic form. Consumers have the right to receive a hard copy of electronic documents and also to withdraw their consent to receiving their information digitally. Timing requirements for disclosures are the same whether they are made in writing or digitally.

With respect to record retention requirements imposed by law, electronic records will be satisfactory if they accurately reflect the underlying information and if, for at least as long as the record must be retained, the electronic records remain accessible in a format that can be consulted for later reference. Requirements for retaining "checks" can be satisfied by retention of an electronic record of the information on the front and the back of the check.

ENDNOTES

1. *El Paso Natural Gas Co. v. Minco Oil & Gas Inc.,* 8 S.W.3d 309 (Tex. 11/18/99).
2. *JOM Inc. v. Adell Plastics,* 193 F.3d 47 (1st Cir. 1999).
3. *Ionics Inc. v. Elmwood Sensors Inc.,* 110 F.3d 1984 (1st Cir. 1997).
4. *Flatiron Linen Inc. v. First American State Bank,* 68 LW 1179 (Colo. App. 9/16/99).
5. *First Security Bank of New Mexico v. Pan American Bank,* 215 F.3d 1147 (10th Cir. 2000).
6. *In re Cybernectic Services, Inc.,* 239 B.R. 917 (9th Cir. 1999).
7. *National Peregrine, Inc. v. Capitol Federal Savings and Loan Ass'n,* 116 B.R. 194 (C.D.Cal. 1990).

¶300

Employer–Employee Relations

[¶310A] [NEW] EGTRA Changes

One of the major aspects of the 2001 tax bill, EGTRA, P.L. 107-16, is to make changes to the system of retirement savings under IRAs and employer-sponsored qualified plans. Many of these changes concentrate on 401(k) plans, in line with the trend of emphasizing those that are based on employees' voluntary salary deferrals, rather than plans funded by the employer.

Like all EGTRA provisions, the retirement plan provisions are subject to a complex phase-in schedule, and they sunset at the end of 2010, unless Congress makes them permanent in the interim.

[¶310A.1] [NEW] Employer Plans

Several provisions of EGTRA serve to increase plan limits. (Of course, employers are not required to match these limits. They merely represent the maximum amount that can be placed into the plan without penalty, or that qualifies for a tax deduction.) Most of these provisions fall into a pattern: starting in a particular year (often 2002), a plan limit is increased. Further increases are scheduled for succeeding years, until a terminal year.

After the terminal year, the amount in question is indexed (i.e., increased to reflect inflation)—not in every year, but only in those years when the indexing formula requires an upgrade of a specified amount such as $500 or $1,000.

Plan Limits

Starting in 2002, the amount of compensation that can be taken into account in calculating plan benefits under Code §401(a)(17), as amended by EGTRA §611, is $200,000. In later years, it will be indexed in increments of $5,000. (The 2001 limit, under pre-EGTRA law, was $170,000.)

The amount of elective deferrals (e.g., under 401(k) plans) goes up to $11,000 in 2002, as compared to the pre-EGTRA limit of $10,500 for 2001. For 2003, the maximum permitted elective deferral is $12,000; for

2004, it's $13,000; for 2005, it's $14,000; and for 2006, it's $15,000, at which time it will be indexed in increments of $500.

For plan years that end after 12/31/01, the Code §415(b) limit on annual benefits that can be provided under a defined benefit plan goes up to $160,000, which will be indexed in increments of $5,000. Pre-EGTRA law required an actuarial reduction in the size of the maximum benefit provided at early retirement (after age 62, before age 65) to account for the larger number of payments that would be made, but EGTRA allows payment of an unreduced benefit at early retirement as long as the retiree has reached age 62.

Under EGTRA, the maximum annual contribution under a defined contribution plan goes up to $40,000, indexed in increments of $1,000 (it was $35,000 under prior law). EGTRA also abolishes the limitation of contributions to a defined contribution plan to 25% of compensation, so employers can contribute up to 100% of the employee's salary to such a plan. This provision is effective for years that begin (not years that end) after 12/31/01.

The rule has always been that employees are always 100% vested in their own elective contributions to a pension plan. EGTRA §633 changes the vesting schedule for the employer's matching contributions that respond to the employee's elective contribution. Vesting must occur either on a three-year cliff schedule, or a six-year graded schedule, beginning with 20% vesting in the second year of the employee's service.

401(k) Changes

EGTRA makes several quite significant changes to the 401(k) plan rules.

Starting in 2006, EGTRA §617 adds a new section, §402A, to the Internal Revenue Code so that participants in 401(k) plans can treat the plans like Roth IRAs. Employees will be allowed to make contributions to the 401(k) plan, in the form of elective deferrals of part of their salary, that will be taxable income when they are made (unlike ordinary 401(k) elective deferrals) but will not be taxed when they are withdrawn.

This technique is referred to as a "qualified plus contribution program." To qualify for this tax relief, the employees must leave the elective-deferral contributions in the account for at least five years after they were contributed, and tax-free distributions can only be made after the plan participant reaches age 59 1/2 or becomes disabled (or to the participant's estate after his or her death).

Mid-life (age 50 and over) employees are allowed to make additional "catch-up" contributions to their 401(k) plans—i.e., they can agree to have especially large amounts deferred from their salary and placed into the plan instead of being paid in cash currently. This provision is effective for taxable years beginning after 12/31/01. The maximum catch-up contribution allowed for 2002 is $1,000, rising to $2,000 in 2003 and up to $5,000 in 2006, after which time the amounts will be indexed in increments of $500.

Low-income contributors of any age (income under $50,000 for a joint return, $25,000 for a single person's return) can get a tax credit for the 401(k) plan deferrals, up to a maximum of $1,000 (50% of a $2,000 contribution) under EGTRA. The tax credit is available for tax years beginning after 12/31/01 and before 1/1/07.

EGTRA also makes it easier for employers to maintain 401(k) plans that benefit highly-compensated employees (HCEs) without running afoul of the rules against discrimination in employee benefit plans: see §§663 and 666.

Rollovers Between Plans

Because it is less and less common for employees to spend their entire career with a single employer, pension portability is an important issue. EGTRA §641 makes it easier to roll over distributions between employer-sponsored qualified plans, IRAs, 401(k) plans, and 403(b) and 457 plans (non-profit and governmental plans).

However, to allow capital gains and income averaging, distributions from a qualified plan must be rolled over to a "conduit IRA" before being rolled over into a qualified plan, rather than just rolled over to the second qualified plan. Employees' after-tax contributions to 401(k) plans can be rolled over to a qualified plan or to an IRA. These provisions are effective for distributions made after 12/31/01.

Employers gain some flexibility under the EGTRA §631 rule, which says that if all employees who have reached age 50 are allowed to make catch-up contributions to 401(k) plans (see above), the amount of the catch-up contributions will not be considered in calculating limits on contributions. Nor will the catch-up amounts be used in non-discrimination testing.

Employer's Deduction

One of the most powerful incentives for a company to maintain pension and other deferred compensation plans is the availability of an income tax deduction for the costs associated with the plan. Therefore, increases in the size of the available deduction tend to be pro-employer. EGTRA

§614 allows employers to contribute more to their plans for years beginning after 12/31/01, because employees' elective deferral contributions to plans are not considered when the deduction limits are calculated—i.e., they do not reduce the amount that the employer can deduct.

EGTRA §616(b) provides that the employee's "compensation" includes these elective deferrals, so they may increase the amount that the employer contributes on the employee's behalf, even though the employee does not have taxable income on account of the salary reductions.

Funding Limitation

An important objective of the Internal Revenue Code and ERISA provisions about defined benefit plans, backed up by PBGC insurance, is making sure that the plans have enough assets to satisfy their obligations to pay benefits. (This is not an issue for defined contribution plans, because there is a separate account for each employee, and the retiree's pension entitlement depends on the investment results of the account.)

Before EGTRA, the "full funding limitation" (what the employer had to contribute to keep the plan economically sound in the long run) was defined as the plan's accrued liability, or 160% of its current liability (whichever is smaller) minus its assets.

EGTRA §651 increases the current liability full funding limit to 165% of current liability for plan years that begin in 2002, and to 170% for plan years that begin in 2003—but repeals the current liability full funding limit for plan years that begin between 2004 and 2010. (Remember, all of the provisions of EGTRA sunset at the end of 2010.) Therefore, for plan years between 2004 and 2010, the full funding limit is simply the difference between the plan's accrued liability and the value of its assets.

Two ERISA Rules Eliminated

EGTRA eliminates two ERISA rules that employers often found burdensome. EGTRA §645 eliminates the ERISA §204(h) "anti-cutback" rule, so that employers are permitted to eliminate certain forms of plan distribution when benefits are transferred to a new plan, as long as employees retain the right to elect a lump-sum payout. EGTRA also streamlines plan administration by permitting elimination of certain optional benefit forms, as long as lump sums are still available, and the rights of participants are not adversely affected. The Department of the Treasury is ordered to issue final regulations by 12/31/03 to carry out these new rules.

Employers that modify their plans must be sure to comply with the new IRC §4980F, added by EGTRA §659, imposing a penalty of $100 a day for failure to provide adequate notice to participants of significant reductions in the rate of future benefit accruals.

The "same desk" rule provides that distributions cannot be made to a terminated employee who has been re-hired and continues to perform the same job functions for a successor employer. For distributions after 12/31/01, EGTRA §646 repeals this rule for 401(k), 403(b), and 457 plans (but NOT for conventional employer-sponsored qualified plans). Note that repeal refers to the date that the distribution was made, not the date when the individual stopped working for the initial employer.

Retirement Advice Fringe Benefit

EGTRA §665 allows "qualified retirement planning services" (retirement planning advice and information) provided to employees and spouses under an employer-sponsored plan that does not discriminate in favor of HCEs to be treated as tax-free fringe benefits. But tax preparation, accounting, legal and brokerage services don't qualify. This section is effective for plan years that begin after 12/31/01.

[¶310A.2] [NEW] IRAs

Before EGTRA, the rules affecting Individual Retirement Accounts had been changed many times, and in some ways the program was liberalized. For example, the Roth IRA options were added so high-bracket taxpayers could forego a tax deduction when they made their IRA contributions, yet receive proceeds from the IRA tax-free after reaching age 59 1/2 (or becoming disabled). However, the overall limit on IRA contributions was not changed for many years.

EGTRA completely revolutionizes IRAs, providing for much larger contribution limits. For the years 2002–2004, contributions to conventional or Roth IRAs can be up to $3,000 per taxpayer, rising to $4,000 in 2005–2007 and $5,000 in 2008. After 2008, the $5,000 limit will be indexed. As noted above, elective deferrals placed into 401(k) plans can receive the same tax-free treatment as Roth IRAs, at the employee's option.

Taxpayers who have reached age 50 are allowed to make slightly larger contributions, on the theory that they need to catch up by the time they reach retirement age. For the years 2002–2005, a catch-up contribution of $500 a year is permitted; for 2006 and later years, the additional allowed contribution is $1,000 a year.

A tax credit provides more benefit than a tax deduction because it has a more powerful effect in reducing tax liability. Low-income taxpayers (defined as joint returns with AGI under $50,000, single taxpayers with AGI under $25,000, and heads of household with AGI under $37,500) are entitled to a tax credit reflecting their conventional and Roth IRA contributions. The maximum credit is $1,000 (50% of a $2,000 contribution); the credit phases down based on AGI levels. The credit is available for tax years that begin after 12/31/00 and before 1/1/07.

Among the many EGTRA provisions that refer to education costs is one that allows contributions to be made to an Education IRA of up to $2,000 per designated beneficiary per year—four times the previous limit of $500 per beneficiary. Furthermore, married taxpayers filing a joint return can contribute to education IRAs if their modified AGI is as high as $220,000; prior law phased out eligibility at modified AGI of $190,000. The provisions about Education IRAs take effect for taxable years beginning after 12/31/01.

[¶310] Labor Law

In 2000 and 2001, labor arbitration issues were prominent. The Supreme Court decided in March, 2001 that the Federal Arbitration Act is generally applicable to employment contracts. Although the language of the FAA exempts "contracts of employment of seamen, railroad employees, or any other class of workers engaged in foreign or interstate commerce," the exemption is limited to transportation workers and does not extend to all workers involved in interstate commerce. Therefore, pre-dispute arbitration clauses are not necessarily unenforceable whenever they involve workers in interstate commerce.[1]

Several recent cases permit enforcement of pre-dispute arbitration requirements.[2]

The Tenth Circuit ruled that instead of submitting a case about job reductions to arbitration, the District Court should first have rendered a decision as to whether the matter was arbitrable at all, because courts, not arbitrators, must decide the question of whether a Collective Bargaining Agreement mandates arbitration—unless the CBA clearly and unequivocally demands arbitration.[3]

The Fourth Circuit held in early 2001 that an arbitration agreement dividing fees and costs between the employer and employee is not per se unenforceable. A case-by-case analysis should be made, involving the employee's ability to pay and whether the costs are likely to be substantial enough to deter employees from pursuing worthwhile claims.[4]

In August, 2000, the NLRB issued a decision that reversed its long-standing policy that temporary workers could be organized in the same bargaining unit with permanent workers if, and only if, both the "supplier employer" (e.g., temp agency) and "user employer" (locus where services were provided) concurred. The 2000 decision gave unions the right to show that the supplier and user employers are actually joint employers that both control the terms and conditions of employment.[5]

The WARN Act requires 60-day notice whenever there is a plant closing, even though the employees lose their jobs more than 30 days before the actual closing. As long as there is a plant closing, the 30-day aggregation period is irrelevant to who has to be notified.

The employer in this case (which closed down an unsafe mine) said that it has to give notice only to employees whose actual layoff comes within the 30-day aggregation period that defines plant closing. But in the Fourth Circuit view, the class of persons entitled to notice is everyone affected by the closing; the 30-day period relates to whether or not 50 people are affected.[6]

The WARN Act and the Labor-Management Relations Act (LMRA) preempt state-law liens that relate to sanctions for WARN Act noncompliance (as well as unpaid wages and amounts claimed under a collective bargaining agreement—CBA). LMRA §301 preempts CBA claims, so employee claims to bankruptcy priority liens arising out of vacation pay, wages, pension contributions, or health claims under a CBA are necessarily preempted.[7]

Hiring private investigators to pose as employees to monitor whether employees were stealing, committing vandalism, or using drugs at the warehouse could be a tortious violation of an employee's right to privacy. (The Illinois Court of Appeals characterized the tort as "intrusion on seclusion."[8]) The investigators gave the employers reports including highly personal information that employees revealed in conversation, with no expectation that it would get back to the boss. Because the employer is treated as having a special relationship with the employee, the public disclosure element of the tort was satisfied.

An employer subcontracted out its transportation department; the union representing the company's employees did not object. When the employer re-took control of the subcontracted tasks, rehiring most of the subcontractor's employees, it was required to recognize the union. According to the Tenth Circuit, the collective bargaining agreement between union and employer remained in effect,[9] because the union did not waive its representation rights by not trying to organize the subcontractor's employees. Nor did the employer become a successor of the non-union subcontractor. The work remained the same, even though there were different people within the bargaining unit.

A dispute about whether a railroad would hire subcontractors that employed union members is a "labor dispute" as defined by the Norris-LaGuardia Act, and therefore the District Court could not enjoin the union against its threatened picketing of the railroad's hub.[10] To the Ninth Circuit, reversing the District Court, the test of a labor dispute is whether the employer–employee relationship is central to the controversy.

A bankrupt company that rejects a collective bargaining agreement under Bankruptcy Code §1113 need not do so before rather than after it sells its assets. The Eighth Circuit did not require the bankruptcy filer to prove that rejection of the contract was part of a workable strategy for surviving as a going concern. [11]

When a union operates an exclusive hiring hall, any breach (even a negligent breach) of its established procedures that results in loss of hiring for an applicant is a breach of the duty of fair representation. [12]

In January, 2001, the NLRB announced a new policy to expedite rendition and distribution of its decisions. The agency stated that it had made strides in reducing its case backlog for unfair labor practice and representation cases. At the end of fiscal 1998, the agency had 693 unresolved cases, which was reduced to 580 by the end of FY 2000. Looking only at representation cases, the backlog declined from 163 to 72 cases in the same time period.[13]

A union violates its duty of fair representation if it fails to give a detailed explanation of how nonmembers are charged union dues in an agency shop situation.[14] Notice is required both to new employees and to nonmembers who might object to the allocation. New employees and full-dues nonmembers are entitled to an explanation of how much less they'd pay if they exercised their right to object to paying for nonrepresentational expenditures, so it was inadequate to give the objectors nothing but a one-page list of 19 general categories of expenditures and how much of each was charged to nonmembers.

An April, 2000 decision of the Eleventh Circuit[15] conflicts with an earlier Seventh Circuit decision.[16] The Eleventh Circuit denied punitive damages in a private suit for Fair Labor Standards Act (FLSA) retaliation, because the FLSA employee suit provisions are compensatory, aimed at making the plaintiff whole. (The plaintiff was a waiter who alleged that he was fired for contacting the Department of Labor about wage and hour violations.)

At trial, the jury awarded him $35,000 in punitive damages (much higher than the compensatory damages for wages and overtime lost because of retaliation). The District Court struck the punitive damage award. The Eleventh Circuit reading of FLSA §216(b) is that it provides legal and equitable relief, but doesn't specify punitive damages. The ADEA language tracks the FLSA, and the ADEA has also been read to exclude punitive damages.

[¶315] Other Statutes Affecting the Employment Relationship

The Workers Economic Opportunity Act, P.L. 106-202 (5/18/00), amends the Fair Labor Standards Act, so that stock options are not included in the "regular rate of pay" when FLSA calculations are made.

On November 3, 1999, the SEC published an order approving NASD's proposal for changing its arbitration procedures for the employment discrimination claims of securities industry employees.[17] All employment discrimination claims must go to a qualified, nonindustry arbitrator. Claims up to $100,000 can be heard by one arbitrator, rather than a panel. The arbitrator can award reasonable attorneys' fees. The procedure allows employers to stave off bifurcation of claims (especially those joined with claims other than discrimination) between litigation and arbitration.

[¶340] Pensions

IRS Proposed Regulations appearing at 66 *Federal Register* 3928 (January 17, 2001) relate to required minimum distributions from qualified plans, IRAs, and 403(b) and 457 plans. They greatly simplify the planning task for individuals who wish to take smaller distributions from these plans in order to accumulate more funds for their estates. The new rules create a single, easy-to-use table for calculating the minimum distribution, irrespective of whether the named beneficiary is a spouse, a natural person who is not the spouse, a trust, or a charitable organization. Earlier rules made the calculations much more complex if any beneficiary other than the spouse were designated.

EGTRA directs the Treasury to adopt new tables, reflecting current demographic realities, but does not otherwise address this issue.

This table compares plan limits for the 2000 and 2001 tax years. For 2000 figures, see IR-1999-80; for 2001 figures, see IR-2000-82; for later figures, see EGTRA.

Description	2000 Limit	2001 Limit (pre-EGTRA)	EGTRA Limit
Maximum Annual Benefit (Defined Benefit Plan)	$135,000	$140,000	$160,000 (years ending after 12/31/01), then indexed
Maximum Annual Contribution (Defined Contribution Plan)	$30,000; 25% of compensation	$35,000; 25% of compensation	$40,000 (as of 2002); 100% of compensation
Compensation of Highly Compensated Employee	$85,000	$85,000	$85,000
Maximum 401(k) Deferral	$10,500	$10,500	$11,000 (2002) rising to $15,000 (2006) then indexed

In 2000, the IRS announced an updated and consolidated EPCRS (Employee Plans Compliance Resolution System)—another voluntary mode for plan sponsors to correct plan problems before they are detected (and penalized) by federal regulators.[18]

An employer's benefit plan allowed severance to anyone terminated "other than for cause or voluntary separation, due to the exigencies of the business situation." The Seventh Circuit held in early 2000 that employees who were terminated by the employer when the employer's sale of its assets became effective were entitled to severance, even though in fact they were immediately hired by the purchaser of the assets and were never actually unemployed.[19]

To the D.C. Circuit, the employer did not breach ERISA fiduciary duty by telling employees who asked that retirement benefit incentives would not be provided, then announcing a benefit program after the plaintiff employees retired.[20]

There was no "plan," because this was a one-time arrangement, under which the employer had no responsibility other than writing checks. The severance didn't supplement the pension plan, and was not tantamount to a welfare benefit plan on its own because of the lack of administrative integrity.

The Supreme Court struck down a Washington State law that made all beneficiary designations (in employee benefit plans and life insurance) invalid when the couple divorced. The Supreme Court view is that ERISA preempts such a statute, because it "relates to" an ERISA plan, and states are precluded from making rules in the ERISA plan area.[21]

Whether there has been a partial termination of an ERISA plan is a question of law, to be reviewed by the Court of Appeals de novo. Both vested and nonvested participants should be considered in determining whether there has been a partial termination, and terminations of employees in more than one plan year can also be used in the calculation.[22]

A court order that divides a pension incident to divorce can operate as a valid QDRO even if it fails to satisfy all the statutory requirements completely,[23] as long as the order supplies the essential elements: i.e., makes it clear who gets how many payments or gets payments in what period. The statutory purpose for permitting QDROs is making sure that money goes to a legitimate alternate payee, and that the plan doesn't have an additional payment burden or make payments that conflict with an existing QDRO. An order that is technically defective (here, by omitting the wife's address, which was known to the administrator in any case) can nonetheless be a valid QDRO.

The IRS has issued an updated text that can be used as a safe harbor explanation by plan administrators to satisfy the §402(f) requirement of notice to the recipients of eligible rollover distributions of the tax consequences of the various available elections.[24]

The valuation and forfeiture provisions of ERISA are violated by calculating lump-sum balances under a cash balance pension plan by using a projection rate that is lower than the interest credits guaranteed by the plan.[25]

Converting a defined benefit plan to a cash balance plan does not violate ERISA's ban on age discrimination in benefit accruals (or the ADEA).[26]

T.D. 8894, 2000-33 IRB 162 gives Final Regulations under IRS §72 as to when a loan from a qualified plan will be treated as a distribution from the plan. Loans that must be repaid in not more than five years, in substantially level installments, generally will not be treated as §72 "deemed distributions."

With respect to a Chapter 13 debtor who borrowed from his retirement account, repaying the plan loan is not considered reasonable and necessary for the debtor's maintenance or support, and therefore can't be deducted from the debtor's disposable income that is considered available to pay the unsecured creditors.[27]

A spouse who executes a valid prenuptial agreement that waives pension rights on divorce can't use ERISA to cancel the waiver. To the District of Columbia court, then, ERISA doesn't preempt state matrimonial laws that allow and govern prenuptial agreements.[28]

This is only the second case on the issue; the other one[29] says that ERISA has a consent requirement on waiver of survivor benefits, but is silent on waiver of other types of pension benefits, and therefore an ex-spouse is certainly able to waive his or her interest.

Under a 2000 Maine case[30] a divorcing wife was held not to be entitled to a 50% share of the marital part of an early retirement subsidy that was available to the employee-husband at age 55, notwithstanding the separation agreement incorporated in the divorce decree and dividing the "pension" equally. The early retirement subsidy was not included in the valuation of benefits at the time of the divorce, because the husband was not yet eligible. The wife was aware of the possibility, but did not insist on a share.

However, a Pennsylvania case from the Spring of 2000 treats early retirement incentive benefits paid to the husband post-divorce as part of the marital estate. Because he did not do any additional work to earn the incentive benefits, they were counted as an adjustment to pension rights earned during the marriage.[31]

Pension benefits earned by the husband during his first marriage are not marital property with respect to the dissolution of his second marriage—even though this case had the unusual fact pattern that both marriages and both divorces involved the same woman! In the analysis of the

Pennsylvania Superior Court[32] the pension rights were acquired prior to the current marriage and therefore are separate property.

A woman awarded half of the pension earned during marriage is not entitled to "surviving spouse" benefits after the death of the husband (who had remarried).

This Arizona case[33] holds that her community interest was extinguished, even though the husband and his second wife executed a purported irrevocable assignment of all retirement benefits, including death benefits, to the first wife. In this reading, only the person married to the employee at the time of his or her death can be considered a surviving spouse.

[¶345] Health Benefit Plans

Given the dominance of employer-sponsored managed care plans within the U.S. health care system, it is inevitable that HMOs and their uneasy relationship with both employers and insured employees would be a focus of legal attention.[34]

The Supreme Court decided the crucial case of *Pegram v. Herdrich*[35] in June of 2000. The petitioner in this case was an insured employee who suffered a ruptured appendix and peritonitis after her managed care physician delayed approval of a diagnostic test for eight days. The petitioner sued her HMO in state court; the basic claim was one of fraud (denying access to care without disclosing the financial incentives given to participating physicians to limit the number of diagnostic procedures ordered). The case was removed to the federal system on ERISA preemption grounds.

According to the Supreme Court, the petitioner in effect had no forum to bring her complaint against the HMO (although the state-law malpractice claim against the physician remains a possibility). ERISA preempts state litigation, but the Supreme Court held that the petitioner did not assert a valid ERISA claim against the HMO, because an HMO does not serve as fiduciary when, acting through its physicians, it makes decisions about treatment and subscriber eligibility for desired medical interventions.

In the Supreme Court view, courts are not able to distinguish between "good" and "bad" HMOs as they exercise their function of rationing care. Although the petitioner's contention was that it is inherently wrong for HMOs to give their physicians financial incentives to restrict care, the Supreme Court treats rationing of care as essential to managed care itself.

Furthermore, in the Court's analysis, HMOs are not fiduciaries of the employer-sponsored health care plan, because they do not administer the plan, and decisions about eligibility for care do not fit into the traditional fiduciary framework, which has evolved from the role of the trustee vis-a-vis a trust.

Because so many Americans depend on employment for health coverage, the relationships among patients, physicians, HMO plans, and employers are crucially important. Patients' rights have been the focus of a great deal of state legislation, and multiple bills have been introduced in Congress, seeking various ways of protecting patients' rights without entirely neglecting provider, employer, and insurer interests.

ERISA's authorization of nationwide service of process doesn't automatically give the federal court personal jurisdiction over every entity that has minimum contacts with the United States—it's still necessary to determine whether personal jurisdiction is fair and reasonable.

This Tenth Circuit case[36] involves coverage of psychiatric care that was not provided by one of the plan's preferred providers. The plan pre-certified care in Utah for a plan beneficiary who lived in Tennessee with her guardian, who was the employee covered by the plan. The employer's headquarters was in Georgia, and the plan was administered by Blue Cross/Blue Shield of Alabama. The Tenth Circuit held that personal jurisdiction, unlike service of process, requires contacts with the forum, but deemed Utah to be an adequate forum.

The Third Circuit vacated the preliminary injunction granted by the District Court, requiring the employer to maintain full funding of health benefits for 136 retirees, on the grounds that irreparable harm was shown as to only two of the retirees (who testified as to financial hardship caused by medical bills), not the rest.[37] The plaintiffs charge that the employer breached its fiduciary duty by inducing them to retire early by misleading them as to the continued availability of retiree health benefits.

The Second Circuit has joined the Third, Fourth, and Seventh, holding that denials of ERISA benefits are reviewed de novo as to both their facts and issues of plan interpretation unless the plan reserves discretion to decide those issues.[38] The plan called for payment of benefits on satisfactory proof of total disability—which was not a reservation of discretionary authority sufficient to prevent administrators' decisions from being reviewed de novo.

The plaintiff was a director of nursing services until suffering an automobile accident. She received long-term disability benefits for 15 months, at which point the plan administrator terminated benefits on the grounds that she could return to work, based on the DOL's characterization of the nursing director's job as "sedentary."

In the Second Circuit reading, "own occupation" total disability determinations involve a factual issue of the material duties of the occupation, plus the plan interpretation question of what the allegedly disabled person's own occupation is—and both the factual and the interpretive issues are reviewed de novo. It was not clear whether proof of disability had to be objectively satisfactory, or satisfactory to the insurer—an ambiguity that had to be resolved against the insurer.

The Second Circuit also determined that the plaintiff was entitled to disability benefits, because the determination of one's regular occupation involves consideration of the individual workplace (not just outside characterizations), and the plaintiff's actual job called for standing, performing clinical duties, and responding to emergencies, and therefore was not sedentary.

It was an abuse of discretion for a plan administrator to deny long-term disability benefits to a litigator with high blood pressure.[39] The administrator erred in describing the core duties of a trial lawyer too narrowly and saying the attorney was not disabled because she was capable of working a 40-hour week; in practice, the litigator often worked 16- to 20-hour days, which her health could no longer tolerate.

It does not violate the Americans with Disabilities Act (ADA) for a long-term disability plan to provide less coverage for mental than for physical disabilities, on the theory that Congress could have but did not impose an explicit statutory ban on this near-universal practice.[40]

According to the Eighth Circuit, ERISA doesn't preempt a state claim of negligent misrepresentation against doctors premised on a theory that doctors had an undisclosed conflict of interest in that their contract with the HMO induced them to limit the decedents' access to specialists.[41]

The court construed the case as less about denial of a referral sought by the patient, than about preventing the patient from even seeking referral. Therefore, it was essentially a simple medical malpractice claim not calling for construction of the plan.

In the Tenth Circuit view, ERISA was violated by the employer's modification (ten years after the plaintiffs took early retirement) of the health plan.[42] The employer sent letters to employees before their retirement and, although the letters were marked "for informational purposes only," their language indicated a clear intent on the employer's part to provide lifetime health benefits. The employer agreed to pay retiree health premiums, and the employer had ongoing administrative responsibility, so there was an enforceable "plan."

See 65 FR 70246 (November 21, 2000) for the Pension and Welfare Benefit Administration's Final Rule on claims procedures for ERISA health and disability benefits. Under this rule, plans must expedite decision-making about health claims and must also render faster decisions when employees appeal denied claims. The timetables are shorter for "pre-service claims" (i.e., where approval of treatment is sought—and the employee might have to delay or forgo treatment if approval is not granted) than for "post-service claims," where the employee has already received treatment and the issue is merely one of payment.

[¶348] ERISA Enforcement

At the end of its 2000 term, the Supreme Court decided the case of *Harris Trust & Savings Bank v. Salomon Smith Barney Inc.*, #99-579, 120 S.Ct. 2180 (Sup.Ct. 2000), interpreting ERISA §406 [prohibited transactions with a party in interest]. The Supreme Court resolved a circuit split by determining that even an individual or business that is not a fiduciary as to the plan can be sued for "appropriate equitable relief" by any participant, beneficiary, or fiduciary of the plan.

The IRS can impose tax penalties for prohibited transactions on a plan, even though the plan entered into a consent decree with the Department of Labor which found that the transaction was not prohibited with respect to ERISA. In other words, acceptability under ERISA doesn't settle the question of whether the transaction was prohibited under Code §4975.[43]

In the Seventh Circuit view,[44] plan administrators should not have gotten summary judgment, because the plan language didn't give them the power of discretionary judgment over benefits. Therefore, de novo review rather than arbitrary and capricious review was appropriate.

One of the plans at issue said that the benefit will be paid "upon receipt of satisfactory written proof that you have become disabled," but that didn't make it clear that the proof had to be satisfactory to the administrator acting in a discretionary capacity; the other plan said that total disability occurs when all these conditions are met, but listed objective and not subjective factors, so discretionary power could not be assumed.

The Seventh Circuit suggests the following as safe harbor language for ERISA plans: "benefits under this plan will be paid only if the plan administrator decides in his discretion that the applicant is entitled to them."[45]

The Pennsylvania case of *Pappas v. Asbel*, decided in April, 2001 after a remand to conform to *Pegram*, holds that ERISA does **not** preempt state-law claims of negligence and malpractice arising out of an HMO's reluctance to authorize out-of-network neurological treatment. The plaintiff alleged that his permanent quadriplegia resulted from the treatment delay that resulted from the coverage dispute. On remand[46] the Pennsylvania Supreme Court read *Pegram* to dictate an analysis of three types of decisions made by doctors operating under managed care systems.

The first type of decision is the patient's eligibility for treatment; the second is a purely medical treatment decision (e.g., which antibiotic should be prescribed for a patient in a particular condition); and the third is a mixed decision. The Pennsylvania Supreme Court also cited *Pegram* for the proposition that ERISA does not preempt state negligence concepts when it comes to these mixed eligibility/treatment decisions.

However, on March 27, 2001, the Third Circuit ruled that ERISA preempts a claim by an HMO patient that the HMO was negligent when it delayed necessary back surgery. Hence, claims against the HMO, and against various physicians, were properly dismissed.[47]

The Third Circuit uses a "quality vs. quantity" analysis, i.e., ERISA preempts claims about the extent of treatment given, because that is a question of enforcement of benefits that should be available under an employer-sponsored plan. But claims about the quality of benefits are not completely preempted, because they involve issues such as negligence in treatment.

According to the Fifth Circuit, a Texas state statute that renders health plans (including HMOs) vulnerable to suit for malpractice or negligent treatment decisions is not preempted by ERISA. The rationale is that the statute excludes coverage decisions (which are preempted), and the quality of medical care is traditionally regarded as a state-law purview.[48] The Third Circuit rejected RICO claims against an HMO.[49]

Thirteen types of ERISA violations can be corrected voluntarily by employers:[50] e.g., making a below-market loan to a party in interest; buying or selling assets to and from parties in interest. A participating plan must restore any losses or lost profits with interest, and must notify participants and beneficiaries of the changes and file an application with the PWBA regional office.

If the plan carries out the correction, the Pension and Welfare Benefit Administration (PWBA) will issue a no-action letter, will not take any further enforcement action about the corrected problem, and will not impose Civil Money Penalties (CMPs). However, IRS excise taxes will still apply, because the PWBA has no jurisdiction over the IRS.

[¶350] Employment Discrimination

In March, 2000, the Eighth Circuit upheld DOL regulations defining the "serious health condition" triggering entitlement to Family and Medical Leave Act (FMLA) leave,[51] and also ruled that continuing treatment of the plaintiff's stomach ailment came within the definition. The employer's company policy allowed firing anyone who was absent for any reason whatever, for more than five percent of the scheduled work hours in any twelve-month period.

The plaintiff employee was out sick for two work days and came back on Monday with a doctor's note saying no work until Monday. She worked a few hours, went to the doctor who ordered tests, and came back a week later with another doctor's note, but was fired for excessive absence.

The District Court granted summary judgment to the employee. On appeal, the employer's contention was that the plaintiff's condition (diagnosed as an upset stomach and minor ulcer) was not a serious illness, because 29 CFR 824.114(c) uses these conditions as examples of health problems that are **not** serious unless complications arise. To the Eighth Circuit, the need for two doctor visits showed objectively that continued treatment was required. The plaintiff's absence and the doctor's note put the employer on notice that FMLA leave might be required. Therefore, it was up to the employer to require the employee to obtain medical certification on issues such as diagnosis, onset, duration of condition, and ability to work. The employer's failure to ask for certification meant that there was no genuine issue of material fact as to the employee's ability to work on the days she was absent.

An employee could lawfully be fired shortly after he requested and got leave for alcoholism treatment.[52] He was already on administrative supervision for coming to work drunk, contrary to the state substance abuse policy. The jury had substantial evidence that he would have been terminated anyway, with or without the request for FMLA leave, so the employer was not liable.

In FMLA litigation, the employee retains the burden of proving the right to reinstatement, even if the employer asserts that the employee would have been dismissed even if no FMLA leave had been taken.[53] Therefore, a jury instruction that requires the employer to prove a nondiscriminatory reason for the dismissal is incorrect.

In the Seventh Circuit, in FMLA retaliation cases, the issue is whether the employer had an impermissible retaliatory or discriminatory animus. The substantive FMLA right doesn't include any right, benefit, or condition the employee would not have been entitled to absent the FMLA leave, and the ultimate burden of proof is always on the employee.

According to the Commonwealth Court of Pennsylvania, illegal aliens who are not certified to work in this country are nevertheless "employees" entitled to receive Worker's Compensation benefits if and when they suffer employment-related injuries.[54]

[¶351] Title VII

A neutral seniority system is not an absolute defense to a Title VII religious discrimination claim.[55] Religious beliefs must be accommodated if they don't disrupt the seniority system, or if they do not cost the employer more than a de minimis amount (either in dollar cost or lost efficiency).

This case arose when an applicant, after being offered a job, said she couldn't work Saturdays for religious reasons, but offered to split her days off. The department said it couldn't accommodate that request in light of the existing seniority system (which did not allow trading shifts on a regular basis). She withdrew her application and sued for religious discrimination under Title VII.

The job applicant suggested two accommodations: voluntary shift trades and split shifts. In the court's view, trading shifts would impose undue burdens on the employer, because of unacceptable costs and logistic and personnel problems. But the case was remanded to determine whether split shifts would burden the employer unduly.

An employer's fitness test that imposes a cutoff rather than a range of acceptable scores, and that is likely to exclude women and members of minorities, is acceptable only if the test accurately represents minimum qualifications needed for the job.[56] The District Court found the test valid, because expert studies correlated aerobic fitness with effective performance as a transit police officer.

The Third Circuit view is that, although business necessity is a defense to a disparate impact charge, an employee-plaintiff can nevertheless demonstrate an alternative business practice that reduces the disparate impact on the plan, but still fulfills business needs. After *Wards Cove* (main volume), business practices can survive challenge even if they are not essential or indispensable to the business—as long as they will stand up to reasoned review.

In the view of the Southern District of New York, Title VII was not violated when a male employer yielded to his wife's demands and fired a female employee with whom he had had a consensual sexual relationship.[57] Improper though his conduct was in an ethical sense, it did not constitute severe or pervasive conduct creating a hostile work environment.

The Sixth Circuit rejected an employee's contention that she was subjected to pregnancy discrimination in violation of Title VII.[58] Although the employee's supervisor told her that she would be paid more if she stopped having children, that was not the reason for adverse employment action against her. A complicating factor was that, although she earned less than her non-pregnant colleagues, she received a larger raise than they did. Furthermore, the employee had criticized her supervisors and threatened to quit if she didn't get a larger raise, which the court deemed to be adequate nondiscriminatory reason for her firing.

An employer that did not question a supervisor about a female employee's sexual harassment complaints about him, and that denied the employee's requests for a transfer did not act reasonably or perform a reasonable investigation, and therefore could not be relieved of liability for the harassment.[59]

Four Circuits permit suits by at-will employees under 42 USC §1981 (the Civil War–era statute that gives all citizens the same right to make contracts as "white citizens") when they allege termination of the at-will employment for racially discriminatory reasons.[60]

Whether a person is an employee or an independent contractor for Title VII purposes depends on the extent of the employer's (or independent contractor's client) control over the manner and means in which job tasks are performed—and not whether the individual qualifies for employee benefits or is taxed as an employee.[61]

Punitive damages can be imposed on an employer whose general manager told an employee who made frequent complaints about sexual harassment that the harassers were revenue producers and she was not.[62] The employer's contention was that the manager violated the company's articulated anti-harassment policy, but the court found that the manager who was at fault had final decision-making authority for enforcing the anti-harassment policy, and therefore the company should be held liable.

The Second Circuit has permitted Title VII punitive damages in a sexual harassment case in which the plaintiff was not entitled to compensatory damages—thus widening a Circuit split between the Seventh Circuit (which also allows punitives in the absence of compensatory damages) and the First, which does not.[63]

The Third Circuit did not require a former employee charging retaliation to show antagonism or retaliatory animus during the three- to four-week period between rejection of the supervisor's sexual advances and the employee's termination. An employee can prove the causal connection circumstantially, e.g., by showing inconsistent explanations for the termination.[64]

The Second Circuit view is that, as long as the employee can show a causal connection between protected activity and retaliation, the employee can assert unlawful retaliation by Employer #2 based on the employee's opposition to an unlawful practice, or participation in investigation of wrongdoing, by Employer #1.[65]

[¶353] ADEA

A Supreme Court ADEA case from early in 2000 strikes down 1974 ADEA amendments that abrogated states' sovereign immunity against age discrimination suits filed by their own employees.[66] In this view, Congress exceeded its powers, because abrogation is so disproportionate to state conduct that the amendments were not "appropriate legislation" that Congress is empowered to enact by Section 5 of the Fourteenth Amendment.

In June, 2000, the Supreme Court[67] eased the burden of age discrimination plaintiffs somewhat. The issue in this case is whether an ADEA defendant can obtain a judgment as a matter of law (JMOL; see F.R.C.P. 50) after a plaintiff's case limited to a prima facie case of discrimination and rebuttal evidence going to the employer's defense that it had a legitimate nondiscriminatory rationale for the challenged conduct.

The petitioner was a 57-year-old who was one of three supervisors of a department that allegedly suffered from poor management and impaired productivity. He was fired after an audit of the department. The employer contended that his poor performance was at fault; he claimed that the employer's response was pretextual. At the District Court level, he was awarded $35,000 in compensatory damages, plus an additional $35,000 in liquidated damages for willfulness. The employer sought but did not receive a JMOL, and the employee also received two years' front pay.

The Fifth Circuit reversed the District Court, on the basis that the plaintiff introduced insufficient evidence. The Supreme Court reversed yet again, and allowed the trier of fact to conclude that unlawful discrimination occurred based on a prima facie case plus evidence justifying the trier of fact in treating the employer's explanation as pretextual.

However, the Supreme Court did not compel the trier of fact to find for the plaintiff in such situations—it only allowed it. The employer would be able to get a JMOL based on a record that made it conclusive that the asserted nondiscriminatory reason for the employment action was valid. Furthermore, consideration of the JMOL motion should include consideration of evidence favorable to both the moving and nonmoving parties.

Some retirees are over 65 and, therefore, qualify for Medicare. Retirees who have not yet reached age 65 do not qualify for Medicare unless they have been disabled for two years. The Third Circuit held in 2000 that it violates the ADEA for an employer to offer retiree health benefits to Medicare-eligible employees in HMO form, while offering a more liberal Point of Service plan to non-Medicare-eligible retirees.[68]

Transferring an over-40 teacher from junior high school to high school special education classes was not an adverse employment action for ADEA purposes, because he continued to teach the same subject in both settings.[69] A transfer can be an adverse employment action if it involves a significant change in responsibilities, but not if the second job is not materially less prestigious, less suitable for the individual, or less likely to result in career advancement.

It does not violate the ADEA to give some employees subject to a Reduction in Force (RIF) the choice between severance pay and a special retirement option enhancing the value of the pension based on age and service requirements.[70] The plaintiff employee said it was discriminatory to make him choose because of his age, when employees under 50 automatically received severance. The Fourth Circuit did not find this persuasive: as long as employees are not selected for RIF on the basis of age, they are better off having more choices, so there is no ADEA violation.

[¶354] ADA

In another ruling that Congress exceeded its powers, the Supreme Court decided in February, 2001 that Congress improperly abrogated Eleventh Amendment immunity when it permitted ADA suits against state government employers. The Court's rationale was that Congress acted without adequate evidence that handicap discrimination in state employment was a serious problem.[71]

The ADA requires the employer to assign disabled employees to vacant jobs for which they are qualified if the employer is unable to provide accommodation in the current job. The Tenth Circuit position is that the ADA would not be very meaningful if it merely obligated employers to consider applications for reinstatement.

The Tenth Circuit sitting en banc rejected its earlier panel decision that a person who can no longer perform the original job, even with accommodation, is no longer qualified. (In this case, the employee's occupationally-induced skin condition prevented him from continuing to assemble brake components.)

The en banc position is that a person is qualified (whether or not able to do current job under any circumstances) if he or she can perform the essential tasks of other jobs within the company that he or she wants to fill: 42 USC §12111(8) refers to the employment position that the person holds or desires, and the ADA definition of reasonable accommodation refers to reassignment to a vacant position.

The Tenth Circuit en banc adopts the EEOC position that the employer, subject to a requirement of reasonableness, must reassign a disabled worker to a vacant job that the employee wants and is capable of performing. It is not necessary, however, to bump another employee or create a new job. Accommodation within the original job is the preferred option, so reassignment need not be considered until all other measures have failed, and the employer must engage in an interactive process to evolve the accommodation.

In the spring of 2001, both the Fourth and the Fifth Circuits held that a qualified person with a disability can bring suit for harassment on the basis of disability that rises to the level of a hostile work environment.[72]

Another important issue is whether an acute health or disability plan is required to treat different conditions on a parity. According to the Fourth Circuit, the ADA does not require a private employer's long-term disability plan to provide the same level of benefits for mental as for physically-caused disabilities,[73] based on an earlier holding that the ADA does not impose a parity requirement on a plan for state employees[74] and the court saw no rationale for distinguishing between state and private employers in this context.

The Fifth Circuit held that Title III of the ADA (public accommodations) is not violated by a health insurance policy that sets lower limits for

AIDS and AIDS-related conditions than for other conditions.[75] This is also the Seventh Circuit position,[76] but the Second Circuit ruled in 1999 that Title III applies to the content of insurance policies as well as physical access to the places where they are sold.[77]

AIDS is a handicap under Texas Insurance Code Art. 21.21-3, which forbids insurers to limit the amount of coverage available to an individual because of handicap (unless the limitation is based on sound actuarial principles or actual or reasonably anticipated experience). But the Fifth Circuit rationale is that the insurer didn't know the plaintiff-purchaser had AIDS. Policy provisions were the same for everybody.

In this analysis, the Title III claim was unsustainable, because the plaintiff's ability to enjoy goods and services was limited by the disability itself, not the insurer. For instance, there is no requirement that bookstores carry only Braille books, even though blind people are impaired in their ability to enjoy printed materials.

A utility worker's bad back kept him from doing the overtime that was mandatory for his position as an installer. (Workers have to be available for long hours, because utility connections have to be done as soon as possible.) Therefore, to the Eleventh Circuit, he was not qualified under the ADA. Although the published description for the job doesn't mention hours or overtime, the job application does say that overtime is a condition of employment. The Eleventh Circuit treated overtime as the equivalent of reliable attendance as a prerequisite of qualification for the job.[78]

[¶355] Litigation Issues

According to the D.C. Circuit, a Title VII plaintiff must wait 180 days after filing of his or her charge before bringing suit. A mid-1999 D.C. Circuit decision[79] says that the EEOC's regulation at 29 CFR §1601.28(a)(2), allowing earlier issuance of the right to sue letter, is invalid, in that the EEOC has a duty to investigate, which can't be avoided via an early right to sue letter. However, the Ninth and Eleventh Circuits agree with the EEOC about the desirability of expediting litigation.

When a motion for summary judgment is made in an ADA diversity case, the District Court must apply the federal burden-shifting rule, not the state rule.[80]

A claim of harassment based on sexual orientation can be brought by a public employee[81] (in this case, a gay police officer) under §1983, as an equal protection violation. Harassing conduct by other officers and supervisors is impermissible status-based conduct that is not justified by any defensible state objective.

In its defense, the Police Department cited a case holding that a gay postal worker did not have a cause of action for sexual orientation-based harassment,[82] but the Eastern District of New York did not find that Title VII case compelling in the §1983 context. Title VII enacts a list of categories for which discrimination is forbidden; sexual orientation is not included. The equal protection clause doesn't have the same limitation, and protects similarly situated individuals from invidious and irrational orientation discrimination.

A sexual harassment complainant can only litigate claims relating to incidents occurring during the 300-day period that ended with the filing of a claim with the EEOC. Complaints to management that did not result in an EEOC filing will not permit testimony about earlier incidents to be used to demonstrate the presence of a hostile work environment. In this particular case, without that testimony, the evidence was insufficient to show regular, pervasive harassment. Nor could the presence of sexually offensive material on company computers be used to prove the hostile environment, because the material was neither specifically aimed at the plaintiff (she discovered it through a search of the site) or made available to the general public.[83]

Under a March 2000 decision,[84] when an employee won both federal and state discrimination claims, the court could allocate the compensatory damage award to the state law claim, so that the $300,000 cap applies only to the federal punitive damage award. The plaintiff received a general verdict with duplicative damages, so the court had discretion over allocation of the damages. In this case the employee lost promotions and received unfavorable evaluations after complaining about sexist treatment by coworkers. The jury awarded $100,000 in back pay, $2 million in front pay, and $1 million compensatory damages for emotional distress.

The District Court allocated the compensatory damages and front and back pay to the state claims, then reduced the punitive damages to $300,000 in compliance with the Civil Rights Act of 1991 (CRA '91). The Ninth Circuit held that compensatory damages for non-Title VII claims are not subject to the CRA '91 cap, because the Congressional intention was to permit states to maintain damage remedies greater than those provided under Title VII.

Employees who prevail in the sense of settling employment discrimination claims at the administrative level do not have the right to bring a separate Title VII action in District Court for recovery of attorney's fees, in that there is no federal jurisdiction over such claims.[85] In this reading, jurisdiction over "actions under this subchapter" means proceedings to enforce substantive employment rights. Fee awards are only discretionary and ancillary to these proceedings.

[¶360] Wrongful Termination

An employee who can be terminated only for cause can assert a tort cause of action for wrongful discharge,[86] and can bring the tort suit even without exhausting administrative or contractual remedies. Some earlier Washington decisions suggested that only at-will employees (or only private rather than government employees) can bring a common law wrongful discharge claim, but that blurs the fundamental distinction between tort and contract claims. The tort wrongful discharge claim isn't based on contract terms; rather, it stems from the employer's duty to conform to public policy—and public employers are not exempt from this duty.

Texas maintains the concept of at-will employment, and employers do not have a generalized duty of good faith and fair dealing to employees.[87] Police officers, whose jobs were reclassified as civilian positions, claimed they were being retaliated against because they had filed ADA and state discrimination suits. In Texas, the employment relationship is not a fiduciary or special one, and the only recognized exception to the at-will doctrine is firing an employee for refusing to carry out an illegal act.

ENDNOTES

1. *Circuit City Stores, Inc. v. Adams*, #99-1379, 69 LW 4195 (Sup. Ct. 3/21/01).
2. See Michael Delikat and Rene Kathawala, "Enforcing Pre-Dispute Arbitration Agreement," *N.Y.L.J.* 5/1/01, available through law.com, citing, e.g., *Chanchani v. Salomon/Smith Barney, Inc.*, 2001 WL 204214 (S.D.N.Y. 3/1/01) [enforcing arbitration policy in employee handbook]; *Wright v. SFX Entertainment Inc.*, 2001 WL 103433 (S.D.N.Y. 2/7/01) [written employment agreement with arbitration clause]; *Marcus v. Masucci*, 118 F.Supp.2d 453 (S.D.N.Y. 2000) [U-4 arbitration clause].

3. *Oil, Chemical & Atomic Workers Int'l Union v. Conoco Inc.*, 69 LW 1553 (10th Cir. 3/7/01).

4. *Bradford v. Rockwell Semiconductor Systems*, 69 LW 1480 (4th Cir. 1/22/01).

5. *M.B. Sturgis Inc.*, 331 NLRB No. 173 (8/25/00).

6. *United Mine Workers v. Martinka Coal Co.*, 202 F.3rd 717 (4th Cir. 2000).

7. *In re Bluffton Casting Corp.*, 186 F.3d 857 (7th Cir. 1999).

8. *Johnson v. Kmart Corp.*, 723 N.E.2d 1192 (Ill.App. 2000).

9. *NLRB v. F&A Food Sales Inc.*, 202 F.3d 1258 (10th Cir. 2000).

10. *Burlington Northern & Santa Fe RR v. IBT Local 174*, 203 F.3d 703 (9th Cir. 2000).

11. *United Food & Commercial Workers Union Local 211 v. Family Snacks Inc.*, 69 LW 1469 (8th Cir. 1/31/01).

12. *Jacoby v. NLRB*, 233 F.3d 611 (D.C. Cir. 2000).

13. See 69 LW 2444.

14. *Penrod v. NLRB*, 203 F.3d 41 (D.C. Cir. 2000).

15. *Snapp v. Unlimited Concepts Inc.*, 208 F.3d 928 (11th Cir. 2000).

16. *Travis v. Gary Community Mental Health Center Inc.*, 921 F.2d 108 (7th Cir. 1990).

17. "SEC Approves Changes to Arbitration of Securities Industry Employment Disputes," (no by-line) 68 LW 2288.

18. Adv Rev Proc 2000-16, 2000-6 IRB 518. Also see Rev. Proc. 2000-17, 2000-11 IRB 766.

19. *Anstett v. Eagle-Picher Industries Inc.*, 203 F.3d 501 (7th Cir. 2000).

20. *Young v. Washington Gas Light Co.*, 206 F.3d 1200 (D.C. Cir. 2000).

21. *Egelhoff v. Egelhoff*, #99-1529, 69 LW 4206 (Sup. Ct. 3/21/01).

22. *Matz v. Household Int'l Tax Reduction Investment Plan*, 227 F.3d 971 (7th Cir. 2000).

23. *Stewart v. Thorpe Holding Company Profit Sharing Plan*, 207 F.3d 1143 (9th Cir. 2000).

24. IRS Adv. Notice 2000-11, 2000-6 IRB 572.

25. *Esden v. Bank of Boston*, 229 F.3d 154 (2nd Cir. 2000).

26. *Eaton v. Onan Corp.*, 117 F.Supp.2d 812 (S.D. Ind. 2000).

27. *Anes v. Dehart*, 195 F.3d 177 (3rd Cir. 1999).

28. *Critchell v. Critchell*, 746 A.2d 282 (D.C. 2000).

29. *Rahn v. Rahn*, 914 P.2d 463 (Colo.App. 1995).

30. *Greenwood v. Greenwood*, 746 A.2d 358 (Maine 2000).

31. *Meyer v. Meyer*, 26 Family Law Reporter 1303 (Pa. 4/17/00).

32. *Smith v. Smith,* 26 Family Law Reporter 1260 (Pa.Super. 3/17/00).
33. *Parada v. Parada,* 26 Family Law Reporter 1309 (Ariz. 4/19/00).
34. Gary M. Ford and Jennifer E. Eller's paper, "Managed Care Litigation Review," originally presented at the ALI-ABA ERISA Litigation Conference, May 3-5, 2001, is available at their law firm's Web site, http://www.groom.com. The paper provides an excellent summary of litigation issues after *Pegram,* including class action suits against HMOs by both patients and health care providers and prescription drug litigation.
35. #98-1949, 530 U.S. 211 (Sup.Ct. 2000).
36. *Peay v. Bellsouth Medical Assistance Plan,* 205 F.3d 1206 (10th Cir. 2000).
37. *Adams v. Freedom Forge Corp.,* 204 F.3d 475 (3rd Cir. 2000).
38. *Kinstler v. First Reliance Standard Life Ins.,*181 F.3d 243 (2nd Cir. 1999).
39. *Rosenthal v. Long-Term Disability Plan of Epstein, Becker & Green PC,* 68 LW 1544 (C.D. Cal 2/23/00).
40. *EEOC v. Staten Island Savings Bank,* 207 F.3d 144 (2nd Cir. 2000). On January 25, 2000, the Supreme Court affirmed *Doe v. Mutual of Omaha,* main volume, without opinion, as Docket #98-4112.
41. *Shea v. Esensten,* 208 F.3d 712 (8th Cir. 2000).
42. *Deboard v. Sunshine Mining & Refining Co.,* 208 F.3d 1228 (10th Cir. 2000).
43. *Baizer v. CIR,* 204 F.3d 1231 (9th Cir. 2000).
44. *Herzberger v. Johnson,* 205 F.3d 327 (7th Cir. 2000).
45. In "Evidentiary Scope of Judicial Review of Discretionary Employee Benefit Plan Decisions," http://www.groom.com/Ar&Br_HC-1st11th cirdc.htm, John P. McAllister and Alvaro I. Anillo outline the issues involved in determining whether a court will review a plan administrator's decision de novo, or merely determine whether there has been an abuse of discretion by the administrator.
46. *Pappas v. Asbel,* 69 LW 2183 (Pa. 4/3/01), discussed in Ruth Bryna Cohen, "After Remand, Pennsylvania Supremes Affirm Landmark HMO Decision," *The Legal Intelligencer* 4/5/01, available on law.com.
47. *Pryzbowski v. U.S. Healthcare,* No. 99-5920 (3rd Cir. 3/27/01). The Third Circuit suggested that seeking a preliminary mandatory injunction was a better way of getting an HMO to approve treatment

desired by the plaintiff, citing, e.g., *Marro v. K-III Communications Corp.*, 943 F.Supp. 249 (E.D.N.Y. 1996).

48. *Corporate Health Insurance Inc. v. Texas Dep't of Insurance*, 215 F.3d 526 (5th Cir. 2000).

49. *Maio v. Aetna Inc.*, 221 F.3d 472 (3rd Cir. 2000) denies RICO claims by HMO subscribers based on the HMO's alleged failure to disclose its practices of limiting coverage to enhance its own profits. The claims were deemed improper because RICO requires actual and not merely hypothetical injury to plaintiffs' "business or property".

50. Pension and Welfare Benefits Administration (DOL) Voluntary Fiduciary Correction (VFC) program, 65 FR 14,164-14,179 (3/15/00).

51. *Thorson v. Gemini Inc.*, 205 F.3d 370 (8th Cir. 2000).

52. *Renaud v. Wyoming Family Services Dept.*, 203 F.3d 723 (10th Cir. 2000).

53. *Rice v. Sunrise Express Inc.*, 209 F.3d 1008 (7th Cir. 2000).

54. *The Reinforced Earth Co. v. Worker's Compensation Appeal Board*, discussed in Danielle Rodier, "Illegal Aliens Can Receive Workers' Compensation Benefits," *The Legal Intelligencer* 4/14/00, available at http://www.law.com. But cf. *Granados v. Windson Development Corp.*, 257 Va. 103, 509 S.E.2d 290 (1999), which reaches precisely the opposite conclusion.

55. *Balint v. Carson City*, 180 F.3d 1047 (9th Cir. 1999).

56. *Lanning v. Southeastern Pennsylvania Transp. Auth.*, 181 F.3d 478 (3rd Cir. 1999).

57. *Kahn v. Objective Solutions International*, 86 F.Supp. 2d 377 (S.D.N.Y. 2000).

58. *Miller v. American Family Mutual Ins. Co.*, 203 F.3d 997 (6th Cir. 2000)

59. *Smith v. First Union National Bank*, 202 F.3d 234 (2nd Cir. 2000).

60. *Lauture v. IBM*, 216 F.3d 258 (2nd Cir. 2000); *Perry v. Woodward*, 199 F.3d 1126 (10th Cir. 1999); *Spriggs v. Diamond Auto Glass*, 165 F.3d 1015 (4th Cir. 1999); *Fadeyi v. Planned Parenthood*, 160 F.3d 1048 (5th Cir. 1998).

61. *Eisenberg v. Advance Relocation & Storage Inc.*, 237 F.3d 111 (2nd Cir. 2000).

62. *Deters v. Equifax Credit Information Services*, 202 F.3d 262 (10th Cir. 2000).

63. *Cush-Crawford v. Adchem Corp.*, 98-CV-67 (2nd Cir. 2000); see Daniel Wise, "No Compensatory Damages Required for Punitive Award," *N.Y.L.J.* 5/5/00, http://www.law.com. Cf. with *Timm v. Steel Plating Inc.*, 137 F.3d 1008 (7th Cir. 1998) and *Kerr-Salgas v. American Airlines Inc.*, 69 F.3d 1205 (1st Cir. 1995).

64. *Farrell v. Planters Lifesavers Co.*, 206 F.3d 271 (3rd Cir. 2000).

65. *McMenamy v. Rochester*, 69 LW 1536 (2nd Cir. 3/2/01).

66. *Kimel v. Florida Board of Regents,* 528 U.S. 62 (Sup.Ct. 2000).

67. *Reeves v. Sanderson Plumbing Products,* 530 U.S. 133 (Sup.Ct. 2000).

68. *Erie County Retirees Ass'n v. Erie County, PA,* 200 F.3d 193 (3rd Cir. 2000).

69. *Galabya v. NYC Board of Education,* 202 F.3d 636 (2nd Cir. 2000).

70. *Stokes v. Westinghouse Savannah River Co.,* 206 F.3d 420 (4th Cir. 2000).

71. *Board of Trustees of the University of Alabama v. Garrett,* #99-1240, 69 LW 4105 (Sup.Ct. 2/21/01).

72. *Flowers v. Southern Regional Physician Services*, No. 99-31354 (5th Cir.); *Fox v. General Motors*, No. 00-1589 (4th Circuit), discussed in Marcia Coyle, "ADA: New Tool for Bias Suits," *National Law Journal* 5/7/01, available on law.com

73. *Lewis v. Kmart Corp.,* 180 F.3d 166 (4th Cir. 1999).

74. *Rogers v. Dept. of Health and Environmental Control,* 67 LW 1672 (4th Cir. 1999).

75. *McNeil v. Time Insurance Co.,* 205 F.3d 179 (5th Cir. 2000).

76. *Doe v. Mutual of Omaha Ins. Co.,* 179 F.3d 557 (7th Cir. 1999), affirmed without opinion by the Supreme Court in 2000.

77. *Pallozzi v. Allstate Life Ins. Co.,* 198 F.3d 28 (2nd Cir. 1999).

78. *Davis v. Florida Power & Light Co.,* 205 F.3d 1301 (11th Cir. 3/10/00).

79. *Martini v. FNMA,* 178 F.3d 1336 (D.C. Cir. 1999).

80. *Snead v. Metropolitan Property & Casualty Ins. Co.,* 237 F.3d 1080 (9th Cir. 2001).

81. *Quinn v. Nassau County Police Dep't.,* 53 F.Supp.2d 347 (E.D.N.Y. 1999).

82. *Simonton v. Runyon,* No. CV 96 4334, 1999 WL 345956 (E.D.N.Y. 5/26/99).

83. *Cronin v. Martindale Andres & Co.,* discussed in Shannon P. Duffy, "No 'Continuing Violation' If Plaintiff Delays EEOC Filing," *The Legal Intelligencer* 4/3/01, available on law.com.

84. *Passantino v. Johnson & Johnson Consumer Products Inc.*, 68 LW 1583 (9th Cir. 3/10/00).
85. *Chris v. Tenet*, 68 LW 1087 (E.D. Va 7/28/99).
86. *Smith v. Bates Technical College*, 991 P.2d 1135 (Wash. 1/27/00).
87. *Midland, Texas v. O'Bryant*, 68 LW 1635 (Texas 4/6/00).

¶400

Business Taxes

[¶401]

The Tax Relief Extension Act, P.L. 106-170, provided that for sales and other dispositions occurring after the effective date of the Act, §453(a) would prevent accrual basis taxpayers from using the installment method to report installment sale income that would otherwise be accrued. The object was for profits to be taxed in the year of the sale, even if income comes in over several years.

However, the Installment Sale Tax Correction Act of 2000, P.L. 106-573, repeals this provision, retroactive to 12/16/99, which was supposed to be its effective date.

The Economic Growth Tax Relief and Reconciliation Act of 2001 (EGTRA) primarily deals with individual income taxes, not corporate taxes. However, EGTRA §801 provides that the corporate estimated tax payment that would otherwise be due on September 17, 2001 can be deferred until October 1, 2001. For the corporate estimated tax payment due on September 15, 2004, it is permissible to divide the payment into two parts: 80% paid by 9/15/04, the balance not paid until 10/1/04.

See T.D. 8896, 2000-36 IRB 249 for Temporary Regulations governing disclosure of corporate tax shelters.

A 2000 case from Michigan holds that taxing authorities satisfied due process by following the procedures of the property tax statute and mailing notices of delinquency and tax sale to the corporate taxpayer's address of record. There was no burden of inquiry when the notice was returned as undeliverable.[1]

See http://www.irs.gov/elec_svs/qa-bus.html for the IRS' plain-English "Q and A for Businesses Filing Taxes Electronically," explaining how to file Form 941 with a personal computer, using Electronic Data Interchange Format, or with a touch-tone telephone; electronic filing of information returns such as 1099 and W-2G; how to file Form 940 electronically or on magnetic tape, and how to "e-file" the Form 5500 series of employee benefit plan returns. IR-2000-83, which appears in the *Federal Register* for December 6, 2000, publishes temporary and final regulations for deposit of federal employment taxes. Certain employers can avoid making deposits by remitting the full amount of tax liability with a timely return.

[¶410] Partnership Taxation

In mid-1999, the Second Circuit held that taxpayers can't raise a statute of limitations defense to adjustments to partnership items, because anything about a partnership item must be raised at the partnership, and not the individual-partner, level.[2]

T.D. 8841[3] comprises Final Regulations implementing the Taxpayer Relief Act of 1997's changes in partnership reporting requirements. All domestic partnerships must file partnership returns; this Treasury Decision explains the circumstances under which foreign partnerships must also file.

Effective January 1, 2000, a foreign partnership with under $20,000 in U.S. source income and no income that is effectively connected to business in the United States need not file unless 1% or more of any item of gain, loss, deduction, or credit is allocable to direct U.S. partners. A partnership return is not required if there are no U.S. partners or income effectively connected to business in the United States—even if there is some U.S. source income.

T.D. 8847, 1999-52 IRB 701 finalizes Regulations under Code §§734, 743, 751, 755 dealing with optional adjustment to the basis of partnership property, after partnership interests have been transferred to harmonize the transferee's economic and tax consequences.

[¶450] Corporate Tax

A taxpayer with average annual gross receipts under $1 million, and that uses the cash method on its books, is now permitted to use the cash method for tax purposes. Such a taxpayer will no longer be required to account for inventories or use the accrual method for purchases and sales of merchandise.[4]

Notice 2000-43, 2000-35 IRB 209 announces a six- to twelve-month pilot program for companies with open cases in the Large and Mid-Sized Business Division to resolve all open issues, for all open years examined by the IRS either currently or in the past.

[¶451] Income Items

In February, 2000, the Supreme Court struck down[5] California's scheme for allocating the interest expenses of foreign corporations between California and non-California income. The system was invalid because it has the effect of imposing tax on non-California income, rather than reasonably allocating the expense deduction to the income it generates.

[¶452] Business Deductions

Most of the costs incurred in gaining ISO 9000 certification (proof of satisfaction of international quality standards) are deductible as ordinary and necessary business expenses.[6]

[¶453] Treatment of Capital Expenditures

Adv.Rev.Rul. 99-23, 1999-20 IRB 3 provides that the expense of trying to acquire a specific business is not a startup expense, and therefore is ineligible for amortization over 60 months under §195. Instead, the acquiring company has to capitalize the expenses incurred after the decision to acquire a particular business, even if they occur before a legally enforceable agreement has been put in place.

T.D. 8865 provides Final and Proposed Regulations under §197 (dealing with 15-year amortization of purchased intangibles such as goodwill) and under §167(f) (36-month recovery period for certain software; amortization of items that do not come under §197). The new rules are generally applicable to intangibles acquired after January 25, 2000.

Environmental remediation costs that made the taxpayer's real property safely usable for a broader range of purposes provided "permanent improvements" to the property and, therefore, had to be capitalized rather than currently deducted as ordinary and necessary business expenses.[7]

Similarly, legal fees encountered by a store chain that acquired another store chain, related to negotiating an FTC consent order and settling state antitrust litigation that went all the way to the Supreme Court, had to be capitalized and not deducted because of the long-range implications of the acquisition.[8]

[¶458] Reorganizations and Related Transactions

In two fact situations (in which the target corporation does not cease to exist), corporate transactions that are really divisive transactions will not qualify as tax-free A Reorganizations as prescribed by §368(a)(1)(A) even though they are state-law mergers.[9] However, some divisive transactions qualify for tax-free status in another way, under §355, so taxation is not inevitable.

T.D. 8898, 2000-38 IRB 276, issues Final Regulations under §368, explicating the effect of redemptions and distributions before the reorganization. Distributions and redemptions by the target are taken into effect for continuity of interest purposes to the extent that consideration received by the target shareholders constitutes boot, or would be if the target shareholders had also received stock of the issuing corporation in exchange for their target shares.

In a 2000 Tax Court case, the sole shareholder of a trucking company sold the company's operating assets. He was also majority shareholder in another trucking company. The two companies were merged. The taxpayer could not treat the transaction as a tax-free reorganization, because there was no continuity of business enterprise. The merged company did not continue the historic business of its predecessor (the first company had not operated for five years as of the time of the merger) and did not use the predecessor's historic assets in its business. Instead, the taxpayer had cashed out and invested the proceeds of the sale of the operating assets in tax-exempt bonds. Because the transaction was not an exempt reorganization, the taxpayer had to recognize gain equal to the fair market value of the property received for stock in the first corporation, less his basis in the stock.[10]

[¶459.1] Subchapter S Corporations

Under the circumstances laid out in T.D. 8869 (65 FR 3843, 1/25/00), a Subchapter S corporation can liquidate and reabsorb its corporate subsidiary by making an election. The process will not be treated as a step transaction.

Early in 2001, the Supreme Court ruled that discharge of the indebtedness of an insolvent S Corporation is not gross income for the corporation. However, it is an item of income that passes through to the shareholders under §1366(a)(1), thus increasing their basis in the stock. [11]

ENDNOTES

1. *Smith v. Cliffs on the Bay Condominium Ass'n*, 617 N.W.2d 536 (Mich. 2000).
2. Chimblo, 83 AFTR2d ¶99-851 (2nd Cir. 5/17/99).
3. 1999-48 IRB 593, 64 FR 61,498 (11/12/99).
4. Rev.Proc. 2000-22, 2000-20 IRB 1008.
5. *Hunt-Wesson Inc. v. Franchise Tax Board of California*, #98-2043 120 S.Ct. 1022 (Sup.Ct. 2/22/00).
6. Rev.Rul. 2000-4, 2000-4 IRB 331.
7. *Dominican Resources, Inc. v. U.S.*, 219 F.3d 359 (4th Cir. 2000).
8. *American Stores Co. v. Comm'r*, 114 TC No. 27 (5/26/00).
9. Rev.Rul. 2000-5, 2000-5 IRB 436.
10. *Honbarrier v. Comm'r*, 115 TC No. 23 (9/29/00).
11. *Gitlitz v. CIR*, #99-1295, 69 LW 4060 (Sup.Ct. 1/9/01).

¶600

Securities Regulation

[¶601]

On June 7, 1999, the Ninth Circuit reversed its earlier ruling about Matsushita's buyout of MCA Incorporated.[1] This time, the Ninth Circuit says that a Delaware judgment, confirming settlement of both state and federal securities claims about the buyout, is entitled to full faith and credit. The Delaware suit was the first to be filed, making breach of fiduciary duty claims under state law.

The federal suit was filed in California. While it was on appeal to the Ninth Circuit, the parties to the Delaware class action, who included the federal plaintiffs, settled and released their federal claims. The U.S. Supreme Court said that the judgment approving the settlement was entitled to full faith and credit in the federal suit, but a footnote said that claims about adequacy of representation of federal plaintiffs in Delaware were outside the scope of the case.

The case was remanded to the Ninth Circuit. In its second decision, the Ninth Circuit held that Constitutionally infirm judgments violate due process, but the Supreme Court signaled that the Delaware courts had resolved the due process issues. (The dissent said that the Delaware court didn't explicitly decide whether the absent federal plaintiffs were adequately represented, and the representatives had no incentive to get the federal claims fairly valued, because they couldn't be asserted in state court anyway.)

Another 1999 Ninth Circuit case[2] holds that the SEC should not have affirmed "parking" charges against a broker, because there was no violation in making legitimate sales of securities in a falling market to shift loss from one party to another. (A broker, with proprietary accounts, sold and bought back a particular stock five times to meet minimum net capital requirements, without taking the required "haircut" [deduction] from market value.) The NASD said the broker had violated its Rules of Fair Practice but the allegedly improper trades did not follow a pattern; they occurred anywhere from one to seven days apart and didn't have the same terms.

In October, 1999, the SEC adopted an extremely significant scheme of new rules for communications in connection with mergers and acquisitions ("the Regulation M&A Release");[3] the SEC described it as the biggest reform in a generation.

The current system imposes a quiet period after the announcement of a merger, until the registration or proxy statement is approved.

The new rules allow merging companies additional freedom to communicate with the investing public. After a merger is announced, the merging companies are allowed to make public statements while waiting for the registration and proxy statements to become effective, as long as any written communication is immediately filed with EDGAR. Oral communications (a category deemed to include speeches, conference calls, and slide shows) can be made without filing, although the SEC is reviewing whether these should be treated as writings.

The release also attempts to bring the treatment of cash and stock tender offers closer to parity. Traditionally, the SEC has treated a stock offer as a sale of securities, so a registration statement must be filed. But the SEC doesn't want regulatory hurdles to mandate cash takeovers in situations where the acquiror prefers to use stock.

The new rule allows "early commencement": the offeror can file the registration statement and start the exchange offer immediately, unlike current rule which requires a delay until the registration becomes effective. However, the purchase of the tendered securities has to wait until effectiveness; the 20-business-day tender offer period has expired; and the security holders get disclosure of all material changes to the offering documents in adequate time to review and act on the changes.

The new rule combines all existing schedules for issuer and third-party tender offers into a single Schedule TO. A plain English summary term sheet must be furnished for all tender offers, mergers, and going-private transactions. The financial statement disclosures for business combinations are somewhat streamlined.

In November, 1999, the SEC permitted changes in the mechanisms for arbitration of employment disputes within the securities industry.[4] The SEC approved NASD's proposal for strengthening the arbitration process and resolving disputes about claims that might potentially be either arbitrated or litigated.

Claims up to $100,000 can be heard by one arbitrator, not a panel. All employment discrimination claims must go to qualified, nonindustry arbitrators. The arbitrator can award reasonable attorneys' fees; and employers are at less risk that claims will be bifurcated between litigation and arbitration (e.g., discrimination claims joined with other employment-related claims).

State-law breach of fiduciary duty claims were reinstated by Delaware against a brokerage firm alleged not to have fully disclosed to customers that it made money when their money market sweep accounts were transferred to a company that had a joint venture agreement with the brokerage.[5]

The broker claimed that the state claims were preempted by the NASD rule which lets brokers use "negative option" letters to customers when sweep accounts are moved. The brokerage sent a letter saying unless the customer gave instructions to the contrary, the firm would move the sweep accounts to a company with which it had a joint venture and in which it owned a 20% interest. (The SEC position is that negative option letters are efficient and provide adequate protection for investors.)

The Delaware court said that the full disclosure obligation doesn't conflict with the NASD rule, which is supposed to relieve brokers of unreasonable burdens, but is not a safe harbor. A form letter can be used to disclose the identity of the transferee. State-law fiduciary duty requires acting in the customer's best interest and abstaining from self-dealing unless the customer has freely consented after full disclosure.

Omitted information is material if it would have had actual significance in a reasonable shareholder's decision-making process. So the question becomes whether investors, knowing that the broker could profit from the move, would want to understand the structure of the joint venture deal. There were two reasonable inferences of how the broker acquired an interest in the joint venture: by investing its own money or transferring customer money, and customers are entitled to facts so they can decide which explanation they favor.

[¶605] [NEW] What is a "Security"?

A Web site described as a "virtual stock exchange," where "players" using real money could trade "virtual shares" of "virtual companies" in order to "double your money," was held by the District Court for the District of Massachusetts to be a gambling site rather than a locus for unregistered investments; therefore, it was not subject to securities regulation.[6]

[¶610] [NEW] The '33 Act and Its Registration Process

In August, 2000, the Tenth Circuit joined the First, Second and Ninth Circuits in holding that fraud in the initial registration statement will support a '33 Act §11 action against the issuer by investors who bought on the secondary market rather than in the initial issue, on the grounds that the text of §11 does not limit the cause of action to the initial issue.[7]

SEC Release No. 33-7943 creates a safe harbor for integrated offerings under Rule 155. An issuer that initiates either a private or public offering, but does not sell any securities, can abandon the private offering and go public instead—but the prior, unsuccessful offering must be disclosed. In general, the issuer must wait 30 days between terminating one form of offering and adopting the other.

[¶630] The Securities Exchange Act

Regulation FD (for Fair Disclosure) was promulgated by the SEC on August 10, 2000. The purpose is to require companies that disclose material information (thus making it public) to do so broadly to the entire market of investors and potential investors, rather than selectively to institutional investors and Wall Street analysts. The new rule was heavily criticized by the securities industry, which predicted that it would lead to information boycotts rather than broader dissemination of information.

Generally speaking, Regulation FD applies to securities that are already on the market; communications in connection with most registered offerings are exempt. But once the senior officials of an issuer know (or are reckless not to know) that material nonpublic information is about to be selectively disclosed, the company must disclose the information to the public. Furthermore, if an improper selective disclosure is made (e.g., important information is given to analysts in a conference call), the issuer has an obligation to make a public disclosure within 24 hours.

There are two routes to disclosure. The issuer can file a Form 8K with the SEC, and the company can use any means of communication that is accessible to the public on a broad, nonexclusionary basis—typically, a press release. The SEC's position is that, under current conditions, placing information on a corporate Web site does not constitute adequate disclosure, although it may in the future.

Regulation FD is a disclosure regulation, so violations are not subject to anti-fraud enforcement. The SEC has the power to file an administrative proceeding to get a cease-and-desist order against a violator. The SEC can also bring a civil suit for injunction or civil penalties, but there is no private right of action strictly for Regulation FD violations.

Earlier in 2000, the SEC issued Release Nos. 34-42974, IC-24543, and IA-1883[8] to implement the financial reform statute, the Gramm-Leach-Bliley Act. This particular SEC Release deals with the protection of the privacy of investors' financial information. Brokers, dealers, investment companies, and registered investment advisors are obligated to set up procedures to protect the security, confidentiality, and integrity of customer records and information (e.g., to prevent computer hackers from gaining access to sensitive information). The securities firms must disclose to these customers what the company's policy is for protection of personal information, including the mandatory choice of opting out of having information disclosed to third parties (e.g., sale of customer information to marketers).

In Staff Accounting Bulletin No. 99 (8/12/99),[9] the SEC staff says that an income misstatement of a line item in a financial statement cannot automatically be ignored as immaterial merely because it does not exceed 5%. All factors, and the impact on the financial statement as a whole, must be considered, even if egregious circumstances such as management self-dealing are not present.

Mere percentages are not enough to determine materiality. The SEC staff says that a matter is material if there is a substantial likelihood that it would be of interest to a reasonable person. Qualitative factors may make even a very small misstatement material: e.g., if it hides a trend (such as a change in earnings); could and should have been accurately measured; tilts a negative item into the positive, or vice versa; conceals an unlawful transaction; or affects a compliance burden. And even an immaterial but intentional misstatement can be unlawful.

Exchange Act §13(b) requires accurate and complete books and records that reflect events in "reasonable" detail. Reasonableness analysis is not exactly the same as that for materiality; §13(b) may be involved if issuer fails to correct a known misstatement, depending on the significance of the misstatement, how it happened, how much it would cost to correct it, and how clear the accounting rules are that it was misstated.

A broker's delivery of a prospectus to the customer after a sale won't cure misrepresentations made during the sales pitch.[10] Even if the prospectus offers adequate disclosure, it still can't cure a purchase induced by prior fraud, and it doesn't matter that federal law permits delivery of the prospectus at the time the sale is confirmed.

[¶630.1] [NEW] Anti-Fraud Rules

According to the D.C. Circuit, a scheme of wash and match trades that defrauds brokers rather than investors is still subject to Rule 10b-5, because the fraud occurs in connection with a purchase or sale. In this case, a broker was deemed to have scienter because she continued to execute trades involved in the fraud, ignoring suspicious factors, and thus her state of mind was reckless. (The person committing the fraud received the proceeds of sales before having to pay for the securities bought in wash transactions; in effect, the scheme was similar to kiting checks.)[11]

However, the Fourth Circuit held that a broker convicted of 13 counts of wire fraud for converting the account balance of a mentally disabled customer was not subject to SEC penalties for 10(b), 10b-5, and Securities Act §17(a) violations.[12]

A corporate officer who signs filings on behalf of the company makes a "statement" for 10(b) purposes whether or not the officer is involved in preparing the filings; anyone who signs a document attesting to its truth can be held liable for the contents of the document.[13]

The fraud on the market theory assumes that investors rely on the integrity of the market to set stock prices. The theory is not available in a New Jersey common-law fraud action, which requires actual reliance. Furthermore, the Mississippi Supreme Court is the only state court to accept this litigation theory, and merely in dictum.[14]

Materiality is a mixed question of fact and law—for instance, it is not possible to give a simple answer as to whether misstating an item representing only 1.7% of corporate revenues is material. At least at the pleading stage, a bright-line test cannot be used to assess materiality; all factors must be considered.[15]

[¶630.2] [NEW] Insider Trading

On August 10, 2000, the SEC announced two rules under 10b-5 dealing with insider trading.[16] Under new Rule 10b5-1, trading "on the basis" of inside information occurs if the individual is "aware" of the inside information at the time of the purchase or sale. However, affirmative defenses are available if the information, although known, was not a factor in the decision to enter into the transaction. Rule 10b5-2 imposes a duty of trust and confidence (and therefore potential liability for misrepresentation) when:

- The potentially liable person agreed to keep the information confidential
- The person who communicated the non-public information had a reasonable expectation of confidentiality based on, e.g., a history or pattern of shared confidences
- The alleged tipee got the information from a close family member (spouse, parent, child, sibling) although it is an affirmative defense that the actual relationship within the family did not create a reasonable expectation of confidentiality

[¶640] [NEW] Proxy Regulation

Shareholders who make 10(b) claims about proxy fraud, like plaintiffs under the §14(a) proxy fraud provision, must prove both loss and transaction causation—i.e., that their loss was caused by the misleading proxy statement.[17]

Under Release 33-7912, an issuer can satisfy the proxy delivery requirement by sending a single proxy statement to two or more investors who share a household—although a separate proxy card must be issued for each shareholder account.

[¶650] [NEW] Tender Offer Disclosure (Williams Act)

In the view of the Southern District of New York, the purpose of the '34 Act §13(d) [obligation to disclose acquisition of 5% or more of the target's securities] is to protect the target shareholders. Therefore, shareholders of the would-be acquiror do not have standing to sue; the statutory scheme doesn't even entitle them to receive Schedule 13D.[18]

[¶660] [NEW] The Investment Companies Act of 1940

Effective April 16, 2001, SEC Release No. 33-7941 amends the requirements for disclosing a mutual fund's after-tax returns. Mutual fund advertisements and sales materials have until October 1, 2001 to comply with amended Rule 482 and Investment Company Act Rule 34b-1.

According to the Third Circuit[19], Investment Company Act §36(b) does not preempt state-law claims of breach of fiduciary duty and deceit when a customer alleges that a fund investment adviser fails to provide adequate disclosure of fee calculations and conflicts of interest. The Third Circuit held that Congress did not intend preemption, because the state remedy is not in conflict with the federal one.

[¶680] SEC Enforcement

Commodity Exchange Act §4m(l) requires registration with the Commodity Futures Trading Commission of persons who are paid to advise others (in print or electronically) about the value or advisability of trading commodities futures. But it doesn't apply (for First Amendment reasons) to a publisher of general investment advice.[20] Imposing the requirement on a publisher of impersonal trading advice is an impermissible prior restraint on speech. Making the plaintiff register before engaging in publishing activities would be a prior restraint because communication is made contingent on approval from government officials.

A 1999 case from the District Court for the District of Columbia[21] invalidates (also on First Amendment grounds) the CFTC's rule requiring Internet operators and other publishers of information about futures trading to register. The publisher gives the same information to all subscribers; doesn't have discretion over customer accounts; doesn't trade on behalf of customers; and doesn't specifically advise following its recommendations. However, publishers are still subject to the antifraud requirements, because there's no element of prior restraint in applying these rules.

[¶690.1] Private Securities Litigation Reform Act (PSLRA)

F.R.E. 201 lets a court take judicial notice of publicly filed SEC documents for purpose of determining the contents of a document. Therefore, according to the Eleventh Circuit,[22] a defendant can rely on the documents if a motion to dismiss is based on cautionary statements in the document. Adding the documents to a 12(b)(6) motion to dismiss doesn't turn it into a motion for summary judgment.

The decision also voices the Eleventh Circuit's concepts about scienter under the PSLRA. In this conventional reading, motive and opportunity to commit fraud are relevant, but are not sufficient to prove severe recklessness. In this case, the plaintiffs charge that the corporation concealed and affirmatively misrepresented the harm that the company's expansion strategy did to its earnings per share.

Allegedly, concealment was done to satisfy analysts and prevent the stock price from declining. When the announcement was finally made, the stock price dropped 40%. The defendant's contention was that the safe harbor for forward-looking statements was applicable, and the SEC documents attached to the motion to dismiss showed that the firm "bespoke caution" about its corporate prospects.

The District Court granted plaintiffs' motion to strike the exhibits, on the theory that the exhibits embodied matters outside the pleadings and therefore could not be considered without converting the motion into one for summary judgment, giving the defendants a chance to reply on that level.

In the Eleventh Circuit view, any document that a company is legally obligated to file with the SEC is entitled to judicial notice at the dismissal stage, because SEC filings are recognized as the most accurate and authoritative source of information about a corporation, and there is no real question as to their authenticity.

With respect to the question of scienter, the Eleventh Circuit deems a complaint that alleges with particularity that the defendant acted with a severely reckless state of mind is sufficient to allege scienter. Therefore, the Eleventh Circuit disagrees with the Ninth Circuit to the extent that the Ninth reads the PSLRA to increase the substantive state of mind requirement.

The Ninth Circuit's July, 1999 *Silicon Graphics* decision[23] is the strictest of the recent PSLRA cases. It says that a satisfactory pleading must plead in detail facts showing deliberate or conscious recklessness, not just ordinary recklessness with no heightening factors. Therefore, the class action had to be dismissed because the Ninth Circuit standard is higher than the Second Circuit pleading standard, which calls for showing either simple recklessness or motive plus opportunity.

In the Ninth Circuit, proof of fraudulent intent requires "great detail" on facts "that constitute circumstantial evidence of deliberately reckless or conscious misconduct." Proof of mere recklessness or motive for fraud creates a reasonable inference of intent but is not tantamount to the required strong inference of intent.

The Ninth Circuit amended that opinion slightly in August, 1999, saying that the plaintiff must show "particular facts giving rise to a strong inference of deliberate recklessness, at a minimum." In order to show a strong inference of deliberate recklessness, the plaintiffs must produce facts that come closer to demonstrating intent than a mere showing of motive and opportunity would provide.

The Sixth Circuit takes an intermediate approach:[24] the presence of mere motive and opportunity for fraud isn't sufficient, but allegations giving rise to a strong inference of recklessness are adequate. In this case, the plaintiffs charged officers of the defendant corporation with selling stock while knowing about, or disregarding, inappropriate corporate accounting in the form of premature recognition of sales revenue that inflated the stock valuation.

A mid-1999 Third Circuit case[25] treats the PSLRA requirement of statement with particularity to permit the plaintiff to allege scienter by means of particular facts giving rise to a strong inference of the defendant's motive and opportunity to commit fraud, or the defendant's intentional, conscious, or reckless behavior.

But in this case, the stockholders did not satisfy the burden as to whether the firm's statements about earnings potential and the value of stock were misleading. The company's $20 million loss in one quarter led to a 25% drop in value of stock. The stockholders charged that the company withheld information about its risky business practices that led to the losses.

According to the Third Circuit, in the post-PSLRA environment, merely alleging that management stood to benefit from wrongdoing and had the opportunity to commit fraud is not adequate. Motive and opportunity must be supported by facts alleged with particularity, not merely stated as a conclusion. The alleged false statement also qualified for the forward-looking safe harbor, because the plaintiffs failed to prove that the executive knew the statement was false or misleading when made. An accurate statement of past earnings does not create 10(b) liability, and a general expression of optimism is understood by investors as puffery, so it can't be a material misstatement.

In the Sixth Circuit view, PSLRA didn't change the underlying law of scienter governing victory in a securities case, only what the plaintiff must plead to survive a motion to dismiss. Under the underlying 10(b) rule, recklessness can constitute scienter.

The First Circuit's entry in the PSLRA scienter sweepstakes[26] holds that the PSLRA doesn't change definition of scienter, which the First Circuit reads to include a narrowly defined concept of recklessness that approaches a lesser form of intent. Merely pleading motive and opportunity is not sufficient, but in the appropriate case facts showing motive and opportunity can create the necessary strong inference of scienter.

On another PSLRA issue, the Northern District of California decided[27] that a group of unrelated investors with nothing in common other than their attorney were not suitable lead plaintiffs for a class action. In this reading, institutional investors are presumptive lead plaintiffs because of their greater capacity to manage the case. The PSLRA has not really achieved its objective of reducing lawyer domination of the securities class action; the race to the courthouse has been replaced by an attempt to sign up the largest number of plaintiffs, then race to the courthouse and publish the required disclosures.

Although plaintiffs' attorneys have interpreted the PSLRA's use of the term "group" to mean that the attorney representing the largest number of plaintiffs should be lead counsel, the court says that the legislative intent is to presume that the normal lead would be an institutional investor with a substantial stake in the defendant corporation. In this case, the Board of Pensions and Retirement of the City of Philadelphia was named as the presumptive lead.

The Second Circuit's position, as articulated in mid-2000, is that the PSLRA embodies the long-standing Second Circuit position that a proper pleading must state with particularity the facts giving rise to a "strong inference" that the defendant's state of mind constituted scienter. [28]

The order that names a PSLRA lead plaintiff is not a collateral order that can be immediately appealed by would-be lead plaintiffs. According to the Ninth Circuit, the order does not conclusively determine the question being litigated; does not resolve an important issue separate from the merits; and can be reviewed on appeal from the final judgment.[29]

Although PSLRA §107 eliminates securities fraud as a RICO predicate act, an investor can nonetheless maintain a RICO suit about a fraud that occurred before the PSLRA's enactment in 1995—even though the suit was filed after PSLRA became effective.[30]

[¶690.2] Securities Litigation Uniform Standards Act (SLUSA)

Even after the Securities Litigation Uniform Standards Act, which is supposed to direct breach of duty to disclose cases into the federal system, the Southern District of New York has permitted shareholders to bring a state class action against a corporation and its directors[31] under the "Delaware carve-out" for state class actions involving the state-law fiduciary disclosure obligations of directors.

The Southern District of California has held[32] that the Securities Litigation Uniform Standards Act preempts a state-court class action against a broker. The plaintiff claimed that the defendant misrepresented the risks of using an online trading system that promised immediate execution, and should have known that there would be too much order volume to execute trades immediately. The causes of action asserted were unfair trade practices, false advertising, unjust enrichment, negligent misrepresentation, and fraud.

The plaintiff said that the state court action was not preempted because the suit stemmed from the broker/customer relationship and not from an issuer's fraud with respect to an individual security. This argument was not found persuasive, because the suit was still "in connection with the purchase or sale of a covered security." The statute does not include a limitation to issuer transactions, and trading systems necessarily operate in connection with the sale or purchase of securities.

Also on the Delaware carve-out, see *Gibson,*[33] a securities fraud class action, alleging breach of fiduciary obligations with respect to the proxy materials for an acquisition. The case was remanded to the state (California) court.

The Securities Litigation Uniform Standards Act (1998) includes a "Delaware carve-out" (15 USC §77p(d)(1)) allowing certain class actions for breach of the fiduciary duty of disclosure to shareholders, to be brought in state courts (not necessarily Delaware). Some legislative history suggests that the case has to be brought in the defendant's state of incorporation, but the court did not mandate this, because the statute does not require venue to be laid in the state of incorporation.

The plaintiff in this case sued in California on behalf of shareholders and investors in the defendant corporation, based on alleged misstatements in the proxy statement. The defendants used SLUSA to remove the case to District Court, saying that the complaint alleges a state-law violation involving misrepresentations in connection with purchase and sale of stock. The plaintiff's rationale was that the suit was not preempted by SLUSA because he was merely seeking equitable relief, not money damages, and SLUSA exempts breach of fiduciary duty claims in connection with a merger vote.

The Southern District of California permitted remand of the case, deeming it to be a covered class action within the meaning of the SLUSA removal provisions. The Uniform Standard Act wouldn't have much practical effect if plaintiffs could defeat removal merely by amending their complaints to remove the player for money damages.

[¶695] [NEW] Securities Activities on the Internet

See http://www.sec.gov/news/studies/online.htm for an SEC staff report on examinations of on-line trading services offered by registered broker-dealers. The staff recommended that all trading sites should provide basic information in plain English about securities in general, margin accounts in particular, and the risks of trading. The staff also identified problems with duplicate orders that arise where cancellations are not transmitted fast enough.

ENDNOTES

1. *Epstein v. MCA Inc.,* 179 F.3d 641 (9th Cir. 1999).
2. *Yoshikawa v. SEC,* 192 F.3d 1209 (9th Cir. 8/20/99).
3. Neil Hare, "SEC Adopts 'Sweeping' Rule Changes, Eases Curbs on Communications During Mergers," 68 LW 2233.
4. See 68 LW 2288.
5. *O'Malley v. Boris,* 742 A.2d 845 (Del. 1999).
6. *SEC v. SG Ltd.,* 2001 U.S. Dist. Lexis 1011 (D.Mass. 1/25/01).
7. *Joseph v. Wiles,* 223 F.3d 1155 (10th Cir. 2000).
8. June 23, 2000; the text is available at http://www.sec.gov/rules/final/34.42974.htm.
9. "SEC Staff Bulletin Spells Out 'Materiality' Criteria in Calculating Earnings," (no by-line), 68 LW 2128.
10. *Crowell v. Morgan Stanley Dean Witter Services Co.,* 68 LW 1512 (S.D. Fla. 1/27/00).
11. *Graham v. SEC,* 69 LW 1123 (D.C. Cir. 8/18/00).
12. *SEC v. Zandford,* 238 F.3d 559 (4th Cir. 2001).

13. *Howard v. Evarex Systems Inc.*, 2000 U.S. App. Lexis 23973 (9th Cir. 9/29/00).
14. *Kaufman v. i-Stat Corp.*, 754 A.2d 1188 (N.J. 2000). This case arose pre-SLUSA; after SLUSA, the fraud cause of action is exclusively federal.
15. *Ganino v. Citizens Utilities Co.*, 2000 U.S. App. Lexis 22493 (2nd Cir. 9/22/00).
16. See 69 LW 2094.
17. *Grace v. Rosenstock*, 228 F.3d 40 (2nd Cir. 2000).
18. *In re Dow Chemical Securities Bhopal Litigation*, 69 LW 1429 (S.D.N.Y. 12/28/00).
19. *Green v. Fund Asset Management LP*, 2001 U.S. App. Lexis 3975 (3rd Cir. 3/16/01).
20. *Commodity Trend Service v. Commodity Futures Trading Comm'n*, 68 LW 1222 (N.D.Ill. 9/27/99). Under *Lowe v. SEC*, 472 U.S. 181 (Sup.Ct. 1985), publishers of nonpersonalized advice about stock trading don't have to register as investment advisors.
21. *Taucher v. Born*, 68 LW 1028 (D.D.C. 1999).
22. *Bryant v. Avado Brands*, 187 F.3d 1271 (11th Cir. 1999).
23. *Janas v. McCracken, In re Silicon Graphics*, 183 F.3d 970 (9th Cir. 1999); amended opinion of 8/4/99, 195 F.3d 121 (9th Cir. 1999).
24. *Hoffman v. Comshare Inc.*, 183 F.3d 542 (6th Cir. 1999).
25. *In re Advanta Corp. Securities Litigation*, 180 F.3d 525 (3rd Cir. 1999).
26. *Greebel v. FTP Software Inc.*, 194 F.3d 185 (1st Cir. 1999).
27. *In re Network Associates Inc. Securities Litigation*, 68 LW 1315 (N.D. Cal. 11/12/99).
28. *Novak v. Kasaks*, 216 F.3d 300 (2nd Cir. 2000).
29. *Z-Seven Fund Inc. v. Ehrlich*, 69 LW 1254 (9th Cir. 10/18/00).
30. *Scott v. Boos*, 68 LW 1784 (9th Cir. 6/8/00).
31. *Lalondriz v. USA Networks Inc.*, 68 LW 1080 (S.D.N.Y. 6/30/99).
32. *Abada v. Charles Schwab & Co.*, 68 LW 1171 (S.D. Cal 9/7/99).
33. *Gibson v. PS Group Holdings Inc.*, 68 LW 1588 (S.D. Cal 3/8/00).

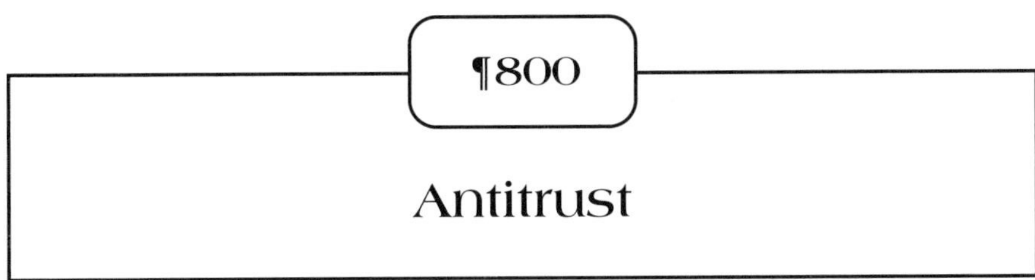

Antitrust

[¶801]

In February, 2000, the Eastern District of New York certified a rather large (four million member!) class of retailers in an antitrust suit on the issue of whether the issuers of Visa and MasterCard illegally forced stores accepting their credit cards to accept debit cards as well.[1]

The plaintiffs allege that, although they pay the same fee to the issuers for debit and credit cards, the debit card fee is much higher than that charged by competitors. Therefore the demand is an illegal tie (made possible by defendants' 90% market share) that forces the plaintiff merchants to pay excessive fees.

The class was certified based on a showing that common proof can show injury in fact; and that substantive claims and the issue of the defendant's market power can be resolved class-wide. This leaves open the option of decertification if the individual damages later are found to outbalance the common issues.

Certainly the biggest antitrust story of the last few years is the Justice Department's litigation against Microsoft, discussed in ¶810, below. The 2001 Supplement went to press after the District Court for the District of Columbia ruled that Microsoft had indeed been guilty of predatory anti-competitive behavior. The main remedy ordered was the breakup of the software giant into two companies: one selling the Windows operating system, the other one selling applications programs and other products. However, on June 20, 2000, Judge Jackson granted a stay of the judgment pending appeal, and certified the case for appeal to the Supreme Court under the Federal Expediting Act. As of press time for the 2002 supplement, however, the appeals process still had not been completed, and Microsoft had not undergone divestiture.

As a footnote to the massive Microsoft case, the Middle District of Tennessee has ruled[2] that state court is the proper place for a class action seeking a mandatory injunction requiring Microsoft to unbundle the Internet browser from the operating system. The amount in controversy wasn't over \$75,000, which precludes the federal action. Microsoft said that it would cost over \$58 million to pull out the browser, but the amount in controversy is the value of the right the plaintiffs sought to enforce, which is insufficient.

The same litigation, pursued in Tennessee state court, yielded a mid-2000 decision that Tennessee's antitrust and consumer protection laws apply to all conduct that is not covered by federal statutes. Therefore, indirect purchasers can sue Microsoft in the state court system, even though Microsoft characterizes most of the challenged conduct as interstate. In contrast, a Kentucky state decision forbids suits by indirect purchasers under Kentucky antitrust law. The court did not accept the argument that indirect purchasers should be allowed to sue because direct purchasers are afraid to endanger their relationship with the powerful Microsoft Corporation.[3]

The District Court for the District of Columbia has held[4] that the FTC has the power to order disgorgement of illegal profits derived from large increases in the prices of two generic drugs. The FTC claimed that long-term exclusive licenses excluded competitors from access to materials for manufacturing the drugs.

The FTC sued under the FTC Act §5 and for unfair competition. However, the court required that the companion case brought by 32 states, charging Sherman Act violations and price fixing, be narrowed down to prevent the possibility of duplicate recovery and to exclude purchases from competitors from the calculation of monetary relief.

The position of the defendants was that FTC Act §13(b), which permits a permanent injunction to be granted in "proper cases," applies only to per se antitrust violations. However, the District Court said that any violation of law can be enjoined. Although §13(b) does not explicitly refer to disgorgement or other monetary relief, the D.C. district court treated monetary relief as a natural and proper extension of the statutory remedies.

However, the portion of the states' complaint brought under Clayton Act §16 for disgorgement or restitution was dismissed. That phase of the case was limited to Clayton Act §4 claims about direct purchases of generic drugs from the defendants made by state entities or state citizens. The court did not accept the state plaintiffs' argument that competitors raised their prices in response to the defendants, and therefore the "price umbrella" theory should be applied, making the defendants liable for responsive price increases posted by their competitors.

The Southern District of New York refused to permit a federal antitrust suit against brokerage houses for conspiracy to restrict private retail customers' ability to re-sell their shares purchased in Initial Public Offerings.[5] In this reading, the SEC is the appropriate enforcement authority for such conduct, and it has chosen not to act.

A lawsuit that is not fraudulent or baseless cannot be treated as a sham. Therefore, under *Baltimore Scrap Corp v. David J. Joseph Co.,*[6] *Noerr-Pennington* immunity is available when a company sues one of its competitors—even if the suit was in fact brought for anticompetitive purposes. In this case, summary judgment was granted to an antitrust defendant that secretly instigated and funded an unsuccessful citizen suit that attempted to prevent a competitor from getting zoning approval for a facility that would compete with one of the defendant's facilities.

The defendant in a private antitrust suit is not entitled to immediate appeal when summary judgment is denied based on the state action or *Noerr-Pennington* doctrines.[7] Assertion of the state action doctrine by a private defendant is only a defense to liability, not immunity against being sued.

Public policy does not require immediate appeal under the collateral order doctrine. (A District Court's interlocutory order is appealable under the collateral order doctrine if it conclusively determines the disputed question; resolves an important issue that is completely separate from the merits of the action; and cannot be reviewed on an appeal from the final judgment.) Assertion of the *Noerr-Pennington* doctrine is also a mere affirmative defense, not a method of preventing the trial from occurring at all.

[¶810] The Sherman Act

On April 3, 2000, the District Court for the District of Columbia issued conclusions of law[8] stating that Microsoft indeed maintained monopoly power in the relevant market (defined as the Intel-compatible operating system for personal computers) by anticompetitive means, and violated Sherman Act §2 by attempting to monopolize the browser market. Tying the browser to the operating system was also held to violate Sherman Act §1. In addition, various state antitrust laws were violated by this conduct.

The District Court did not accept Microsoft's contention that it had numerous competitors in the operating systems market, such as America Online, Sun, Linux, Apple, the Internet, and the emerging market for non-PC devices. Microsoft also cited the high degree of competition in the modern software industry, claiming that consumers benefit from such competition.

The Findings of Fact note that Microsoft has a 95% share of the worldwide licensed market for Intel-compatible PC operating systems; there is no viable substitute for the Windows platform, nor did the court expect one to emerge.

Monopoly power was found on the basis of a dominant, persistent market share protected by substantial entry barriers. The court did not believe that Microsoft had effectively rebutted the government's prima facie case.

Under this analysis, contractual and technical linkage of the browser to the operating system forced customers to take the Internet Explorer browser as a condition of installing the Windows operating system.

However, Microsoft prevailed on §1 allegations of illegal exclusive dealing in connection with marketing agreements with computer manufacturers and other businesses, because non-Internet Explorer browsers were not denied access to the relevant market.

The decision on remedies was issued on June 7. As noted above, the Sherman Act remedy was division of the company into operations and applications companies, which would be forbidden to engage in joint ventures with one another.

It was held that Microsoft was guilty of tying violations (based on the connection between operating system and Web browser). Microsoft was ordered to make applications available separately from the browser, and to release technical information that would allow developers to work on these products separately. Microsoft's practice of giving away its browser was held to constitute predatory pricing, and Microsoft was ordered to make Windows available under a uniform price structure, although prices can be adjusted for volume and for different languages.

As noted above, Judge Jackson moved under the Expediting Act (which has been used only twice, both times in connection with the breakup of AT&T) to have the Supreme Court consider whether it will hear the appeal of Jackson's decision or have the case reviewed by the D.C. Circuit. The federal government preferred immediate Supreme Court review, whereas Microsoft preferred to be heard again by the D.C. Circuit (which ruled for Microsoft in earlier antitrust litigation). The District Court also held that Microsoft's contracts with other companies contributed to monopolistic practices, but not that these contracts were unlawful. Nevertheless, certain exclusive contracts were forbidden for the future.

In early 2001, the District Court for the District of Maryland dismissed federal claims for money damages in 63 consolidated actions against Microsoft for abuse of monopoly power.[9]

In the view of the Second Circuit,[10] it is not a violation of Sherman Act §§1 and 2 for the Associated Press (whose basic business is distribution of news and photographs to newspapers) to enter, and eventually dominate, the business of electronic distribution of advertisements to newspapers.

The Second Circuit defined the market broadly, to include physical delivery of advertising (which still represented 80% of all ad delivery when the complaint was filed). Associated Press had no potential for achieving monopoly power in the market as defined, so summary judgment was granted for Associated Press on the charge of attempted monopolization.

Associated Press admitted that it had monopoly power in the wire service market and the market for electronic transmission of photographs, but summary judgment was granted on the claim that AP leveraged those monopolies in the ad delivery market, because there was no evidence that Associated Press' conduct harmed competition.

Initially, Intergraph Corporation secured a preliminary injunction obligating chip manufacturer Intel to share trade secrets about its unreleased chips and technical services, before the June 2000 trial. But in November, 1999, the Federal Circuit vacated the preliminary injunction[11] because the court did not believe Intergraph was likely to prevail on its Sherman Act §§1 and 2 claims against Intel. In this interpretation, Intergraph is an Original Equipment Manufacturer, whereas Intel is a microprocessor manufacturer, which means that they are not competitors for antitrust purposes.

The case arose because, in 1994, Intergraph became a "strategic customer" of Intel, entitled to proprietary information about Intel products. In late 1996, Intergraph sued several Intel customers for infringing Intergraph's patents on the Clipper microprocessor. The defendants asked Intel to defend and indemnify them; meanwhile, Intel terminated Intergraph's strategic customer status, and Intergraph sued Intel for patent infringement.

The District Court granted the preliminary injunction based on Intel's monopoly status and the likelihood of Intergraph prevailing on its Sherman Act allegations.

In contrast, the Federal Circuit focused on market definition. Sherman Act §2 forbids use of monopoly power and anticompetitive power to affect the relevant product market, which is the area of effective competition between plaintiff and defendant. Intergraph isn't a competitor in either of the relevant markets—high-end microprocessors or Intel microprocessors—because Intergraph stopped manufacturing microprocessors in 1993. If they are not competitors in a relevant market, then it doesn't matter whether Intel has monopoly power in the market. Intel's actions were not helpful to Intergraph's business but negative behavior is not necessarily an antitrust violation.

Intergraph asserted that its dependence on Intel raised an essential facility theory, but the Federal Circuit required assertion of competition for a Sherman Act case, even where it is alleged that an essential facility was present.

Preliminary injunction was denied on the refusal to deal claim, because Intergraph didn't allege that Intel withheld its strategic customer benefits for the **purpose** of enhancing its own competitive position. The monopoly leveraging doctrine was also held inapplicable, because even though Intel certainly has a dominance in the microprocessor field, Intergraph failed to demonstrate market power in the two leveraged markets (graphics subsystems and workstations) identified by the District Court. The Federal Circuit rejected the District Court's contention that downstream integration by an alleged monopolist into new markets is an antitrust violation.

Xerox did not commit an antitrust violation by refusing to sell patented parts to independent service organizations or license its copyrighted manuals and software used in servicing its products. In early 2000, the Federal Circuit ruled[12] that the plaintiff didn't meet its burden of showing that the owner of the intellectual property lacked valid business judgment for denying access. (The patent claim was reviewed under Federal Circuit law, whereas copyright claims were reviewed under the regional law of the Tenth Circuit.)

In general, patent holders who sue to enforce their statutory right to exclude are exempt from antitrust scrutiny. There are two exceptions to the rule: if the defendant proves that the patent was fraudulently obtained; or when the infringement suit is a sham brought for the purpose of interfering with the defendant's business relationships. In this case, the patent was concededly valid, and even though misuse was alleged, it was not alleged that the counterclaims were sham.

On the issue of manuals and software, the court said that copyright concepts can't be used to extend the marketplace, and there was no Tenth Circuit law governing whether a unilateral refusal to sell or license copyrighted expression violates the Sherman Act.

[¶810.2.1] Predatory Pricing

Consumers adequately pleaded antitrust injury (in the form of higher prices and reduced competition) and therefore summary judgment was denied in a case alleging a conspiracy to fix minimum prices for shoes.[13]

Market power was irrelevant because the plaintiffs alleged a per se violation of §1. The court also held that the Clayton Act's four-year statute of limitations was tolled by the plaintiffs' allegations of fraudulent concealment by the defendants and due diligence by the plaintiffs.

In contrast, summary judgment was granted with respect to claims of conspiracy to fix potash prices.[14] To get to trial, the plaintiff must show not only consciously parallel pricing but also additional factors that make it more likely that there was a price fixing conspiracy and not independent pricing decisions made separately by the defendants.

In this case, the plaintiffs did find evidence of high-level communications among the firms, verifying pricing, but the court did not detect a causal relationship between such communications and the price increases, because the discussions involved consummated sales rather than future pricing policies.

[¶830] The Robinson-Patman Act

The Robinson-Patman Act §2(a) gives the seller an affirmative defense to the prima facie price discrimination case: that the lower price that was available to only some customers was offered in good faith to match a competitor's price.

In a late 1999 opinion, the Fourth Circuit held[15] that the defense depends on meeting a particular competitor's price, not market factors in general. A seller can assert the defense based on a good-faith belief that the lower price was offered; absolute certainty is not required. But evidence of actual pricing behavior of competitors, not a mere assertion that the market is very competitive, is necessary to assert the defense.

The Southern District of New York has permitted an independent book retailer to pursue Robinson-Patman Act claims against the major bookstore chains, with respect to the bookstore chains' ability to coerce lower prices from publishers (an alleged violation of §2(f)), including advertising allowances and promotional payments.[16]

The District Court for the Eastern District of Wisconsin found diversity jurisdiction to be present in a treble-damage class action asserting a 15-year conspiracy of price fixing. The court ruled that it would require only

$25,000 per person (or $1,700 a year) in damages to meet the jurisdictional minimum, which the court believed was attainable. Therefore, the case should not be remanded to state court.[17]

[¶840] Antitrust Aspects of Mergers

On October 1, 1999, the Department of Justice and Federal Trade Commission released for public comment their proposed antitrust guidelines dealing with joint ventures, strategic alliances, and other collaborative relationships among competitors.[18]

The agencies' stated purposes were to encourage pro-competitive forms of collaboration that will allow businesses to lower their costs, pursue innovation that might be too expensive without technology sharing, and expand into foreign markets. The Guidelines are designed to furnish safe harbors (including one for joint research and development efforts) so companies contemplating a pro-competitive collaboration will not shy away from the transaction on the grounds of legal uncertainty. But even transactions outside the safety zone could have procompetitive or at least neutral effects, so they will not necessarily be presumed anticompetitive. Each case is judged on its own facts; the agencies do not intend to rule out judgment and discretion in enforcement.

The Guidelines define competitor collaboration as "a set of one or more agreements, other than merger agreements, between or among competitors to engage in economic activity, and the economic activity resulting therefore." Competitors include firms that actually or potentially compete in a defined market.

Analysis under per se and rule of reason tests will continue. Practices that always or almost always have the effect of raising prices or limiting output, such as price fixing, bid rigging, and allocation of markets or customers, will continue to be subjected to per se illegality analysis, irrespective of their claimed business purposes, benefits, or even their overall effect on competition.

However, rule of reason analysis is applied to assess the overall competitive effect of agreements that are reasonably related to and reasonably necessary to achieve pro-competitive efficiencies. The analysis is performed by examining competition in the market with and without the proposed agreement. The central question is whether competition is likely to be harmed because of increasing ability or incentive to get additional profits by raising prices above, or cutting output, quality, service, or innovation below the level that would otherwise prevail.

On April 7, 2000, the two agencies released further guidelines for antitrust analysis of broad horizontal agreements among competitors, such as joint ventures and strategic partnership.[19]

Because collaborations usually have a different competitive effect from mergers, their antitrust scrutiny is different. The usual effect of a merger is to terminate competition between the merged entities entirely, whereas collaboration maintains at least some competition. In general, mergers are at least intended to be permanent, whereas joint ventures and strategic partnerships are usually meant as temporary measures, opening up the potential for further post-termination competition.

In cases suitable for rule of reason analysis, the two federal agencies won't challenge an agreement that doesn't harm competition and where market power is absent. However, if harm has already occurred, the agreement will be challenged even without a detailed market analysis unless there are overriding countervailing benefits.

If the real effect of the transaction is the same as if there had been a partial or total merger, then the merger guidelines will be applied. A constructive merger occurs, e.g., where the participants compete in the relevant market; the collaboration enhances integration in the market in a way that promotes efficiency; the integration wipes out all competition in the market; and the collaboration doesn't have a stipulated term or doesn't end within a limited period.

The agencies have identified safety zones where there will probably not be a challenge: where the market shares of all collaborators are under 20% of each relevant market, or the arrangement's effect is to promote research and innovation. The safety zone is not available to per se illegal agreements or merger-type agreements. Outside the safety zone, either per se or rule of reason analysis will be applied as appropriate.

Late in 2000, the District Court for the District of Columbia refused to grant the FTC a preliminary injunction against a proposed merger of the Heinz and Beech-Nut baby food businesses. Although the court conceded that the FTC had made out a prima facie case under Clayton Act §7 that the merger greatly increases concentration in an already highly-concentrated industry (with 65% of the market going to only three firms), and thus is anticompetitive, the D.D.C. considered that on balance the merger (between the #2 and #3 firms in the market) would be pro-competitive because it would create a counterbalance to Gerber, the existing market leader.

The D.C. Circuit, however, reversed this ruling in April 2001, and Heinz terminated its plan to acquire Beech-Nut. The D.C. Circuit considered that a preliminary injunction was justified.[20]

ENDNOTES

1. *In re Visa Check/MasterMoney Antitrust Litigation,* 68 LW 1516 (E.D.N.Y. 2/22/00).
2. *Sherwood v. Microsoft Corp.,* 68 LW 1575 (M.D. Tenn. 2/22/00).
3. Compare *Sherwood v. Microsoft,* 69 LW 1095 (Tenn. 7/5/00) with *Arnold v. Microsoft,* 69 LW 1096 (Ky. 7/21/00).
4. *FTC v. Mylan Labs Inc.,* 68 LW 1046 (D.D.C. 7/7/99).
5. *Friedman v. Salomon/Smith Barney,* 69 LW 1400 (S.D.N.Y. 12/7/00).
6. 81 F. Supp. 2d 602 (D. Md. 2000).
7. *Acoustic Systems Inc. v. Wenger Corp.* 207 F.3d 287 (5th Cir. 2000).
8. See 68 LW 1595.
9. *In re Microsoft Corp. Antitrust Litigation; Gravity Inc. v. Microsoft Corp.,* 69 LW 1495 (D. Md. 1/12/01).
10. *AD/SAT v. Associated Press,* 181 F.3d 216 (2nd Cir. 1999).
11. *Intergraph Corp. v. Intel Corp.,* 195 F.3d 1346 (Fed. Cir. 1999).
12. *CSU LLC v. Xerox Corp.,* 203 F.3d 1322 (Fed. Cir. 2000).
13. *In re Nine West Shoes Antitrust Litigation,* 80 F.Supp.2d 181 (S.D.N.Y. 1/7/00).
14. *Blomkest Fertilizer Inc. v. Potash Corp. of Saskatchewan Inc.,* 203 F.3d 1028 (8th Cir. 2000).
15. *Hoover Color Corp. v. Bayer Corp.,* 199 F.3d 160 (4th Cir. 1999).
16. *Intimate Bookshop Inc. v. Barnes & Noble Inc.,* 68 LW 1543 (S.D.N.Y. 2/15/00).
17. *West Bend Elevator Inc. v. Rhone-Poulenc SA,* 69 LW 1207 (E.D. Wis. 9/15/00).
18. *http://www.ftc.gov/os/1999/9910/jointventureguidelines.htm.*
19. *http://www.ftc.gov/os/2000/04/ftcdojguidelines.pdf.*
20. *FTC v. H.J. Heinz Co.,* 116 F.Supp.2d 190 (D.D.C. 2000) and 69 LW 1319 (D.C. Cir.); Mark Wigfield and John R. Wilke, "Court Blocks Heinz Bid for Beech-Nut," *Wall Street Journal,* 4/30/01 p. B7.

¶1200

Environmental Law

[¶1210] CERCLA

Putting a site on the National Priorities List is rulemaking that is subject to judicial review under CERCLA §113(a). However, a challenge to the expansion of a Superfund site is treated as a challenge to putting the site on the List in the first place, and therefore §113(a) confers exclusive jurisdiction on the District Court.[1]

There is a circuit split on the CERCLA statute of limitations. In late 2000, the Fifth Circuit joined the Tenth Circuit in holding that the statute of limitations for a contribution action applies unless a statutory event occurs to trigger the statute of limitations.[2]

As for the statute of limitations in a suit against Potentially Responsible Parties (PRPs) for response costs, a consent decree with the federal government involving the same owner and site is an "initial action" for which the case against the PRPs can be a "subsequent action," even if the consent decree includes neither a finding nor an admission of liability.[3]

Under California law, a liability insurer's obligation to indemnify the insured for "all sums that the insured becomes legally obligated to pay" is limited to payments under a court order. Therefore, the insurer need not cover the cost of complying with an administrative cleanup order.[4]

[¶1210.1] [NEW] Potentially Responsible Parties

Ohio state common law makes the sole shareholder who controls a corporation's polluting activities personally liable for CERCLA cleanup costs, in that the state's rules for piercing the corporate veil are comparable to CERCLA's conditions for imposing direct liability on an individual.[5]

A lessee, the full extent of whose control over the contaminated property is to sub-lease it to someone else, is not an "owner" subject to CERCLA liability. According to the Second Circuit, if this was sufficient to subject the lessee to liability, the statute would not require separate categories for "owner" and "operator" liability.[6]

Under the Superfund Recycling Equity Act of 1999, a recycler is not treated as arranger or transporter of the materials. SREA has been held to apply retroactively to state cost-recovery actions that were pending on its enactment date.[7]

[¶1210.2] Contribution

When a defendant sends waste to a disposal facility, where it becomes commingled with other wastes to the extent that segregation is impossible, the defendant's CERCLA allocated share of contribution liability cannot be limited to the cost of disposing of the particular waste that it contributed. All wastes are considered in the allocation.[8]

When calculating the cost of a cleanup for which contribution is available, the Seventh Circuit instructs the court[9] to calculate the amount spent by the plaintiff, minus amounts received or due under third-party settlements involving the same site.

The Seventh Circuit says that this approach is consistent with the text of RCRA and is also easier for the District Court to apply than proportionate share methodology, which requires a difficult and perhaps unproductive assessment of contribution of absent parties. In this case, the District Court (using the Uniform Comparative Fault Act, which does not take the liability of nonparties into account) ordered Akzo to reimburse Aigner for 12.56% of its cleanup costs, whereas Akzo says if it is liable at all, liability should be limited to 9%, the proportion of the solvents that they dumped on the site.

In the Seventh Circuit view, that is the wrong analysis. CERCLA says contribution claims are decided under "federal" law, and the Uniform Comparative Fault Act is not federal. Another possibility is to apply the Uniform Contribution Among Tortfeasors Act, which reduces liability in contribution actions by the amount of third-party settlements.

CERCLA §113(f)(2) says that settlement with the United States or an individual state doesn't discharge a PRP unless the terms provide for discharge, but does reduce potential liability of the others by the amount of the settlement (which is closer to the UCATA analysis than the UCFA concepts). The case was remanded, for Akzo to be ordered to pay 12.56% of cleanup costs minus whatever Aigner received from settlements.

However, the Seventh Circuit did approve the District Court's treatment of the site as a unit, rather than analyzing the source of contamination of smaller parts of the site. It was also deemed permissible to treat all solvents the same way, because it's hard to link expense and toxicity. It could be easier and less costly to clean up some substances that are more toxic than others that are harder to deal with even though they are less dangerous.

The Eastern District of Virginia has joined the other courts[10] holding that the Supreme Court's 1998 *Apfel* decision[11] (that retroactive application of 1992 Coal Industry Retiree Health Benefits Act to the facts of that case was an unconstitutional taking) cannot be extended to CERCLA or be used to avoid cleanup liability.

When lawyers pay for soil testing as part of the preparation for a CERCLA case, the plaintiff does not have compensable "response costs" because of the potential obligation to reimburse the attorneys if the CERCLA suit is won. The costs have not yet been incurred until the CERCLA case is concluded.[12]

Nor do the fees paid by the purchaser of property to an environmental consultant supervising the cleanup performed by the seller constitute response costs. According to the Third Circuit, the consultant's true role was as an expert witness, and such costs are not consistent with the national contingency plan for environmental clean-up.[13]

The Second Circuit also ruled that the cost of hiring expert witnesses on causation is not a response cost because their reports were intended for use in litigation, not for the actual clean-up of the site. The same decision[14] holds that the plaintiff should not have been awarded a lump sum for future response costs, because CERCLA limits the recovery to a declaratory judgment action.

Courts have the power, under CERCLA §113(f), to immunize de minimis contributors to the hazardous condition of a site from liability.[15] In this reading, imposing joint and several liability is not fair to companies that didn't create serious environmental harm; those who did not dispose of a meaningful amount of waste did not cause the plaintiffs to incur measurable response costs to cope with those wastes. The discretion to allocate liability based on equitable factors is extensive enough to provide forgiveness for contributing trace amounts.

A title company that receives contaminated property under a tax deed does not become an "owner" for CERCLA purposes, according to the Northern District of Illinois.[16] The CERCLA third-party defense refers to contamination caused by a third party with whom the defendant did not have a "contractual relationship," and a deed or transfer instrument is deemed a contract for this purpose, but a tax deed is not, because it removes title from the previous owner and vests it in the purchaser. In this situation, the ex-owner and the title company were not in privity, and there was no "transfer" because that refers to voluntary events rather than involuntary ones like tax foreclosure.

In the Seventh Circuit, joint (not just several) liability can be imposed in a CERCLA contribution suit, based on the statutory mandate of "equitable" allocation of liability exposure.[17] Defendant TerMaat was the president and principal shareholder of landfill operating companies.

The District Court found that 55% of cleanup costs were allocable to landfill operators and transporters of the waste dumped there. The District Court also allocated liability severally between two companies that operated the landfill, on the theory that joint liability was not appropriate.[18] The Sixth Circuit felt constrained to apply federal law to CERCLA contribution, even though state law calls for joint liability.

The Sixth Circuit ruled that it is proper to impose operator liability personally on the president and principal shareholder if, but only if, he operated the landfill personally. Directing general operations doesn't create operator liability for the site without day-to-day supervision of site operations, such as negotiating the dumping contracts.

The court refused to pierce the corporate veil, because there was no voluntary creditor in the picture, only an imposed "creditor" that obeyed the EPA's command to clean up the site. Nor did the facts justify piercing the veil based on the corporation's having deceived its creditors about its solvency, or because it disregarded corporate formalities.

Undercapitalization sometimes justifies piercing the corporate veil, but only if the company lacks funds for normal operations; it would be unfair to require all companies to retain enough funds to handle the potentially enormous expenditures related to a major cleanup or lawsuit. Nor could the veil be pierced based on the corporation's maintaining a thin capital structure in order to save taxes, because (within lawful parameters) saving taxes is a legitimate corporate objective.

[¶1210.3] [NEW] Property Issues

In September, 2000, the Ninth Circuit widened the circuit split on the question of whether a site owner can be liable under CERCLA for "disposal" of hazardous substances on the basis of passive spread of contaminants. The Fourth and Ninth say yes, but the Second, Third, and Sixth require active human conduct before "disposal" will be deemed to have occurred.[19]

[¶1220] Clean Water Act

A January, 2000 Supreme Court decision[20] holds that a decrease in the aesthetic and recreational value of a waterway is adequate to prove injury, even without proof of actual harm to the water. Both injury and traceability can be shown with circumstantial evidence (e.g., closeness to polluting sources; past pollution; predictions of influence the discharge will have).

Although the Army Corps of Engineers has regulatory jurisdiction over "navigable waters," that phrase cannot properly be interpreted to include non-navigable, intrastate, isolated waters merely because they furnish migratory bird habitat.[21]

The Court of Federal Claims treated denial of a Clean Water Act wetlands permit as a partial regulatory taking interfering with the owner's reasonable investment interest in the land.[22] Therefore, the Fifth Amendment requires that compensation be paid. Despite the CWA's valid regulatory purpose, the taking had the effect of penalizing a single company for a burden that should have been shouldered by the public at large.

The Fourth Circuit's decision, in a case brought by local environmental groups against a copper smelter, is that direct scientific evidence of impairment to the waterway in question is not mandatory to prove injury in fact sufficient to support a citizen suit.[23]

CWA §505(g) authorizes a "citizen" (a person or persons having an interest which is or may be adversely affected) to bring suit. A group's standing to sue on behalf of its members depends partly on the members' standing to sue in their own right. A plaintiff has to show injury in fact, that the alleged offensive conduct caused the injury, and that the courts can redress the injury.

An intervenor (in this case,[24] an environmental group) in a successful CAA §113 EPA enforcement action is not entitled to get attorneys' fees under CAA's citizen suit provision, §304, because an intervenor in a government suit hasn't "brought" an action.

An earlier Seventh Circuit case[25] does allow a fee award to citizen group intervenors in an EPA RCRA action, even though there was no statutory provision for the award, but in the Ninth Circuit view, the CAA does not manifest a Congressional intent to provide fees in this context. Furthermore, the Ninth Circuit reads the legislative intent to be encouraging citizen suits only in situations in which the government has not become involved—obviously not true when an EPA suit has been filed.

CWA §309(a)(6) rules out federal citizen suits when a state is "diligently prosecuting" an environmental action under a "comparable state enforcement scheme." According to the Sixth Circuit, Tennessee law does not provide adequate scope for citizen participation. Therefore, citizens can bring their own federal suit in an effort to expedite enforcement of the CWA discharge permit.[26]

[¶1230] Clean Air Act

Early in 2001, the Supreme Court upheld CAA §109(b), finding that it does not improperly designate legislative power to the EPA. The Supreme Court also held that the EPA is not allowed to consider how much implementation will cost when the agency sets NAAQS. However, the Court of Appeals has jurisdiction to review the EPA's interpretation of particular NAAQS (in this case, for ozone). The Supreme Court found that the EPA's ozone implementation policy was unlawful because the agency's interpretation is unreasonable in that it goes beyond the text of the statute.[27]

Section 304 of the Clean Air Act says that nothing in federal law shall prohibit, exclude or restrict suits in state court brought by state or local enforcement authorities. Therefore, the federal government does not have the power to use 28 USC §1442(a)(1), the general removal statute, to remove a case involving air quality to federal court.[28]

According to the D.C. Circuit, the EPA's final rule for CAA compliance assurance monitoring satisfies Congress' 1990 increased requirements for emission monitoring (CAA §114(a)(1)),[29] so the EPA can require major sources of air pollution to generate the appropriate type and amount of compliance monitoring data.

When the EPA considers the adequacy of a State Implementation Plan (SIP), the cost of reducing a pollutant is a legitimate factor in determining whether that pollutant contributes significantly to a state's nonattainment of its goals. According to the D.C. Circuit, the EPA did not exceed its discretion by requiring 22 states to reduce ozone precursors, but only to the extent attainable with highly cost effective controls.[30]

[¶1240] RCRA

A Ninth Circuit case from 1999[31] arose when the defendants contracted for disposal of eleven truckloads of waste. Although two truckloads did go to a permitted facility, the rest were kept in the company's warehouse, as the EPA discovered after a tip from a company employee.

RCRA §3998(d)(1) penalizes knowing transport of waste, or causing it to be transported, and §(d)(2) penalizes knowing treatment, storage, or disposal of waste. The government contention is that receiving hazardous waste after it's been shipped from the generating facility constitutes causing it to be transported.

The Ninth Circuit ruled that the statute would not contain both §§(d)(1) and (d)(2) unless they penalized different activities, but declined to accept the defense's contention that only a party in business of generating or transporting waste can incur (d)(1) liability. An intended recipient of waste could be liable based on personally undertaking transportation or getting a third party to do it.

In this reading, merely receiving hazardous waste isn't "causing transportation of waste" for RCRA purposes, but the defendants' convictions were nevertheless affirmed—there was enough evidence that they were vital to the effort to transport and dispose of wastes, so receiving waste wasn't critical to the equation.

After a state has applied its own hazardous waste program to a violation, RCRA doesn't authorize a subsequent federal enforcement action ("overfiling").[32]

The defendant in this case was a circuit board company that voluntarily reported RCRA violations and arranged a cleanup plan. It entered into a state consent decree, waiving civil penalties. The EPA maintained its own enforcement action, seeking over $2 million penalties, and the ALJ imposed $586,000 in penalties. In the Eighth Circuit view, RCRA is supposed to give states primary enforcement authority, not to subject businesses to overlapping enforcement efforts. RCRA §3006 says that an approved state enforcement effort acts in lieu of the federal system, and the EPA is supposed to enforce if, and only if, the state enforcement effort is inadequate.

But in late 2000, the District Court for the District of Colorado ruled that the EPA can initiate a RCRA enforcement action even though a state with an approved RCRA program has initiated action on the same violation.[33]

[¶1240.1] State Regulation of Solid Waste Disposal

During the supplement period, the Eighth Circuit twice tackled the perennial question of how states and localities can regulate waste without violating the Commerce Clause.

The Eighth Circuit found an Iowa statute requiring municipal waste flow programs in cities and towns to satisfy the Commerce Clause.[34] Municipalities are given complete discretion to contract with landfill operators and haulers of their choice, and can send waste out of state. Municipalities that do send waste within Iowa have to choose a single depository within Iowa. The statute is Constitutionally acceptable because its impact on interstate commerce is remote and minimal.

However, a Nebraska municipal ordinance dealing with solid waste flow control was struck down because of impermissible restrictions it placed on interstate commerce in recyclables.[35]

The ordinance required all garbage collected within the city not destined to be sent out of state to be processed at a city-owned transfer station. The transfer station inspects the waste for hazardous materials, which are removed before the waste goes to the landfill.

C&A Carbone v. Clarkstown, N.Y.,[36] says that it's per se invalid to discriminate in favor of local business or investment, and against interstate commerce, unless that is the only way to advance the legitimate local interest. An earlier decision, *Pike v. Bruce Church Inc.,*[37] holds that an ordinance can violate the Commerce Clause even without overtly discriminating against interstate commerce, if the actual burden on interstate commerce clearly outweighs the local benefits.

The Nebraska ordinance in question exempts waste sent out of state, so there is no explicit discrimination against interstate commerce, but it fails to satisfy the *Pike* balancing test. The Eighth Circuit was unimpressed by the city's arguments (that the ordinance raised revenue needed to pay off debt incurred to build the transfer facility; that the ordinance prevented the city from incurring tort liability related to hazardous materials) because interstate commerce has to prevail over cities' fiscal needs, and the ordinance hasn't been proved to have any effect on the risk of hazardous waste accidents. The interstate market in recyclables would be seriously impaired if such ordinances were generally adopted;

and the stated goals could have been achieved in other ways less burdensome to commerce.

The Eastern District of Virginia applied strict scrutiny[38] to a Virginia law limiting the amount of solid waste that regional landfills can accept, and also barring barge transport of waste until Regulations are published. The statute was held to violate the Commerce Clause, given discrimination against out-of-state commerce in solid waste, with no valid state objective shown. Nor did the state show that there were no valid nondiscriminatory methods available.

[¶1260] Environmental Class Actions

West Virginia law provides a cause of action for recovery of medical monitoring costs, upon proof that the expenses are both necessary and reasonably likely to be incurred as a proximate result of environmental torts committed by the defendant.[39] There are six prerequisites:

- Significant exposure
- Proven risk of the substance to which exposed
- Tortious conduct by the defendant
- The defendant's conduct increased the risk of latent disease (as compared with nonexposed population)
- The exposed population needs some kind of diagnostic testing not needed by the general population
- There are effective monitoring procedures for early diagnosis of the tortiously induced disease.

The West Virginia court refused to adopt the defense suggestion that the plaintiff be required to prove the existence of a current effective treatment for the disease allegedly caused by the environmental tort. It would be a perverse incentive for environmental tortfeasors to derive an advantage from causing irreparable harm!

The First Circuit says[40] that a citizen group that is allowed to intervene in a class action is not entitled to a hearing when it challenges the consent decree that settles various environmental allegations. The intervenor was given the chance to respond in writing during the public comment period on the proposed consent decree, providing them with due process. Although the trial court told the intervenors that they would have a chance to testify at an evidentiary hearing, that statement is not binding on the court system.

[¶1270] [NEW] Environmental Tax Issues

The Fourth Circuit ruled in 2000 that environmental remediation costs of the taxpayer's real property were "permanent improvements," in that they make the land safe for a broader range of uses. Therefore, the costs had to be capitalized, rather than deducted as ordinary and necessary business expenses.[41]

ENDNOTES

1. *U.S. v. ASARCO Inc.*, 214 F.3d 1104 (9th Cir. 2000).
2. *Geraghty v. Miller*, 234 F.3d 917 (5th Cir. 2000), following *Sim Co. v. Browning-Ferris Inc.*, 124 F.3d 1187 (10th Cir. 1997).
3. *U.S. v. Findett Corp.*, 220 F.3d 842 (8th Cir. 2000).
4. *Certain Underwriters at Lloyds' London v. Superior Court of Los Angeles County*, 69 LW 1477 (Cal. 2/1/01).
5. *Carter-Jones Lumber Co. v. LTV Steel Co.*, 69 LW 1480 (6th Cir. 1/23/01).
6. *Commander Oil Corp. v. Barlo Equipment Corp.*, 68 LW 1775 (2nd Cir. 6/12/00).
7. *Dep't of Toxic Substances Control v. Interstate Non-Ferrous Corp.*, 68 LW 1768 (E.D. Cal. 5/25/00).
8. *U.S. v. Pesses,* 68 LW 1624 (W.D. Pa 3/21/00).
9. *Akzo Nobel Coatings Inc. v. Aigner Corp.,* 197 F.3d 302 (7th Cir. 1999).
10. *Combined Properties/Greenbriar Limited Partnership v. Morrow,* 58 F.Supp.2d 675 (E.D. Va. 1999). Semble: *U.S. v. Vertac Chemical Corp.,* 33 F.Supp.2d 769 (E.D. Ark 1998); *U.S. v. Alcan Aluminum Co.,* 67 LW 1735 (N.D.N.Y. 1999).
11. *Eastern Enterprises v. Apfel,* 524 U.S. 498 (Sup.Ct. 1998).
12. *Trimble v. ASARCO Inc.*, 232 F.3d 946 (8th Cir. 2000).
13. *Black Horse Land Ass'n v. Dow Chemical Co.*, 228 F.3d 275 (3rd Cir. 2000).
14. *Gussack Realty Co. v. Xerox Corp.*, 224 F.3d 85 (2nd Cir. 2000).
15. *Acushnet Co. v. Mohasco Corp.*, 191 F.3d 69 (1st Cir. 1999).

16. *Continental Title Co. v. Peoples Gas Light and Coke Co.* 68 LW 1224 (N.D. Ill. 9/15/99).

17. *Browning-Ferris Industries of Illinois Inc. v. TerMaat,* 195 F.3d 953 (7th Cir. 1999).

18. The Seventh Circuit cited *Carter-Jones Lumber Co. v. Dixie Distributing Co.,* 166 F.3d 840 (6th Cir. 1999) to support joint liability for CERCLA contribution, although the Seventh Circuit did not accept the Sixth's rationale for this.

19. *Carson Harbor Village v. Unocal Corp.,* 227 F.3d 1996 (9th Cir. 2000).

20. *Friends of the Earth v. Laidlaw,* 528 U.S. 1674 (Sup.Ct. 2000).

21. *Solid Waste Agency of Northern Cook County v. Army Corps of Engineers,* #99-1178, 69 LW 4048 (Sup.Ct. 1/9/01).

22. *Florida Rock Industries v. U.S.,* 68 LW 1192 (Fed.Cl. 8/31/99).

23. *Friends of the Earth Inc. v. Gaston Copper Recycling Corp.,* 204 F.3d 149 (4th Cir. 2000).

24. *U.S. v. Stone Container Corp.,* 196 F.3d 1066 (9th Cir. 1999).

25. *U.S. v. Environmental Waste Control,* 917 F.2d 327 (7th Cir. 1990).

26. *Jones v. Lakeland, TN,* 69 LW 1106 (6th Cir. 8/9/00).

27. *Whitman v. American Trucking Ass'ns Inc.,* #99-1257, 69 LW 4136 (Sup.Ct. 2/27/01).

28. *California v. U.S.,* 215 F.3d 1005 (9th Cir. 2000).

29. *Natural Resources Defense Council Inc. v. EPA,* 68 LW 1266 (D.C. Cir. 10/29/99).

30. *Michigan v. EPA,* 68 LW 1536 (D.C. Cir. 3/3/00).

31. *U.S. v. Fiorillo,* 68 LW 1054 (9th Cir. 7/14/99).

32. *Harmon Industries Inc. v. Browner,* 191 F.3d 894 (8th Cir. 1999).

33. *U.S. v. Power Engineering Co.,* 69 LW 1352 (D. Colo. 11/24/00).

34. *United Waste Systems of Iowa Inc. v. Iowa Dept. of Natural Resources,* 189 F.3d 762 (8th Cir. 9/7/99).

35. *U&I Sanitation v. Columbus,* 205 F.3d 1063 (8th Cir. 2000).

36. 511 U.S. 383 (Sup.Ct. 1994).

37. 397 U.S. 137 (Sup.Ct. 1970).

38. *Waste Management Holdings v. Gilmore,* 68 LW 1496 (E.D. Va. 2/3/00).

39. *Bower v. Westinghouse Electric Corp.,* 68 LW 1127 (W.Va. 7/19/99).

40. *U.S. v. Comunidades Unidas Contra La Contaminacion,* 68 LW 1576 (1st Cir. 2/25/00).

41. *Dominion Resources, Inc. v. U.S.,* 219 F.3d 359 (4th Cir. 2000).

¶1300

Intellectual Property

[¶1301]

Many of the most cogent intellectual property issues currently under review and development involve computers and the Internet, so also see ¶7540.

A click wrap (part of a Web site) arbitration agreement has been deemed enforceable by the Northern District of Illinois[1] in a case involving the software's advertised ability to track the Internet sites the user visits. The court did not accept the argument that the issues were not arbitrable because they were not grounded in the contract.

Although both shrink wrap (in packaged software) and click wrap (on Web site) agreements have been found to be valid and enforceable [2], the District Court for the District of Kansas treated a computer dealer's standard terms (including an arbitration requirement), packed in the box with the computer, as "proposed alterations to the sales agreement" (UCC 2-207). Therefore, they could be enforced only if the customer explicitly agreed to them. The District of Kansas believed that it is unfair to impose on the consumer the burden of finding the contract and its arbitration clause, and returning the merchandise if the contract terms are unacceptable.

Note, however, that the Northern District of Illinois treated a pop-up license agreement displayed by a Web browser as a "writing" for Federal Arbitration Act purposes. Although they were not conspicuous, the "save" and "print" features could be used to create a hard copy; so the arbitration agreement could be enforced in a suit alleging trespass to property. [3]

According to the Federal Circuit,[4] Xerox did not commit any antitrust violations by refusing to sell patented repair parts to independent service organizations, or by refusing to license copyrighted manuals and software used to service Xerox products. The plaintiff failed to meet the burden of showing that the owner of the intellectual property lacked valid business judgment for denying access to it.

The case involved both patent claims (reviewed under Federal Circuit law) and copyright claims (reviewed under the regional law of the Tenth Circuit).

In general, patent holders who sue to enforce their statutory right to exclude others are exempt from antitrust scrutiny. There are two exceptions: if the defendant proves that the plaintiff's patent was fraudulently obtained; or when the infringement suit is a sham brought for the purpose of interfering with the defendant's business relationships.

Here, the patent was concededly valid, and even though misuse was alleged, it was not alleged that the counterclaims were sham.

As for manuals and software, the court said that copyright can't be used to extend the marketplace, and there was no Tenth Circuit law on whether a unilateral refusal to sell or license copyrighted expression violates the Sherman Act.

[¶1310] Copyright

[¶1310.1.1] The Bundle of Rights

Electronic manipulation was not sufficient to turn an unlicensed photograph into a licensed illustration.[5] Because the defendant's license merely permitted creating illustrations based on the photograph, actual use of the photograph itself violated the license and thus was infringing. The final product did not have enough artistic intervention to render the original copyrighted photograph unrecognizable or create a genuinely new work.

[¶1310.2] Copyrightable Subject Matter

A compilation of wholesale prices of coins is copyrightable, as product of the author's creative process in analyzing the price information.[6] It doesn't even matter if the selection and arrangement is original enough to be protectable; the prices themselves are original enough for their compilation to be copyrightable.

The California Court of Appeals decided, in February 2000, that state law claims can be maintained for misappropriation of a person's likeness and image, when photographs are used on the Internet without consent of the subjects,[7] despite the defendants' argument that federal copyright law preempts such state-court claims. But the decision said that the likeness itself is not subject to copyright, even if it is embodied in a copyrighted photograph, and the tort here was misappropriation of the image (by placing it on a Web site). There is no requirement that the individual whose image is used be a celebrity in order to maintain the cause of action.

The Southern District of New York ruled that the style of a diamond ring (using a bridge motif) is entitled to copyright protection, in that diamond rings are not "utilitarian articles," and the design options are greater for jewelry designers than, e.g., compilers of telephone directories or case law reports. [8]

In Louisiana, the economic benefit of a copyrighted work is community property that can be divided in a divorce proceeding, and the Copyright Act does not preempt because this is a matter of family law (a traditional state purview) and not of intellectual property law (where federal law must prevail).[9]

[¶1310.3] Music Recording Rights

The Third Circuit held that a copyright registration was invalid because a work that should have been described as a "song" was incorrectly described as an "audiovisual work."[10] Given the invalidity of the registration, there was no subject matter jurisdiction over the infringement suit. The error was material, because the Copyright Office's decision to issue the registration would reflect the registrant's lack of authorship of the audiovisual work. Furthermore, the error could not have been inadvertent, because songs and audiovisual works are different enough to prevent mix-ups.

A preliminary injunction was granted against "Napster" (a software program that made it simple to download music files without payment and often included copyrighted music whose copyright proprietor had not agreed to make the files available) and upheld by the Ninth Circuit in February, 2001.[11]

Although preliminary injunctions are rather uncommon, this one was deemed necessary because of the likelihood that the Napster service would be held liable for contributory and vicarious infringement (the persons downloading the files committing the direct infringements). However, the Ninth Circuit did trim down the preliminary injunction, making Napster liable only to the extent it had actual notice of specific infringing files that it did not remove from its server.

P.L. 106-379, the Work Made for Hire and Copyright Corrections Act of 2000, removes 1999 amendments that added sound records to the list of creations that could be works for hire. The purpose of the 2000 legislation is to return to the status quo, where courts and the Copyright Office were responsible for deciding which musical compositions are works for hire.

[¶1310.5] [NEW] Term of Protection

Early in 2001, the D.C. Circuit upheld the 20-year extension of copyright under the Copyright Term Extension Act of 1998. The court was not persuaded by First Amendment arguments and found the extension consistent with the copyright clause of the Constitution, although it did concede that the plaintiffs, who sought to use works that would fall into the public domain if the extension were invalid, did have standing to maintain the suit.[12]

[¶1310.6] Digital Millennium Copyright Act

The Digital Millennium Copyright Act amendments to Copyright Act §117, permitting software to be loaded into computer memory for repair purposes, operate retroactively. To the Northern District of Georgia[13] retroactivity is appropriate because the amendments don't impose any new duties; if anything, they reduce liability; and they clarify the inapplicability of some unwisely decided court decisions.[14]

[¶1310.7] Fair Use

Summary judgment was granted for newspapers whose articles were placed on a Web bulletin board site for comments and criticism from users of the site. Such a use was not fair use, although it would have been permissible either to provide summaries of the articles on the site, or to link to sites maintained by the newspapers.[15]

A professional photographer took many pictures of a beauty contest winner, some of them showing her scantily clad. A local TV station reproduced the photographs and taped interviews with local residents expressing their opinion as to whether or not the photographs were pornographic. The local newspaper reported the scandal (with, of course, another look at the shocking pictures).

The photographer's suit for copyright infringement was unsuccessful. The First Circuit found that the newspaper made fair use of the images in the course of reporting on a newsworthy event, engaging in transformative fair use by placing photographs taken to publicize the beauty contest winner in an editorial context. Because the photographer distributed the photographs widely without compensation, his market for the photographs was not affected.[16]

It did not constitute fair use for ministers breaking away and setting up their own church to copy the writings of the church's original founder verbatim, and to distribute the writings. The schismatic group "profited" from the copyrighted works by attracting new members, and the original church had the right to terminate publication of materials that they now adjudged outmoded and racist.[17]

[¶1310.10] Remedies and Copyright Litigation

In yet another victory for state immunity from lawsuit, the Fifth Circuit decided early in 2000 that the Copyright Remedy Clarification Act (which makes the states subject to suit for copyright infringement) is invalid, because Congress lacked the authority to abrogate Eleventh Amendment immunity in a situation where there had been no documented pattern of abuses requiring redress.[18]

In another of a line of recent decisions expanding the rights and immunities of states and state agencies, see also the Fifth Circuit's earlier decision on the issues.[19] The Patent and Plant Variety Protection Remedy Clarification Act was struck down by the Supreme Court in 1999.[20] Both statutes aimed at protecting the same interest, and the abrogation provisions in both were more or less identically phrased, so both statutes should stand or fall together.

[¶1310.11] Technology and Copyright

In February, 2000, the Southern District of New York granted a preliminary injunction against the distribution of DeCSS, a computer program used to circumvent the Content Scramble System of encryption for DVDs[21] in order to make digital copies of movies in the DVD format. Injunction was granted based on the likelihood that a violation of 17 USC §1201(a)(2), the DMCA anti-circumvention provision, would be found. The DMCA provisions have survived a First Amendment challenge based on restrictions on distribution of the program to the public.

DeCSS was made available on the Internet. The MPAA and its members moved under DMCA to have it taken off the servers. The Southern District agreed with them that DeCSS conforms to the DMCA definition, and it has no commercially significant purpose other than accessing copyright materials without consent of the copyright proprietors.

The program is not entitled to a reverse engineering defense because that relates to copyrighted computer programs, not "technological copyright protection schemes" within the meaning of the Act. The DMCA does provide exemptions for encryption research and security testing, but both require the consent of the copyright holder, which was signally lacking in this case.

The Southern District also rejected First Amendment-based arguments, because the First Amendment doesn't protect infringement, and the government interest in protecting copyrighted works is greater than the burden on DeCSS imposed by restricting its online distribution.

At press time, the Second Circuit had heard arguments on, e.g., First Amendment issues involved in an attempt to suppress a form of communication; a decision had not been rendered when the 2002 Supplement went to press.[22]

A defendant's creation of links to sites containing copyrighted expression, and encouragement of others to view and copy the copyright materials, constitutes active encouragement of infringement and likely contributory infringement. The District of Utah held[23] that browsing creates a "copy" for Title 17 purposes, but the court wouldn't go so far as to say that mere linking generates liability for contributory copyright infringement. A preliminary injunction issued against the defendants posting URLs that they knew or had reason to know contained material infringing on the plaintiff's copyrights.

The Second Circuit heard the plaintiff's appeal from dismissal of her complaint against a Native American tribe for copyright infringement, breach of contract, and various state tort causes of action.[24] (The case involved disputes about a film to be made about the Pequot War. The contract between the plaintiff and the tribe was terminated; the tribe made its own film; and the plaintiff, alleging that the tribe used her copyrighted script, sought injunctive and other remedies.)

The District Court, following *Shapolsky*[25] dismissed the copyright claims for lack of jurisdiction, finding that they did not "arise" under the Copyright Act for purposes of 28 USC §1338 (exclusive District Court jurisdiction over copyright claims); instead, they were only incidental to breach of contract claims. Furthermore, tribal immunity led to dismissal of the contract and tort claims.

An infringement complaint alleging factually related copyright and contract claims arises under the Copyright Act for jurisdictional purposes only if the complaint seeks a remedy expressly granted by the Copyright Act, or requires construction of the Copyright Act itself.

The Second Circuit was not persuaded by *Shapolsky*. The exclusively federal nature of copyright litigation means that anyone whose case was transferred out of federal court because the copyright claims were incidental to contract claims would have no forum to pursue the copyright claims.

A composer who granted a nonexclusive license to use a jingle she wrote doesn't have to wait for the 35-year period under Copyright Act §203 (allowing termination of a nonexclusive license during the five-year period that begins 35 years after the grant of the license) to expire before bringing suit for infringement.[26]

Although there is a circuit split[27] on this point, the Eleventh Circuit position is that the license can be canceled while the 35-year period is still running, as long as this is permitted by state contract law.

The Eleventh Circuit's reading is that §203 permits termination of any license that happens still to be in effect after 35 years, but doesn't prevent parties from contracting for a shorter license term. A statutory provision permitting license termination under certain circumstances does not necessarily preclude termination under all other circumstances. The Eleventh Circuit copes with the language in §203(b)(6), "unless and until termination is effected under this section, the grant, if it does not provide otherwise, continues in effect for the term of copyright provided by this title" by saying that any state law governing contracts of indefinite duration does provide otherwise.

The Ninth Circuit affirmed a grant of summary judgment,[28] thus holding that substantial contributors to the movie *Malcolm X* were not "joint authors," for copyright purposes, because that requires more than copyrightable creative contribution to the finished work. Joint authors have to have control over the final work, plus proof that their collaborators intended them to have co-author status. In other words, it doesn't take much to find a copyrightable "work," but once there is a work, "authorship" of it requires a higher standard.

According to the Third Circuit,[29] the Copyright Act preempts a state (Pennsylvania) statute limiting the duration of the exclusive first-run engagement of a movie. The statute is invalid because it prevents the copyright holder from full exercise of the rights granted by the Copyright Act.

The Copyright Act (at §301) provides for exclusive federal jurisdiction over legal or equitable rights "equivalent" to any exclusive right specified in §106. With respect to movies, the §106 rights include distributing copies of the movie by sale, rental, lease, or loan; public performance; and public display of individual images.

The Third Circuit ruled that the state law must fall because of its limits on the distributor's federally provided right to control licensing for exhibition. States have the power to regulate unfair market practices in the film industry, including blind bidding, but the statute as enacted actually limits the federally granted scope of licensing, and is not a mere market regulation to prevent unfair business practices.

State-court claims by musicians, alleging that a music producer and the distributor of audio recordings violated their right of publicity, are not preempted by the Copyright Act.[30] An individual's name and likeness can't be copyrighted, and the state misappropriation tort doesn't conflict with federal copyright law. The state tort deals with the persona of the artist, which is outside copyright law. Preemption exists only when the content of the protected right falls within the subject matter of copyright, and the state law right purports to cover any of the exclusive rights under the federal copyright statute.

Nor, to the California Court of Appeals, was federal preemption present in a state-law right of publicity claim made by the assignee of models whose erotic photographs were used without their permission.[31] Such claims were not preempted because the action did not interfere with exclusive rights of the copyright owner. The right of publicity was not asserted against the copyright owner, but against a person displaying the photographs without authorization.

The Digital Theft Deterrence and Copyright Damages Improvement Act, P.L. 106-160 (12/9/99), increases some penalties for copyright infringement by 50%, so that the range of damages is from $750 to $30,000, or $150,000 in the case of willful violation. In large part, the statute implements the digital piracy provisions of the No Electronic Theft Act, on the theory that prosecutors might be deterred from bringing meritorious cases if the appropriate penalty is in doubt. The 1999 statute gives the Sentencing Commission 120 days to come up with emergency sentencing guidelines for piracy offenses.

The Ninth Circuit vacated[32] a preliminary injunction that Sun obtained against Microsoft for breach of its license to use Java, and remanded the case. If the allegedly breached items in a copyright license were limitations on the scope of the license (not covenants of independent contractors), then irreparable harm can be presumed from the breach. However, the breach is a question to be decided under state copyright law.

The Second Circuit reversed[33] the *Tasini* decision noted in the main volume. To the Second Circuit, the Copyright Act forbids putting freelance articles into a database or CD-ROM without the consent of the author. Such reuse is not part of the publisher's statutory right to reproduce a revision of a collective work.

According to the Second Circuit, 17 USC §201(c) provides that the owner of a copyright in the entire collective work (as opposed to the individual components of it), absent an express transfer of the copyright or of rights, has only the "privilege" of reproducing and distributing the item as part of that collective work, "any revision of that collective work," and any later collective work in the same series.

The Second Circuit defines "revision" for this purpose to mean separate editions of the same newspaper; the legislative history shows that a completely different periodical or anthology cannot be considered a revision. Nor would the statute refer to "a later collective work in the same series" as a separate entity if databases are mere revised digital copies of the collective work.

Dr. Martin Luther King's "I Have a Dream" speech was given in front of the Lincoln Memorial on August 28, 1963. A copyright application was made on September 30, 1963, pursuant to the Copyright Act of 1909, then in effect. A copyright certificate was issued shortly afterwards.

In 1994, CBS produced a documentary which included film footage of about 60% of the speech, without permission or royalty payments to the King estate. The estate sued CBS for copyright infringement. The District Court granted summary judgment for the network, in light of the public performance and wide dissemination of the speech.

Under the 1909 Act, common-law copyright protection was automatic upon creation of a work, and lasted until general publication (when the work became available to the public at large without regard to identity or their intentions for using the work). A limited publication, which would not constitute dedication to the public domain, involved communicating the contents of the work, for a limited purpose, to a select group, who did not have the right to transmit, reproduce, distribute, or sell the work.

The plurality opinion of the Eleventh Circuit[34] holds that performance of a work is not general publication, because there are no tangible copies distributed to the general public so that they can exercise dominion and control over the work. Distribution to the news media is only a limited publication, if it is done for the purpose of facilitating reporting of a newsworthy event.

In 1963 (before widespread use of video cameras and VCRs), performance did not constitute publication. Neither the importance of the speech nor the Southern Christian Leadership Council's desire for news coverage made the speech exempt from the "performance is not a publication" doctrine. The size of the audience and the news significance of the event did not constitute general publication. The case was remanded to the District Court to see if there were any other factors leading to general publication of the speech, and to cope with fair use arguments.

It is not a copyright violation for a generic drug manufacturer to issue a user's guide and audiotape nearly identical to those copyrighted by the manufacturer of the proprietary drug,[35] because the Food, Drug and Cosmetic Act requires generic drug manufacturers to use the "same labeling" approved by the FDA for the underlying patented drug. The Second Circuit didn't think that conventional fair use concepts (e.g., scholarship or criticism) applied.

The Food, Drug and Cosmetic Act as amended requires generic drugs to carry approved labels, and FDA regulations define labeling broadly enough to include booklets and sound recordings describing the drug.

Furthermore, if the copyright claim were upheld, nobody would ever be able to get a license to manufacture generic drugs, because it would be impossible to satisfy both copyright and drug labeling law; federal law seeks to enhance competition in the manufacturing of drugs whose patent has expired; manufacturers of generic drugs can get to market faster by using materials that have already received FDA approval. Drug manufacturers make most of their money during the period of exclusivity; they suffer little financial loss from the re-use of copyrighted materials by the manufacturers of generic drugs.

[¶1330] Trademarks

See ¶7540 for a discussion of trademark issues with respect to URLs (Web site "addresses").

A March, 2000 Supreme Court case says that in a §43(a) Lanham Act (trade dress infringement) case dealing with product design, the product design is distinctive (and hence protectable) only if it has secondary meaning.[36] Product design isn't inherently distinctive; it's like product color, in that consumers have no predisposition to use it to identify the source of the goods. But in 1995 the Supreme Court found that color, although not inherently distinctive, can acquire protectable secondary meaning[37] for identification of source.

The Supreme Court returned to trade dress issues about a year later, ruling that the fact that a product feature was disclosed in a now-expired utility patent is strong evidence that the feature is functional, and therefore not protectable as trade dress. (The burden of proving non-functionality is on the party asserting trade dress protectability.)[38]

A copyright or design patent might be available for elements that do identify source but have not yet developed secondary meaning.[39]

However, Virginia law doesn't provide for direct transfer of property from judgment debtor to judgment creditor, and it is not yet clear how domain names can be seized. In the Eastern District of Virginia analysis, a trademark is only a right to prevent other parties from using an owner's mark to confuse the public; a trademark doesn't really trade independently of its goodwill. The Eastern District viewed registration of a nontrademark domain name as a contract between the registrar and registrant, not a property right. Usually, domain names are valueless other than the way they're used by the owning entity, although some do have independent value even without attached goodwill.

Unlike the Fourth Circuit[40] the Second Circuit permits[41] proof of trademark dilution without proof of actual, consummated harm. Therefore, the grant of a preliminary injunction was affirmed against a maker of goldfish-shaped crackers, based on several factors involving likelihood of confusion. In the Second Circuit, the anti-dilution statute applies whether or not the goods are competing.

The Fifth Circuit held that *Polo* magazine infringed Ralph Lauren's Polo trademark when the magazine began to cover equestrian sports and lifestyles, not just the sport of polo itself. However, actual harm is required for a dilution claim. The lower court's permanent injunction was vacated, and the case was remanded to determine a more appropriate remedy because of the First Amendment rights involved in selecting titles for literary works.[42]

The federal anti-dilution statute doesn't necessarily give the owner of a famous trademark the right to use its trademark as a domain name (in this case, "Clue Computing" versus Hasbro's "Clue" board game).[43] Even the fact that consumers will find out that they've gone to the wrong site, and will have to do a search to find the right one, is not substantial enough to constitute confusion for legal purposes.

Lanham Act trade dress protection is not available for the overall appearance, design, and configuration of an unpatented multi-purpose tool.[44] Despite the competitors' admission that it copied the appearance of the tool almost exactly, the Ninth Circuit held that design and physical details of a product are protectable only if nonfunctional. A patent is the only available form of protection for utilitarian features that are the essence of the product.

In this reading, a functional feature is the actual benefit that the consumer buys the product for, whereas a trademark is an identification of the source or endorsement of a product. Only a completely nonfunctional configuration can constitute a trademark or trade dress; adding nonfunctional arbitrary features cannot be used to enhance protection.

Late in 2000, the Third Circuit ruled that Lanham Act §43(a) protection of trade dress extends to non-identical items within a product line—as long as there is a consistent overall look that conveys one continuing commercial impression. Protection is not available if the trade dress varies so widely that consumers would not perceive a single source for the goods.[45]

Various phrases including "Playboy" were fair use for a one-time Playmate of the Year to describe herself on her personal Web site.[46] According to the Southern District of California, the terms were used in a nontrademark manner, as an accurate description of her past connection with the magazine. Despite Playboy's evidence of initial confusion, the former Playmate's inclusion of Playboy in the metatags (identifying description) of her site also constituted fair use.

Despite the likelihood of success at trial on the issue of trademark dilution, the Second Circuit denied Federal Express a preliminary injunction against "Federal Espresso Inc.," because of the low risk of trademark erosion or actual confusion of two such dissimilar services.[47]

Even after a trademark has become incontestable, functionality can still be raised as a defense to a claim of infringement. According to the Eleventh Circuit,[48] the defense of functionality (that no trademark can be granted in the functional features or shapes of a product) is a judicially created doctrine that predates the Lanham Act. The doctrine, which serves to explicate the interface between trademark and patent law, has never been repealed and achieved statutory authority under 1998's Trademark Law Treaty Implementation Act, P.L. 105-330 (albeit prospectively only).

In this case, a U.S. company alleges that the configuration of German-made fuses infringes the trade dress of the U.S. products, and wants the company to stop importing the fuses to the U.S. The German manufacturer sought declaratory judgment of noninfringement. To the District Court, the individual features of the U.S. configuration were functional, so the trademark registration was invalid and unenforceable.

If the phrase "You have mail" is merely used to alert e-mail users to the presence of messages, it is generic and cannot be protected as a trademark. Therefore, the Fourth Circuit ruled in favor of AT&T rather than AOL, in that AOL did not use the phrase consistently to describe a service. Furthermore, even if AOL could establish de facto secondary meaning in that the public associated the phrase with AOL, it could not prevent functional use of common English words by others.[49]

15 USC §1065 makes a trademark registration incontestable based on five years of continuous post-registration use with no challenge posed, plus an affidavit from the user, within one year after the end of the five-year period, that the mark is still in use. The Eleventh Circuit notes that the concept of functionality is not mentioned in the Lanham Act at all, so its omission from the list of Lanham Act defenses is not dispositive. The court also noted that the functionality defense was applied long before the 1998 amendments, and found it unlikely that Congress would enact only part of the doctrine and not all of it.

A trademark using "XXXX" as a placeholder for missing elements cannot be registered, because the Lanham Act limits each application to only one mark.[50] The court's rationale is that allowing registration of a "phantom mark" would impair trademark searching, and would not put other potential users of the mark on notice of what had been claimed.

To the Ninth Circuit, a showing of distinctiveness is not sufficient to prove that a trademark is "famous" and thus entitled to anti-dilution protection. Under this decision, using a surname as a domain name (even if the surname is also a trademark) does not constitute "using a trademark in commerce" with respect to whether the trademark has been diluted.

The defendant in this case operated a company that registered vanity domains, mostly surnames, and mostly in the .net and .org Top Level Domains.

Avery Dennison, which has registered both Avery and Dennison as trademarks, brought suit for dilution under 15 USC §1125(c). It obtained summary judgment at the District Court level, on the grounds that the marks were famous as a matter of law, and granted summary judgment.

The Ninth Circuit distinguishes the *Toeppen* case discussed in the main volume, involving .com registration and the defendant's concession that the mark was famous.

In this case, Avery Dennison contended that registration on the principal register is prima facie evidence of distinctiveness, which in turn makes a trademark famous for dilution purposes. However, the Ninth Circuit[51]held that a famous mark has to be truly prominent and renowned; allowing dilution protection on a mere showing of distinctiveness would give too much protection to trademarks and implicate too many noninfringing uses.

The court was unwilling to provide additional protection based on Avery Dennison's long-term history of using and advertising the marks, in that they were not famous marks. The court's rationale was that more than 200 businesses use "Avery" or "Dennison" in some form in a business name, so neither of them can really be famous for dilution purposes.

The Ninth Circuit reversed the summary judgment for the plaintiff, and in fact awarded summary judgment for the defense, on the grounds that the defendant capitalized on the surname status of "Avery" and "Dennison," rather than their trademark status, and thus commercial use did not occur.

It was not a trademark infringement to use a 30-second clip from a Three Stooges movie that had fallen into the public domain in a movie (as background on a TV set). The Ninth Circuit does not allow assertion of trademark to be used to revive what is in effect an expired copyright claim.[52]

A television commercial for golf clubs used swing music and the caption "Swing swing swing" to emulate Benny Goodman's "Sing, Sing, Sing (With a Swing)." The advertiser had considered licensing the Goodman song but was unwilling to pay the licensing fees. EMI, the owner of the rights to the Goodman song, sought to have the song itself protected under Lanham Act §43(a), but the Second Circuit refused.[53] In this reading, trademark law is concerned with protection of symbols of identity and the source of goods, whereas copyrighting is the correct way to protect the rights in a musical composition. However, titles cannot be copyrighted, but they can be protected against unfair competition by Lanham Act §43(a). The Second Circuit allowed an unfair competition suit to proceed with respect to whether "Swing, swing, swing" was fair use in that it was descriptive of the product.

Fee awards, available under Lanham Act §35(a) in "exceptional cases," are not limited to willful infringement. They can be granted against a party guilty of vexatious litigation conduct, by analogy with patent cases where the statutory language about attorneys' fees is similar.[54] In contrast, a Tenth Circuit case from mid-2000 holds that a prevailing Lanham Act defendant was properly denied a fee award because the subjective good faith of the plaintiff is a factor, even if the plaintiff's suit was objectively unfounded.[55]

[¶1350] Patents

A District Court's construction of a patent claim (even in a case that is resolved through settlement) has collateral estoppel effect on lawsuits on the same claims.[56] *Markman* (see main volume) only increases the finality of claim construction, because the issue is decided separately by the court (often pre-trial) and doesn't involve a jury verdict.

The Administrative Procedures Act calls for review on a "substantial evidence" standard when PTO findings of fact are appealed to the Federal Circuit.[57] *Zurko*[58] calls for application of the APA and not the "clearly erroneous" standard.

However, the APA includes two tests, "substantial evidence" and "arbitrary and capricious"; the Federal Circuit opted for the former (whether a reasonable finder of fact could have reached the same decision). This standard is less deferential than the "arbitrary and capricious" test, which requires a clear error of judgment for reversal.

The PTO has an obligation to issue a detailed opinion that explains its factual conclusions, and Federal Circuit review is confined to that record. Doctrine of equivalents infringement can be asserted even though asserted equivalent structure consists of pre-existing technology.[59] Although *Chiuminatta*[60] rules out equivalents infringement when the accused product is a pre-existing technology, in this case the Federal Circuit limits preclusion to means-plus-function claims.

To the District Court for the District of Massachusetts,[61] *Dickinson v. Zurko* doesn't change the standard that District Courts use to assess the validity of reissue patents. (*Zurko* says that PTO findings are reviewable by the Federal Circuit to see if they are backed up by substantial evidence.) Reviewing an "original patent" under 36 USC §251 to see if there has been an impermissible recapture in a reissue patent doesn't have to consider all the applications related to the patent that is corrected by the reissue.

Federal patent law preempts state law standards as to the determination of inventorship,[62] to prevent states from awarding property rights to persons who do not count as inventors under federal standards, or from granting relief broader than that allowed by federal patent law.

An offer to sell creates personal jurisdiction if and only if specific product descriptions and pricing information are purposefully released within the forum state. Mailing one catalog to a person in New Jersey, and having a Web site accessible in New Jersey has been held by the District of New Jersey to be insufficient grounds for jurisdiction. Neither mode is an offer to sell because they don't provide specific descriptions or pricing information.[63]

[¶1350.1] Patentable Subject Matter

Making one product imitate another one is "utility" as defined by 35 USC §101, and the imitation product is not rendered unpatentable by deceptiveness.[64] Patent Act §101 doesn't involve moral considerations, and many imitation products (e.g., artificial fibers; cubic zirconia) have been patented.

Seeds and seed-grown plants are patentable under 35 USC §101, even though protection is also available under the Plant Patent Act and Plant Variety Protection Act, and even though the same subject matter could have different rights and obligations depending on the patentee's choice of statute. A legal or property interest can be governed by more than one statute, e.g., ornamental designs can come under either design patent or copyright.[65]

[¶1350.1.1] Novelty; Nonobviousness

Although Excel's system literally infringed AT&T's patented method for billing long-distance calls, the District Court for the District of Delaware held that AT&T's patent was invalid because it had been anticipated by MCI's Friends and Family system.[66]

The Western District of Washington granted Amazon.com a preliminary injunction (based on the likelihood of prevailing on the patent claim) against Barnes & Noble's one-click ordering system. The Western District held[67] that Amazon's one-click ordering patent is valid, not obvious, and not anticipated. The grant of the injunction aided Amazon during the critical end-of-year holiday ordering season. The court held that one-click ordering differs significantly from the order methods cited by Barnes & Noble as prior art, because those require multiple actions rather than a single action.

This case discusses secondary issues in assessing nonobviousness: commercial success; felt need that was not previously satisfied (i.e., shopping cart abandonment because of difficulty of completion); failure by others to achieve the same objective. The Western District of Washington applied the presumption of irreparable harm, based on infringement of multiple claims of a valid patent, finding that Barnes & Noble was a direct competitor; Amazon invested heavily in developing the market; and toleration of one infringement would encourage other infringers.

The Federal Circuit ruled that the patent on the popular psychoactive drug Prozac is invalid as an obvious case of double patenting, because an earlier, expired patent covers the drug.[68]

[¶1350.2] The Patent Application

It's comparatively easy to assess the patentability of an allegedly novel piece of machinery or manufacturing process, but it was not clear that business methods were patentable until the 1998 *State Street* decision.[69]The validity of AT&T's patent for "call message recording" was upheld by the Federal Circuit.[70]

The PTO has granted a number of business methods patents for computer and commercial techniques used on the Internet, and some of these patents have been challenged by competitors and have attracted criticism.

In March, 2000, the PTO announced that it would tighten the scrutiny to be applied to applications for business method patents, and a secondary level of review would be applied. The agency announced plans to staff up with technologists who understand e-commerce and online financial techniques.[71]

The PTO is altering its practices in other regards as well. On December 20, 1999, the PTO announced that its pilot project, for online filing of utility patent applications, was well-received by the IP community and would probably be expanded. The pilot started with biotechnology patents for gene sequence listings, and was extended to all kinds of utility patents that can be created with an "authoring template." The PTO issues software called "electronic packaging and validation engine" (ePAVE) for submitting electronic files to the PTO, which then prints them out and handles them in paper form.[72]

Also in December, 1999, the PTO proposed examination guidelines for assessing patent applications for DNA segments that are alleged to be patentable because of their utility in discovering other DNA segments. Such patents are controversial in the scientific community, because there is an ethic that this information should be publicly released to ease the tasks of other researchers.[73]

[¶1350.5] Patent Transfers

A security interest in a patent can be perfected by complying with state law requirements for perfecting a security interest, even if the interest is not recorded in the PTO.[74] Because a security interest usually doesn't shift title, it is not the kind of "assignment" that is only valid under Patent Act §261 if it is filed in the PTO. Nor does the PTO's filing system supersede UCC Article 9.

In this case, a Chapter 7 debtor's only real asset was a patent. The creditor had a security interest in all of the debtor's assets, including general intangibles. Both sides stipulated that this was sufficient to create a security interest in the patent.

The creditor filed a state UCC-1 and UCC-2 (continuation statement), appropriate under state law, but didn't file with PTO. The debtor's bankruptcy trustee's position was that the interest in the patent was unperfected, and therefore the trustee as hypothetical lien creditor had a superior interest.

The bankruptcy court, affirmed by the Ninth Circuit, said that the state practice was sufficient; there had been no change of title. In this analysis, most post-UCC-adoption security interests in personal property don't involve transfer of title, because such concepts are not very meaningful for personal property security interests. But the patent situation is quite different from the copyright situation because of the statutory language.

"Transfer" of copyright ownership (see 17 USC §101) includes "hypothecation," which in turn means pledging property as security or collateral for debt. Copyright Act §205 makes recordation of a document in the Copyright Office constructive notice of the facts in the document to anyone affected by a transfer of copyright ownership, so state-law methods of recording the security interest are preempted.

UCC 9-302(3)(a) says that the Article 9 filing requirements don't apply if there is a federal statute prescribing a national registration of security interest or a centralized repository located someplace other than the place for the Article 9 filing. Comment 8 to this section says there are three federal systems in this category: for copyright, aircraft, and railroads. But the Ninth Circuit says the Patent Act isn't comprehensive enough to preempt state-law recordation. The Patent Office records security interests on a purely discretionary basis, and this doesn't provide constructive notice.

[¶1350.6] Interference Proceedings

If a District Court, reviewing a Board of Patent Appeals and Interferences interference ruling, takes live testimony on all the matters that the Board considered, the Board's factual findings are reviewed de novo.[75] The District Court has a considerable advantage, because the Board can't hear live testimony. Review of interference decisions is governed by 31 USC §146.

Dickinson v. Zurko, which is discussed in the main volume, dealt with direct appeals from the PTO to the Federal Circuit; it didn't resolve this interference issue. Nor does this *Winner International* decision instruct District Courts how to review factual findings in a case where the testimony relates to only some, not all, of the facts or issues that were before the Board.

[¶1350.7] Patent Infringement

When a patent infringement claim is dismissed without prejudice as part of a bifurcation order, the Federal Circuit does not have appellate jurisdiction under 28 USC §1338 over the state law claims that remain, only supplemental jurisdiction under 28 USC §1337. And, because the case no longer arises under patent law, the Federal Circuit does not have jurisdiction under 27 USC §1295(a)(1).[76]

Even if a patent infringement suit is not objectively baseless with respect to *Noerr-Pennington* immunity, a later action for malicious prosecution is not collaterally estopped.[77] A ruling that the infringement suit was not baseless did not settle allegations of fraud and false testimony, and in the infringement action, the alleged infringer can raise evidence that the patent was obtained fraudulently.

[¶1350.7.2] Doctrine of Equivalents

The Eastern District of Pennsylvania refused to find collateral estoppel effect, and thus allowed a patentee to relitigate another court's interpretation of a claim construed in a *Markman* hearing.[78] The patentee won in the earlier suit on equivalents infringement, and lost on claim interpretation, but the claim interpretation issue couldn't be appealed separately.

The Eastern District said that there will be issue preclusion on claim interpretation only if the interpretation was the reason for the loss.

Structural equivalents for literal infringement, under 35 USC §112 paragraph 6, are determined by the overall structure disclosed (corresponding to the claimed function) rather than the individual components of the structure. Therefore, in mid-1999, the Federal Circuit reversed the District Court's judgment of noninfringement as a matter of law, and reinstated a $70.6 million jury verdict.[79]

ENDNOTES

1. *Lieschke v. RealNetworks Inc.*, 68 LW 1543 (N.D. Ill. 2/10/00).
2. The leading case is *Zeidenberg*, 86 F.3d 1447 (7th Cir. 1996); see main volume; followed by, e.g., *M.A. Mortenson Co. v. Timberline Software Co.*, 998 P.2d 305 (Wash. 2000).
3. Compare *Klocek v. Gateway, Inc.*, 69 LW 1080 (Dolcan. 6/16/00) with *In re Real Networks Inc. Privacy Litigation*, 68 LW 1767 (N.D. Ill. 5/8/00).
4. *CSU LLC v. Xerox Corp.*, 203 F.3d 1322 (Fed. Cir. 2000).
5. *Mendler v. Winterland Production Ltd.*, 207 F.3d 1119 (9th Cir. 2000).
6. *CDN Inc. v. Kapes,* 197 F.3d 1256 (9th Cir. 1999).
7. *Enterprises v. Matthews,* #B127931 (Cal.App. 2/17/00), discussed in Mike McKee, "Naked Ambition No Excuse for Internet Piracy," *The Recorder/Cal Law* 2/18/00, available at *http://www.law.com.*
8. *Weindling Int'l Corp. v. Kobi Katz Inc.*, 69 LW 1271 (S.D.N.Y. 9/29/00).
9. *Rodrigue v. Rodrigue*, 218 F.3d 432 (5th Cir. 2000).
10. *Raquel v. Education Management Corp.*, 196 F.3d 171 (3rd Cir. 1999).
11. *A&M Records Inc. v. Napster Inc.*, 69 LW 1487 (9th Cir. 2/12/01).
12. *Eldred v. Reno*, 69 LW 1516 (D.C. Cir. 2/16/01).
13. *Telecomm Technical Services Inc. v. Siemens Rolm Communications Inc.*, 68 LW 1080 (N.D. Ga. 7/6/99).
14. E.g., *MAI Systems Corp. v. Peak Computer Inc.*, 991 F.2d 511 (9th Cir. 1993).
15. *L.A. Times v. Free Republic*, 68 LW 1335 (C.D. Cal. 11/8/99).
16. *Nunez v. Caribbean Int'l News Corp.*, 235 F.3d 18 (1st Cir. 2000).
17. *Worldwide Church of God v. Philadelphia Church of God*, 227 F.3d 1110 (9th Cir. 2000).
18. *Chavez v. Arte Publico Press,* 204 F.3d 601 (5th Cir. 2000).

19. *Rodriguez v. Texas Commission on the Arts,* 199 F.3d 279 (5th Cir. 2000).
20. *Prepaid Postsecondary Education Exp. Bd. v. College Savings Bank,* 527 U.S. 666 (Sup.Ct.1999).
21. *Universal City Studios Inc. v. Reimerdes,* 82 F.Supp.2d 211 (S.D.N.Y. 2000).
22. See Mark Hamblett, "2nd Circuit Weighs DVD Copying," *N.Y.L.J.* 5/2/01, available on law.com.
23. *Intellectual Reserve Inc. v. Utah Lighthouse Ministry Co.,* 73 F.Supp.2d 1290 (D. Utah 1999).
24. *Bassett v. Mashantucket Pequot Tribe,* 204 F.3d 343 (2nd Cir. 2000).
25. *Schoenberg v. Shapolsky Publishers Inc.,* 971 F.2d 926 (2nd Cir. 1992).
26. *Korman v. HBC Florida Inc.,* 182 F.3d 1291 (11th Cir. 1999).
27. *Rano v. Sipa Press Inc.,* 987 F.2d 580 (9th Cir. 1993) interprets §203 to mean that a license of indefinite duration has a minimum term of 35 years; *Walthal v. Rusk,* 172 F.3d 481 (7th Cir. 1999) doesn't deem there to be any minimum term, and this is the position adopted by the Eleventh Circuit.
28. *Aalmuhammed v. Lee,* 202 F.3d 1227 (9th Cir. 2000).
29. *Orson Inc. v. Miramax Film Corp.,* 189 F.3d 377 (3rd Cir. 1999).
30. *Brown v. Ames,* 201 F.3d 654 (5th Cir. 2000).
31. *KNB Enterprises v. Matthews,* 92 Cal. Rptr.2d 713 (Cal. App. 2000).
32. *Sun Microsystems Inc. v. Microsoft Corp.,* 188 F.3d 1115 (9th Cir. 1999).
33. *Tasini v. N.Y. Times Corp.,* 192 F.3d 356 (2nd Cir. 1999).
34. *Estate of Martin Luther King Jr. Inc. v. CBS,* 194 F.3d 1211 (11th Cir. 1999).
35. *SmithKline Beecham Consumer Healthcare L.P. v. Watson Pharmaceuticals Inc.,* 68 LW 1634 (2nd Cir. 4/4/00).
36. *Wal-Mart Stores Inc. v. Samara Bros. Inc.,* 529 U.S. 205 (Sup.Ct. 2000). See, e.g., Inna Fayenson, "A Turning Point for Trade Dress Protection," *N.Y.L.J.* 4/11/00 p. 1; Julius Rabinowitz, "Wal-Mart Clarified Product Appearance Trade Dress," *Nat.L.J.* 5/1/00 p. C4.
37. *Qualitex v. Jacobson Products Co.,* 514 U.S. 159 (Sup.Ct. 1995). *Two Pesos Inc. v. Taco Cabana Inc.,* 505 U.S. 763 (Sup.Ct. 1992) doesn't say that product design trade dress can never be inherently distinctive; in that case, the trade dress was the décor of a restaurant, which was more like packaging than the product design here.

38. *TrafFix Devices Inc. v. Marketing Display Inc.*, #99-1571, 69 LW 4172 (Sup.Ct. 3/20/01).
39. These issues are canvassed in Robert S. Kate and Helen Hill Minsker, "Design Patent + Trademark = Better Protection," *Nat.L.J.* 5/1/00 p. C19.
40. *Ringling Bros-Barnum & Bailey Combined Shows Inc. v. Utah Div. Of Travel Development,* 170 F.3d 449 (4th Cir. 1999).
41. *Nabisco Inc. v. PF Brands Inc.*, 191 F.3d 208 (2nd Cir. 1999).
42. *Westchester Media Co. v. PRL USA Holdings Inc.*, 214 F.3d 658 (5th Cir. 2000).
43. *Hasbro Inc. v. Clue Computing Inc.*, 66 F.Supp.2d 116 (D.Mass. 1999).
44. *Leatherman Tool Group Inc. v. Cooper Industries,* 199 F.3d 1009 (9th Cir. 1999).
45. *Rose Art Industries Inc. v. Swanson*, 235 F.3d 165 (3rd Cir. 2000).
46. *Playboy Enterprises Inc. v. Welles,* 78 F.Supp.2d 1066 (S.D. Cal. 1999). Also see *Bihari v. Gross*, 69 LW 1240 (S.D.N.Y. 9/25/00): use of another party's trademark in the metatags (indexing information) for a Web site, but not in the part of the site visible to casual Web users, does not violate the Anticybersquatting Consumer Protection Act (ACPA), because it falls within the ambit of fair use. Because of the low probability of confusion, there was no Lanham Act §43(a) violation either.
47. *Federal Express Corp. v. Federal Espresso Inc.*, 189 F.3d 914 (2nd Cir. 2000).
48. *Wilhelm Pudenz GMBH v. Littlefuse Inc.,* 177 F.3d 1204 (11th Cir. 1999).
49. *AOL v. AT&T*, 69 LW 1543 (4th Cir. 2/28/01).
50. *In re International Flavors & Fragrances Inc.*, 183 F.3d 1361 (Fed. Cir. 1999).
51. Citing *IP Lund Trading ApS v. Kohler Co.*, 163 F.3d 27 (1st Cir. 1998).
52. *Comedy III Productions Inc. v. New Line Cinema,* 200 F.3d 593 (9th Cir. 2000).
53. *EMI Catalogue Partnership v. Hill, Holiday, Connors, Cosmopoulous Inc.*, 225 F.3d 942 (2nd Cir. 2000).
54. *Secura Comm Consulting Inc. v. Secura-Com Inc.*, 224 F.3d 273 (3rd Cir. 2000).
55. *Nat'l Ass'n of Professional Baseball Leagues Inc. v. Very Minor Leagues Inc.*, 223 F.3d 1143 (10th Cir. 2000).

56. *TM Patents L.P. v. IBM,* 72 F.Supp. 2d 370 (S.D.N.Y. 1999).

57. *In re Gartside,* 203 F.3d 1305 (Fed. Cir. 2000).

58. *Dickinson v. Zurko,* 119 S.Ct. 1816 (Sup.Ct. 6/10/99).

59. *Kraft Foods Inc. v. International Trading Co.,* 203 F.3d 1362 (Fed. Cir. 2000).

60. *Chiuminatta Concrete Concepts v. Cardinal Industries,* 145 F.3d 1305 (Fed. Cir. 1998).

61. *United States Filter Corp. v. Ionics Inc.,* 68 F.Supp.2d 48 (D.Mass. 1999).

62. *University of Colorado Foundation Inc. v. American Cyanamid Co.,* 196 F.3d 1336 (Fed. Cir. 1999).

63. *VP Intellectual Properties LLC v. Imtec Corp.,* 68 LW 1400 (D.N.J. 12/8/99). Also see *HollyAnne Corp. v. TFT Inc.,* 199 F.3d 1304 (Fed.Cir. 1999): an offer to donate the allegedly infringed devices in the forum state is not an offer to sell that gives rise to personal jurisdiction. There were no commercial elements (product description, price quote, or indication that donee could purchase the product) in the donative transaction, so the case had to be dismissed.

64. *Juicy Whip v. Orange Bang Inc.,* 185 F.3d 1364 (Fed. Cir. 1999).

65. *Pioneer Hi-Bred International Inc. v. J.E.M. AG Supply Inc.,* 200 F.3d 1374 (Fed. Cir. 2000).

66. *AT&T Corp. v. Excel Communications Inc.,* 68 LW 1320 (D.Del. 10/25/99).

67. *Amazon.com Inc. v. Barnesandnoble.com Inc.,* 68 LW 1346 (W.D. Wash. 12/1/99).

68. *Eli Lilly & Co. v. Barr Laboratories Inc.,* 222 F.3d 973 (Fed. Cir. 2000).

69. *State Street Bank & Trust Co. v. Signature Financial Group,* 149 F.3d 1368 (Fed. Cir. 1998).

70. *AT&T Corp. v. Excel Communications Inc.,* 172 F.3d 1352 (Fed. Cir. 1999).

71. See, e.g., Brenda Sandburg; "PTO Ups the Ante," *The Recorder/CalLaw* 3/30/00, available at *http://www.law.com;* Gary M. Hoffman and Gabriela I. Coman, "Business Method Patents," *Nat'l L.J.* 2/14/00 p. 8.

72. See Dugie Standeford, "First Electronic Utility Patent Filed in Pilot Project," *IP Law Weekly* 12/28/99, available from *http://www.law.com.*

73. See Veronica Slind-Flor, "PTO's New Guide to DNA Info," *Nat.L.J.* 1/11/00, available at *http://www.law.com.*

74. *Moldo v. Matsco Inc. (In re Cybernectic Services Inc.)*, 239 B.R. 917 (9th Cir. 1999).
75. *Winner International Royalty Corp v. Wang*, 202 F.3d 1340 (Fed. Cir. 2000).
76. *Nilssen v. Motorola Inc.*, 203 F.3d 782 (Fed. Cir. 2000).
77. *Hydranautics v. FilmTec Corp.*, 204 F.3d 880 (9th Cir. 2000).
78. *Graco Children's Products Inc. v. Regalo International*, 77 F.Supp.2d 660 (E.D. Pa. 1999).
79. *Odetics Inc. v. Storage Technology Corp.*, 68 LW 1064 (Fed.Cir. 7/6/99).

$$\boxed{\P\,1400}$$

Insurance Law

[¶1410.1] [NEW] Whole Life, Term, and Investment-Oriented Insurance

The New Jersey Superior Court reversed the trial court, certifying a class of buyers of "vanishing premium" life insurance between 1985 and 1989, with respect to claims under the Consumer Fraud Act and common-law fraud claims. Although most states would refuse certification to such a class, New Jersey requires liberal class action practice for common grievances where an individual suit is not feasible.[1]

[¶1440] Automobile Insurance

An insurance policy provision (which follows Illinois insurance law, Comp.Stat. §5/143a) requiring arbitration of uninsured motorist coverage disputes (with arbitral awards under $20,000 becoming binding), is enforceable.[2] The plaintiff failed to secure a declaratory judgment that the mandatory arbitration clause is unconstitutional.

As the Illinois court held in late 1999, the state statute does not violate public policy or Due Process; it does not impair freedom of contract. The arbitration rules are rationally related to the statutory purpose of assisting insured persons injured by uninsured drivers.

Mandatory binding arbitration for small claims reduces litigation costs and speeds up case resolutions. Mandatory arbitration for small claims would be more likely to be rejected if it had been imposed unilaterally by the insurer, but in this case, the requirement is imposed by state law. The enactment of a state statute will not be deemed to impair contracts that don't come into existence until after the statute's effective date. This provision falls into the category of economic legislation, which is acceptable for Due Process purposes if it is rationally related to a legitimate governmental interest.

If an auto insurer exercises its statutory right (here, under Florida law) to make an insured who has Personal Injury Protection (PIP) submit to a medical examination, it must allow the insured to send his attorney or own videographer to approve the examination.[3] The court applied the analogy of cases allowing third parties to be present at medical examinations done in connection with Worker's Compensation or civil discovery. A PIP exam could be a step toward future litigation, because the insured applies for further benefits, which the insurer says are not available, so litigation potential is present.

[¶1460] Liability Insurance

An attorney defending a corporate client charged with intellectual property infringement has no duty to investigate whether the client's CGI policy might provide indemnification or defense costs. There might be an obligation for the lawyer to raise the insurance issue in some contexts, such as automotive personal injury—but in a business case, there is no duty to inquire into the availability of insurance for the client.[4]

The Eighth Circuit required a liability insurer to defend a contractor who punctured an underground storage tank on a neighbor's property, leading to a suit for environmental cleanup costs.[5] The court deemed it essentially a tort cause of action and not a trespass-by-pollution case. Therefore, personal injury coverage and the duty to defend was triggered, and the absolute pollution exclusion did not apply.

According to the California Court of Appeals,[6] California law doesn't require a CGL insurer to indemnify its insured for cleanup costs incurred under state orders. Such costs are not "damages" that the insured is obligated to pay because of property damage resulting from acts covered by the CGL, so the insurer is not responsible.

Here, the insured complied with the administrative orders, so no attempts at judicial enforcement were made. The insured's contention was that it would have been in serious legal jeopardy if it had failed to comply, so it was legally obligated to pay sums for which indemnification is available. But the court held that administrative proceedings, even if coercive, are merely the equivalent of claims or demands, not lawsuits triggering the duty to defend.

The insurer had no duty to defend under a liability insurance policy excluding coverage for suits arising out of the insured's "products" in personal injury and wrongful death suits alleging liability of the entire gun industry. The insured argued that it was being sued because of its "conduct" and not its "products," but the First Circuit found this argument unpersuasive.[7]

The insurer covering a nurse who was not sued in a medical malpractice case against the hospital, but whose negligence might have been a factor in the plaintiff patient's injury, does not have an obligation to contribute either defense or indemnity costs to the hospital's liability insurer.[8]

A 1995 California case[9] holds that the duty to indemnify doesn't arise until an underlying liability is established, and this can only be done through the judgment of a court. "Damages" are the result of a suit, not a lesser proceeding.

A homeowner's insurance company has no duty to defend or indemnify an insured businessman for damages in a sexual harassment suit that he lost.[10] The policy had a "business pursuits" exception, which rules out coverage. The insurer was entitled to summary judgment because the sexual harassment claim arose out of a sexual relationship between the insured and an employee. The policy's business pursuits exclusion is subject to an exception for "activities which are ordinarily incident to non-business pursuits"; the insured said that sexual activity is not a business pursuit, and in this context was not profit-oriented. But the court agreed with the insurer that the liability-creating event was the sexual harassment of an employee, which is work-related and triggers the employment exception.

Insurance for advertising injury that covers "infringement of copyright, title and slogan" doesn't cover patent infringement,[11] because the insurer did not include this type of injury in the list of covered incidents. Obviously the insurer didn't intend to cover patent infringement—it certainly didn't put it into the laundry list. "Title" in this context means the name of a copyrighted work, not title to an invention.

[¶1470] Health Insurance

See ¶345 for discussion of ERISA issues in employment-related health insurance policies, and for discussion of the June, 2000 Supreme Court ruling on rationing of care by HMOs.

On August 20, 1999, HCFA published an interim final rule, effective September 20, 1999: see 64 FR 45,785. The rule explains how HCFA will act as the backup regulator for the Health Insurance Portability and Accessibility Act (HIPAA) if the states fail to meet their enforcement burden. The rule also gives procedures for HCFA "market conduct examinations" of health insurers' HIPAA compliance, and explains the evidence that insurers can submit to clear themselves of allegations of violation. HCFA has already assumed the HIPAA enforcement burden in several states (California, Missouri, Rhode

Island) that failed to provide the required minimum protection for consumers, and HCFA may have to take on a regulatory role in Massachusetts and Michigan, too.

Insurers' "all products" demands have attracted controversy.[12] This practice requires doctors who want to remain in a Preferred Provider Organization (PPO), a type of managed care organization, to join the insurer's HMO. About a dozen medical associations have protested this policy, by lobbying state regulators or supporting legislation. Bills have been introduced in, e.g., Alaska, Illinois, North Dakota, Oregon, and Texas. Massachusetts is the only state to have legislation forbidding PPOs to force their doctors to subscribe to plans other than the PPO.

Nevada's state Division of Insurance issued an advisory, Bulletin 98-004, in October, 1998 calling this tying practice an instance of illegal coercion. The bulletin says, "Requiring a provider to become a member of a provider network for which he does not wish to contract in order to maintain a contractual relationship with an organization with which he chooses to contract is coercion. This practice violates the Unfair Trade Practices Act, Chapter 686A of the Nevada Revised Statutes."

The insurer's contention is that the provision actually protects patients, because it saves them from having to change doctors each time there is a change in their coverage.

In examining Aetna's acquisition of Prudential Health Care Plans Inc., the Department of Justice consent decree declined to impose an outright ban on all products clauses. The DOJ says this is only an issue where market power is present, and proving tying implicates major issues of defining the market and the products.

[¶1480] [NEW] Bad Faith

An insurer accused of breach of the covenant of good faith and fair dealing because it failed to settle a case cannot charge the insured with "comparative bad faith" on the basis of its conduct in the underlying personal injury case. (In this case, the insured, a manufacturer of water slides, did not mention earlier injuries in its response to interrogatories.) In this analysis, breach of the covenant of good faith is usually analyzed as a breach of contract; however, tort theories are applied to breaching insurers (but only to them, and not to the insureds). In this case, the insurer should have settled the case, irrespective of the insured's improper conduct.[13]

ENDNOTES

1. *Varacallo v. Massachusetts Mutual Life Ins. Co.*, 752 A.2d 807 (N.J. Super. 2000). But see, e.g., *Gibbs Properties Corp. v. Cigna Corp.*, 69 LW 1015 (M.D. Fla. 6/16/00) denying class certification in a suit brought by three Florida corporations on behalf of 40,000 state residents, alleging that insurers unlawfully inflated premiums for commercial insurance coverage. The Middle District of Florida found that the class was not identifiable; the criteria of predominance of common issues and class-action superiority were not met; and each of the members of the class would have to prove reliance on the insurer's misrepresentations and would have to prove damages.
2. *Reed v. Farmers Insurance Group*, 720 N.E.2d 1052 (Ill. 10/21/99).
3. *U.S. Security Insurance Co. v. Cimino*, 68 LW 1569 (Fla. 3/9/00).
4. *Darby & Darby PC v. VSI International Inc.*, 701 N.Y.S.2d 50 (N.Y.A.D. 1/13/00).
5. *Royal Insurance Co. of America v. Kirksville College of Osteopathic Medicine*, 194 F.3d 1009 (8th Cir. 1999).
6. *Certain Underwriters at Lloyds v. Superior Court of California*, 69 LW 1477 (Cal. 2/1/01). The decision follows *Foster-Gardner Inc. v. National Union Fire Ins. Co.*, 959 P.2d 265 (Cal. 1998): a CGL carrier has no duty to defend in a state administrative enforcement action that seeks site cleanup.
7. *Brazas Sporting Arms Inc. v. American Empire Surplus Lines Ins. Co.*, 220 F.3d 1 (1st Cir. 2000).
8. *American Continental Insurance Co. v. American Casualty Co. of Reading, Pennsylvania*, 69 LW 1476 (Cal.App. 1/30/01).
9. *Montrose Chemical Corp. v. Admiral Ins. Co.*, 913 P.2d 878 (Cal. 1995).
10. *Zimmerman v. Safeco Insurance Co. of America*, 605 N.W.2d 727 (Minn. 2000).
11. *U.S. Test Inc. v. NDE Environmental Corp.*, 196 F.3d 1376 (Fed. Cir. 1999).
12. See Chad Bowman, "Insurer 'All Products' Clauses Under Fire as Medical Associations Seek State Action," 68 LW 2131.
13. *Kransco v. American Empire Surplus Lines Ins. Co.*, 97 Cal.Rptr.2d 151 (Cal. 2000).

¶2000

Credit, Collections, and Disclosure

[¶2001]

A class of four million retailers was certified by the Eastern District of New York in early 2000[1] in an antitrust suit charging Visa and MasterCard with illegal pressure on retailers to accept the issuers' debit cards as well as their credit cards. The plaintiffs claim that this is an illegal tying action because although the fee for debit and credit cards is the same, Visa and MasterCard use their market domination to impose debit card fees that are much higher than those of their smaller competitors.

The class was certified based on a showing that common proof can show injury in fact, and that charges about the defendants' market power and other substantive claims can be resolved class-wide. The court left open the option of decertification if the individual damages would later be found to outbalance the common questions.

The late-2000 ruling of the Fifth Circuit is that the claims of more than a million debtors against Sears, Roebuck, alleging that Sears coerced bankrupt customers into paying pre-petition debt that had actually been discharged, cannot be maintained in class action form. The rationale is that individual damages, not injunctive relief, represent the predominant interest in the litigation.[2]

Only a couple of weeks later, the same court held that a class of automobile lessees seeking actual damages under TILA could not be certified. The would-be class members alleged that the lessor wrongfully failed to itemize the $400 "acquisition fee" charged to dealers at the beginning of leases. But the Fifth Circuit required proof of actual reliance as a prerequisite of awarding actual damages. These are sustained as a result of the failure to disclose only if the customer can prove that a different, less expensive transaction would have resulted if proper disclosures had been made.[3]

[¶2010] Truth in Lending

An FRB Final Rule published at 65 FR 58,903 (10/3/00) adds to the disclosures required on credit card solicitations and applications. The APR for purchases must be disclosed in 18-point type, under a separate heading from the rates charged as penalties. The disclosures must be readily noticeable, made in 12-point or larger type, and in reasonably understandable form. The APRs for cash advances and balance transfers must be disclosed in the same table as the APR for purchases.

At the beginning of 2000, the Northern District of Illinois held that TIL claims against a lender can be subject to mandatory arbitration, even if the plaintiff borrowers prefer to bring a TILA class action.[4]

The court rejected the borrowers' contention that TILA includes a statutory right to seek relief via class action. The borrowers also objected to being subject to mandatory arbitration, while the lender was allowed to use judicial or other process to enforce payment obligations on default. The court said that contracts don't have to be equal, so this inequality did not render the loan agreements invalid, and the lender's agreement to arbitrate at least some claims furnished consideration for the arbitration clause.

Similarly, in late 2000, the Eleventh Circuit held that neither TILA nor the ECOA is violated by requiring borrowers to arbitrate disputes about their loan agreements, in that there is no non-waivable right to litigate TILA claims either individually or as a class.[5]

Florida's 20-year statute of limitations for actions to enforce in-state judgments has been held also to apply to registration and enforcement under the Uniform Foreign Money Judgments Recognition Act (UFMJRA). The Florida Court of Appeals decided[6] that the policy underlying the statute would be better served by using the local statute of limitations rather than Florida's five-year statutory statute of limitations for enforcement of foreign judgments. The purpose of the statute was to make U.S. judgments enforceable in foreign courts by giving foreign countries reason to believe their judgments would be enforced in the United States.

Pre-UFMJRA law required a judgment creditor to sue in Florida on the foreign judgment, prove it was valid and entitled to enforcement, and get a Florida judgment on the basis of the foreign one.

UFMJRA says that judgments of foreign countries for recovery of a sum of money can be recognized and made entitled to enforcement by filing an authenticated copy of a final and conclusive judgment that could be enforced by the foreign court. The judgment party files an authenticated copy of the judgment with the clerk of the court and records it in the public records where enforcement is sought.

The court clerk has to send notice to the judgment debtor at the address provided by the judgment creditor. The debtor has 30 days to file objections to recognition of the judgment. If none are filed, then the clerk records a certificate. Either side can get a hearing in which the court orders the judgment to be granted or denied recognition. The judgment becomes enforceable after issuance of the certificate or order.

Late in 2000, the Supreme Court answered some—but not all—questions about arbitration of consumer finance agreements. According to the Supreme Court, a District Court's order compelling arbitration and dismissing underlying claims is a "final decision with respect to an arbitration" and therefore is appealable under FAA §16(a)(3)/9 USC §16(a)(3). However, the Supreme Court did not permit the consumer borrower to invalidate the arbitration agreement on the grounds that, because it was silent as to allocation of costs, it put her at risk of encountering prohibitive costs. The party seeking invalidation has the burden of proving the likelihood of costs, a subject on which the consumer introduced little evidence.[7]

The Third Circuit, however, deemed the arbitration provision included in a home improvement contract to be enforceable under the FAA, even though the homeowner had no opportunity to negotiate the provision with the finance company. In this reading,[8] each party gave consideration over and above the promise to arbitrate.

Allegedly, the contract arose out of a high-pressure sales campaign targeting low- and middle-income senior citizens. Building contractors got high-interest secondary mortgages on the homes of customers, and mortgages were assigned or sold to the defendant finance company, with exorbitant charges for credit insurance. The arbitration provision was buried in the fine print. The dissatisfied homeowners brought suit under state consumer protection laws and RICO. The finance company moved to compel arbitration.

The District Court found the contract unconscionable and denied the motion to compel arbitration, but to the Third Circuit, federal law does not require mutuality for an arbitration agreement to be enforceable, as long as mutual consideration is present.

Unconscionability can be procedural (based on the way the contract was obtained) or substantive (contract terms were imposed without choice, and/or unduly favoring one party). The plaintiffs claimed procedural unconscionability based on the small print buried within the agreement. The court found this a sustainable argument under state law, but not one that is supported by the FAA precedents. The agreement was enforceable despite the fact that the lender could litigate certain claims whereas customers were compelled to arbitrate. A late 1999 Alabama case says that arbitration agreements were not unconscionable, and therefore consumers could be obligated to arbitrate their claims.[9] The agreement made arbitration optional in some situations, such as claims under $20,000, and the costs of arbitration were allocated between the parties, so the agreement was not unfairly one-sided.

An automobile dealer remained a TILA "creditor" even though it assigned the Retail Installment Sales Agreement to a lender as soon as it was executed.[10] The contract identified the dealer as Vendor/Creditor, so initially, and on its face, the contract was payable to the dealer despite the assignment. The District Court position was that even though the dealer's credit department investigates applications and makes out the forms, GMAC or another assignee lender actually makes the loan and extends credit. But the Fifth Circuit disagreed. For one thing, there's an official FRB staff interpretation that says that a person to whom an obligation is originally payable is the creditor, even if the terms of the instrument call for simultaneous assignment. The example given is bank/auto dealer.

A borrower of two-week "payday loans" stated a TILA claim that can survive a 12(b)(6) motion to dismiss by alleging that the lender made a practice of stapling cash register receipts to the loan agreement in a way that blocked the disclosure statement,[11] and that the receipts didn't describe the costs as "finance charges." Disclosures can't be "clear and conspicuous" if something blocks them. However, in the Seventh Circuit view, measured from the viewpoint of the ordinary consumer, the statement "Your post-dated check is security for this loan" was an acceptable TILA disclosure.

TILA is violated by disclosing APRs based on the face amount, where borrowers were required to put up cash collateral for the loans (and therefore the effective amount borrowed was lower than the nominal amount). In substantive rather than formal terms, the cash collateral reduced the amount of credit available, and was not really used to secure the loans and was not really held as a deposit.[12]

[¶2030] FCRA

The Eastern District of Texas permitted an alleged child support debtor to bring an FCRA claim against the Texas Attorney General's Office,[13] based on charges that he was harassed over so-called support payments that he didn't even owe. The Eleventh Amendment was not implicated, because he only sought prospective injunctive relief.

Even though the FCRA is usually cited in connection with credit reporting agencies, the statutory text does not limit the Act's scope in that way. In this case, the plaintiff claimed that the defendants were making inaccurate reports about him to credit reporting agencies, which the Eastern District of Texas deemed to be conduct contemplated by the statute.

Under the Gramm-Leach-Bliley Act (GLB), effective July 1, 2001, the credit services industry is severely limited in its ability to market consumer data (e.g., matching up names with addresses and Social Security and phone numbers). Resale of data without consumer consent is forbidden. At press time, the FTC rule, defining the entire credit report, including the "credit header" (address and related data) as subject to the GLB privacy restrictions, had been upheld by federal Judge Ellen Segal Huvelle in litigation brought by agencies (including the Federal Reserve and the FTC) against Trans Union LLC, Equifax, and other generators of consumer credit data.[14]

According to two recent decisions, consumers have an implied private right of action under the FCRA to sue companies that make initial negative reports to credit reporting agencies and then fail to make a proper investigation after a consumer challenge to the information.[15]

[¶2040.1] [NEW] What is a "Debt"?

Whether a loan is a consumer debt rather than a business obligation for FDCPA purposes is determined as of the time of the loan—and not when collection efforts begin. The Seventh Circuit's theory is that the original lender would be more able to characterize the debt accurately at the time of the loan than a third-party collector would be at the time collection is sought.[16]

[¶2040.2] Who is a "Debt Collector"?

In the Sixth Circuit view,[17] an attorney or law firm "regularly" collects debts if it does it as a matter of course for its clients; for certain clients; or if debt collection is a substantial (whether or not it is the principal) part of the practice. The firm in question did 50-75 collections a year, representing about two percent of its practice, and it didn't have any dedicated staff or software for collections, so it was not deemed to be a debt collector.

An attorney who sent out 900 debt collection letters a day did not violate FDCPA §1692e(3) [false representation that a collections communication comes from a lawyer], because he did have direct and personal involvement in the process by reviewing the files and making independent determinations of who should receive which collection letters.[18]

[¶2040.3] Verification Requirement

A dismissal under FRCP 12(b)(6) was not available with respect to a consumer's claim that the debt collection notice confused her about her FDCPA §1692g right to debt verification. Whether a statement is "confusing" is a question of law, not of fact.[19]

According to the Seventh Circuit, a dunning letter that said that the past-due account had been placed for immediate collection could confuse debtors about their rights, because they might fail to understand the relationship between a demand for immediate payment and notification of their right to demand verification. However, the court left open the possibility of dismissal on the pleadings (F.R.C.P. 12(b)(3)) if the debtor failed to produce evidence of confusion.

A letter that gives the basic §1692g information, and does not threaten any further action, is not "deceptive" even if it is sent by a bank in connection with outstanding debts that the bank knew were uncollectable because they were time-barred.[20]

[¶2040.4] Forbidden Conduct

A check authorization and collection agency can legitimately require customers to pay service charges on collection efforts for dishonored checks. The Second Circuit[21] did not interpret the FDCPA to forbid such charges. The charges were treated as incidental damages authorized by the local (Connecticut) version of UCC Article 2. The checks were given at a counter displaying a large sign disclosing that collection charges would be imposed, so consumers were adequately warned of this possibility.

The Seventh Circuit ruled that the District Court should not have approved an FDCPA class action settlement which benefited only the class representative and his attorney, but not the other class members.[22] Three individuals filed separate suits to challenge Equifax Check Service Inc.'s debt collection letters. Two cases were consolidated and certified as class actions; the third was kept separate. Under the settlement, Equifax agreed to stop using the letter. One plaintiff was awarded $500 damages, plus

$1,500 for being the class representative; his attorney received a $78,000 fee. The other class members did not receive any damages, but were permitted to file their own individual suits.

A debt collection letter used in multiple states was permissible under the FDCPA. It included the required Colorado notice describing certain state and federal rights not subject to disclosure under FDCPA. The plaintiff, from Minnesota, said that she was misled into believing that she didn't have the rights in the Colorado disclosure box, but the court didn't accept this interpretation.[23]

[¶2060] Creditors' Remedies

A state (Virginia) court has held[24] that a credit card issuer's late fees did not constitute unlawful liquidated damages. The relevant state statute, Va. Code §6.1-330.63, abrogated the common law of unlawful liquidated damages, allowing lenders to impose a late charge up to 5% of the amount of the installment payment as long as the contract discloses it. A later amendment removed the 5% limitation.

ENDNOTES

1. *In re Visa Check/MasterMoney Antitrust Litigation,* 68 LW 1516 (E.D.N.Y. 2/22/00).
2. *Bolin v. Sears, Roebuck & Co.,* 231 F.3d 970 (5th Cir. 2000).
3. *Perrone v. GMAC,* 232 F.3d 433 (5th Cir. 2000).
4. *Thompson v. Illinois Title Loans Inc.,* 68 LW 1435 (N.D. Ill. 1/6/00).
5. *Bowen v. First Family Financial Services,* 233 F.3d 1331 (11th Cir. 2000).
6. *Le Credit Lyonnais S.A. v. Nadd,* 741 So.2d 1165 (Fla.App. 1999).
7. *Green Tree Financial Corp.-Alabama v. Randolph,* #99-1235, 69 LW 4023 (Sup.Ct. 12/11/00).
8. *Harris v. Green Tree Financial Corp.,* 183 F.3d 173 (3rd Cir. 1999).
9. *Commercial Credit Corp. v. Leggett,* 744 So.2d 890 (Ala. 1999). Also see *Green Tree Financial Corp. of Alabama v. Vintson,* 68 LW 1256 (Ala. 10/1/99): the arbitration agreement was not unconscionable even though the lender could litigate some matters and buyer had to arbitrate all matters. Nor did the court accept the plaintiffs' contention that they were unable to comprehend the agreement.

10. *Riviere v. Banner Chevrolet Inc.*, 184 F.3d 457 (5th Cir. 1999).

11. *Smith v. Cash Store Management Inc.*, 195 F.3d 325 (7th Cir. 1999).

12. *Williams v. Chartwell Financial Services Ltd.*, 204 F.3d 748 (7th Cir. 2000).

13. *Campbell v. Baldwin*, 68 LW 1576 (E.D. Tex. 2/23/00).

14. See Glenn R. Simpson, "Judge Upholds Tough New Restrictions on Sales of Certain Personal-Credit Data," *Wall Street Journal*, 5/8/01 p. A28.

15. *Dornhecker v. Ameritech Corp.*, 68 LW 1771 (N.D. Ill. 6/7/00); *Campbell v. Baldwin*, 90 F.Supp.2d 754 (E.D. Tex. 2000); but contra *Carney v. Experian Information Solutions*, 57 F.Supp.2d 496 (W.D. Tenn. 1999).

16. *Miller v. McCalla, Rayner, Padrick, Cobb, Nichols, and Clark LLC*, 68 LW 1756 (7th Cir. 6/5/00).

17. *Schroyer v. Frankel*, 197 F.3d 1170 (6th Cir. 1999).

18. *Boyd v. Wexler*, 69 LW 1383 (N.D. Ill. 11/17/00).

19. *Walker v. National Recovery Inc.*, 200 F.3d 500 (7th Cir. 1999).

20. *Shorty v. Capital One Bank*, 90 F.Supp.2d 1330 (D.N.M. 2000).

21. *Tuttle v. Equifax Check*, 190 F.3d 9 (2nd Cir. 8/19/99).

22. *Crawford v. Equifax Payment Services Inc.*, 201 F.3d 877 (7th Cir. 2000).

23. *Morse v. Dun & Bradstreet Inc.*, 87 F.Supp.2d 901 (D. Minn. 2000).

24. *Perez v. Capital One Bank*, 522 S.E.2d 874 (Va. 11/5/99).

¶2100

Bankruptcy

[¶2101]

The WARN Act and the Labor-Management Relations Act (LMRA) pre-empt state-law liens with respect to sanctions imposed for WARN Act non-compliance (as well as unpaid wages and amounts claimed under a collective bargaining agreement, or CBA). LMRA §301 preempts CBA claims, so employees' claims of entitlement to bankruptcy priority liens arising out of vacation pay, wages, pension contributions[1] or health claims under the CBA are necessarily preempted.[1]

Several changes to the Federal Rules of Bankruptcy Procedure (F.R.B.P.) were adopted by the Supreme Court on April 17, 2000, effective December 1, 2000. See *http://www.uscourts.gov/about.html:*

- Rule 1017(e): A motion to dismiss a Chapter 7 case (Bankruptcy Code §707(b)) can be extended by the court pursuant to a timely request.
- Rule 2002(a): It is not necessary to notify all creditors of a hearing that requests de minimis compensation or expense reimbursement. De minimis now means $1,000 rather than the earlier limit of $500.
- Rule 4003(b): Again based on a timely request, the court can grant an extension of the time to object to the list of exemptions that are claimed.
- Rule 4004(c)(1): Chapter 7 discharge will no longer be granted as long as there is a motion pending for extended time to file a motion to dismiss.
- Rule 5003: The United States and state jurisdictions are given the power to designate addresses for mailing purposes.

[¶2105] Bankruptcy Pros And Cons

A Chapter 11 petition can be dismissed for cause under Bankruptcy Code §1112(b) if the corporation's motivation for filing is to protect itself against a potentially expensive antitrust suit, and if the company is financially sound and does not have a valid reorganizing purpose. The Third Circuit held in 1999 that such lack of good faith constitutes cause for dismissal.[2]

117

In this reading, although the Bankruptcy Code encourages early filing, and insolvency is not a prerequisite of a Chapter 11 filing, the company must face actual, not merely potential, financial or managerial difficulties.

The Third Circuit also held in 1999 that a Chapter 11 petition should be dismissed if its primary purpose was frustration of a shareholder suit and not reorganization of the company, because such petitions are not filed in good faith; the Eighth Circuit adopted a similar analysis in a 2000 case.[3]

However, in a case from the Western District of Texas, the taxpayer was subject to a default judgment for back tax liability. The court ordered foreclosure of real estate owned by the taxpayer to satisfy the tax liens. The taxpayer filed a bankruptcy petition on the morning of the foreclosure sale, preventing the government from confirming the foreclosure. Because Texas law requires a valid foreclosure sale (and not merely an order of foreclosure) to divest a property interest, the court ruled that the taxpayer still owned the property when the bankruptcy petition was filed. The District Court remanded the government's motion to lift the automatic stay to the Bankruptcy Court, finding that that was the best forum to judge whether the petition was filed in good faith.[4]

[¶2110] Forms of Bankruptcy

Chapter 12, dealing with family farm bankruptcies, was originally enacted in 1986. At that time, it was intended to sunset in 1993. Several extensions were granted, but Chapter 12 was terminated as of July 1, 2000 under P.L. 105-277. It was then revived by P.L. 107-8, but only for the one-year period of June 1, 2000 to June 1, 2001.

[¶2110.1] Chapter 7

The debtor has an absolute right, pursuant to Bankruptcy Code §1307(b), to dismiss a Chapter 13 filing before the case is converted to Chapter 7.[5] (In this case, a month before the Chapter 13 filing, the debtor entered into a contract to sell a building. After filing, the debtor sought court permission to repudiate that contract and sell the building to another party for more money, over the understandable objections of the first would-be buyer.) The bankruptcy court intended to convert the case to Chapter 7; the debtor moved for dismissal.

The bankruptcy court viewed it as more appropriate to convert the case to Chapter 7 than to permit withdrawal or conversion to Chapter 11.

The court had to reconcile the Bankruptcy Code language in §1307(b) (the court "shall" dismiss the action on request of the debtor at any time before conversion to Chapter 7) with §1307(c) (conversion by the court on request of a party in interest) and §105(b) (broad authority to take any action necessary to prevent abuse of process). The Second Circuit treats the "shall" in §1307(b) as mandatory, in contrast with the permissive "may" of §1307(c).

Although it is the only Circuit taking this position, the First Circuit view is that interest on post-petition tax obligations in a Chapter 7 case is not a first-priority administrative expense; it is merely entitled to fifth priority.[6]

A family home in Louisiana was community property. It was awarded to the wife by partition incident to divorce, before the husband filed for bankruptcy. Therefore, it never became part of his Chapter 7 bankruptcy estate.[7]

A wife relinquished her interest in the marital residence. In return, the husband agreed to hold her harmless on two marital debts aggregating $14,000. The Northern District of Ohio held that the obligation was not a "maintenance or support obligation" that would be denied bankruptcy discharge. However, based on the facts of the case (that paying the debts would have a more serious negative impact on the wife's standard of living than on the husband's), discharge was denied in the husband's Chapter 7 bankruptcy case8

In another Chapter 7 case[9] the debtor held a $25,000 judgment lien on the house that used to be her marital home. This lien was deemed exempt in her Chapter 7 case. It would be treated as alimony to the extent it was reasonably necessary for her support. The divorce decree, which is controlling as to the characterization of the lien, treated it as an alimony lien.

A Chapter 7 trustee is not empowered to bring malpractice claims against the accounting firm that represented the debtor in its initial Chapter 11 filing. The fee application hearing in the Chapter 11 proceeding became res judicata, because it has the same nucleus of operative facts as the malpractice claim, and it was the proper point for malpractice claims to have been raised.[10]

Section 330(a) of the Bankruptcy Code has been amended to remove the phrase "or the debtor's attorney" from the list of people eligible to get fees for post-petition services, but a 1999 case from the Ninth Circuit treats this as a scrivener's error,[11] saying that the deletion was inadvertent and renders the statutory language ambiguous.

The Fifth Circuit and some Bankruptcy Courts have ruled that the language is not ambiguous, and the fee award is precluded; the Second Circuit and other Bankruptcy Courts disagree. In the Ninth Circuit view, before 1994, it was clear that Chapter 7 attorneys could collect fees for post-petition services. After the amendment, the list of categories eligible for "reasonable compensation" is different from the categories to whom the court "may award" payment, and the sentence as it stands is grammatically incorrect.

A Chapter 13 plan was not, in the First Circuit view, proposed in bad faith when a debtor who had a fraud claim that was nondischargeable in the Chapter 7 proceeding originally filed wanted to convert to Chapter 13 to get a broader discharge.[12] The Bankruptcy Code does not forbid a second filing while a Chapter 7 case remains open, and the court viewed obtaining greater access to discharge as a legitimate planning objective.

[¶2110.1.2] [NEW] Right of Redemption

Supreme Court precedent from 1997 [*Associates Commercial Corp. v. Rash,* 520 U.S. 953 (Sup.Ct. 1997)] requires a Chapter 13 debtor who seeks to redeem collateral to pay its retail or replacement value. However, according to a late-2000 decision from the Sixth Circuit, a Chapter 7 debtor is required to pay only the wholesale value, on the theory that if the debtor fails to redeem, the creditor will probably sell the collateral (here, a repossessed automobile) at a wholesale auction and therefore suffers no detriment by receiving the wholesale price from the debtor.[13]

[¶2120] Bankruptcy Court Procedures

Although it is not illegal to specify breakup fees (payable if the deal falls through) in a contract for the sale of the debtor's assets, such a provision is permissible only if the fees are necessary to preserve the value of the estate. In other words, merely satisfying the business judgment rule is not enough; the fee must qualify as a Bankruptcy Code §503(b)(1)(A) administrative expense.

A successful fee application under this section requires that the debt must arise from a transaction with a debtor in possession, and the consideration for the claimant's right to payment must benefit the DIP in operation of its business.[14]

A corporate officer of a company in Chapter 11, who allegedly used one of the company's customers to divert funds to himself cannot be prosecuted for criminal bankruptcy fraud 18 USC §157(2). The Eastern District of Pennsylvania refused[15] to apply the law as broadly as mail and securities fraud laws have been applied.

The bankruptcy provision's legislative history says that the intent of the provision is to criminalize the specific intent to defraud using a bankruptcy petition, or making a fraudulent representation for the purpose of carrying out a fraudulent scheme. But it doesn't apply to people who make a misrepresentation on a financial statement and later make a bankruptcy filing that was not contemplated at the time of the representation. Nor does it apply to someone who lies in a bankruptcy proceeding in a way that is not part of a scheme to defraud involving the proceeding itself.

In 2000, the Third and Ninth Circuits disagreed about whether a debtor's bad-faith acquisition of substantial credit-card consumer debt before a Chapter 7 filing justifies dismissal of the petition. The Third Circuit held that such conduct is bad faith that will justify dismissal of the petition pursuant to Bankruptcy Code §707(a), whereas the Ninth Circuit says that §707(b) embodies a presumption in favor of granting debt relief. In the Ninth Circuit view, the Chapter 7 statutory language is different from the language in Chapters 11 and 13 because there is no post-liquidation relationship between debtor and creditors. (The Third Circuit case involved an additional factor: the debtor was also getting a divorce, resulting in dissolution of a tenancy by the entireties and, subsequently, in the debtor's access to cash that could be used to pay debts.)[16]

Service of process under FRBP 7004(b)(9) is valid and effective as long as the documents are mailed to the address disclosed by the debtor on the court documents. Thus, a summons and complaint can be legally effective even if it is not actually received.[17]

[¶2130] [NEW] The Bankruptcy Estate

Although state courts take the leading role in handling domestic relations issues, the Eastern District of Michigan ruled early in 2001 that a uniform federal definition should be used to determine what constitutes "alimony" received from the other spouse that can be excluded from the debtor-spouse's bankruptcy estate under Bankruptcy Code §522(d)(10)(D). In this case, weekly payments identified as "alimony or spousal support" were excluded from the bankruptcy estate because they were intended as spousal support, and because the bankruptcy court deemed the amounts to be reasonably necessary to support the debtor-spouse.[18]

The Oklahoma state undue hardship exemption extends to earnings from personal services—but state and federal tax refunds resulting from excess withholding cannot be traced back. They are considered "taxes," not "wages," and consequently become part of the bankruptcy estate.[19]

When a law firm partner files for bankruptcy protection, the lawyer's interest in the firm (his or her capital contribution and money attributable to pre-petition legal work) must be turned over to the bankruptcy trustee when the firm makes its year-end profit distribution. In this case, the partner's bankruptcy caused a formal dissolution of the firm, but the firm did not wind up its affairs. Bankruptcy Code §541(a) makes the partner's interest in the firm the property of the bankruptcy estate. Although the trustee cannot force the partnership to wind up, the other partners have to account to the trustee for the value of the bankrupt partner's interest.[20]

A legal malpractice claim involving the conduct of the bankruptcy case itself (the debtor says that he directed his attorneys to file in Chapter 11, but they filed a Chapter 7 petition, resulting in loss of control over his assets) belongs to the bankruptcy estate. The claim is not the property of the debtor as an individual.[21]

Alimony payments received after a Chapter 7 filing are not property of the estate, although Bankruptcy Code §541(a)(5)(B) does put property received under a settlement agreement or divorce decree into the estate.[22]

Money embezzled by the debtor does not become part of the bankruptcy estate, but items purchased with the embezzled funds do enter the estate, on the grounds that the debtor did not have legal title to the money, but did have legal title to the legitimately purchased items.[23]

[¶2140] Exemptions

Debtors who were separated but not divorced when they filed a joint Chapter 7 petition are each entitled to claim a separate residence as a homestead.[24] Although their home state (Florida) doesn't recognize legal separation, state court decisions indicate a public policy of allowing two homestead exemptions in situations where no fraud is present.

The Bankruptcy Code §522(d)(11)(D) exemption for the debtor's right to receive up to $15,000 as a payment on account of personal bodily injury is limited to only one $15,000 amount, not one exemption per claim,[25] if the debtor has more than one. The statute refers to "a" payment, not "payments." The First Circuit's analysis is that the legislative intent was to provide reasonable levels of support for the debtor, but this intent is not furthered by favoring debtors who have several small claims rather than one larger one.

Under Bankruptcy Code §522(b), the debtor can choose between the state and federal exemption schemes and make a list of claimed exemptions from the bankruptcy estate. FRBP 4003(b) allows the creditor and any bankruptcy trustee to file objections to the list of exemptions within 30 days of the creditors' meeting. The Second Circuit has ruled that the 30-day period does not start over again when a Chapter 11 case is converted to Chapter 7. FRBP 1019(2) is explicit in stating that the conversion does not re-start the clock.[26]

The holder of a wholly unsecured second mortgage does not get the protection from modification in Chapter 13 given to mortgagees of the debtor's principal residence.[27]

[¶2140.2.2] [NEW] Trusts and Pensions

The Eighth Circuit refused to treat a debtor's individual retirement annuity as exempt under a law that exempts Individual Retirement Accounts. Iowa has opted out of the federal exemption scheme, and the state exemption covers Roth and conventional IRAs but not annuities.[28]

According to the Ninth Circuit, the bankruptcy court erred by denying the debtor's request for a state-law exemption of her IRA. The bankruptcy court accepted the trustee's contention that the debtor used the account to supplement her non-retirement income. California law defines the exemption in terms of principal use for retirement purposes, but the funds need not be devoted entirely to retirement purposes. The case remanded to determine how the funds, and therefore the exemption, should be allocated.[29]

[¶2150] The Role of the Trustee

If a bankruptcy trustee enters into a settlement agreement, the agreement is not binding against a creditor who did not agree to the settlement.[30] The trustee's authority is limited by Bankruptcy Code §363. The trustee needs notice and a hearing to deal with property outside the ordinary course of business, and agreeing to settle claims equals the sale of the claim, which falls outside the ordinary course of pre-filing business.

Setoff, recoupment, and other affirmative contract defenses that arise because of the bankruptcy debtor's default are not "interests" as defined by

Bankruptcy Code §363(f), and therefore they are not necessarily extinguished by a bankruptcy sale.[31] Although the trustee can sell property free and clear of claims and other interests that can be asserted against the estate, a defense is not an interest. However, if an actual setoff (not just a right to setoff) is taken prior to bankruptcy, it can be asserted as a defense.

Yet another Circuit split exists with respect to the trustee's duties. The Fifth Circuit declines to hold the trustee personally liable for damage to the Chapter 11 estate caused by mishandling of the taxes on the estate,[32] unless the trustee's conduct was tantamount to gross negligence. A much earlier case[33] holds trustees personally liable for willful breach of the fiduciary duty of loyalty, but provides no guidance for the treatment of trustee mistakes.

The Bankruptcy Code §546(a) two-year statute of limitations for the trustee to bring an avoidance action begins when the trustee is appointed, rather than when Debtor in Possession status is granted. Although theoretically the DIP has the powers of the trustee, the statute neither refers to the DIP in this context nor limits the DIP's avoidance power to two years.[34]

The Bankruptcy Court said that the bankruptcy trustee always controls the exercise or waiver of the attorney–client privilege with respect to pre-petition, good-faith, affirmative civil claims against third persons with whom the debtor did business. But the Tenth Circuit rejected this approach.[35] To the Tenth Circuit, control over the assertion or waiver of the privilege is not automatic. Each case should be reviewed by the court in camera to determine if the trustee should be allowed to exercise the right.

The size of the estate on which the trustee's commission is calculated does not include the value of a credit bid on property that was sold to a secured creditor.[36] The Third Circuit rationale is that the proper analogy is turnover of the property to the creditor—not a sale of property and distribution of the proceeds; that would generate a commission under Bankruptcy Code §326(a).

According to the Eleventh Circuit, the Chapter 11 trustee's fees, which are based on "disbursements" (see 28 USC §1930) should reflect all of the debtor's disbursements, including those made in the ordinary course of business—not just those made under the confirmed Chapter 11 plan.[37]

Under IRS Regulations proposed October 10, 2000, the IRS accepts the majority view taken by most courts: that as long as the debtor satisfies the IRC §121 requirements (e.g., duration of ownership and use) for exclusion of capital gain on the sale of the debtor's principal residence, the Chapter 7 or Chapter 11 estate will also be entitled to exclusion of gain for tax purposes.[38]

[¶2160] The Automatic Stay

The automatic stay prevents a tax lien from attaching to an asset that the debtor inherits while the proceeding is going on. However, a tax lien that was perfected pre-petition usually attaches to after-acquired assets by operation of law.

In a Fourth Circuit case from 1999,[39] an involuntary Chapter 7 debtor disclosed a contingent interest in a potential inheritance under a trust of which the debtor was a beneficiary. Eventually, the debtor inherited about $150,000.

About a year before the filing of the Chapter 7, the IRS filed notice of tax lien where the debtor's property was located, thus perfecting the lien under Code §6323. The bankruptcy court, District Court, and Fourth Circuit were in agreement: the automatic stay prevents imposition of a tax lien on property received by the estate after filing, even though the lien was filed pre-petition.

The claw-back principle of Bankruptcy Code §541(a)(5)(A) returns property to the bankruptcy estate if it is acquired by the debtor by bequest, devise, or inheritance within 180 days after filing. The trustee's contention was that the bequest went right into the bankruptcy estate, and never became the debtor's property, preventing attachment of the lien.

The trustee also cited the effect of Bankruptcy Code §362(a)(5) automatically staying any "act" to perfect liens against debtors' property, to the extent that they secure pre-filing claims. The IRS said that its lien attached to the property by operation of law, so there was no "act" to be stayed; the Fourth Circuit disagreed. A 1994 amendment adding §362(b)(18) exempts perfection of liens from property taxes (which are statutory) from the stay—showing that Congress had but passed up the opportunity to make an exception for federal tax liens.

Because Bankruptcy Code §362(a) says that criminal proceedings are not stayed, the automatic stay does not apply to criminal proceedings, even if their purpose is debt collection.[40] This overrules an earlier decision which did place criminal proceedings with debt collection purpose within the ambit of the automatic stay.

Sanctions for frivolous litigation (here, a frivolous appeal as defined by F.R.A.P. 38) are not subject to the automatic stay in a lawyer's Chapter 11 case. Bankruptcy Code §362(b)(4) makes the automatic stay inapplicable to actions or proceedings by governmental units to enforce police or regulatory powers, and the Ninth Circuit considers the sanction to carry out government policy, not protect private rights or the government's pecuniary interest in the lawyer's property.[41]

Creditors who violate the automatic stay are not liable for damages for infliction of emotional distress under the Bankruptcy Code §362(h) definition of "actual damages," because the Bankruptcy Code provision is concerned with the protection of the automatic stay, not with the maintenance of tort claims.[42]

[¶2170] Assumption or Avoidance of Obligations

A Chapter 11 debtor who rejects a nonresidential lease is obligated to pay the rent for the full month, even though rejection occurred, and premises were vacated, only two days after the rent was due.[43] The ten-year lease called for rent payment on the first of each month, which is when the debtor's obligation to pay was triggered.

Therefore, the trustee was required by §365(d)(3) to pay for the full month after the debtor gave notice on November 25 that it was rejecting the lease and vacating the premises on December 2 (post-petition).

A debtor's obligation under a divorce judgment to pay third-party debts is not accorded priority under Bankruptcy Code §507(a)(2), which reflects Congressional policy to protect only those support obligations actually owed to family members and not property division obligations.[44]

There is no requirement under Bankruptcy Code §1113 that a company reject its Collective Bargaining Agreements before, rather than after, sale of the company's assets, because the Eighth Circuit does not condition rejection of the CBA on the debtor's having a workable plan for surviving as a going concern.[45]

[¶2175] [NEW] Impact of Bankruptcy on Secured Creditors

Bankruptcy Code §1329(a) allows modification of a confirmed plan, but only to the extent of the amount and timing of the payments, not the amount of the claim itself. Therefore, the debtor is not permitted to surrender the collateral to a secured creditor and then treat the deficiency as an unsecured claim to be paid off at a lower rate.[46]

[¶2180] [NEW] Valuation of Property

To prevent windfalls, the First Circuit requires that whenever a debtor strips down a mortgage (thus frustrating the interests of unsecured creditors), is discharged, and sells the mortgaged property, all proceeds above the stripped value must be disgorged.[47]

[¶2185] [NEW] Improper Transfers

In a September, 2000 Third Circuit case, the DIP sold all of its assets after the petition. The sale did not divest unsecured creditors of their state-law fraudulent transfer claims with respect to pre-petition transfers. The claims belong to the creditors, not the debtor, and therefore do not become assets of the estate.[48]

A Chapter 7 debtor's payments under a debt restructuring agreement are not necessarily made outside the ordinary course of business and, therefore, are not necessarily avoidable as preferences; the Ninth Circuit treats it as a fact determination based on practices within the relevant industry.[49]

The same court ruled in mid-2000 that the 90-day window (Bankruptcy Code §547(b)(4)) for the trustee to recapture preferential transfers includes weekends and holidays. The FRBP 9006(a) extension to the next business day does not apply in this context.[50]

[¶2190] Discharge

A debtor used part of a $22,000 home equity loan to pay off her credit cards, then ran up a further $22,000 in debts. The District Court held that there was no fraudulent intent, and the credit card issuer did not rely on misrepresentations by the debtor to extend credit, so discharge could not be denied on grounds of fraud. The Eighth Circuit affirmed these findings, in that they were not clearly erroneous.[51]

The card issuer's argument was that it was a badge of fraud to use the card heavily right after making a large balance transfer. But there is no single factor that determines fraudulent intent, and the court's analysis was that the financially unsophisticated debtor accepted a heavy interest rate, risked losing her home, did not change her spending habits, and generally acted the same way she always had—she had a history of being severely indebted.

Debtors do not have an implied private right of action to enforce Bankruptcy Code §524 [discharge enjoins attempts to collect debts subject to the discharge; this section also defines acceptable agreements for reaffirming a debt].

The Sixth Circuit also refused to grant a Bankruptcy Code §105 order ["any order necessary or appropriate" to implement the Bankruptcy Code] to debtors who claim that creditors have violated the debt reaffirmation provisions of §524—although the First Circuit did make an order of this type in a case earlier in 2000.[52]

The Fifth Circuit ruled in late 2000 that the claims of more than a million debtors about Sears' alleged coercion to force them to pay discharged pre-petition debt should not have been certified as a class action. The rationale is that their predominant interest is in securing individual damages rather than injunctive relief.[53]

A representative of a decedent's estate can challenge the discharge of a wrongful death claim against a bankruptcy debtor, because the administrator is a "creditor" with standing to object to the discharge.[54] (The facts in this case were somewhat unusual: the debtor shot her husband to death, and her daughter, as administratrix of the husband's estate, filed a wrongful death suit against the mother, who then filed under Chapter 7. The daughter opposed the discharge as a willful and malicious act, denied discharge under Bankruptcy Code §523(a)(6).)

Under Texas law, the administrator is the judicial officer who can enforce claim and right to payment under a wrongful death statute, and therefore has standing to get the wrongful death claim declared nondischargeable.

Creditors who did not contest dischargeability of student loan debts, and did not appeal the order of confirmation of a Chapter 13 plan that discharged student loan debt (because not discharging it would be an undue hardship on the debtor) cannot reopen the issue of dischargeability once the debtor makes payments under the plan and is discharged.[55] The issue is not whether the debtor adequately proved hardship, but whether confirmation of the plan finally resolved the issue of hardship.

[¶2190.1] Exceptions to Discharge

According to the Third Circuit, it is invalid for a reorganization plan to release the debtor company's nondebtor directors and officers and permanently enjoin the shareholders from suing them,[56] because Bankruptcy Code §523(e) does not permit discharge of nondebtor liability.

The District Court justified the release by citing Bankruptcy Code §105(a), which allows the court to take necessary or appropriate actions to enforce Title 11. The Third Circuit did not agree with the District Court that resolving shareholder fraud suits was critical to the success of the reorganization. Any nonconsensual release must satisfy stringent tests (fairness; necessity to the reorganization; supported by specific factual findings) that the Third Circuit did not believe to be present in this case.

According to the Ninth Circuit,[57] post-petition interest on nondischargeable child support obligations is also nondischargeable. The court reached this conclusion by analogy with post-petition interest on a nondischargeable student loan debt, which has been held so both because it remains a personal liability of the debtor, and because interest is integral to a continuing debt.

A noncustodial parent's debt to the county that provided AFDC benefits to the parent's children is not dischargeable—even debt accumulated before the date of the support order. The Ninth Circuit did not find earlier cases on this issue controlling, because of changes in both bankruptcy and social services law. Even though the debt is not directly owed to the ex-spouse and children, it is still treated as support debt under this analysis.[58]

A divorce decree's award of half of the husband's pension benefits to the wife, effective when the employee-spouse becomes eligible for retirement, is not dischargeable in bankruptcy.[59]

Monetary sanctions imposed on a lawyer, under a state-law counterpart of Rule 11, for filing a frivolous suit against a former opponent in litigation are imposed for a "willful and malicious injury" and hence are not dischargeable.[60] The retaliation suit exposed the opponent to expenses for defending itself, proving injury.

The Eleventh Circuit denied[61] discharge of $2 million in tax liability because the debtor transferred assets to his wife as a tax avoidance mechanism. Bankruptcy Code §523(a)(1)(C) forbids discharge of taxes that the debtor willfully attempted in any manner to evade or defeat.

The debtor contended that this only applies to evasion of tax assessment, not tax payment. Eleventh Circuit precedent[62] says this is true for mere nonpayment of tax, or paying other debts instead of giving the appropriate priority to tax payments—but not where there has been affirmative fraudulent conduct.

Government tax claims cannot be discharged if the return was due during the three years prior to filing of the petition: Bankruptcy Code

§507(a)(8). The First Circuit (joining the Third, Seventh, Eighth, Ninth, and Tenth Circuit) says that the three-year period is automatically tolled by a prior bankruptcy proceeding. The Fifth and Eleventh Circuits, joined by the Sixth Circuit in 2000, reject automatic tolling, but do permit case-by-case tolling on equitable grounds.[63]

An innocent partner subjected to fraud liability because of another partner's conduct cannot discharge the liability in bankruptcy. Bankruptcy Code §523(a)(2)(A) forbids discharge in the case of imputed fraud—even if the innocent partner did not receive any financial benefit from the other partner's fraud, and despite whether or not the fraud occurred in the ordinary course of business.[64]

[¶2192] [NEW] Attorneys' Fees in Bankruptcy

There is a Circuit split as to whether the changes to Bankruptcy Code §330(a)(1) made by the Bankruptcy Reform Act of 1994 (which does not include the debtor's attorney in the list of officers eligible to receive fees and expenses from the bankruptcy estate) represent a real change in the law or a mere scrivener's error. The Third and Ninth Circuits allow a fee award to the debtor's attorney based on the established precedent for compensating the attorney, but the Fifth and the Eleventh cite the plain meaning of the statute as a reason for denying the award.[65]

The automatic stay is not violated by a lawyer charging to a client in Chapter 7 a fee for post-petition services that the bankruptcy court later found to be unreasonable, because the attorney had no reason to believe that the fee was unreasonable when it was charged.[66]

Bankruptcy Code §328(a), dealing with retainers, hourly rates, and contingent fees—and not the §330(a)(1) lodestar—is the proper criterion for reviewing special counsel's application for legal fees submitted to the trustee.[67]

An attorney who deliberately refused to comply with Bankruptcy Code §329 and corresponding local rules, requiring approval of fees, was ordered by the Western District of Missouri to disgorge those fees even if they were reasonable.[68] Disgorgement was also required when an attorney delegated too much of the work in bankruptcy cases to a paralegal, because this constituted failure to properly represent clients. The attorney was also ordered to reimburse the U.S. Trustee's investigative costs for the matter.[69]

Because federal and state bar admissions are separate, an Illinois lawyer who is admitted before the District of Arizona but not in the Arizona state courts is entitled to receive fees for work before the Bankruptcy Court of the District of Arizona.[70]

[¶2195] Bankruptcy Appeals

The U.S. Trustee's power under Bankruptcy Code §307, to appear and intervene in Bankruptcy Court proceedings, gives the U.S. Trustee standing to appeal Bankruptcy Court decisions to the District Court.[71]

A bankruptcy court's denial of a claim to exemption is a final order as defined by 28 U.S.C. §158(a)(1). Therefore, the right to appeal is waived if it is not raised within 10 days. In mid-1999, the Ninth Circuit made explicit[72] what was implied by earlier decisions: that not only is immediate appeal available in this context, it is mandatory.

In an adversary bankruptcy proceeding, the Eleventh Circuit says that the losing party needs certification under FRCP 54(b) before appealing.[73] FRBP 7054 incorporates Rule 54(b), so if the bankruptcy order in an adversary proceeding disposes of less than all the claims, it cannot be appealed immediately unless the bankruptcy judge certifies immediate review. This view has also been taken by five other Circuits, but the Seventh Circuit treats the order as final and appealable even without certification.

[¶2196] Tax Issues in Bankruptcy

In the Eighth Circuit's view,[74] the Bankruptcy Court has jurisdiction based on Bankruptcy Code §505 to determine the debtor's post-petition tax liability, and can give the debtor an offset because of restitution against an IRS claim for income tax assessed on embezzlement income. The §505 power does not extend to the estate's right to a refund, but it does extend to tax liability beyond the year stated in the proof of claim, if the liability relates to repayment of embezzled funds.

In general, the Bankruptcy Code calls for compliance with non-bankruptcy statutes of limitations, absent good cause. Therefore, the automatic turnover provision of Bankruptcy Code §542(a) does not obligate the IRS to refund a debtor's tax overpayment to a bankruptcy trustee who failed to file a timely refund claim.[75]

Bankruptcy Code §502(b)(8) and FRBP 3002(c)(1) impose a 180-day limit during which the IRS can file proof of claim against a bankruptcy estate. The doctrine of equitable tolling is not available to the IRS to extend this period.[76]

In a situation where the IRS imposes a valid levy on a debtor whose Chapter 13 reorganization plan is not confirmed (in this case, because it was withdrawn by the debtors), money deposited by the debtor into the reorganization plan must be remitted to the IRS, not returned to the debtor.[77]

In other words, the IRS levy provisions (Code §6331) outweigh Bankruptcy Code §1326(a)(2)'s provisions for distributing funds out of an unconfirmed Chapter 13 plan. The Ninth Circuit also approved the IRS' service of the notice of levy on the bankruptcy trustee rather than the debtor, because any third party who has possession of the debtor's property or has a duty to the debtor can properly be served.

An "insolvent" debtor is permitted by Code §108 to exclude discharged liabilities from income. The Code defines insolvency as having liabilities in excess of the fair market value of assets, but §108 does not contain a definition of "liabilities."

The Ninth Circuit allows[78] contingent liabilities to be used in the determination of insolvency, but only if the taxpayer can show by a preponderance of the evidence that it was more likely than not that the taxpayer would be required to satisfy the contingent liability.

The taxpayers in this case were general partners in a partnership. A bank forgave a $1.4 million nonrecourse note obligating the partnership. The taxpayers reported their distributive share of the discharge of indebtedness, but excluded it from income because they said that their potential liability as guarantors rendered them insolvent before the partnership realized the income. (The bank made no effort to collect on the guarantee.)

The Ninth Circuit affirmed the IRS and District Court position that an obligation isn't a liability unless it exists and is ripe before the indebtedness is discharged.

ENDNOTES

1. *In re Bluffton Casting Corp.,* 186 F.3d 857 (7th Cir. 1999).
2. *Official Committee of Unsecured Creditors v. Nucor Corp.,* 200 F.3d 154 (3rd Cir. 1999).
3. *In re SGL Carbon Corp.,* 200 F.3d 154 (3rd Cir. 1999); *Cedar Shore Resort Inc. v. Mueller,* 235 F.3d 375 (8th Cir. 2000).
4. *U.S. v. Bishop,* 2000-2 USTC ¶50,740 (W.D. Tex. 8/18/00).
5. *Barbieri v. RAJ Acquisition Corp.,* 199 F.3d 616 (2nd Cir. 1999).
6. *U.S. v. Yellin,* 251 B.R. 174 (1st Cir. 2000).
7. *Anderson v. Conine,* 203 F.3d 855 (5th Cir. 2/11/00).

8. *Findley v. Findley,* 26 Family Law Reporter 1247 (N.D. Ohio 3/2/00).

9. *In re Bentley,* 26 Family Law Reporter 1248 (D.Kan. 1/10/00).

10. *Osherow v. Ernst & Young LLP,* 200 F.3d 382 (5th Cir. 2000).

11. *U.S. Trustee v. Garvey, Schubert & Barer,* 195 F.3d 1053 (9th Cir. 11/18/99).

12. *Keach v. Boyajian,* 68 LW 1495 (1st Cir. 1/27/00).

13. *Triad Financial Corp. v. Weatherington,* 254 B.R. 895 (6th Cir. 2000).

14. *Calpine Corp v. O'Brien Environmental Energy Inc.,* 181 F.3d 527 (3rd Cir. 1999).

15. *U.S. v. Lee,* 68 LW 1453 (E.D. Pa. 1/20/00).

16. *Tamecki v. Frank,* 229 F.3d 205 (3rd Cir. 2000); *Neary v. Padilla,* 222 F.3d 1184 (9th Cir. 2000). Earlier Sixth and Eighth Circuit decisions permit the petition to proceed absent misconduct or egregious behavior on the part of the debtor.

17. *Bak v. Vincze,* 230 F.3d 297 (7th Cir. 2000).

18. *Harbaugh v. Sweet,* 27 Family Law Reporter 1138 (E.D. Mich. 1/23/01).

19. *Manchester v. Annis,* 69 LW 1245 (10th Cir. 10/19/00).

20. *Beaman v. Shearin* 224 F.3d 346 and *Beaman v. Vandeventer Black LLP,* 224 F.3d 353 (both 4th Cir. 8/17/00).

21. *Johnson, Blakely, Pope, Bokor, Ruppel & Burns PA v. Alvarez,* 224 F.3d 1273 (11th Cir. 2000).

22. *Kelly v. Jeter,* 27 Family Law Reporter 1148 (8th Cir. 2/1/01).

23. *Kitchen v. Boyd,* 233 F.3d 922 (6th Cir. 2000).

24. *Colwell v. Royal International Trading Co.,* 196 F.3d 1225 (11th Cir. 1999).

25. *Christo v. Yellin,* 192 F.3d 36 (1st Cir. 1999).

26. *In re Bell,* 225 F.3d 203 (2nd Cir. 2000).

27. *Tanner v. First Plus Financial,* 217 F.3d 1357 (11th Cir. 2000).

28. *Huisinga v. Kemmerer,* 69 LW 1127 (8th Cir. 7/26/00).

29. *Jacoway v. Wolfe,* 69 LW 1352 (9th Cir. 10/30/00).

30. *Northview Motors Inc. v. Chrysler Motors Corp.,* 68 LW 1032 (3rd Cir. 6/18/99).

31. *Folger Adam Security Inc. v. DeMatteis/MacGregor JV,* 68 LW 1580 (3d Cir. 3/20/00). Cases such as *In re Lawrence United Corp.,* 221 B.R. 661 (N.D.N.Y. 1998) say that a right of recoupment is a defense, not a claim in a bankruptcy case.

32. *Dodson v. Huff,* 207 F.3d 758 (5th Cir. 2000).

33. *Mosser v. Darrow,* 341 U.S. 267 (Sup.Ct. 1951).

34. *Terlecky v. Helmer*, 214 F.3d 773 (6th Cir. 2000).
35. *Foster v. Hill*, 188 F.3d 1259 (10th Cir. 1999).
36. *Staiano v. Cain*, 192 F.3d 109 (3rd Cir. 1999).
37. *Walton v. Jamko Inc.*, 69 LW 1486 (11th Cir. 2/5/01).
38. REG-105235-99, 65 FR 60,136 (10/10/00).
39. *U.S. v. Gold*, 178 F.3d 718 (4th Cir. 6/28/99).
40. *Gruntz v. Los Angeles County*, 202 F.3d 1074 (9th Cir. 2/3/00), over-ruling *Hucke v. Oregon*, 992 F.2d 950 (9th Cir. 1993).
41. *Berg v. Good Samaritan Hospital*, 230 F.3d 1165 (9th Cir. 2000).
42. *Aiello v. Providian Financial Corp.*, 69 LW 1485 (7th Cir. 2/6/01).
43. *Koenig Sporting Goods Inc. v. Morse Road Co.*, 203 F.3d 986 (6th Cir. 2000).
44. *In re Pearce*, 68 LW 1559 (S.D. Ill. 3/2/00).
45. *United Food & Commercial Workers Local 211 v. Family Snacks Inc.*, 69 LW 1469 (8th Cir. 1/31/01).
46. *Chrysler Financial Corp. v. Nolan*, 69 LW 1243 (6th Cir. 10/24/00).
47. *Barbosa v. Soloman*, 235 F.3d 31 (1st Cir. 2000).
48. *Official Committee of Unsecured Creditors of Cybergenics Corp. v. Chinery*, 69 LW 1165 (3rd Cir. 9/6/00).
49. *Arrow Electronics v. Justus*, 218 F.3d 1070 (9th Cir. 2000).
50. *MBNA America v. Locke*, 69 LW 1096 (9th Cir. 7/12/00).
51. *Universal Bank NA v. Grause*, 68 LW 1500 (8th Cir. 2/16/00).
52. *Pertuso v. Ford Motor Credit Co.*, 233 F.3d 417 (6th Cir. 2000); *Bessette v. Avco Financial Services Inc.*, 230 F.3d 439 (1st Cir. 2000).
53. *Bolin v. Sears, Roebuck & Co.*, 231 F.3d 970 (5th Cir. 2000).
54. *Fezler v. Davis*, 194 F.3d 570 (5th Cir. 1999).
55. *Andersen v. UNIPAC-NEBHELP*, 179 F.3d 1253 (10th Cir. 1999).
56. *Gillman v. Continental Airlines*, 203 F.3d 203 (3rd Cir. 2000).
57. *Sacramento County v. Foross*, 242 B.R. 692 (9th Cir. 1999).
58. *Leibowitz v. Orange County*, 217 F.3d 799 (9th Cir. 2000).
59. *Brown v. Grossman*, 27 Family Law Reporter 1238 (Bank. N.D. 3/7/01).
60. *French Kezelis & Kominiarek PC v. Carlson*, 68 LW 1575 (N.D. Ill. 2/17/00).
61. *Griffith v. U.S.*, 206 F. 3d 1389 (11th Cir. 2000).
62. *In re Haas*, 48 F.3d 1148 (11th Cir. 1994).
63. Compare *Young v. U.S.*, 233 F.3d 56 (1st Cir. 2000) with *Palmer v. U.S.*, 219 F.3d 580 (6th Cir. 2000).

64. *Deodati v. M.M. Winkler & Associates*, 239 F.3d 746 (5th Cir. 2001). Also see *Katz v. Comm'r*, 116 TC No. 2 (1/21/01): the allocation of a bankrupt partner's distributive share of the partnership is not a partnership item under IRC §6231(a)(3)—and therefore the allocation does not have to be resolved through a partnership-level proceeding of the type prescribed by IRC §§6221-6234.

65. Compare *In re Top Grade Sausage*, 227 F.3d 123 (3rd Cir. 2000) and *U.S. Trustee v. Gainey, Schubert & Barer*, 195 F.3d 1053 (9th Cir. 1999) with *Falligant, Horne, Covington & Nash PC v. Moore*, 197 F.3d 1354 (11th Cir. 1999) and *Andrews & Kurtz LLP v. Family Snacks Inc.*, 157 F.3d 414 (5th Cir. 1998).

66. *Sanchez v. Gordon*, 69 LW 1532 (9th Cir. 3/5/01).

67. *Peele v. Cunningham*, 218 F.3d 443 (5th Cir. 2000).

68. *In re Redding*, 251 B.R. 547 (W.D. Mo. 2000).

69. *Walton v. LaBarge*, 223 F.3d 859 (8th Cir. 2000).

70. *Brown v. Smith*, 222 F.3d 618 (9th Cir. 2000).

71. *Stanley v. McCormick, Barstow, Sheppard, Wayte & Carruth*, 215 F.3d 929 (9th Cir. 2000).

72. *Preblich v. Battley*, 181 F.3d 1048 (9th Cir. 1999).

73. *Dzikowski v. Boomer's Sports & Recreation Center Inc.*, 184 F.3d 1285 (11th Cir. 1999).

74. *United States v. Kearns*, 177 F.3d 706 (8th Cir. 1999).

75. *U.S. v. Neary*, 206 F.3d 465 (5th Cir. 2000).

76. *Gardenhire v. U.S.*, 209 F.3d 1145 (9th Cir. 2000).

77. *Beam v. CIR*, 192 F.3d 191 (9th Cir. 1999).

78. *Merkel v. CIR*, 192 F.3d 844 (9th Cir. 1999).

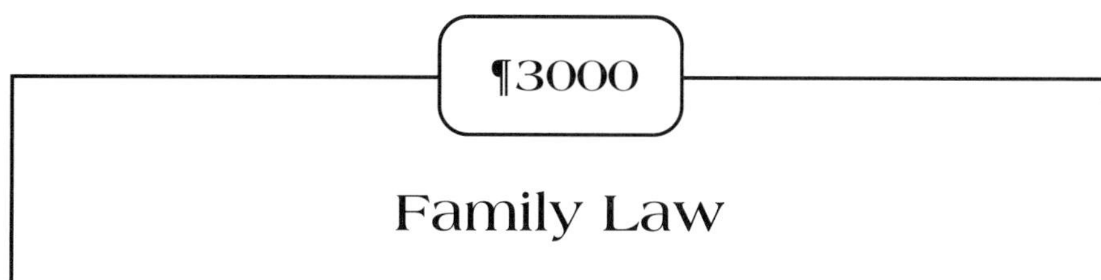

Family Law

[¶3005] Antenuptial Agreements

Pennsylvania is a no-fault state in the sense that, when an engagement is terminated, the fiancee is obligated to return the ring or pay its equivalent in cash, irrespective of which party decided to call off the engagement.[1] A contrary result would obligate courts to decide swearing contests between formerly loving couples.

Under Pennsylvania law, an engagement ring is a conditional gift, conditional on the marriage actually occurring, not just acceptance of a marriage proposal.

A District of Columbia case[2] holds that a spouse who executes a valid prenuptial agreement that waives pension rights on divorce cannot use ERISA to cancel the waiver. In other words, ERISA doesn't preempt state matrimonial laws allowing prenuptial agreements.

An earlier case on the same issue[3] says that ERISA imposes a consent requirement for the waiver of survivor benefits, but is silent on waiver of other types of pension benefits, so waivers by an ex-spouse are certainly permissible.

[¶3010] Marriage

A 1995 state statute, denying marriage licenses to same-sex couples, has been ruled valid[4] by a 1998 amendment to the state (Hawaii) constitution empowering the legislature to reserve marriage to male/female couples. The amendment removed the statute from the equal protection clause of the state constitution.

A 1996 decision noted in the main volume held that the 1995 statute was invalid because it created a sex-based classification, reviewable under a strict scrutiny Equal Protection test. However, in the view of the Hawaii Supreme Court, the constitutional amendment permits the statute to have full force and effect.

A state with a far less agreeable climate in terms of weather, Vermont, proved a more hospitable climate for same-sex marriage. A December, 1999 court decision[5] held that the state constitution requires extending the benefits and protections of marriage to same-sex couples. These benefits are so important that denying them can only be justified by public concerns of unquestionable weight, cogency, and authority. Although there is a traditional link between marriage and procreation, the court noted that heterosexual couples who cannot or choose not to have children are permitted to marry, and some same-sex couples have children, and that denying marital unions to same-sex couples does nothing to protect children or procreation.

However, the court did not accept the contention that the petitioners were entitled to marriage licenses, because the legislative assumption is that a marriage is a male–female relationship. But constitutionally, the "common benefits" clause is broader than the Equal Protection clause.

The court declined to order remedies right away. Instead, the state legislature was given time to decide if the necessary benefits and protections should be offered under the name of "marriage" or a form of registration of domestic partnerships.

Legislation was passed in 2000. H. 847 was signed by Governor Howard Dean on April 26, 2000.[6] Same-sex couples still cannot marry but can enter into "civil unions" that have the same benefits, consequences, and protections of marriage.

Therefore, a civil union partner will have the right to intestate succession of a married person; civil union couples can hold property by the entireties; a survivor can bring suit for wrongful death of his or her civil union partner; and a civil union partner has the status of a parent or stepparent with respect to children raised by the couple. A civil union partner is also considered a spouse for purposes of health care decision making.

Civil union licenses are issued by town clerks, based on proof that the parties are of the same sex and therefore cannot marry; that they are not closely related by blood; and that they are not already parties to another marriage or civil union. Certification of the civil union can be performed by a clergymember, judge, or justice of the peace. Most of the provisions of the law became effective July 1, 2000, but implementation was delayed until January 1, 2001 for provisions affecting insurance and taxes.

[¶3020] Divorce

A guardian has standing to proceed with a dissolution action filed by the ward before the adjudication of incapacity. Illinois joins[7] several other jurisdictions in holding that the guardian's right to do so can be implied, even though it is not explicit in the state statute. Although a guardian cannot initiate a divorce action for the ward, the guardian can maintain an ongoing action.

In the view of South Carolina (and a few other states), an attorney who represents him- or herself in a divorce case is not entitled to an award of counsel fees, because the pro se divorce litigant does not "incur" an obligation to pay fees.[8]

[¶3020.2] Property Distributions

A woman died before her divorce was granted. According to the trial court, her action for equitable distribution vested at the time of the separation and did not abate when she died (although the divorce action did abate). The trial court's theory was that equitable distribution actions can be heard independent of divorce actions, and thus the administratrix of the estate should have been substituted as plaintiff in the equitable distribution action. However, the following year, the trial court's decision was reversed, in that only a living person can be divorced, and the equitable distribution action is inextricably connected to the divorce case.[9]

The federal government interest in forfeiture of tainted property is superior to an innocent divorcing spouse's interest in the same property, as awarded by the state court's divorce decree. The issue, in the Eleventh Circuit view, is whether the government had a valid interest at the time execution was sought, not at the point in time at which the state court rendered its property division decision.[10]

The Southern District of Illinois denied priority under Bankruptcy Code §507(a)(7) to a debtor's obligation, stemming from a divorce judgment, to pay third-party debts.[11] The rationale was that Congress only wanted to protect support obligations actually owed to family members, not property division obligations.

[¶3020.3] Separate vs. Community or Marital Property

A tax loss carry-forward occurring during the marriage is divisible marital property, because the nature of a marital asset is a thing of value arising out of the marital relationship.[12]

A family home in Louisiana was community property. It was awarded to the wife by partition incident to divorce, before the husband filed for bankruptcy. Therefore, it never became part of his Chapter 7 bankruptcy estate.[13]

A wife relinquished her interest in the marital residence. In return, the husband agreed to hold her harmless on two marital debts aggregating $14,000. The Northern District of Ohio held that the obligation was not a "maintenance or support obligation" that would be denied bankruptcy discharge. However, based on the facts of the case (that paying the debts would have a more serious negative impact on the wife's standard of living than on the husband's), discharge was denied in the husband's Chapter 7 bankruptcy case.[14]

In another Chapter 7 case[15] the debtor held a $25,000 judgment lien on the house that used to be her marital home. This lien was deemed exempt in her Chapter 7 case. It would be treated as alimony to the extent it was reasonably necessary for her support. The divorce decree, which is controlling as to the characterization of the lien, treated it as an alimony lien.

[¶3020.3.1] Status of Special Items

The buy–sell agreement between a doctor and his professional association did not control the value of his professional practice for divorce purposes; it was merely one factor to be considered.[16]

Nonvested stock options granted by an employer are marital property. (Nonvested retirement benefits have already been held to be marital property.) In this case,[17] the options were earned during marriage and were granted as compensation and an incentive for continued employment.

In Louisiana, the economic benefit of a copyrighted work is community property and can be divided in a divorce proceeding. The Copyright Act does not preempt the state law in this context, because preemption occurs only with respect to state laws that purport to regulate intellectual property.[18]

[¶3020.4] Pensions and Divorce

Early in 2001, the Supreme Court decided a case on ERISA and retirement benefits. The court ruled that ERISA preempts a Washington State statute automatically revoking beneficiary designations (for life insurance as well as employee benefits) upon the divorce of the employee spouse and the named beneficiary. The analysis behind the decision is that this is a core ERISA area, so state law regulation is preempted.[19]

The New Jersey Court of Appeals ruled that it is improper for a divorce court to order a retirement plan to begin immediate payments to a wife at a time when the employee husband had vested benefits but no plans to retire. The couple's house and the husband's retirement benefits were the only substantial assets available for distribution, and the wife had limited earning capacity—but the Court of Appeals held that since active employees are not entitled to access their pensions before retirement, neither are ex-spouses.[20]

The Wisconsin Court of Appeals permitted a reduction in the husband's maintenance obligation when he retired, equal to the part of the pension that the wife received pursuant to a QDRO. There was no unfair "double counting" because the QDRO was used instead of assigning the pension a value that would be offset by other assets. (If, on the other hand, the present value of the pension is included in the marital estate, the pension benefits themselves are not considered income when maintenance is ordered.) In this reading, early retirement does not eliminate the maintenance obligation, but it is a change of circumstances.[21]

Given the inevitability of some degree of tax liability, the Minnesota rule is that the tax consequences of property division can appropriately be considered, and retirement benefits can be valued on an after-tax basis.[22]

An award of half of the husband's pension benefit to his wife, effective when he becomes eligible to retire, is an award of future benefits that is not dischargeable in bankruptcy.[23]

A husband cashed out his IRA balance and endorsed the check for the proceeds to his wife, based on an agreement to transfer his entire interest in the IRA to his wife incident to their divorce. She did not place the funds in an IRA account. The Tax Court treated the entire $68,000 balance as not only taxable income to the husband in the year of the withdrawal, but also imposed the 10% penalty on premature withdrawals. Although IRC §408(d)(6) makes a "transfer of an interest" in an IRA tax-free if it is pursuant to a divorce or separation agreement, the Tax Court ruled in 2000 that there are only two acceptable methods of transferring the interest: putting the ex-spouse's name on an existing IRA account, or directing the trustee of the payor's IRA to place the funds in the payee's own IRA. Direct payment of cash from one spouse to the other is not an acceptable tax-free transfer.[24]

The wife was not entitled to 50% of the marital portion of the early retirement subsidy the husband could receive by retiring at 55, even though the separation agreement incorporated into the divorce decree divided the "pension" equally. At the time of the divorce, the early retirement benefit was not included in the valuation of his pension interest (because he was not then eligible for the subsidy); the wife knew about the early retirement option, but did not move for a share of it.[25]

However, a Pennsylvania case from the Spring of 2000 places early retirement incentive benefits paid to the husband post-divorce in the marital estate. Because he did not do any additional work to earn the incentive benefits, they were counted as an adjustment to pension rights earned during the marriage.[26]

Pension benefits earned by the husband during his first marriage are not marital property with respect to the dissolution of his second marriage—even though this case had the unusual fact pattern that both marriages and both divorces involved the same woman! In the analysis of the Pennsylvania Superior Court[27] the pension rights were acquired prior to the current marriage and therefore are separate property.

A woman awarded half of the pension earned during marriage is not entitled to "surviving spouse" benefits after the death of the husband (who had remarried). This Arizona case[28] holds that her community interest was extinguished, even though the husband and his second wife executed a purported irrevocable assignment of all retirement benefits, including death benefits, to the first wife. In this reading, only the person married to the employee at the time of his or her death can be considered a surviving spouse.

[¶3020.6] Alimony and Spousal Support

If the parties' circumstances change—for instance, if the recipient becomes wealthier than the obligor—the court can extinguish the permanent alimony obligation, even if the obligor is still alive and the recipient has not remarried. The relevant statute doesn't say that alimony can't be terminated; the word "permanent" is just used to distinguish it from other forms of alimony, and does not necessarily mean that the payments will have to continue until the recipient's death.[29]

Since 1999, New Jersey has provided for "limited duration alimony" in circumstances where one divorcing spouse is in financial need, yet the marriage was so short that granting permanent alimony would be inequitable. This form of alimony must be distinguished from rehabilitative alimony (used to place a divorcing spouse in a position to become self-supporting) and from reimbursement alimony (making a spouse whole from financial sacrifices on behalf of the other spouse). Limited duration alimony is inappropriate in a marriage that lasted for many years.[30]

Where the parties' income is greater than the maximum amount in the tables, state support guidelines do not determine the amount of spousal support to be ordered. Instead, the case should be treated like a high-income child support case: i.e., the obligor's ability to pay should be balanced against the recipient's needs.[31]

A late-2000 Nevada case refuses to treat marital fault (in this case, the wife's affair and leaving her husband to cohabitate with her lover) as a factor in setting alimony, under the state's no-fault divorce law.[32]

In Louisiana, a post-nuptial agreement by one spouse to provide permanent alimony to the other on separation or divorce is not enforceable.[33] Such an agreement violates public policy because it fails to take need, fault, or ability to pay into account. Although Louisiana allows changes in property regime by either ante- or post-nuptial agreement, periodic spousal support is not a property regime and therefore is not amenable to alteration by post-nuptial agreement.

A North Dakota case[34] requires an ex-husband to continue alimony payments despite his ex-wife's cohabitation in Canada, since the ex-wife and her cohabitant were financially independent (i.e., the cohabitant did not provide support to replace the alimony payments), and he failed to prove that their relationship was tantamount to common-law marriage under Canadian law. (North Dakota does not recognize in-state common-law marriages, but would recognize those valid in a foreign jurisdiction.)

A divorce decree requiring the husband to provide the wife with health insurance equivalent to the coverage during marriage required the husband to provide at least the level of his employment-related coverage. He did provide an inferior conversion policy, but that made him a self-insurer, liable for her medical expenses, to the extent of the shortfall.[35]

According to the Missouri Court of Appeals, it was not an abuse of discretion to order a husband to pay the wife's legal fees (including those of the appeal rendering this decision) because of her limited assets and earning abilities—and his conduct during the marriage, including spousal abuse. In contrast, however, North Dakota treated general fault in marriage as an inadequate reason to order the husband to pay the wife's legal fees. (In this case, it was the wife who was the higher earner.) In this analysis, income and litigation conduct (rather than marital conduct) are the most relevant factors.[36]

[¶3020.7] Tax Issues in Divorce

IRSRRA '98, the Internal Revenue Service Restructuring and Reform Act of 1998, P.L. 105-205, added Code §6015, affording relief to innocent spouses who would otherwise face tax penalties because of tax wrongdoing by the other spouse. Rev.Proc. 2000-15, 2000-5 IRB 447 (1/31/00) explains how divorced and separated spouses can obtain equitable relief as "requesting spouses."

Form 8857, Request for Innocent Spouse Relief (and Separation of Liability, and Equitable Relief), must be filed no later than two years after the IRS' first collection activity taken against the requesting spouse.

The Treasury proposed Regulations on innocent spouse relief at 66 FR 3888 (1/17/01). The proposals define an "erroneous item" that gives rise to potential liability as any item that causes the liability to be reduced because of improper reporting. A spouse who knows that an item exists cannot qualify as an innocent spouse—even if he or she does not know its proper tax characterization.

The facts and circumstances considered as to whether the spouse has actual knowledge of the item include whether the would-be innocent spouse owned an interest in the property creating the item; if the other spouse transferred assets to the spouse asserting innocence; and whether the spouse asserting innocence avoided learning the true state of facts.

A person requesting innocent spouse relief can request that the IRS withhold certain identifying information from the notice to the other spouse (e.g., if the claimant fears spousal abuse). The IRS will not treat a return signed under duress as a true joint return, and therefore such a return will not give rise to joint and survivor liability.

The Tax Court decided several innocent spouse cases in 2000. Under these decisions, the Tax Court has jurisdiction to review a request for innocent spouse relief under IRC §6015(f) [discretionary relief that is not available under §6015(b) or (c)] based on a timely petition,[37] and a non-electing spouse has the right to litigate the Commissioner's decision to grant innocent spouse relief to the electing spouse because of the impact this determination has on the non-electing spouse's tax liability.[38]

A wife is not an innocent spouse if she signed a joint return that omitted part of the husband's retirement distributions: she was aware of the existence of the item, even though she relied on her husband's representations that the funds were not taxable income.[39]

Under an early 2001 Tax Court Memo decision, a divorced taxpayer was not liable for the tax on his charge of the capital gain on a former marital home that was allocated to him under the divorce decree, because the property was titled in the wife's name. Therefore, he was not liable for penalties for substantial understatement of tax related to those capital gains.[40]

[¶3030.1] Custody

The Eighth Circuit has recognized a constitutional tort theory under which social workers are liable in a 42 USC §1983 action if they make custody decisions that knowingly put a child in harm's way.[41] Both sides relied (incorrectly, in the Eighth Circuit's view) on *DeShaney v. Winnebago County DSS*,[42] which holds that the Fourteenth Amendment does not impose a requirement that state actors protect private parties from harm caused by other private parties.

In this case, the child was in permanent DSS custody based on evidence of abuse. The social workers let the child's father visit her, accompanied by a friend that the social workers knew was a convicted pedophile. Later, the child was returned to the father's custody, where she was raped by the father's friend. The child ended up in a mental institution, and suit was brought by her Guardian ad Litem.

The Eighth Circuit found that imposition of liability was proper because of the affirmative nature of the social workers' conduct. Although children do not have an enforceable legal right to be protected against parental abuse by the state, the state cannot knowingly place children at risk by delivering them to abusive caregivers.

In this case, unlike *DeShaney*, the issue is not the state's having returned custody to the father. Instead, claims are based on the state's failure to protect the child after custody was relinquished by the state. In other words, the question is not whether the state has to keep citizens from harming other citizens, but whether the state can be absolved for harm that it has caused itself.

In a custody case, the Guardian ad Litem is appointed primarily to serve the best interests of the child. An attorney/GAL also acts as a neutral factfinder for the judge. Where there is no conflict, an attorney/GAL also acts as the lawyer representing the child's own wishes. However, an attorney who perceives a conflict should notify the court to consider appointing an additional attorney specifically to advance the child's viewpoint. However, it is inappropriate for an attorney/GAL also to testify as a fact witness in the case.[43]

The Eighth Circuit required the plaintiff to prove that the social workers acted with deliberate indifference, in a way that shocks the conscience, and that state conduct was the proximate cause of the injuries.

Half-siblings can be separated even without a showing of actual harm if the children were kept together. In this case, a father was awarded custody of a five-year-old boy whose half-brother remained with the mother, based on the father's more stable living situation and greater ability to provide for the child.[44]

Similar "best interests" issues were raised in a Pennsylvania case in which, after the death of a child's mother, primary custody was awarded[45] to the stepfather who raised the child, not the out-of-state father who had little contact with the child. In other words, it is legitimate for a court to award custody to a non-parent if this is what the best interests of the child require, even if the biological parent has not been found unfit.

According to the Minnesota Court of Appeals, a parent is not barred from receiving custody because he or she has alienated the child from the other parent; interference with the parental relationship is only one factor in the determination.[46]

A female couple conceived a child with sperm donated by a man who was also a partner in a same-sex relationship. When the women's relationship ended, the Minnesota Court of Appeals granted them joint legal custody. The biological mother's grant of physical custody was conditioned on her moving back to Minnesota where the former partner and the sperm donor live. (Before the trial, both women agreed to joint legal custody.[47])

A parent with joint custody can be prosecuted for conspiracy and custodial interference for kidnapping a child from the other parent who has joint custody, as long as the knowledge and intent elements of the custodial interference statute are proved beyond a reasonable doubt.[48]

[¶3030.2] Child Support

The controversy over the Child Support Recovery Act (CSRA) continued in full force in 2000 and 2001. Although eight Circuits have upheld the statute over a commerce clause challenge, the Sixth Circuit decided in September, 2000 that the statute is invalid because Congress exceeded its powers by passing it.

In February, 2001, although it is in the Second Circuit (which upheld the statute), the Southern District of New York ruled that the validity of the CSRA must be re-assessed in light of *U.S. v. Morrison*, 529 U.S. 598 (Sup.Ct. 2000), the case that struck down the Violence Against Women Act, and its analysis of Congressional power and its limitations.[49]

There is no private right of action under the CSRA by a custodial parent against a noncustodial parent who moved out of state and failed to comply with the support order.[50]

The rebuttable presumption of 18 USC §228(b), that the existence of a support obligation is equivalent to the obligor's ability to pay, has been struck down by the District Court for the District of Rhode Island,[51] on Due Process grounds. In this analysis, the statute denies the jury the presumption of innocence that should apply, and the burden of persuasion should remain with the government even if it is proper for the defendant to have the burden of production.

Unlike some other states, North Carolina does not absolutely bar[52] a retroactive increase in child support that has already been ordered. However, a retroactive increase will be ordered only if there has been an extraordinary emergency affecting the child's well-being that subjects the custodial parent to expenditures in excess of the existing support obligation.

The automatic stay in bankruptcy does not apply to state criminal proceedings for nonsupport that relate to arrears of child support.[53]

A woman who quit a full-time job so she could work part-time and take care of the children of her current marriage was considered[54] voluntarily unemployed with respect to her support obligation toward the children of her first marriage. However, the court held that after the presumptive support obligation was set, taking voluntary unemployment into account, an adjustment could be made based on the support needs of the children of the second marriage.

Where both parents were fairly affluent, it was permissible to order the out-of-state father to pay half the expenses of the child's state college (not, as the father suggested, limited to an amount equal to half the in-state tuition at the state university), even though the child had funds of her own (from scholarships and UGMA funds from grandparents). The parents' lifestyle also made it reasonable to expect them to pay the child's car insurance and sorority fees while she was at college.[55]

The Oregon Court of Appeals upheld a state statute permitting a divorce court to order either parent, or both parents, to support a child who is college. The court did not find the equal protection argument (that married parents who live together do not have this obligation) unpersuasive, because of the state's interest in a well-educated population, and because divorced people have not experienced a legacy of prejudice that would make them a suspect class. Furthermore, child support is not ordered in intact families, so there is no precedent to draw on.[56]

Although some states use the "income shares model" (i.e., the child's access to each parent's income should not be changed by divorce),

Kentucky refused to apply the child support guidelines in a case where one parent had income far in excess of the guidelines (here, $57,000 a month, whereas the guideline tables only went up to $15,000 a month).[57]

With respect to a father's obligation to support his children, a cohabitant's contribution to the mother's expenses should not be treated as imputed income that reduces the father's obligation. In this case,[58] the cohabitant paid a share of the rent, but he made payments directly to the landlord, not to the children's mother.

Despite an agreement that the mother of a nonmarital child would not seek support from the father, the Pennsylvania Superior Court permitted maintenance of a child support action.[59] The child's right to parental support cannot be given away, even if the discussion about support occurred before conception, and even if the father of the child said that he would not have continued the relationship with the child's mother if he had thought that financial liability was a possibility.

Pennsylvania adopted the majority rule and allowed a state court to award the dependency exemption (for income tax purposes) to the noncustodial parent, where appropriate. The Internal Revenue Code presumes that the custodial parent will claim the exemption, but does not absolutely require this.[60]

An Illinois couple divorced, subsequently re-married one another, and eventually divorced again. The state's Court of Appeals ruled that arrears of child support do not continue to accrue during the second marriage, in that divorce-related obligations cannot be enforced during a marriage. The case also stands for the proposition that a custodial parent does not have the right to force an unwilling non-custodial parent to exercise visitation rights.[61]

New Hampshire allowed the use of part of the father's salary to value his family-owned closely held corporation, and it also allowed the use of his entire salary in the child support calculation, in that part of his salary was excessive and thus dividend-equivalent. The court did not consider this to be inequitable double-counting. However, even though the father had no plans to sell his stock in the family business, the valuation should have reflected discounts for his minority interest and the lack of marketability.[62]

An early 2001 Indiana case holds that inheritances received by a parent can be considered in setting child support. The court has discretion to determine if the inheritance justifies departure from the guidelines, and whether it should be considered an element of income or a changed financial circumstance.[63]

But California took a different approach to another case involving the financial consequences of a death, ruling that a lump sum payment of life insurance proceeds does not constitute "income" that can be taken into account in determining child support; the court treated it as similar to a gift. However, income derived from investing the proceeds would be income that should be included in the calculation.[64]

Once the obligee, the children, and the obligor have all moved out of a state, the state's courts no longer have jurisdiction to modify an in-state child support order, although the issuing court can continue to enforce the order. Any party seeking a change must file in the appropriate state which, according to UIFSA, is the state in which the obligee resides.[65]

Post-petition interest on child support obligations that are nondischargeable is also nondischargeable. The Ninth Circuit ruled[66] based on an analogy with the bankruptcy treatment of post-petition interest on nondischargeable student loan debt which has been judged so both because it remains a personal liability of the debtor, and because interest is integral to a continuing debt.

Bankruptcy issues continued to be prominent in family law in 2000 (and will probably take an even more dominant role in 2001 and 2002 unless the economy recovers). The Ninth Circuit joined the majority of the Circuits, ruling that under Bankruptcy Code §523(a)(15), only a current or former spouse or child of the bankruptcy debtor is entitled to a determination that the debt for unpaid legal fees cannot be discharged in bankruptcy. Therefore, the attorney to whom the fees are owed cannot get such a determination.[67]

A non-custodial parent's debt to the county for welfare benefits received by the children is not dischargeable, even as to debt accumulated before the date of the support order. The Ninth Circuit was not persuaded by earlier cases to the contrary, in light of interim changes in both Bankruptcy and social services law. The Ninth Circuit analysis is that the debt is in the nature of support even though it is not owed directly to the debtor's wife and children, only owed on their behalf.[68]

The Eighth Circuit found that dischargeability under §523(a)(5) depends on the nature of the debt, not the nature of the payee. Therefore, a court order to pay support and certain expenses for an out-of-wedlock child is not dischargeable, even though the child's mother was not a spouse or ex-spouse, and even though the mother rather than the child was the payee.[69]

Alimony payments received after a Chapter 7 filing are not property of the bankruptcy estate, even though Bankruptcy Code §541(a)(5)(B) incorporates property from a settlement agreement or divorce decree into the estate.[70]

The Eastern District of Michigan tackled a controversial issue: what amounts qualify as "alimony" that can be excluded from the bankruptcy estate under Bankruptcy Code §522(d)(10)(D). The Michigan answer is that the federal-law definition of "alimony" is the primary determinant; other factors include whether the payment was supposed to provide support to an ex-spouse, and whether the amount was reasonable for this purpose (excessive amounts would more likely be treated as a property division). In this case, the wife was supposed to receive $48,500 described as "alimony or spousal support," nearly all of it in weekly installments over a period of seven and a half years.

When the wife filed for Chapter 7 bankruptcy protection, the husband owed $42,000 of the payment. The wife sought to exclude this amount from the bankruptcy estate, whereas the trustee argued for its inclusion. The Eastern District Court required a federal rather than state-law definition of bankruptcy to be applied (in the interests of nationwide uniformity)—i.e., sums intended to provide sustenance for a spouse. Therefore, sums do not enter the bankruptcy estate if they are intended as support by the parties and/or the state court and if the bankruptcy court considers the payments reasonably necessary for support purposes.[71]

An alleged child support debtor, who claimed that he was being harassed by the Texas Attorney General's office over child support amounts he did not even owe, was permitted to bring a Fair Credit Reporting Act Claim against the agency.

Although the FCRA is usually invoked against credit reporting agencies, there is no statutory bar on citing other parties. Here, the plaintiff charged the defendants with making inaccurate reports about him to credit reporting agencies, which the court held to be conduct contemplated by the statute. Because the plaintiff sought only prospective injunctive relief, there was no Eleventh Amendment problem.

[¶3030.3] Visitation

In mid-2000, the Supreme Court made one of its rare forays into family law, affirming the Washington State court that struck down Rev. Code §26.10.160(3), a statute permitting state courts to grant visitation to any party, to the extent that is in the best interests of the child.[72] The Supreme

Court agreed with the state court that the statute is unconstitutional because of its overbreadth (any person can petition for visitation) and its interference with the parental right to control association with their children (which is a Due Process right).

Recent cases in New Jersey and Maryland[73] stand for the proposition that after termination of a lesbian relationship, a partner who acted as "psychological parent" has standing to seek visitation with the children of the ex-partner. Under the facts of the Maryland case, however, visitation was denied as contrary to the best interests of the child, because it caused behavior problems.

[¶3035] Issues of Jurisdiction, Forum, and Choice of Law

The Hague Convention requires federal courts to make every effort to find alternatives to returning a wrongfully abducted child to a home where the child is at risk of harm.

The mother admitted that she wrongfully removed the children from France and forged the father's signature to get passports for them, but she claimed this was done to protect at-risk children.

When the father petitioned the United States court system for return of the children, the District Court cited grave risk of harm to them, despite the violation of Hague Convention. The Second Circuit ruled[74] that the District Court's conclusion was supported by adequate factual evidence.

Hague Convention Article 13(b) justifies withholding return based on clear and convincing evidence of grave risk of physical or psychological harm or an otherwise intolerable situation for the child. However, the Convention also requires the court to at least consider ways to return the children to their home country without subjecting them to danger, based on an assumption that the home-country courts will be able to issue any necessary protective orders.

The Second Circuit instructed the District Court to contact the French government to evolve a method for returning the children to a safe setting in France; the father's petition could be denied if there would be no effective way for the District Court to carry this out.

A court that assumes jurisdiction over a registered foreign child support order still has to apply its own law when modification of the order is sought. In this case[75] the child never lived in Alaska, the home state of the obligor parent. However, UIFSA requires application of the law of the forum state. Official Comment to UIFSA §611 says that the substantive law of the state that has jurisdiction to modify is controlling.

[¶3040] Other Family Law Issues

After a man died intestate, his long-term same-sex partner was not permitted[76] to use the state's procedure for dividing community property after the death of a participant in a "meretricious relationship." The court limited this category to quasi-marital male/female relationships, involving parties who chose not to get married. Marriage was not an option for the male couple, so their relationship did not give rise to a property division.

The causes of action of alienation of affection and criminal conversation have been abolished in Maryland, thus precluding a husband from suing his wife for fraud and intentional infliction of mental distress by committing adultery and passing off another man's children as his.[77]

Like most states, Maryland does not have a wrongful life cause of action (brought by a child asserting that he or she should never have been born) because it is too difficult to calculate damages for the difference between a normal and an impaired life. (Wrongful life cases can be maintained in California, New Jersey, and Washington.) However, the majority rule (also followed in Maryland) is that a wrongful birth cause of action, for the additional costs of raising a disabled child, can be maintained.[78]

In September, 2000, Ohio refused to allow disabled children to recover either wrongful life or wrongful pregnancy damages against their parents' allegedly negligent physicians. The wrongful life cause of action was denied in the case of a child born with spina bifida, because the doctor neither caused the condition nor was able to correct it.

The wrongful pregnancy suit (subsequent to an unsuccessful sterilization) could not be maintained, because the heart defect resulting in the child's death was not reasonably foreseeable as of the time of the sterilization and, therefore, negligence in performing the sterilization was not the proximate cause of the infant's death.[79]

P.L. 106-395, The Child Citizenship Act of 2000, amends Immigration and Naturalization Act §320 to increase the number of children who qualify for automatic U.S. citizenship or certificates of naturalization based on their relationship to at least one parent who is a native or naturalized U.S. citizen.

Indiana wiretap law covers the unpermitted recording of one estranged spouse's telephone conversations by the other spouse.[80]

[¶3050] Establishment of Paternity

A son was born to a cohabiting couple. Later they married and eventually divorced. At the time of the divorce, the wife said that the husband was not the father of the child. The husband filed a paternity action. The trial court ordered DNA tests without first holding a hearing on the child's best interests in the matter. The tests showed that the husband was not the father of the child. However, according to the Kansas Court of Appeals,[81] DNA tests should not be ordered without consideration of whether the paternity determination is in the best interests of the child.

In cases such as this one, where the child of the marriage is no longer a minor at the time the paternity question arises, the child must also be named as a party to the action and given the right to counsel (appointed counsel if he or she cannot afford to hire counsel). Appointment of a Guardian ad Litem for a child who is a minor at the time of the paternity case (the more common situation) was also held appropriate.

[¶3060] Adoption

Late in 2000, the United States implemented the Hague Convention on Protection of Children and Co-Operation in Respect of Intercountry Adoption: see P.L. 106-279, the Intercountry Adoption Act of 2000 (October 6, 2000). The law is designed to control inappropriate adoption practices, such as adoption of children in the United States who have been wrongfully taken from families in other countries; excessive fees to international adoption "facilitators," and failure to disclose the medical and psychological condition of adopted children which would prepare adoptive parents to care for them properly.

In late 1999 and early 2000, perhaps the prime issue in adoption law was the extent to which adoptees could obtain access to adoption records.

A September, 1999 Tennessee case[82] upholds a state law that allows disclosure of sealed records once they reach age 21. The holding was that the law does not impair vested rights of surrendering birth parents who thought that the records would remain sealed, because the statute includes a "contact veto" provision that bars contact by the adoptee, so the only risk to surrendering birth parents is that someone who is forbidden to approach them will learn their identity.

A similar voter initiative from Oregon (1998's Measure 58) that opens birth records to adoptees who have reached adulthood has similarly been upheld.[83] The court found that the potential for such access does not violate birth mothers' privacy rights or the contracts clauses of either state or federal Constitution.

There has never been a recognized state-law contractual right to total anonymity for birth mothers. Disclosing the information doesn't violate the constitutionally protected right to bear children. The group of surrendering birth mothers claimed that when they surrendered children for adoption, doctors and social workers (acting as state agents) explicitly promised them continued anonymity.

Under this analysis, neither the federal nor the state Constitution confers an absolute right to concealment of the birth mother's identity; adoption did not even exist at common law. Nor is surrendering children for adoption a fundamental right, so there is no corresponding fundamental right to have the adoption handled in a manner that completely prevents disclosure of the birth parents' identity.

Adoption records can be unsealed only if the adoptee (who wants medical background information for health treatment) shows the need by clear and convincing evidence of a cause sufficient to justify release of the records, balancing the needs of the adoptee against those of biological and adoptive parents and the integrity of the adoption process.[84]

A same-sex life partner is not a "spouse" under state law—and therefore cannot be a stepparent who is entitled to adopt the other life partner's biological child without the birth parent surrendering parental rights.[85]

P.L. 106-324, the Strengthening Abuse and Neglect Courts Act of 2000, implements a provision of the Adoption and Safe Families Act of 1997 that requires states to move to terminate parental rights with respect to children who have been in foster care for 15 of the previous 22 months. (The intention is to expedite adoption of the children.) In order to reduce court backlog, the 2000 legislation calls for a computerized case tracking system; more family court judges; longer court hours; better training for judges; and volunteer CASA (court appointed special advocate) programs.

[¶3060.2] [NEW] Foster Parents

New York law does not give foster parents a protectable liberty interest with respect to removal, return, or visitation with children whom they have fostered. Therefore, administrative discretion as to removal or visitation is not subject to due process liberty interest analysis.[86]

[¶3070] Reproductive Technology

A married couple who went to an in vitro fertilization clinic signed a series of consent forms specifying that, if they separated, the wife would be entitled to receive and implant the frozen pre-embryos stored at the clinic. Massachusetts' highest court refused to enforce the agreement[87] to the extent that it could make one now-divorced spouse become a parent involuntarily.

Only three states have laws about the enforceability of "custody agreements" for pre-embryos (fertilized eggs). Appellate courts in Tennessee and New York have concluded that pre-embryos should usually be disposed of in accordance with agreements between egg and sperm donors.

In this case, the Massachusetts court said that the contract was intended to govern the relationship between the couple and the clinic, not to adjust rights between the spouses. The court also said that the contract includes the phrase "should we become separated" but fails to define it.

A Maryland Attorney General's opinion[88] denied enforcement to a provision in a surrogacy contract calling for payment of a fee to the birth mother. However, payment of a fee will not prevent approval of the adoption contemplated by the contract.

A woman who was erroneously implanted with another couple's embryo, and who gave birth to one of her own babies and one of the other couple's babies, was held not to have visitation rights after the other baby was ordered returned to his genetic parents. The New York Appellate Division treated the case as analogous to babies mixed up by a hospital.[89]

ENDNOTES

1. *Lindh v. Surman,* 742 A.2d 643 (Pa. 11/23/99).
2. *Critchell v. Critchell,* 746 A.2d 282 (D.C. 2000).
3. *Rahn v. Rahn,* 914 P.2d 463 (Colo.App. 1995).
4. *Baehr v. Miike,* 68 LW 1368 (Hawaii 12/9/99).
5. *Baker v. State,* 744 A.2d 864 (Vermont 12/20/99).
6. See 68 LW 1316 (5/2/00); Carey Goldberg, "Forced Into Action on Gay Marriage, Vermont Finds Itself Deeply Split," *New York Times* 2/3/00 p. A16.
7. *In re Burgess,* 26 Family Law Reporter 1211 (Illinois 2/17/00).
8. *Calhoun v. Calhoun,* 26 Family Law Reporter 1262 (S.C. 3/6/00).

9. *Brown v. Brown,* 26 Family Law Reporter 1151 (N.C.App. 1/18/00), reversed *Brown v. Brown,* 27 FLR 1126 (N.C. 12/21/00).
10. *U.S. v. Kennedy,* 201 F.3d 1324 (11th Cir. 2000).
11. *In re Pearce,* 68 LW 1559 (S.D. Ill. 3/2/00).
12. *Finkelstein v. Finkelstein,* 701 N.Y.S.2d 52 (Appellate Division 1/13/00).
13. *Anderson v. Conine,* 203 F.3d 855 (5th Cir. 2/11/00).
14. *Findley v. Findley,* 26 Family Law Reporter 1247 (N.D. Ohio 3/2/00).
15. *In re Bentley,* 26 Family Law Reporter 1248 (D.Kan. 1/10/00).
16. *Harmon v. Harmon,* 26 Family Law Reporter 1243 (Tenn.App. 3/2/00).
17. *Keff v. Keff,* 26 Family Law Reporter 1133 (Ala.Civ.App. 1/7/00).
18. *Rodrigue v. Rodrigue,* 218 F.3d 432 (5th Cir. 2000).
19. *Egelhoff v. Egelhoff,* #99-1529, 69 LW 4206 (Sup.Ct. 3/21/01).
20. *La Sala v. La Sala,* 760 A.2d 1122 (N.J. App. 2000).
21. *Wettstaedt v. Wettstaedt,* 27 FLR 1219 (Wis.App. 3/8/01).
22. *Maurer v. Maurer,* 27 FLR 1233 (Minn. 3/22/01).
23. *Brown v. Grossman,* 27 FLR 1238 (Bank. N.D. 3/7/01).
24. *Jones v. Comm'r,* TC Memo 2000-219 (7/20/00), relying on *Bunney v. Comm'r,* 114 TC 259 (2000)'s explanation of acceptable transfer methodologies.
25. *Greenwood v. Greenwood,* 746 A.2d 358 (Maine 2/28/00).
26. *Meyer v. Meyer,* 26 Family Law Reporter 1303 (Pa. 4/17/00).
27. *Smith v. Smith,* 26 Family Law Reporter 1260 (Pa.Super. 3/17/00).
28. *Parada v. Parada,* 26 Family Law Reporter 1309 (Ariz. 4/19/00).
29. *De Grazia v. De Grazia,* 26 Family Law Reporter 1132 (D.C. 12/16/99).
30. *Cox v. Cox,* 27 FLR 1089 (N.J. Super. 12/12/00).
31. *Mascaro v. Mascaro,* 27 FLR 1088 (Pa.Super. 12/13/00).
32. *Rodriguez v. Rodriguez,* 13 P.3d 415 (Nev. 2000).
33. *Williams v. Williams,* 26 Family Law Reporter 1308 (La.App. 4/11/00).
34. *Pearson v. Pearson,* 606 N.W.2d 128 (N.D. 2/22/00).
35. *Blair v. Blair,* 26 Family Law Reporter 1226 (Georgia 2/21/00).
36. Compare *Brady v. Brady,* 27 FLR 1237 (Mo.App.3/29/01) with *Reiser v. Reiser,* 27 FLR 1153 (N.D. 1/31/01).
37. *Fernandez v. Comm'r,* 114 TC No. 21 (5/10/00), acq.; *Charlton v. Comm'r,* 114 TC No. 22 (5/16/00).
38. *Corson v. Comm'r,* 114 TC No. 24 (5/18/00).

39. *Cheshire v. Comm'r*, 115 TC No. 15 (12/21/00).
40. *Suhr v. Comm'r*, TC Memo 2001-28 (2/8/01).
41. *D.S.S. v. McMullen* 68 LW 1071 (8th Cir. 7/21/99).
42. 489 U.S. 189 (Sup.Ct. 1989).
43. *Meekins v. Corbett*, 26 Family Law Reporter 1231 (D.C. Super. 2/17/00).
44. *Viamonte v. Viamonte*, 748 A.2d 493 (Md.Spec.App. 2000).
45. *Charles v. Stehlik*, 744 A.2d 1255 (Pa. 1/19/00).
46. *Lemcke v. Lemcke*, 27 FLR 1249 (Minn.App. 4/3/01).
47. *La Chapelle v. Mitten*, 26 Family Law Reporter 1259 (Minn.App. 3/14/00).
48. *State v. Vakilzaden*, 251 Conn. 656, 742 A.2d 767.(Conn. 12/21/99).
49. *U.S. v. Faasse*, 227 F.3d 660 (6th Cir. 2000); *U.S. v. King*, 69 LW 1544 (S.D.N.Y. 2/8/01).
50. *Salahuddin v. Alaji*, 232 F.3d 305 (2nd Cir. 2000).
51. *U.S. v. Grigsby*, 85 F.Supp.2d 100 (D.R.I. 2/24/00).
52. *Biggs (Greer) v. Greer*, 524 S.E.2d 577 (N.C. App. 1/18/00).
53. *Gruntz v. Los Angeles*, 202 F.3d 1074 (9th Cir. 2/3/00).
54. *Pollard v. Pollard*, 991 P.2d 1201 (Wash.App. 1/27/00).
55. *Saliba v. Saliba*, 26 Family Law Reporter 1219 (Miss. 2/24/00).
56. *In re McGinley*, 27 FLR 1207 (Ore.App. 2/28/01).
57. *Downing v. Downing*, 27 FLR 1259 (Ky.App. 4/6/01).
58. *Allred v. Allred*, 744 A.2d 70 (Md.App. 1/13/00).
59. *Kesler v. Weniger*, 744 A.2d 794 (Pa.Super. 1/7/00).
60. *Piso v. Piso*, 761 A.2d 1215 (Pa.Super. 2000).
61. *In re Mitchell*, 27 FLR 1247 (Ill.App. 3/2/01).
62. *Rattee v. Rattee*, 27 FLR 1178 (N.H. 2/15/01).
63. *Gardner v. Yrttima*, 27 FLR 1172 (Ind.App. 2/8/01).
64. *Scheppers v. Scheppers*, 27 FLR 1136 (Cal.App. 1/26/01).
65. *Jurado v. Brashear*, 27 FLR 1231 (La. 3/19/01).
66. *Sacramento County v. Foross*, 242 B.R. 692 (9th Cir. 11/30/99).
67. *Ashton v. Dollaga*, 27 FLR 1261 (9th Cir. 3/23/01).
68. *Leibowitz v. Orange County*, 217 F.3d 799 (9th Cir. 2000).
69. *Williams v. Kemp*, 232 F.3d 652 (8th Cir. 2000).
70. *Kelly v. Jeter*, 27 FLR 1148 (8th Cir. 2/1/01).
71. *Harbaugh v. Sweet*, 69 LW 1138 (E.D. Mich. 1/23/01).
72. *Troxel v. Granville*, 530 U.S. 57 (Sup.Ct. 2000).
73. *VC v. MJB*, 26 Family Law Reporter 1284 (New Jersey 4/6/00); *SF v. MD*, 26 Family Law Reporter 1319 (Md.App. 5/2/00).

74. *Blondin v. Dubois,* 189 F.3d 240 (2nd Cir. 8/17/99).
75. *State Child Support Enforcement Division v. Bromley,* 987 P.2d 183 (Alaska 9/17/99).
76. *Vasquez v. Hawthorne,* 26 Family Law Reporter 1212 (Wash.App. 2/11/00).
77. *Doe v. Doe,* 26 Family Law Reporter 1231 (Md. 3/7/00).
78. *Kassama v. Magat,* 27 FLR 1195 (Md.App. 2/28/01).
79. *Hester v. Dwivedi,* 733 N.E.2d 1161 (Ohio 2000) and *Simmerer v. Dabbas,* 733 N.E.2d 1169 (Ohio 2000).
80. *State v. Lombardo,* 738 N.E.2d 653 (Ind. 2000).
81. *Ferguson v. Winston (Lindsay),* 26 Family Law Reporter 1222 (Kan.App. 2/11/00).
82. *Doe v. Sundquist,* 2 S.W.3d 919 (Tenn. 9/27/99).
83. *Does v. Oregon,* 68 LW 1390 (Ore.App. 12/29/99).
84. *In re Long,* 745 A.2d 673 (Pa.Super. 1/21/00).
85. *In re Adoption of RBF,* 27 FLR 1027 (Pa.Super. 11/8/00).
86. *Rodriguez v. McLoughlin,* 68 LW 1776 (2nd Cir. 6/5/00).
87. *AZ v. BZ,* 725 N.E.2d 1051 (Mass. 2000).
88. Md. AG Op. No. 00-035 (12/19/00); see 27 FLR 1150.
89. *Perry-Rogers v. Fasano,* 715 N.Y.S.2d 19 (N.D.A.D. 2000).

$$\boxed{\P 3100}$$

Estate Planning

[¶3101]

Estate planning for benefits from qualified plans and IRAs was greatly simplified by the Proposed Regulations the IRS published on January 17, 2001 (starting at 66 *Federal Register* 3928). The proposals are especially significant for high-income individuals who wish to reduce the minimum distribution they must take each year in order to accumulate more funds in the estate.

The proposals include a single, easy-to-use table, based only on the age of the employee, irrespective of whether the beneficiary is a person (and whether the person is the spouse or someone else), a trust, or an entity such as a charitable organization. The rules for distribution of balances after the death of the original owner are also greatly simplified.

For the year 2001, special use valuation under §2032A is available for amounts up to $800,000. The annual exclusion remains at $10,000; the present interest gift that can be made tax-free to a noncitizen spouse is $106,000. The exemption under the Generation Skipping Trust provisions rises to $1,060,000. Attorneys' fees of $140/hour can be awarded to prevailing taxpayer plaintiffs.[1]

Also see Advance Announcement 2000-25,[2] containing corrections to the official actuarial tables, the June 12, 2000 Final Rule on the use of those tables, published at 65 FR 36908, and T.D. 8886, 2000-27 IRB 3, giving actuarial factors for valuation under Sections 642, 664, and 2031.

A decedent's will called for half of his residuary estate to be placed in trust for the surviving wife for her lifetime. In fact, the wife elected against the will; litigation was settled when she received a lump sum settlement. According to the Tax Court, the wife did not have an enforceable right under New Jersey law to enter into a lump sum settlement, because that would require terminating the trust and contravening the decedent's intent. The Tax Court ruled that the money and real estate the surviving spouse received did not pass from the decedent to the surviving spouse under §2056(a), because they were not received under a bona fide recognition of enforceable rights in the decedent's estate. Nor was QTIP treatment available, because no QTIP election was made.[3]

[¶3101A] [NEW] EGTRA Estate and Gift Tax Provisions

During the Clinton administration, both Houses of Congress passed measures repealing the estate tax, but President Clinton vetoed this legislation and there were not enough votes to overturn the veto. However, estate tax repeal legislation eventually passed and was signed into law by President Bush on June 7, 2001 as the Economic Growth Tax Reform and Reconciliation Act of 2001 (EGTRA), P.L. 107-16.

Although it is not entirely untrue to say that EGTRA repeals the estate tax, this statement is true only with a number of caveats. During the period 2001–2010, the number of federally taxable estates will be reduced, because the amount exempt from estate tax will increase. Furthermore, those few estates that continue to be taxed will be subject to a smaller tax liability, because the highest estate tax rates will be phased out.

On the face of the legislation, estate taxes will be abolished as of 2010. But because of the sunset date of the entire EGTRA legislative package, the repeal of the estate tax will sunset at the end of 2010. So, unless Congress moves in the interim to make the repeal permanent, the estate tax will in fact be repealed for only a single year. For the year 2010 only, although there will be no estate tax, there will be a gift tax, equivalent to the highest income tax bracket.

In calendar years 2002 and 2003, the unified credit (and the amount exempt from generation-skipping transfer taxes) will be $1 million. This will increase to $1.5 million for 2004–2005, $2 million for 2006–2008, and then peaking at $3.5 million for 2009, the last year before the scheduled one-year repeal of the estate tax in 2010. Although much of the rhetoric in favor of estate tax repeal centered around small family-owned businesses, EGTRA in fact repeals the deduction for qualified interests in family-owned businesses as of 2004.

Under EGTRA, the maximum estate/gift tax rate will be 50% for calendar 2002, shrinking an additional 1% each year until 2007, when the top rate stabilizes at 45% until repeal in 2010.

The Conference Report for EGTRA says that, except as provided by regulations, as of 2010, all transfers into trust will be treated as taxable gifts (i.e., taxed at the highest income tax rate) except for grantor trusts that are deemed to be wholly owned by the grantor or the grantor's spouse.

For the year of estate tax repeal, EGTRA adds rules about basis of inherited property. Under pre-EGTRA law, decisions had to be made about whether a potential donor/testator and donee/heir would be better off with a lifetime gift or a bequest. One of the major factors in the decision was the basis of the property to be transferred.

Prior law called for the donee of a lifetime gift to receive the same basis in the property that the donor had. Inherited property, however, was subject to a carryover basis (under Code §1014(b)), valued as of either the date of death or the alternate valuation date six months later. This was often referred to as a stepped-up basis, reflecting the assumption that assets would appreciate rather than depreciate over time. Because the income tax calculation of profit on the sale of any asset begins with the price received minus the seller's basis, a higher basis means less potentially taxable profit.

Under EGTRA, each decedent's estate gets a single $1.3 million "step-up" in basis that the executor can use to enhance the basis of estate assets. Property transferred to the surviving spouse qualifies for an additional step-up of up to $3 million, and both spouses' shares of community property can be stepped up. Some losses belonging to the decedent (e.g., net operating losses) can also be used by the executor to increase basis of inherited assets. For joint or entireties property, half is deemed to belong to the decedent and, therefore, qualifies for the basis step-up.

However, the basis step-up will not be granted to certain types of securities (e.g., in certain types of foreign companies) or property that was acquired by the decedent by gift (not purchase or inheritance) during the three-year period before his or her death. Inter-spousal gifts, however, qualify for the basis step-up no matter when they were made.

EGTRA also adds reporting requirements. A donor who makes a non-charitable gift worth more than $25,000 must inform the IRS as to who has received the property; what it consists of; the donor's adjusted basis for the property when the gift was made; the donor's holding period in the property; and whether selling the property would result in ordinary income or capital gain. Most of the same information must also be given to the donee to facilitate tax compliance.

[¶3108.1] [NEW] Applicability of Tables

Even though a married couple died simultaneously (in a plane crash) before the effective date of Reg. §20.7520-3(b), which forbids use of the tables in case of common accident, the tables could not be used to calculate the value of their reciprocal life estates. There were earlier cases and rulings precluding use of the tables. Because they died simultaneously, their reciprocal life estates had no value, and neither estate could claim a §2013 credit.[4]

[¶3120.1] §§2053, 2054: Debts, Expenses, Taxes, and Losses

Payments to the decedent's female companion, made over many years, were taxable gifts and not compensation for household services and caring for the decedent's disabled daughter. Nor could bequests to the companion operate as claims against the estate on the basis of a prior written agreement.

The Tax Court treated this as a quasi-marital, not an employment, relationship.[5] The Tax Court rejected the estate's contention that the decedent was a party to a contract to make a will, promising certain property to his companion in consideration of past and future services. The court treated it as an attempt to protect the companion in the event of a will contest. Also, the estate didn't prove that the decedent received adequate and fair consideration; the value of the services to be rendered in the future; that the services were in fact provided in consideration of the agreement.

The estate tax administration expense deduction for executors' fees is limited by the compensation allowable under state law. In Maryland, therefore, it is based on the value of probate property under administration (not the gross estate).[6] The estate in question consisted of $11,000 worth of probate property and an $865,000 revocable trust passing outside probate. Therefore, the deductible fee was only $1,000, not $17,000, and nearly all of the miscellaneous administrative expenses that were claimed were nondeductible because they related to the trust rather than the probate property.

T.D. 8845, 1999-51 IRB 684 (12/2/99), promulgates Final Regulations on the effect of certain administrative expenses on the valuation of property that gets qualified for a marital or charitable deduction under §§2055 or 2056. The Regs. enact *Estate of Hubert,*[7] as to the effect of material limitations on the surviving spouse's right to use income.

Under the Regs., estate expenses are divided into estate transmission expenses and estate management expenses. Transmission expenses are those that would not have been incurred if the decedent had not died. Transmission expenses reduce the value of the property with respect to the marital and charitable deductions; management expenses do not.

[¶3120.3.1] QTIPs

The Eleventh Circuit ruled[8] that the estate of the decedent included terminable interest property received from the decedent's husband, for whom a marital deduction was taken (although no QTIP election was made), because taxpayers have a duty of consistency. Estate inclusion was not mandated by §2044 absent an election, but the husband's estate made a representation of fact (as to deductibility) in one tax year; the IRS relied on the fact in that year; and the estate sought to change the representation of fact after the statute of limitations had closed for that tax year, thus triggering a duty of consistency.

Rev.Rul. 2000-2, 2000-3 IRB 305, permits an executor to treat an IRA payable to a trustee as QTIP property if the surviving spouse has the right to compel the trustee to withdraw all the income earned on the IRA from the IRA at least annually and distribute it to the surviving spouse.

The Ruling uses the example of a testamentary trust paying all income annually to the surviving spouse. The trustee was named beneficiary of the decedent's IRA. The trust terms gave the surviving spouse the power to compel the trustee to withdraw an amount equal to IRA income from the IRA, and distribute it through the trust. No one could appoint any IRA or trust property to anyone except the surviving spouse. If the survivor exercised the power, the trustee was obligated to withdraw from the IRA either the income for the year or the minimum required distribution from the IRA (whichever was greater). The IRS decided that the surviving spouse had a qualifying income interest in both the IRA and the trust, but required the executor to make a valid QTIP election as to both, because the trust was a conduit for payments equal to the IRA income.

In a Technical Advice Memorandum (TAM 200014004), the IRS has treated excessive fees paid to QTIP trustees (children of the surviving spouse) as taxable gifts to the trustees. Ordinary business transactions have no gift tax implications (see Reg. §25.2512-8), but these fees were not set by arm's length bargaining. Nor did they reflect the market value of administering a trust largely funded with Treasury bills, for which little administrative work was required. The transaction was really a way to transfer funds to the beneficiary's children, and had to be taxed as such.

[¶3120.4] Valuation Issues

To the Tax Court, the value of a family-owned and -operated corporation was best represented by a combination of earnings-based value (capitalization of net cash flow) and asset-based value (fair market value of the assets). The court used a straight average of earnings, because a weighted average would give too much importance to the low point of the business cycle.[9]

The value of closely held corporation stock exchanged between the decedent and his father should have been set using the Reg. §20.2031-1(b) standard of a hypothetical willing buyer and seller. The expert witness erred in using the standard of actual buyers and sellers and by computing the control premium incorrectly.[10]

In a memorandum decision, the Tax Court accepted the estate's valuation rather than the IRS' for close corporation stock. The court approved of a 30% discount for lack of marketability, a 5.2% small stock premium and a 5% growth rate used in calculations. The court said that the capital asset pricing model was inappropriate for a company that had no meaningful chance of going public.[11]

Late in 2000, the Tax Court allowed minority and marketability discounts for estate purposes, for both the decedent's 99% interest in a limited partnership and his 47% (i.e., minority) interest in the corporate general partner that held the other 1% of the limited partnership. Nor was there a taxable gift when the taxpayer transferred cash, securities, and other property to the limited partnership in exchange for his 99% interest—even though in effect he traded $10 million in assets for an interest worth $6.5 million, because he never surrendered control of the assets; the partnership was valid under Texas law; and his contribution was allocated to his own account.[12]

[¶3120.4.1] Valuation Under Chapter 14

Even though it occurred only two days before the decedent's death, the District Court for the District of Texas treated a transfer of securities and an interest in the family ranch, in exchange for an interest in a Family Limited Partnership (FLP), as a bona fide business transaction and not an intrafamily transfer for less than full and adequate consideration.[13]

The transaction was deemed bona fide because the primary purpose of forming the FLP was efficient management of the family ranch; the family planned to raise cattle in the future; the partnership had objectives other than reducing estate tax; and although the decedent was being treated for cancer, she had not been diagnosed as terminally ill when she died of a sudden heart attack.

There was no gratuitous transfer because the partnership agreement had substantial economic effect, and the partnership interests were distributed pro rata, based on family members' relative contributions to the FLP.

In a similar case, the FLP satisfied all requirements of Texas law, so gifts of partnership interests to trusts benefiting the donor's children were transfers of partnership interests under state law and could be recognized for gift tax valuation purposes. The FMV of the transferred interests was the pro rata net asset value of the partnership, adjusted by a 15% discount for lack of marketability.[14]

[¶3130] Gift Tax

T.D. 8845, 1999-51 IRB 684 prescribes "adequate disclosure" of a gift sufficient to prevent its revaluation with respect to gift tax on a later gift. The disclosure must include:

- Description of the transferred property
- Consideration, if any, received by transferor
- Identity of each transferee; relationship with the transferor
- If trust is involved, the trust's TIN and a brief description of terms (or copy of trust instrument)
- Either an appraisal or a description of how the property was valued
- Disclosure of any position taken contrary to IRS positions

The T.D. holds that any completed transfer to a family member in the ordinary course of operating a business is adequately disclosed even if it is not reported on a gift tax return, as long as all the family members involved report it properly for income tax purposes.

Because substance rather than form is controlling, late in 2000 the Tax Court decided that annual transfers of close corporation stock by a decedent to the wives of her sons and grandson were really made to the sons and grandson themselves (who had already received annual exclusion gifts). The Tax Court reached this conclusion because the donor knew that the wives were subject to agreements to transfer the stock to their husbands; the donor's will disposed of her remaining stock to her sons, not to their wives; and she did not make any lifetime gifts to her daughters (whom she did not consider to be committed to the family business). Therefore, for gift tax purposes, the lifetime transfers to the in-laws were not deemed to qualify for the annual exclusion because the real recipients, the sons and grandson, had already received annual exclusion gifts.[15]

A similar concept, the reciprocal transaction doctrine, was applied to re-characterize gifts of close corporation stock to members of the decedent's brother's family as gifts to the decedent's own family, because the brother engaged in mirroring transactions. There was no real change in corporate ownership; the purported transactions merely existed to increase the number of annual exclusions to be claimed.[16]

The District Court for the District of Virginia ruled early in 2001 that for gift tax purposes, the value of gifts cannot be reduced to account for the possible liability of the donees as transferees under Code §6324(a)(2)[because of application of the §2035(b) gross-up rule, the possibility of future estate tax liability is too speculative to alter valuation]. Similarly, no account was taken of an agreement under which the donor's children assumed liability for additional gift tax if the value of the stock was later determined to be greater than the value reported on the gift tax return, because of the speculative nature of the potential obligation.[17]

[¶3140] §2518: Disclaimers

As already noted, Supreme Court cases involving estate planning are rather rare. The December, 1999 case of *Drye v. U.S.*[18] holds that the taxpayer's interest as heir to his mother's estate was a right to property under Code §6321, so that merely carrying out a disclaimer under state law isn't enough to defeat the federal tax lien.

At the time of the taxpayer's mother's death (when he became sole heir to her $323,000 estate), the taxpayer was insolvent and owed $325,000 in taxes, with liens already in place. The state probate court allowed the disclaimer; the property went to the taxpayer's daughter, who set up a trust with herself and father as beneficiaries.

The IRS filed a lien against the trust and a notice of levy on the trust's bank accounts. The trust filed a wrongful levy action. But Code §6321 imposes a lien on all property and rights to property (real or personal) belonging to someone who neglects or refuses to pay a tax after demand. The Supreme Court's *Drye* decision says that Congress expected property to be broadly available for the satisfaction of tax liens. Thirteen categories of levy exemptions have been enacted, making other categories subject to levy.

Drye also involves the interaction between state disclaimer law and federal tax law. State law controls the ultimate issue of whether the taxpayer has a beneficial interest in the property, but federal law governs the applicability of Code §6321. In this case, the right to disclaim had considerable economic value. It was not like an inter vivos gift, which could be returned to the donor to restore the status quo. It was this "control rein" aspect that brought the disclaimer within the reach of §6321.

[¶3150] Trusts

At the end of 1999, the IRS published final regulations explaining the §663(c) "separate share" rules: the circumstances under which the interests of trust beneficiaries are treated as if they were separate estates when trust distributable net income (DNI) is calculated and trust distributions are made under §§661 and 662.[19] The final regulations also treat a surviving spouse's elective share of the decedent's estate as a separate share. Therefore, that portion (e.g., one-third to one-half) is the only part of the estate's gross income on which the surviving spouse can be taxed.

Notice 2001-26, 2001-13 IRB 942 explains that a qualified revocable trust that has elected to be treated and taxed as part of the estate (rather than as a qualified trust) can avoid filing a separate Form 1041 as long as the trust items attributable to the decedent are reported on the estate's Form 1041, filed before the due date of what would be the trust's Form 1041 if a separate return were filed.

With respect to Grantor Retained Annuity Trusts and Unitrusts (GRATs and GRUTs), T.D. 8899, 2000-38 IRB 288 promulgates Final Regulations effective September 5, 2000. The definition of "qualified interest" under §2702 has been tightened up so that a note, option, debt instrument, or something similar cannot be used to pay the grantor's annuity or unitrust interest. A retained interest will not be treated as a qualified interest unless the trust instrument expressly prohibits the use of such measures for payment.

On August 3, 2000, the NCCUSL approved the Uniform Trust Code (text available at http://www.law.upenn.edu/bll/alc/uta/trst00ps.htm), the first attempt at codifying trust concepts nationwide. In the NCCUSL view, the Restatement (2nd) of Trusts fails to cope with some important practical issues. The Uniform Trust Code concentrates on the powers and duties of the trustee and incorporates the Uniform Prudent Investor Act. Article 6 of the Uniform Trust Code deals with revocable trusts, a subject that is little-explored in state probate codes.

[¶3151.5] Estate Inclusion

Thirty-eight inter vivos gifts of $10,000 each (i.e., typical annual exclusion gifts) made by an attorney-in-fact were included in the principal's gross estate. Under California law, the attorney-in-fact lacked the power to make the gifts, thus making them revocable by the decedent and includible in the estate. The Durable Power of Attorney document did include language permitting the agent to "give or accept any property and/or money," but the Court of Federal Claims did not consider this to be an adequate gifting power.[20]

TAM 1999944005 provides that assets transferred by a DPA agent to two trusts were a completed gift and hence not in the decedent's estate. The agent under the DPA (the decedent's daughter) was granted specific powers including executing deeds, collecting income, paying debts, and acting with respect to the decedent's bank accounts, but the document did not include a gifting power.

The agent-daughter put the mother's house into a Qualified Personal Residence Trust (QPRT), with the daughter as beneficiary, and funded another trust with cash, benefiting the decedent's grandchildren.

Despite the absence of a formal gifting power, the IRS conceded that a state court would probably have allowed the gifts:

- It was broad enough to be a GPA.
- The gifts were only a small part of the estate.
- The decedent didn't suffer by the daughter's actions.
- The gifts were consistent with intent of the decedent.
- The gifts followed decedent's history of gift-giving.

Gifts of real estate made by an agent were excluded from the principal's estate in *S. Pruitt Estate*[21], although the DPA did not have an express gifting power. The Tax Court inferred the gifting power from the general language of the instrument. Oregon state law does not forbid gifts by an agent, and the agent acted consistently with the principal's established pattern of giving. The gifts were not fraudulent, and they did not deplete the principal's estate to a detrimental extent. Therefore, the gifts were in the principal's best interests and carried out her intentions.

Under a late 1999 Tax Court Memo decision[22] a decedent's gross estate included gifts that a state court allowed the decedent's guardian-conservator to make on behalf of the decedent before her death, because the gifts weren't actually made until after her death. As of the time of death, the decedent still had dominion and control over property that the intended donees had not yet received. Furthermore, the state court authorized—but did not compel—the gifts.

The guardian had court approval to make annual exclusion gifts to the ward's daughter-in-law and grandchildren, and to gift $20,000 worth of real estate to himself and his wife. But at the time of death, the estate was too illiquid to make the cash gifts. The court didn't accept a constructive trust theory that would argue that the cash transfers were completed premortem. The cash gifts could not be related back to the pre-death date when the guardian conveyed the realty to himself.

Checks drawn on the decedent's checking account by her attorney-in-fact before her death, but not accepted or paid by the drawee bank until after her death, had to be included in her gross estate. The D.C. Circuit affirmed the Tax Court, which treated gifts to noncharitable donees as incomplete because, as long as the decedent remained alive, she could have stopped payment on the checks.[23] The principle of Metzger[24] [that the relation-back doctrine determines the date on which noncharitable gift checks become completed gifts] was not applied, because the donor was alive when the checks were presented and paid.

Under TAM 200014002, a testamentary trust was not included in the decedent's gross estate, despite the decedent's status as both life beneficiary and co-trustee. The decedent's predeceased spouse left his estate in trust for the decedent and their child. The decedent, as co-trustee, was entitled to receive income as necessary for her comfort and support and the child's comfort, support and education. Invasion was permitted by the trust document if trust income was insufficient for the stated purposes. However, the applicable state (Missouri) statute would not let the decedent exercise any power to distribute corpus for her own benefit, even subject to an ascertainable standard. Because the decedent could not appoint corpus for herself or her own benefit, §2041 did not mandate inclusion of trust assets in her estate.

[¶3152] Charitable Trusts

Early in 2001, the IRS finalized anti-abuse regulations for both charitable lead and charitable remainder trusts. T.D. 8923 (2001-6 IRB 485) rules out "ghoul trusts" (more formally, trusts *pour autre vie*—for another life). The abusive tactic was to choose as measuring life a young person who, although not terminally ill, was nevertheless seriously ill enough to have less than a normal life expectancy. Under the Treasury Decision, the only acceptable measuring lives for charitable lead trusts are the donor, the donor's spouse, or a person who is a lineal ancestor (or spouse of a lineal ancestor) of all of the noncharitable remaindermen.

A different problem was addressed with respect to charitable remainder trusts (CRTs) in T.D. 8926, 66 FR 2001-6 IRB 492. To prevent the use of CRTs to cash out appreciated assets without paying tax, the T.D. treats the trust as having sold a pro rata portion of the trust assets if the trustee borrows money, makes a forward sale of trust assets, or makes use of a similar device to obtain cash to pay the annuity or unitrust amount to the beneficiary.

[¶3170.3] Tax Aspects of Estate Administration

The automatic stay prevents a tax lien from attaching to an asset that the debtor inherits in the course of a bankruptcy proceeding, although a tax lien that is perfected pre-petition usually attaches to after-acquired assets by operation of law.

In a 1999 Fourth Circuit case,[25] an involuntary Chapter 7 debtor listed a contingent interest in potential inheritance under a trust of which the debtor was a beneficiary; eventually, the debtor inherited about $150,000. About a year before the bankruptcy filing, the IRS filed notice of a tax lien where the debtor's property was located (i.e., the lien was perfected under Code §6323).

The claw-back principle of Bankruptcy Code §541(a)(5)(A) returns property to the bankruptcy estate if it is acquired by a debtor by bequest, devise, or inheritance within 180 days after filing.

In this case, the trustee's contention was that the bequest went right into the bankruptcy estate, and never became the debtor's property, so the lien couldn't attach. The trustee also cited Bankruptcy Code §362(a)(5), automatically staying any "act" to perfect liens against the debtor's property, to the extent that the liens secure pre-filing claims. The IRS said that its lien attached to the property by operation of law, so no "act" was performed, but the Fourth Circuit disagreed. Section 362(b)(18), added by a 1994 amendment, exempts perfection of property-tax liens (which are statutory liens), showing that Congress could have exempted federal tax liens, but declined.

At the time of the decedent's death, his estate owed $2.3 million in federal estate tax and $429,000 in state estate tax. Nine months later, when it was time to pay, the estate was tied up in trusts and only had about $1 million in liquid assets.[26] The estate satisfied the state liability fully, and applied the remaining $572,000 toward the federal estate tax. The IRS denied the estate's request for an extension, and the estate didn't appeal the denial. Eventually the estate paid the balance of approximately $1.7 million.

The Fifth Circuit subjected the estate to additional liability for untimely payment, because it did not prove that the delay had a reasonable cause that was not willful neglect. It said that government evidence was admissible as to the estate's failure to get a loan, and failure to appeal the denial. The evidence was probative on issue of reasonableness, and outweighed prejudice to the estate.

Using the principle of equitable recoupment, the Tax Court permitted two estates to offset a time-barred overpayment of estate tax against the decedent's federal income tax liabilities.[27]

The estate tax deduction was not claimed for the income tax debts; by the time the income tax deficiency was determined, it was too late to apply for an estate tax refund. The IRS position[28] was that the defense of equitable recoupment is cognizable in District Court, but not before the Tax Court. The Tax Court holding was that if the case were appealed, the appeal would go to the Eleventh Circuit, which accepts equitable recoupment[29] so the defense can be raised before the Tax Court.

In April, 1993, when the decedent died, the maximum estate tax rate was 50%. In August, 1993, the Revenue Reconciliation Act was enacted, raising the top rate to 55%, thus costing the decedent's estate an additional $175,000 in tax. The District Court for the District of Nebraska rejected a challenge to retroactive application of the tax increase, finding it acceptable in light of the Constitution's apportionment clause, ban on ex post facto laws, the Fifth Amendment Takings clause, and Due Process.[30]

Under a 1999 Tax Court case,[31] the personal representative of an estate was not held personally liable for the estate's unpaid income tax liabilities of more than $60,000, because of his reasonable, good-faith reliance on advice from the estate's attorney that there was no federal tax liability.

The personal representative (a friend of the decedent, who did not inherit anything) therefore used estate funds to pay other claims.

A Tax Court Memo decision from early 2001 permits the IRS to collect estate tax liability from a transferee of estate assets. The IRS sent a notice of deficiency to the estate 26 days before §6501(a)'s three-year statute of limitations expired. The estate filed a Tax Court petition. Therefore, under §6503(a)(1)(A), the limitations period was suspended from the mailing of the notice of deficiency until 60 days after the Tax Court decision became final. The transferee was liable because the notice of transferee liability satisfied the §6901(c) one-year limitations period. The IRS was not guilty of laches (there had been no inexcusable delay) and the beneficiary had unclean hands, because he was aware of the tax liability when he received the assets from the estate.[32]

[¶3180] Intestate Administration

Although divorce actions abate when a party dies, some states permit an equitable distribution action (which vests at the time of marital separation) to be maintained independent of a divorce action. Therefore, the administratrix of an estate should have been substituted for the decedent in an equitable distribution action that was pending at the time of the decedent's death.[33]

According to the Fifth Circuit, a representative of a decedent's estate can challenge the discharge of a wrongful death claim against a bankruptcy debtor, because the administrator is a "creditor" with standing to object to discharge. Under Texas law, the administrator is the judicial officer who can enforce a claim and right to payment under the wrongful death statute, and therefore has standing to get the wrongful death claim declared nondischargeable.[34]

ENDNOTES

1. Rev.Proc. 2001-13, 2001-3 IRB 337
2. 2000-14 IRB 855.
3. *G. Mergott Estate*, 2000-2 USTC ¶60,383, 60,387 (D.N.J. 9/19/00, adopting recommendation of the magistrate judge).
4. *J. Harrison Estate*, 115 TC No. 13 (8/22/00).
5. *L. Cavett Estate,* TC Memo 2000-91 (3/15/00).
6. *C. Grant Estate,* TC Memo 1999-396 (12/7/99).
7. 520 U.S. 93 (Sup.Ct.1997).

8. *M. Letts Estate*, 2000-1 USTC ¶60,374 (11th Cir. 2000).
9. *B. Dunn Estate*, TC Memo 2000-12 (1/12/00).
10. *Estate of Magnin*, TC Memo 2001-13 (2/12/01).
11. *E. Klauss Estate*, TC Memo 2000-191 (6/27/00); also see *M. Cranor Estate*, TC Memo 2001-24 (2/2/01), allowing a 40% discount for the combination of minority and lack of marketability, rather than the 65% asserted by the estate's expert witness. The Tax Court said that the potential delay and transaction costs of the exit event should have been considered by the IRS' expert witness.
12. *A. Strangi Estate*, 115 TC No. 35 (11/30/00).
13. *E. Church*, 2000-1 USTC ¶60,369 (D.C. Tex. 2000).
14. *I. Knight*, 115 TC No. 36 (11/30/00).
15. *Estate of Bies*, TC Memo 2000-338 (11/2/00).
16. *R. Schuler Estate*, TC Memo 2000-392 (12/28/00).
17. *F. Armstrong, Jr., Trust*, 2001-1 USTC ¶60,392 (D.Va. 1/10/01).
18. #98-1101, 68 LW 4005 (Sup.Ct. 12/7/99).
19. 64 FR 72540 (12/28/99).
20. *S. Swanson Estate*, 2000-1 USTC ¶60,371 (Fed.Cl. 2000).
21. TC Memo 2000-287 (9/12/00).
22. *L. Devlin Estate*, TC Memo 1999-406 (12/14/99).
23. *S. Newman Estate*, 99-2 USTC ¶60,358 (D.C. Cir. 1999). Also see *R. Rosano*, 99-2 USTC ¶60,359 (S.D.N.Y. 1999), in which the District Court adopts the Magistrate Judge's findings that checks delivered to donees but not presented for payment until after her death were not completed gifts, and therefore had to be included in her estate. Semble *F. Christensen*, TC Memo 2000-368 (12/6/00).
24. 100 TC 204, *aff'd* 38 F.3d 118 (4th Cir. 1994).
25. *U.S. v. Gold*, 178 F.3d 718 (4th Cir. 1999).
26. *W. Sowell Estate*, 99-2 USTC ¶60,364 (5th Cir. 1999).
27. *H. Orenstein Estate*, TC Memo 2000-150 (4/26/00).
28. Based on *B. Mueller Estate*, 98-2 USTC ¶60,325 (6th Cir. 1998).
29. *R. Bokum II*, 992 F.2d 1139 (11th Cir. 1993).
30. *U.S. Bank NA*, 99-2 USTC ¶60,361 (D. Neb. 1999), following *J. Quarty*, 99-1 USTC ¶60,338 (9th Cir. 1999).
31. *Estate of Little*, 113 TC No. 31 (1999).
32. *E. Fridovich*, TC Memo 2001-32 (2/12/01).
33. *Brown v. Brown*, 26 Family Law Reporter 1151 (N.C. App. 1/18/00).
34. *Fezler v. Davis*, 194 F.3d 570 (5th Cir. 1999).

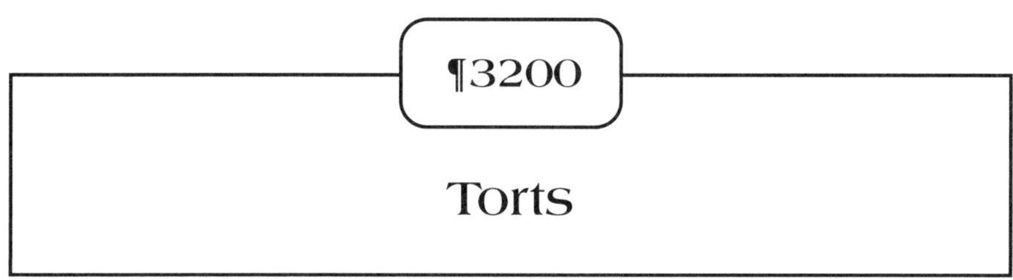

[¶3201]

The Supreme Court seldom decides tort cases, making each one especially notable. Its February, 2001 ruling in *Buckman Co. v. Plaintiffs' Legal Committee*, #98-1768, 69 LW 4101 (Sup.Ct. 2/21/01), is that state courts are not the proper forum for claims that a manufacturer defrauded the FDA in its application for exemption from pre-market approval of a medical device. The FDA's regulatory role in policing fraud means that such cases are subject to implied preemption by the Medical Device Amendments to the FDA Act.

The Department of Justice's Bureau of Justice Statistics released a survey, "Civil Trial Cases and Verdicts in Large Counties,"[1] showing that in the 75 largest counties in the United States, judges were almost twice as likely to find for plaintiffs as juries were (70% vs. 36% of cases), but jury awards were typically much larger.

In nonasbestos products liability cases, the median award from a judge was $56,000, versus $379,000 from a jury. In asbestos cases, juries found for the plaintiff 55% of the time, with a median award of $227,000. (There were no court trials for comparison, because jury trial was elected in all cases.)

About two-thirds of civil cases studied were tort cases, but product liability cases represented less than 3% of the overall caseload. Of all jury trials, 48.7% resulted in a plaintiff verdict, as did 61.6% of bench trials, with an average award of $35,000 (jury) and $28,000 (court trial).

[¶3210] Negligence

A 1999 California case holds[2] that dissatisfied homeowners cannot use their contract with a builder to recover tort damages from their building contractor for emotional distress. The rationale is that there wouldn't be any meaningful tort-contract distinction if every negligent breach of contract was held to be punishable in tort. Conduct constituting breach of contract is tortious only if it violates a duty independent of the contract, and stemming from tort principles—or if it violates a duty that arises from intentional conduct that is intended to harm.

In this case, the contractor performed very badly under the contract, but had no intention to cause harm. Even though it is foreseeable that emotional harm will result from physical harm, the court did not deem such foreseeability to create a new duty. The relationship between contractor and client is an ordinary business relationship, not a special or fiduciary relationship.

Nor are emotional distress damages recoverable as consequential or special damages to the homeowners' contract claim. Consequential damages are usually limited to circumstances the contract parties could reasonably foresee, and emotional damages are not central to a contract to build a house.

In Hawaii, a claim for negligent infliction of emotional distress is cognizable when a plaintiff is exposed to AIDS-contaminated blood.[3] Damages can be awarded entirely based on emotional distress; physical injury is not required. However, the period of damages is limited from the time of discovery of the actual exposure to the time of the first reliable test showing the exposed person's HIV-negative status. Liability attaches only to the extent that the mental distress does not exceed what a reasonable person would feel under the same circumstances.

California law does not impose a duty on the owner of premises (here, an underground parking garage) to hire security guards or otherwise prevent crimes by third parties (in this case, rape of the plaintiff), unless the owner is on notice because of a history of comparable crimes on the premises.[4]

In the premises in question, there had been no assaults during the period 1982-1993, but the property had been a crime scene: there were seven armed robberies of the ground-floor bank during a two-year period.

The California court did not consider underground parking garages to be inherently dangerous, apart from the general prevalence of crime throughout society.

The plaintiff introduced evidence of deteriorating conditions in the garage (dirt, broken security cameras, burned-out lights) but the court did not find this persuasive, on the grounds that better maintenance would not necessarily have deterred a rapist.

[¶3215] Strict Liability

For strict liability purposes, a telephone pole is a "product."[5] Poles are fixtures under real estate law, but they're still products under the Alabama Extended Manufacturer's Liability Doctrine. The plaintiff in an automotive wrongful death case had enough evidence to get to a jury on her strict liability claim that the pole, which broke, resulting in contact of live phone lines with the highway, was defective.

In 2000, Nebraska overruled a 24-year-old decision that had given prescription drug manufacturers blanket immunity from strict liability. However, the court declined to adopt Restatement (3rd) of Torts §6(c), which uses a "reasonable physician" test for claims of defective design of prescription drugs, on the grounds that it is not flexible enough and is too hard to apply in practice.[6]

Under Oklahoma law, sellers of used products who merely re-sell products in the same condition they acquired them are not strictly liable to persons injured by the products, in that the defects (if any) were caused by the manufacturer and not the seller.[7]

[¶3220] Medical Malpractice

Oklahoma recognizes a cause of action for the wrongful death of a non-viable fetus that was nevertheless born alive, but not for the loss of a non-viable fetus that was stillborn. The theory is that life begins at conception.[8]

Unless the patient actually asks, a doctor has no legal duty to disclose factors of his/her personal life that could have negative impact on the patient's treatment, such as illegal drug use.[9]

According to the Georgia Supreme Court (which dismissed fraud and battery claims against a surgeon who failed to disclose cocaine use to a patient), professionals don't have a duty to disclose drug abuse or other negative factors in their personal life. The state's informed consent statute specifies six categories of information that must be given; personal information about the health care provider is not included.

However, evidence of use of illegal drugs is admissible on the medical malpractice claim. The battery cause of action was not available, because improperly obtained consent can support a battery claim, but only if it is directly related to the subject matter of the professional relationship (e.g., diagnosis or treatment).

[¶3225] Malpractice Litigation

The Indiana state constitution has been held to prevent application of the medical malpractice statute of limitations to a plaintiff whose condition had such a long latency period that it couldn't have been discovered within the two-year limit.[10] In this analysis, precluding the suit would deprive the plaintiff of the privileges and immunities and guarantee of open courts promised by the state constitution.

Strict application of the statute of limitations is unacceptable because it is not uniformly applicable to all victims of malpractice, and puts people like the plaintiff in an impossible situation in which valid claims cannot be pursued.

Michigan Comp.L. §600.2169 rules out expert testimony on the standard of care in medical malpractice cases against a specialist from anyone other than another practitioner (or professor) of the same specialty, and has been upheld.[11] In other words, clinicians and educators can testify on the standard of care, but professional expert witnesses cannot.

The statute did not improperly usurp the judge's ability to regulate procedures in state court. This case holds that judges are in charge of procedural rules of evidence but not the evidentiary rules of substantive law, and §2169 is substantive, not mere direction of judicial business.

[¶3240] Intentional Torts

The American Medical Association did not defame Jack Kevorkian by calling him a "killer" who engaged in "criminal activities."[12] Kevorkian's reputation was not impaired, because he is a public figure with a national reputation dealing with assisted suicide; he has been sentenced to 10-25 years for second-degree murder; and members of the public probably had already formed ideas about him before the AMA's comments were made.

A defamation case arose when a directory of lawyers who handle employment discrimination suits described one particular lawyer as an "ambulance chaser" who only took "slam dunk" cases (citing "at least one client" as authority for the statements).

At the District Court level, this was treated as a nonactionable statement of opinion, but the Second Circuit reinstated the lawyer's defamation suit on the grounds that, in the context of a directory that deals with facts, it could reasonably be understood to imply that lawyer unethically solicited clients, which is a statement of fact.[13]

Declining to draw a distinction between media and nonmedia defendants, the court required a private plaintiff suing over a matter of public concern to prove the falsity of the alleged defamatory matter (at least if the statement is directed toward members of the public with interest in that subject). Sex discrimination is a matter of public concern, and so is legal ethics. "Ambulance chaser" is a factual term that reasonably implies unethical solicitation practices, so its use was an actionable fact, not a nonactionable opinion, particularly because publication in the directory gave it the imprimatur of a respected organization.

Lawyers' absolute privilege in judicial proceedings doesn't insulate them against defamation liability for communications with news media about a pending case. The purpose of the privilege is encouraging zealous advocacy, a value that is not served by unrestricted contact with the press. In fact, a lawyer can be sued for defamation based on communications that more or less restate the allegations of the client's pleading.[14]

An administrator, as the representative of the decedent's estate, is a "creditor" who has standing to object to the discharge in bankruptcy of a wrongful death claim against a bankruptcy debtor.[15] Under Texas law, the administrator is the judicial officer who can enforce claims and rights to payment under the wrongful death statute, and therefore has standing.

An action for malicious prosecution was not collaterally estopped by an earlier finding that a patent infringement suit was not objectively baseless for purposes of *Noerr-Pennington* immunity.[16] In the infringement action, the alleged infringer can present evidence that the patent was obtained fraudulently, and ruling that the infringement suit was not baseless did not resolve allegations of fraud and false testimony.

In 1999, Ohio recognized a new independent tort of improper unauthorized disclosure of nonpublic medical information. A hospital that made improper disclosures to a law firm that collected data about patients eligible for Supplemental Security Income benefits, was liable.[17] Even though the duty of confidentiality is not absolute, the disclosures in this case were not made pursuant to any privilege.

Instead of looking for a way to apply conventional legal theories, the Ohio court held that there is an independent tort of improper disclosure of information learned by a doctor or hospital in the course of a physician–patient relationship. Disclosure of otherwise confidential information is permitted in special situations where there is a statutory mandate or common-law duty to disclose, or where there is a countervailing interest supporting disclosure and outweighing the patient's interest.

[¶3240.5] [NEW] "Life Torts"

Like most states, Maryland does not have a wrongful life cause of action (brought by a child asserting that he or she should never have been born) because it is too difficult to calculate damages for the difference between a normal and an impaired life. (Wrongful life cases can be maintained in California, New Jersey, and Washington.) However, the majority rule (also followed in Maryland) is that a wrongful birth cause of action, for the additional costs of raising a disabled child, can be maintained.[18]

In September, 2000, Ohio refused to allow disabled children to recover either wrongful life or wrongful pregnancy damages against their parents' allegedly negligent physicians. The wrongful life cause of action was denied in the case of a child born with spina bifida, because the doctor neither caused the condition nor was able to correct it.

The wrongful pregnancy suit (subsequent to an unsuccessful sterilization) could not be maintained, because the heart defect resulting in the child's death was not reasonably foreseeable as of the time of the sterilization and, therefore, negligence in performing the sterilization was not the proximate cause of the infant's death.[19]

[¶3260] Products Liability

The Executive Branch has made no secret of its desire to have the FDA take steps to reduce tobacco sales to minors. Despite this, in March, 2000, the Supreme Court ruled that the FDA does not have authority to regulate tobacco products.[20]

The FDA's theory was that nicotine is a drug delivered in cigarette form, thus supporting its right to regulate. But to the Supreme Court, Congress already has a comprehensive statutory scheme for coping with tobacco health risks, and the FDA doesn't fit into it. The Supreme Court noted that adopting the FDA analysis would require suppression of cigarettes, which remain legal. Furthermore, the FDA position, upheld for many years, was that the agency lacked authority to regulate tobacco unless the manufacturers made health claims in favor of tobacco.

The Eastern District of Pennsylvania ruled that a Pennsylvania resident's negligence and strict products liability claims against an out-of-state cigarette manufacturer, and local cigarette retailer, could not be brought in federal court.[21] The plaintiff alleged that the decedent's wrongful death was caused by cigarettes manufactured by Philip Morris and sold by Rite Aid. Philip Morris got the case removed from state to federal court, arguing that diversity was still present because the plaintiff's joinder of the local defendant was fraudulent, intended solely to defeat diversity.

But the Eastern District said that as long as there was a colorable cause of action against the local defendant under local law, joinder was not fraudulent. The claim doesn't have to be good enough for the plaintiff to win, as long as it is not wholly insubstantial and frivolous.

The plaintiff's allegation that the design of the defendant's cigarettes failed to reduce carcinogens was an allegation of a specific defect (stating a colorable cause of action in Pennsylvania), not just an allegation of the inherent dangerousness of tobacco. The plaintiff's charges against Rite Aid (negligent breach of the duty to sell only products that are reasonably safe) did not constitute a mere failure to warn claim that would be preempted by the Federal Cigarette Labeling and Advertising Act.

Also with respect to tobacco, the California Superior Court certified a class of approximately 1.5 million regular smokers who began to smoke in California when they were minors. The suit calls for disgorgement of unjust enrichment allegedly obtained from underage smokers, and dedication of all profits from underage smoking to providing programs for smoking cessation and medical monitoring of smokers. The court granted certification of the class pursuant to California statutory claims, finding that arguments against class certification in common-law cases are not applicable.[22]

If the plaintiff is negligent over and above mere failure to discover product defects, then the principle of comparative responsibility applies in Texas strict liability cases.[23]

Imposing a duty to discover defects would violate public policy, because it would vitiate the principle of strict liability. But a person who breaches an existing duty, such as the duty to use due care, should not be rewarded for the breach. In the case at bar, $4 million compensatory damages were reduced to $2 million, based on the driver's 50% responsibility for his fatal accident—although the truck slipped into reverse, he was not adequately careful when exiting the vehicle.

The Third Circuit decided in 1999[24] that the Port Authority is not entitled to tort damages from the manufacturer of the fertilizer component of the bomb used in the 1993 attack on its property, the World Trade Center. Neither New York nor New Jersey law imposes a duty to protect the Port Authority against criminal acts.

Even if liability had been appropriate, the fertilizer was not the proximate cause of the damage to Port Authority property. Two of the fertilizers in question aren't even explosive when sold; they have to be mixed with other substances. The Port Authority's contention was that the manufacturer was on notice that fertilizer could be used to make bombs and that technology had long been available to process ammonium nitrate fertilizer to prevent detonation.

The Third Circuit response was that neither New York nor New Jersey law obligates a manufacturer to prevent a buyer from taking a product that is not dangerous in itself and incorporating it into a dangerous device. Nor could manufacturers objectively foresee the criminal misuse of their products. Following the Tenth Circuit decision about the Oklahoma City bombing,[25] the Third Circuit held that as a matter of law, the bombing was not a natural or probable consequence of anything wrong with the defendant's product design. Terrorism is an intervening act breaking the chain of causation.

The Alabama Circuit Court rejected a limited fund class action settlement that it had previously approved against tobacco company Liggett Group and its parent company the Brooke Group, because of the intervening Supreme Court *Ortiz* decision. In this case, the settlement was inadequate because it would leave Liggett with substantial assets, and would not equally compensate all potential claimants (who didn't have the chance to opt out).[26]

A Texas statute (Civ.Prac. §82.004(a)), immunizing the manufacturers of products known to ordinary consumers to be inherently unsafe, requires dismissal of the wrongful death suit brought by the family of a smoker who died of throat cancer.[27]

Texas uses the "single-action" rule: that is, the plaintiff has one, indivisible cause of action stemming from a defendant's single breach of legal duty. However, the single action related to the consequences of asbestos exposure in the workplace. Thus, a person who recovered damages for asbestosis could maintain a subsequent suit against asbestos manufacturers after he contracted cancer. The court ruled that it was more expeditious to start a separate limitations period if and when cancer develops than to require all defendants in asbestosis cases to have to defend against allegations of the potential development of cancer.[28]

The California Court of Appeals allowed plaintiffs to get to a jury on the question of whether a gun manufacturer was negligent in the manufacture, marketing, and distribution of assault weapons used by a psychotic to kill eight people. This[29] is the first case finding a duty of care on a gun maker's part to people injured by criminal misuse of its product. The court treated it as fundamentally fair for those who profit by selling dangerous instrumentalities to face consequences when their conduct unreasonably increases the risk of injury beyond what is necessary to the enterprise.

Four critical elements of duty were defined under a negligence theory:

- Morally offensive conduct;
- Foreseeable harm;
- Connection between conduct and injury; and
- Ability to prevent future harm.

The court treated the shooting as foreseeable, because Navegar is a preferred brand among criminals, and the advertising served to enhance this reputation. Another factor is that a company officer violated federal gun laws by conspiring to distribute information about converting weapons to full automatic.

Merely manufacturing weapons that are attractive to criminals is not negligence, but negligence can be inferred from the combination of manufacturing such weapons, distributing them to the general public, and advertising in a way that promotes criminal use. The issue of causation (whether the gunman would have been able to wreak so much havoc if a convertible semi-automatic weapon had not been promoted and made publicly available) was permitted to go to the jury. However, the court rejected the plaintiffs' contention that manufacture and distribution of guns is an ultrahazardous activity subject to strict liability, finding instead that the manufacturer could have eliminated or at least seriously reduced the hazards by exercising a higher standard of care.

In contrast, however, the First Circuit held that there is no duty to defend under a general liability insurance policy that excludes coverage for suits arising out of the insured's "products," when personal injury and wrongful death suits allege liability on the part of the entire gun industry. The gun manufacturers were in the paradoxical position of trying to prove that they were sued because of their "conduct" and not their "products," in order to obtain coverage.[30]

A nationwide class action against the gun manufacturer Glock was decertified by the Fifth Circuit for lack of common questions of law. The conduct alleged to have caused the injury was a design defect that caused the guns to jam. Any design defect occurred in Austria, whereas the injury occurred throughout the United States where guns were purchased.[31]

Asymptomatic individuals who took diet drugs fenfluramine and phentermine have a cause of action in Florida for medical monitoring, on the grounds that low-income individuals should not be denied access to the medical system until they develop extreme symptoms.[32] Although there is no cause of action for the enhanced risk of eventually developing a disease, medical monitoring is available because it is much less speculative and does not require the jury to determine whether disease will eventually ensue.

In August, 2000, the Eastern District of Pennsylvania approved a class action settlement with respect to the diet drugs Pondimin and Redux for plaintiffs who have, or are at risk of developing, diseased heart valves. The court found the proposed settlement to be better-crafted than, for instance, tobacco and asbestos class action settlements that were invalidated. The diet drug settlement creates two funds: $1 billion for medical monitoring, and $2.55 billion in compensation. Plaintiffs will receive anywhere from $7389 to $1.5 million apiece, based on factors such as their degree of injury, duration of drug use, and age.

The court accepted this settlement because the class was adequately cohesive; only one manufacturer, not an entire industry, was sued; and the settlement provided objective criteria for allocating proceeds among plaintiffs.[33]

However, with the stated objective of expediting tobacco settlements, the Eastern District of New York denied class certification of consolidated personal injury suits. The requested class would have allowed plaintiffs to opt out with respect to punitive damages. The court preferred a broader class covering both compensatory and punitive damages, allowing opt-out for individual compensatory damages but not for punitive damages.[34]

Plaintiff property owners alleged that a particular type of plumbing system was completely inadequate; that it caused property damage; and that the manufacturers lied about the materials. But the Fifth Circuit ruled that the plaintiffs could not maintain a civil RICO cause of action without proving reliance on fraudulent misrepresentations about the quality of the plumbing system. In a RICO case, the racketeering injury must be the proximate cause of the injury. In this case, the fraud (if any) did not induce the purchase of the plumbing system. The court refused to extend the "fraud on the market" theory outside the context of securities regulation.[35]

RICO (as well as the antitrust laws) could not be used by public hospital districts to force tobacco manufacturers to pay the otherwise unreimbursed costs of tobacco-related illnesses because of a lack of nexus between the injury and the defendants' conduct.[36]

Plaintiffs who alleged that manufacturers, distributors, and others in the chain of distribution of allegedly defective bone screws did not present a cognizable conspiracy cause of action under the Food, Drug & Cosmetic Act. The Third Circuit would not permit a claim of civil conspiracy premised on violation of a federal statute for which there is no private right of action.[37] The plaintiffs claimed that manufacturers, distributors, doctors, and other health care professionals conspired to market and sell devices lacking necessary FDA approval, as shown by intensive marketing of the devices to surgeons, and the incentives provided to surgeons.

However, there was no individual defendant who could be sued for violating the Food, Drug & Cosmetic Act. Conspiracy suits are impossible without conduct that would be actionable if one person did it alone: there must be a separate, underlying predicate tort. Although there are numerous holdings that violating federal law is negligence per se under state law, those cases merely use the federal statute to establish the standard of care; they don't create an independent basis of tort liability.

The Illinois Court of Appeals refused, in late 1999, to permit a mother to sue video game makers for failure to warn that long-term game playing can induce epileptic seizures in children.[38] Although the child first had seizures in 1987, the evidence in the case did not show that the manufacturer was aware of the risk until 1989. (The company started formulating a package warning in 1991.) The manufacturer could not be required to have foreseen the connection between game play and epileptic seizures.

According to the Washington Court of Appeals, promulgation of industry-wide standards that were voluntarily adopted by manufacturers created a duty on the part of a swimming pool trade association to warn the public of the risks of diving boards and pools.[39] The association then violated this duty by failing to revise the safety standards or issue warnings when tests showed that a particular combination of jump board and pool created a risk of serious injury.

[¶3260.2] [NEW] Warranty Issues

In 1999, Alabama took the position that Magnuson-Moss invalidates arbitration provisions in written warranties, but the court reversed itself in June, 2000, finding arbitration provisions acceptable.[40]

The Seventh Circuit ruled that expert testimony from engineers and an expert on metal behavior about the allegedly faulty steering mechanism of a Ford van should have been admitted, because it related to facts at issue in the case: how and when the steering mechanism failed. Their testimony was admissible even though they were not qualified automotive engineers and could not testify whether design or manufacturing was at fault in the accident.[41]

The Southern District of New York refused to permit a plaintiff who alleged that Viagra damaged his vision and led to a car accident to compel production of testimony from FDA employees who allegedly expressed concern over the drug's safety. The FDA approval constituted the agency's official verdict on Viagra safety, so testimony by employees would merely be their personal opinion. This would be misleading because the jury might accord it too much credence given their status as FDA employees.[42]

[¶3260.4] [NEW] Preemption Issues

According to the Third Circuit, FIFRA preempts claims that the manufacturer didn't provide proper labeling about how the product should be opened and stored.[43] However, FIFRA doesn't preempt claims of negligent packaging of the product. FIFRA is broad enough to cover the labeling issue, but not the packaging claim, because the EPA packaging regulations (40 CFR §157.20) are limited to concerns of child safety.

The plaintiff alleged that her throat, lungs, and breathing were injured when she opened a container of chlorine tablets for swimming pools. She claimed that the manufacturer should have warned of the risk of offgassing from decomposed product, and should have changed the packaging to eliminate or at least limit the risk.

A late-2000 Montana case limits FIFRA preemption to requirements enacted by positive law, thus holding that FIFRA does not preempt state common law failure-to-warn actions.[44]

A Sixth Circuit heart pacemaker case holds that the Medical Device Amendments to the FDA Act preempt state tort claims, because the state tort claims are different from, or in addition to, the federal claims. Claims of fraud on the FDA (e.g., during the approval process) are also preempted.[45]

[¶3280] Tort Damages

A personal injury plaintiff whose medical bills are paid in full by an insurer can recover only the amount actually paid for the care by the insurer plus the plaintiff's own co-payments. The nominal amount of the medical bill is not recoverable because the patient doesn't have to pay any amount that the health care provider writes off, and therefore should not be able to collect such amounts as windfall damages.[46]

The Ninth Circuit permits "cede-back" agreements (in which settling plaintiffs agree to remit to the defendant their share of any punitive damages awarded to nonsettling plaintiffs) in mandatory class actions. It is not necessary to disclose such an agreement to jury members; in fact, it should not be revealed to them, because of the likelihood that they will merely order higher damages to make up for the impact of the agreement. In this view, cede-back agreements do not violate public policy and do serve to encourage settlements and thus promote judicial economy.[47]

An award of $1 million in compensatory damages to a breast implant user who suffered muscle and joint pains when the implants ruptured was upheld by the Eleventh Circuit at the end of 2000.[48] It was not an abuse of discretion for the District Court to admit certain testimony of plaintiff's experts. Although they did not testify directly on causation, they did testify as to the disease process resulting from the formation of silica and the body's reaction to silica.

The Bankruptcy Code §522(d)(11)(D) exemption of $15,000 for a debtor's right to receive payment on account of personal bodily injury is limited to only one $15,000 sum, not one per tort claim, if the debtor has more than one. The statutory language is "a payment." According to the First Circuit,[49] the legislative intent was to provide reasonable levels of support for the debtor, an intent that is not served by favoring debtors who have several small claims rather than one larger claim (which implies more serious damage).

Under West Virginia law, a cause of action is available for recovery of medical monitoring costs that are proved to be both necessary and reasonably likely to be incurred as a proximate result of a defendant's tort, with these prerequisites:

- Proven risk of the substance to which the plaintiffs were exposed;
- Tortious conduct by the defendant;
- The defendant's conduct increased the risk of latent disease (as compared with the nonexposed population);

- The exposed population needs some kind of diagnostic testing that the general population doesn't; and
- There are effective monitoring procedures for early diagnosis of the tortiously-induced disease.

The court refused to adopt the defense's contention that the plaintiff must be required to prove the existence of a current, effective treatment for the condition allegedly caused by the defendant's tort.

[¶3290] Tort Reform

A deeply divided Ohio Supreme Court held the state's entire comprehensive tort reform law to be unconstitutional.[50] Given the judiciary's power to decide constitutionality, the Ohio Supreme Court disapproved the state legislature's passage of tort reform legislation that embodied provisions the court had already found unconstitutional.

The reform legislation capped punitive damages at the lesser of three times compensatory damages, or $100,000 for small, $250,000 for large companies. The statute says that caps are needed to prevent cruel and unusual punishment. The state Supreme Court found the cap unconstitutional because it denies plaintiffs the benefit of a jury determination of their claims.

The Ohio Supreme Court also ruled against the statutory cap on noneconomic damages (set at the greater of $250,000 or three times the economic loss, subject to a maximum of $500,000; for some permanent injuries, the cap was set at $1 million or $35,000 per year of the plaintiff's remaining life expectancy). The rationale here was that the cap merely expanded on an existing medical malpractice statute that was itself constitutionally defective. The tort reform law's principles of limitations and treatment of collateral source benefits were also rejected.

In mid-1999, Oregon's Supreme Court rejected the state's statutory cap on noneconomic damages of $500,000 per plaintiff (Rev.Stat. §18.560(1)).[51] The court found the statute to be an impermissible interference with the right to a civil jury trial as guaranteed by the state constitution. The court interpreted this to mean that jury trial must be available whenever it was an option in 1857, when the state constitution was adopted.

The manufacturer-defendant said that the cap was similar to the accepted common-law concept of remittitur, but the court did not accept this argument because application of the cap is mandatory rather than discretionary, and remittitur is available only for an award that has been held to be unreasonable. A prevailing party can reject remittitur and accept another jury trial.

Although Oregon has upheld a cap on wrongful death damages,[52] this court was not persuaded, because the wrongful death cause of action is statutory and did not exist at the time the state Constitution was adopted.

ENDNOTES

1. *http://www.ojp.usdoj.gov/bjs*, discussed at 68 LW 2253.
2. *Erlich v. Menezes*, 87 Cal.Rptr. 2d 886 (Cal. 8/23/99).
3. *Roe v. FHP Inc.*, 985 P.2d 661 (Haw. 1999).
4. *Sharon P. v. Arman Ltd.*, 91 Cal. Rptr. 2d 35 (Cal. 1999).
5. *Bell v. T.R. Miller Mill Co.*, 68 LW 1528 (Ala. 2/4/00).
6. *Freeman v. Hoffman-LaRoche Inc.*, 618 N.W.2d 827(Neb. 2000).
7. *Allenberg v. Bentley Hedges Travel Service Inc.*, 69 LW 1555 (Okla. 3/6/01).
8. *Nealis v. Baird*, 68 LW 1366 (Okla. 12/7/99).
9. *Albany Urology Clinic PC v. Cleveland*, 68 LW 1553 (Ga. 3/6/00).
10. *Martin v. Richey*, 711 N.E.2d 1273 (Ind. 1999).
11. *McDougall v. Schanz*, 597 N.W.2d 148 (Mich. 1999).
12. *Kevorkian v. American Medical Association*, 602 N.W.2d 233 (Mich. App. 8/6/99).
13. *Flamm v. American Ass'n of University Women*, 201 F.3d 144 (2nd Cir. 1/4/00).
14. *Kennedy v. Zimmerman*, 601 N.W. 2d 61 (Iowa 1999).
15. *Fezler v. Davis*, 194 F.3d 570 (5th Cir. 1999); Bankruptcy Code §523(a)(6) denies discharge of liability resulting from "willful and malicious acts."
16. *Hydranautics v. FilmTec Corp.*, 204 F.3d 880 (9th Cir. 2000).
17. *Biddle v. Warren General Hosp.*, 715 N.E.2d 518 (Ohio 1999).
18. *Kassama v. Magat*, 27 FLR 1195 (Md.App. 2/28/01).
19. *Hester v. Dwivedi*, 733 N.E.2d 1161 (Ohio 2000); *Simmerer v. Dabbas*, 733 N.E.2d 1169 (Ohio 2000).
20. *FDA v. Brown & Williamson Tobacco Corp.*, #98-1152, 68 LW 4194 (Sup.Ct. 3/21/00).
21. *Carter v. Philip Morris Corp.*, 68 LW 1524 (E.D. Pa. 2/23/00).
22. *In re Tobacco Cases II*, 69 LW 1400 (Cal.Super. 11/30/00).
23. *G.M. Corp v. Sanchez*, 68 LW 1080 (Tex. 7/9/99).

24. *Port Authority of NY and NJ v. Arcadian Corp.,* 189 F.3d 305 (3rd Cir. 1999).
25. *Gaines-Tabb v. ICI Explosives USA Inc.,* 160 F.3d 613 (10th Cir. 1998).
26. *Fletcher v. Brooke Group Ltd.,* 68 LW 1128 (Ala.Cir.Ct. 7/22/99).
27. *Sanchez v. Liggett & Myers Inc.,* 187 F.3d 486 (5th Cir. 8/25/99).
28. *Pustejovsky v. Rapid-American Corp.,* 69 LW 1364 (Tex. 11/30/00).
29. *Merrill v. Navegar Inc.,* 89 Cal.Rptr. 2d 146 (Cal. App. 1999).
30. *Brazas Sporting Arms Inc. v. American Empire Surplus Lines,* 220 F.3d 1 (1st Cir. 2000).
31. *Spence v. Glock GmbH,* 227 F.3d 308 (5th Cir. 2000).
32. *Petito v. A.H. Robins Co.,* 68 LW 1416 (Fla. Dist. App. 12/22/99).
33. *In re Diet Drugs Products Liability Litigation,* 69 LW 1136 (E.D. Pa. 8/28/00).
34. *Simon v. Philip Morris Inc.,* 69 LW 1319 (E.D.N.Y. 11/6/00).
35. *Summit Properties Inc. v. Hoechst Celanese Corp.,* 68 LW 1782 (5th Cir. 6/7/00).
36. *Ass'n of Washington Public Hospital Districts v. Philip Morris Inc.,* 69 LW 1523 (9th Cir. 2/22/01).
37. *In re Orthopedic Bone Screw Products Liability Litigation,* 193 F.3d 781 (3rd Cir. 1999).
38. *Coursey v. Nintendo of America,* 68 LW 1416 (Ill. App. 12/15/99).
39. *Meneely v. S.R. Smith Inc.,* 69 LW 1144 (Wash. App. 8/3/00).
40. *Southern Energy Homes Inc. v. Lee,* 732 So.2d 994 (Ala. 1999), overruled *Southern Energy Homes Inc. v. Ard,* 68 LW 1784 (Ala. 6/2/00).
41. *Smith v. Ford Motor Co.,* 215 F.3d 713 (7th Cir. 2000).
42. *Moran v. Pfizer,* 69 LW 1160 (S.D.N.Y. 8/4/00).
43. *Hawkins v. Leslie's Pool Mart Inc.,* 184 F.3d 244 (3rd Cir.1999).
44. *Sleath v. West Montana Home Health Service Inc.,* 16 P.3d 1042 (Mont. 2000).
45. *Kemp v. Medtronic Inc.,* 231 F.3d 216 (6th Cir. 2000).
46. *Hull v. Jackson,* 69 LW 1445 (Ala. 1/12/01).
47. *Icicle Seafoods v. Exxon Corp.,* 229 F.3d 790 (9th Cir. 2000).
48. *Toole v. Baxter Healthcare Corp.,* 235 F.3d 1307 (11th Cir. 2000).
49. *Christo v. Yellin,* 192 F.3d 36 (1st Cir. 1999).
50. *State ex rel Ohio Academy of Trial Lawyers v. Sheward,* 715 N.E.2d 1062 (Ohio 8/16/99).
51. *Lakin v. Senco Products Inc.,* 68 LW 1062 (Ore. 7/15/99).
52. *Greist v. Phillips,* 906 P.2d 789 (Ore. 1995).

¶3300

Immigration

[¶3301]

For immigration statistics dating from 1994 to 2000, such as estimates of the number of foreign-born persons and illegal aliens in each state, and annual reports on refugees, asylees, and legal immigrants, see http://www.ins.usdoj.gov/graphics/aboutins.

The 245(i) program (8 USC §1255(i)), permitting applications for legal U.S. residency by illegal immigrants, on payment of a $1,000 penalty, but without the requirement of returning to the home country to apply for entry at the U.S. consulate in the home country, expired on April 30, 2001. More than half a million immigrants took advantage of this provision—often by marrying U.S. citizens shortly before the expiration date. President Bush favors its extension, so it may be reinstated.

A Final Rule on professional conduct by attorneys and representatives appearing before the Executive Officer for Immigration Review (EOIR) was published at 65 FR 39,513 (6/27/00). The rule imposes sanctions for frivolous conduct in immigration proceedings and details the mechanism for investigating complaints against immigration practitioners. The reviewing body for disciplinary determinations has been changed: this responsibility now belongs to the BIA, not the Disciplinary Committee.

[¶3310] [NEW] Visa Categories

Two statutes from 2000 affect family-related immigration. P.L. 106-279, the Intercountry Adoption Act of 2000, authorizes the United States to implement the Hague Convention on Protection of Children and Co-Operation in Respect of Intercountry Adoption. The Department of State serves as the Central Authority for liaison under the Hague Convention. Congress found it necessary to subscribe to this treaty to control abuses in international adoption, such as exorbitant fees to "facilitators," adoption of children who are not available for adoption, failure to prepare adoptive families to carry out their responsibilities, and failure to disclose the medical condition of potential adoptees.

The Child Citizenship Act of 2000, P.L. 106-395, amends INA §320 to make automatic U.S. citizenship available to children under 18, when at least one of the parents is a U.S. citizen by birth or naturalization, if the children are in the United States in the legal and physical custody of the citizen parent, pursuant to lawful admission for permanent residence. A citizen parent can also get a certificate of naturalization for a child born outside the United States who normally lives outside the United States, but who is temporarily lawfully present within the U.S.

The International Patient Act of 2000, P.L. 106-406, amends the INA (at 8 USC §1229c(a)(2)) to set up a three-year pilot project. Under this program the Attorney General has discretion for humanitarian purposes to extend the period for voluntary departure of non-immigrants who were admitted under the INA §217 visa waiver program, if the individuals require medical treatment (and the treatment will not be provided by Medicaid or other U.S. public benefit programs).

[¶3315] Refugees and Asylum

The Ninth Circuit reversed the BIA and granted review to a Colombian woman who had been persecuted by guerillas because she belonged to an anti-guerilla peasant group. When she was still in Colombia, she complained to the police about the harassment, but the police were allied with the guerillas. A reasonable factfinder would have to conclude that guerillas persecuted her because of her political opinions.[1]

Another Ninth Circuit case involves a Filipino who applied for asylum, claiming persecution by Communist guerillas, after serving as an undercover anti-drug police officer and informant to police about guerilla activities. He received death threats and was shot at before eventually moving to the United States. Although the BIA believed his testimony, it said there was no proof of future persecution because of changed conditions in his home country.

The Ninth Circuit ruled[2] that the BIA erred by making the petitioner prove well-founded fear of future persecution; he had already proved past persecution and so was entitled to a presumption that he could continue to fear future persecution. The State Department profile can only corroborate, not disprove, future fear. Also, BIA had to do an individual analysis of the effect of changed conditions on the petitioner.

A Guatemalan immigrant testified that he suffered beatings and threats because of his status as vice president of a political party.[3] The

Ninth Circuit treats a specific death threat as persecution or grounds for a well-founded fear of future persecution, if there is reason to believe that the threat is serious. Corroboration of credible testimony by an asylum-seeker is not required.

Asylum was denied to a Fijian who was beaten and sexually attacked by soldiers, whose father was arrested and severely beaten, and who was forced to state that she would convert to Christianity after being dragged out of the temple of her own faith by soldiers. The Immigration Judge, as affirmed by the BIA, did not feel that these experiences rose to the level of persecution,[4] and conditions in the country have changed since those times. The Ninth Circuit agreed that Fijian conditions were now different enough to rebut her fear of persecution. Nor did she qualify for special humanitarian relief, because her suffering was not great enough to overcome the change in conditions.

Another case brought by a Fijian, this time an ethnic Indian applying for political asylum based on racial persecution, was also denied by the INS, on the basis that all minority groups in Fiji were at risk for the same reason.[5] But harassment of other members of the same group does not detract from the asylum petition, and specific instances of individual harassment can still give rise to a fear of persecution, even if the victimized ethnic population is a large rather than a small one.

In the Second Circuit view, an asylum seeker (or person seeking withholding of deportation) has to present whatever corroborating evidence he or she would reasonably be expected to introduce—or to explain failure to furnish corroboration.[6] In contrast, the Ninth Circuit finds credible testimony from the alien automatically sufficient, even absent corroboration.

The Ninth Circuit has held that gay Mexican men with female sexual identities are an identifiable social group at risk of sexual assault by police in their home country. Therefore, they are entitled to asylum based on a well-founded fear of persecution.[7] The First, Third, and Seventh Circuits define "social groups" more narrowly, requiring immutable common characteristics fundamental to identity. In contrast, the Ninth will allow a social group to be defined by voluntary associational relationships.

An alien who is "firmly resettled" in a country other than the U.S. and his or her country of origin is not entitled to asylum in the United States. The key factor is whether any form of permanent resident status is available in that country, not the totality of the alien's circumstances in that environment.[8]

See 65 FR 76, 121 (12/6/00) for a Final Rule on asylum procedures, prescribing the factors in exercising discretion when past persecution has been shown but fear of future persecution might not be well-grounded, or where the applicant could escape persecution by moving within the home country.

[¶3330] Employment of Immigrants

The EEOC issued enforcement guidance dealing with employment discrimination against undocumented workers: see *http://www.eeoc.gov/docs/undoc.html*. The agency's contention is that undocumented workers are nevertheless entitled to back pay, hiring, and reinstatement as remedies for employment discrimination (under Title VII, the ADEA, ADA, or EPA) as long as this can be granted without direct conflict with IRCA and other immigration laws.

According to the Commonwealth Court of Pennsylvania, despite their lack of lawful employment status, illegal immigrant workers are nonetheless "employees" entitled to receive Worker's Compensation benefits for job-related injuries.[9]

P.L. 106-313, the American Competitiveness in the Twenty-First Century Act of 2000, keeps the number of H-1B visas at 195,000 a year for fiscal 2001, 2002, and 2003. This limit does not apply to employees of institutions of higher education, their affiliate nonprofit entities, nonprofit research centers, or government research organizations. This law also makes H-1B visas more "portable," by allowing a new employer to file a new petition to re-employ a person who entered this country to work for someone else. P.L. 106-311 increases the fee for the petition to employ an H-1B worker from $500 to $1,000, for petitions filed on or after December 17, 2000.[10]

[¶3350] [NEW] Naturalization

Under the Immigration and Naturalization Act, 8 USC §1421(c), the District Court has the power of de novo review of denial of naturalization applications. There is no time limit given in the statute. The Tenth Circuit struck down an INS regulation (8 CFR §336.9(b)) that imposes a 120-day time limit, because the INA does not give the INS the power to limit the judicial power of review of administrative decisions about naturalization.[11]

Another INS regulation, 8 CFR §340.1, was found to be invalid by the Ninth Circuit, which found that giving the U.S. Attorney General (acting through the INS) the power to reopen naturalization proceedings and revoke naturalization is an impermissible statutory interpretation that lacks foundation in the underlying statute.[12] In this reading, naturalization can be revoked only if the U.S. attorney litigates in the District Court; administrative revocation is not available.

[¶3360] Border Patrols and Other INS Searches

In late 1999, the Ninth Circuit decided a class action against U.S. Border Patrol agents.[13] The case arose when the plaintiffs were stopped along the Mexican border in Arizona. The plaintiffs sought class-wide equitable relief for Hispanic individuals stopped on Arizona highways at night.

The District Court, affirmed by the Ninth Circuit, awarded summary judgment to the government as to the plaintiffs' lack of standing to seek equitable relief that would alter border patrol practices. There was no showing of irreparable injury. Plaintiffs were only stopped once, with no proof of risk of future stops—a showing insufficient to require the patrol to alter its procedures. Given the lack of proof of future injury, the claim for declaratory relief was unripe, and systemic injunctive relief is not available for alleged injuries to unnamed members of a proposed class.

[¶3370] Removal

A December 21, 2000 Final Rule amends the INS Regulations with respect to aliens whose removal has been ordered. It creates a uniform review process for detention of criminal, inadmissible, or other aliens who are the subject of a final administrative order of removal, deportation, or exclusion, but who are still in the United States after the 90-day removal period has elapsed. The Final Rule, 65 FR 80, 281 (12/21/00), gives INS officials the power to release aliens from custody or issue stays of removal. However, the Final Rule eliminates the BIA's appellate role in final custody order determinations.

About a month later, another Final Rule was published (66 FR 6436, 1/22/01), this time instituting a uniform procedure for applying AEDPA so that aliens who are the subject of deportation proceedings commenced before 4/24/96 can apply for discretionary relief from deportation under INA §212(c), although those convicted of certain crimes (such as aggravated felonies, drug and firearm offenses) after AEDPA's effective date are precluded from obtaining discretionary relief.

The BIA is not bound by the Court of Appeals' interpretation of INA §101(a)(43) definition of "aggravated felony" for purposes of sentence enhancement when the agency implements civil immigration laws within the Circuit.[14]

The respondent in this case entered the United States as a refugee from Vietnam. In 1992, he pleaded guilty to cocaine possession, then violated his probation and was sentenced to five years' imprisonment. At the removal hearing, the Immigration Judge decided he was guilty of an aggravated felony, analogous to a drug trafficking crime, and not eligible for any relief from removal.

However, for immigration purposes, the BIA says that a state drug offense that is analogous to an 18 USC §924(c)(2) offense punishable as a felony under federal law is an aggravated felony, but a state drug offense that is not analogous to a federal felony is not an aggravated felony. Simple possession would have been a federal misdemeanor, so the defendant was not convicted of an aggravated felony and was not removable.

Even excludable aliens are protected by the Fifth Amendment, and substantive due process is violated by indefinite detention of aliens by the INS after they have completed a prison sentence in the U.S. when their country of origin refuses to take them back.[15]

In 2000, the Second Circuit joined the Third and Ninth Circuits in holding that aliens who are removable because of certain drug offenses are entitled to invoke habeas corpus in the District Court to challenge the legality of deportation—although the Fifth and Eleventh Circuits disagree.[16]

According to the First Circuit, habeas jurisdiction under 28 USC §2241 survives both the IIRIRA transitional and final rules.[17]

Under 28 USC §2243, a writ of habeas corpus is directed to the person having custody of the detainee. For a detained alien pending deportation, this would be the District Director of the INS Service Center where the alien is detained, not the U.S. Attorney General.[18]

In April 2001, the California Supreme Court permitted immigrants to raise claims of ineffective assistance of counsel if they assert that they were inadequately informed of the consequences of pleading guilty to criminal charges within the United States—even though judges are also obligated to inform non-citizen defendants that a guilty plea is likely to result in deportation.[19]

[¶3370.1] [NEW] Discretionary Relief

The Second Circuit allowed a person who pleaded guilty to a crime before the effective date of IIRIRA to apply for discretionary relief from exclusion, on the theory that his guilty plea was premised on an assessment of the consequences of the plea at a particular point in time.[20]

[¶3370.2] [NEW] Appeals

The 90-day deadline imposed by 8 CFR §3.23(b)(1) for reopening deportation proceedings is not jurisdictional. It is subject to equitable tolling for ineffective assistance of counsel—as long as the alien is diligent in pursuing the case throughout the tolling period.[21]

ENDNOTES

1. *Acosta v. INS,* 1999 US App Lexis 34503 (9th Cir. 1999).
2. *Ramirez de Guzman v. INS,* 1999 US App Lexis 34507 (9th Cir. 1999).
3. *Massella v. INS,* 2000 US App Lexis 1713 (9th Cir. 9/13/99).
4. *Kumar v. INS,* 204 F.3d 931 (9th Cir. 3/2/00).
5. *Krishna v. INS,* 2000 US App Lexis 3280 (9th Cir. 3/1/00).
6. *Diallo v. INS*, 232 F.3d 279 (2nd Cir. 2000).
7. *Hernandez-Montiel v. INS*, 69 LW 1134 (9th Cir. 8/24/00).
8. *Abdille v. Ashcroft*, 69 LW 1552 (3rd Cir. 3/7/01).
9. *The Reinforced Earth Co. v. Workers' Compensation Appeal Board,* discussed in Danielle Rodier, "Illegal Aliens Can Receive Workers' Compensation Benefits," *Legal Intelligencer* 4/14/00, *http://www.law.com.* However, the earlier case of *Granados v. Windson Development Corp.,* 257 Va. 103, 509 S.E.2d 290 (1999) reaches the opposite conclusion.
10. For a discussion of INS requirements for employers of H-1B workers, see Daniel C. Horne and Sarnata M.B. Reynolds, "Getting a Visa's Half the Battle," *Natl'l L.J.* 4/23/01 p. B15.
11. *Nagahi v. INS,* 219 F.3d 1166 (10th Cir. 2000).
12. *Gorbach v. Reno,* 219 F.3d 1087 (9th Cir. 2000).
13. *Hodgers-Durgin v. De La Vina,* 1999 US App Lexis 33093 (9th Cir. 12/21/99).
14. *Matter of KVD,* 1999 BIA Lexis 49 (BIA 1999).

15. *Rosales-Garcia v. Holland*, 238 F.3d 704 (6th Cir. 2001).
16. *Calcano-Martinez v. INS*, 69 LW 1153 (2nd Cir. 9/1/00).
17. *Goncalves v. Reno*, 144 F.3d 110 (1st Cir. 1998) [transitional] and *Mahadeo v. Reno*, 226 F.3d 3 (1st Cir. 2000) [final].
18. *Vasquez v. Reno*, 233 F.3d 688 (1st Cir. 2000).
19. *In re Resendiz*, 01 C.D.O.S. 2643 (Cal.Sup. 4/2/01), discussed in Sonia Giordani, "California Justices Split on Advice for Immigrants," *The Recorder* 4/3/01, available on law.com.
20. *St. Cyr v. INS*, 229 F.3d 406 (2nd Cir. 2000).
21. *Iavorski v. INS*, 232 F.3d 124 (2nd Cir. 2000).

$$\boxed{\P4100}$$

Personal Income Tax
and Tax Planning

[¶4101]

Tax changes in 1999 and 2000 were rather modest, but 2001 brought epochal changes in personal income taxation, including a very large tax cut.

For 2001 tax changes before the Economic Growth Tax Reform and Reconciliation Act (EGTRA), see Revenue Procedure 2001-13, 2001-9 IRB 752. EGTRA (in addition to major changes in pension and IRA taxation and dramatic estate tax changes, discussed in the appropriate chapters of this Supplement) cut tax brackets, offered some degree of marriage penalty relief, and offered tax assistance for the costs of secondary and college education.

[¶4101.2 Tax Brackets]

In the years 2000 and 2001, there were four personal income tax brackets: 15%, 28%, 31%, and the top bracket at 39.6%.

EGTRA cut taxes somewhat, but increased the complexity of the system by adding a new bracket (10%) at the bottom of the tax structure and gradually reducing the other brackets over a period of six years. (The importance of tax cuts to EGTRA can be assessed by the fact that the tax bracket changes are §101 of the legislation.)

At first, the 10% bracket applies to the first $6,000 of taxable income (single persons), $10,000 (heads of household), or $12,000 (joint returns), but the amount of income subject to the 10% bracket will increase over time: $7,000 for single filers, $14,000 for joint returns for 2008, at which time the amount of income subject to the 10% bracket will be indexed for inflation.

EGTRA also provides a one-time credit for the year 2001, to represent the phasing in of the 10% bracket. Most taxpayers received refund checks ($300 for single persons, $600 for married persons filing jointly) in the summer and fall of 2001.

For the period from July 1, 2001 to the end of 2003, the tax brackets will be 10%, 15%, 27%, 30%, 35%, and 38.6%. For calendar 2004 and 2005, the brackets will be 10%, 15%, 26%, 29%, 34%, and 37.6%. For

2006 until 2011 (when all EGTRA provisions sunset), the brackets will be 10%, 15%, 25%, 28%, 33%, and 35%.

Pre-EGTRA law provided for a reduction in most types of itemized deductions for high-income taxpayers (IRC §68). The 2001 definition for the phase-out was income of $132,950 for a joint return or $66,475 for married persons filing separate returns. EGTRA §102 provides additional tax relief for high-income filers by phasing out the limitation on itemized deductions between 2006 and 2009. In 2009, the limitation is repealed— but will be restored in 2011 when EGTRA sunsets.

Another pre-EGTRA provision, IRC §151(d)(3), reduced the personal exemption of high-income taxpayers below its normal level of $2,900 per taxpayer, spouse, or dependent. EGTRA §103 phases out the reduction in the personal exemption, starting in 2006, until high-income taxpayers will be entitled to claim an unreduced personal exemption for the year 2010.

EGTRA §301 provides some relief from the "marriage penalty" (tendency of high-income joint returns for couples with roughly equal income to have a greater tax liability than the spouses would have if they were unmarried). For one thing, the standard deduction for a joint return is lower than the sum of two standard deductions on single persons' returns.

For tax years beginning after 12/31/04, the standard deduction will be increased until 2009, at which point the standard deduction on a joint return will be exactly twice the standard deduction on a single person's return. However, this provision does not affect the numerous taxpayers who itemize their deductions instead of claiming the standard deduction.

For tax years beginning after 12/31/04, EGTRA §302 provides additional marriage penalty relief by making the 15% tax bracket available to joint return filers at a higher level of income; for 2008-2010, the 15% bracket for married joint filers will include twice as much income as the 15% bracket for single filers. Also see EGTRA §303 amending IRC §32 with respect to increases in the earned income credit for low-income parents who are also married and filing joint returns.

[¶4102] [NEW] Other EGTRA Changes

In addition to changes in brackets and treatment of the standard deduction, EGTRA changes the Internal Revenue Code in many respects, especially tax breaks for parents (related to education and otherwise).

EGTRA includes a provision dealing with the Alternative Minimum Tax (§701, amending IRC §55), which gives joint-return filers and heads of household an additional $4,000 AMT exemption amount and single persons and married persons filing separate returns an additional AMT exemption of $2,000. Note, however, that this provision takes effect for tax years beginning after 12/31/00, but is only applicable to tax years that begin before 1/1/04.

Even when the additional exemption is in place, the number of taxpayers subject to AMT will increase significantly. (One estimate is that six times as many taxpayers will be subject to AMT by the time EGTRA sunsets as before it was enacted.) This is because the new 10% bracket will reduce the ordinary income tax obligation of many taxpayers to the point that the AMT is triggered.

It should also be noted that, although low-income taxpayers will benefit from the new lower bracket, EGTRA does not reduce FICA taxes, which for many working poor people represent a larger obligation than their income taxes.

Tax Relief for Parents

The "child tax credit" of $500 per qualifying child (IRC §24) is increased by EGTRA to $1,000. However, the increased credit does not take effect at once—instead, the higher credit level is phased in over the 10 years from 1/1/00 to EGTRA's sunset date. (For 2001–2004, the credit will be $600 per child; it will be $700 per child for 2005–2008, $800 for 2009, and $1,000 for 2010.)

EGTRA §202 amends IRC §§23 and 137 [effective for tax years beginning after 12/31/02] to make the adoption credit permanent for all children. (Pre-EGTRA law eliminated the credit except for adoption of special-needs children.) The maximum credit is $10,000 of out-of-pocket expenses (for either an ordinary or a special-needs adoption), although the credit is phased down for high-income taxpayers and for taxpayers with modified Adjusted Gross Income over $190,000. Up to $10,000 in adoption assistance provided by an employer under an adoption assistance employee benefit plan can be excluded from the employee's taxable income.

IRC §21 allows a tax credit for some of the costs that a person encounters in paying for care of a child or handicapped dependent, so that the taxpayer can maintain a paid job. For tax years beginning after 12/31/02,

EGTRA §204 increases the amount of the credit and makes it available to taxpayers with somewhat higher income than under prior law. The maximum post-EGTRA dependent care tax credit is 35% of $3,000 in qualifying expenses for one dependent or of $6,000 in qualifying expenses for two or more dependents. Taxpayers with AGI over $43,000 are only entitled to a maximum credit of 20% of the allowable expenses.

To create an incentive for employers to assist employees with their child care needs, EGTRA §205 adds new IRC §45D, giving employers a tax credit of 25% of expenses for direct provision of child care (e.g., by maintaining a day care center) and 10% of expenses for providing employees with information about their child care options. However, no matter how much the employer spends for this purpose, the maximum credit is a comparatively modest $150,000 a year. This provision is effective for employers' tax years (which are not necessarily calendar years) that begin after 12/31/01.

Education Provisions

It's a commonplace of financial planning that paying for children's college education is one of the major economic challenges that the family faces. For many families, private elementary and secondary education must also be paid for. EGTRA includes several provisions providing at least some relief for taxpayers who are financing their own or family members' education.

For tax years beginning after 12/31/01, taxpayers can make contributions of $2,000 per beneficiary per year (rather than the earlier $500) to "Education IRAs," which are accounts used exclusively to pay for a designated beneficiary's (e.g., child or grandchild) qualified education expenses. In addition to college costs, qualified education expenses can include elementary and secondary education expenses for a special-needs child (EGTRA §401; IRC §530). However, like many tax provisions, the benefits to higher-income taxpayers phase down or out.

EGTRA §402 amends Code §529 to increase the scope of state-run programs under which family members can invest in advance for the anticipated costs of education.

The IRC §127 provision, under which employees are entitled to exclude from taxable income education expenses paid by their employer as an employee benefit, has been amended many times. The current version, under EGTRA §411, makes the exclusion from income permanent (previous provisions had expiration dates, and had to be renewed by Congress) and extends it to both undergraduate and graduate education, with respect to academic courses that begin after 12/31/01.

Taxpayers who have student loan obligations (a very large group of people!) can deduct interest paid on qualified education loans after 12/31/01 if their income does not exceed $65,000 (single person) or $130,000 (joint return) according to EGTRA §412.

The general pre-EGTRA rule was that the expenses of a taxpayer's own education might be deductible under IRC §162 if they enhance the taxpayer's ability to perform an existing profession (but not expenses of qualifying for a new profession). Furthermore, taxpayers could qualify for two tax credits, HOPE and Lifetime Learning, for certain college and graduate school expenses. EGTRA §431 modifies these rules by giving taxpayers with AGI up to $65,000 (single return)/$130,000 (joint return) a deduction of up to $4,000 (tax years 2004 and 2005) for certain post-secondary education expenses—although the deduction cannot be claimed in the same year as a HOPE or Lifetime Learning credit for the same student. (It might, however, be permissible for a taxpaying parent to take a deduction for his or her own tuition expenses and a credit for expenses of a spouse or child.)

For the year 2000, the tax brackets remain unchanged at 15%, 28%, 31%, topping out at 39.6%. These charts compare figures for the years 1999 and 2000:

[¶4105.1] Electronic Filing

In FS-2000-03, the IRS authorized the use of a credit card to make a tax payment associated with an automatic extension of the time to file. (Of course, the automatic extension does not extend the time to pay the tax liability.) As of March 1, 2000, the IRS has accepted credit card payments for estimated tax as well, and a preauthorized direct debit can be used to satisfy liability under a balance-due tax return.

Credit card charges can be made by phone to an American Express, Discover, or MasterCard, and provisions are made for taxpayers to file their returns as soon as they are complete, but defer phoning in the credit card payment authorization until the due date of the return. (The IRS benefits by getting returns faster, thus speeding up processing.)

[¶4120] Income Items

Code §108 allows an "insolvent" debtor to exclude discharged indebtedness from income. In the Ninth Circuit view[1] a contingent liability can be included in the determination of insolvency, but only if the taxpayer can show that it was more likely than not that the contingent liability would become an actual one. Insolvency is defined as liabilities in excess of the fair market value of assets, but Code §108 does not define liabilities.

The taxpayers in this case were general partners in a partnership. A bank forgave a $1.4 million nonrecourse partnership note. They reported their distributive share of the discharge of indebtedness, but excluded it from income because they said that they were insolvent before the partnership realized the income. They took this position because they were potentially liable as guarantors, although the bank made no effort to collect from them.

According to the Ninth Circuit, to make use of §108, the taxpayer must prove by a preponderance of evidence that he or she will be called upon to pay the amounts described as liabilities. The taxpayers in this case failed to prove that, because their obligation as guarantors was contingent on bankruptcy, and they didn't prove that bankruptcy was a likely outcome.

Withdrawals that a taxpayer took from his IRA to pay amounts owed to his ex-wife under their divorce judgment constituted taxable income for the IRA holder.[2] Because the taxpayer withdrew the money and only paid it out later, the withdrawal did not qualify under §408(d)(6) as a transfer of the IRA incident to divorce.

A married taxpayer from Arizona, who did not cohabit with his wife, but was not legally separated from her, had community income under local law, and therefore was entitled to income splitting for federal income tax purposes.[3]

[¶4120.1] Taxation of Damages

Because a corporation's settlement with a fired staff attorney for release of the ADEA and all other tort and contract claims did not refer to any specific claim or establish an allocation among them, the amount paid under the release was taxable income and not entitled to exclusion under Code §104.[4]

A pesticide manufacturer's payment to an orchid farmer was in settlement of negligence and products liability claims rather than personal injury claims, and therefore the §104 exclusion was not available.[5]

This was a particularly lively issue for the Tax Court in 2000. In a Memo decision from May, the full amount received by a university professor whose tenure was bought out to settle an ADEA claim had to be included in gross income. It was not received because of a "personal injury," because this characterization does not apply to ADEA claims, and the agreement failed to allocate between state-law contract and tort damages and the employment claim.[6]

There was a dispute about the handling of an incapacitated person's trust, which was settled when the beneficiary's children agreed to pay him $2,000 a week to settle his claims. According to the Tax Court, the determinative issue is not what claims are filed, but what claims are settled. Therefore, even though a RICO claim was never filed (and probably could not have succeeded), the nature of the claims essentially sounded in tort (stress, emotional distress, damaged health) and, therefore, the weekly payments could be excluded from the father's gross income.[7]

The entire sum received as sexual harassment damages from a pre-CRA '91 case was includible in the recipient's income. The damages were not personal injury damages (the fact that Missouri recognizes torts of assault and battery is irrelevant in a federal employment discrimination case).

Even the part allocated to the plaintiff's attorney under a contingent fee agreement constituted taxable income for the taxpayer, in that the attorney's lien in the claim did not constitute an ownership or proprietary interest in the cause of action. Nor was the attorney's lien superior to the government's right of set-off against the taxpayer. In fact, the entire amount, including the contingent fee, was subject to Alternative Minimum Tax.[8]

Another theory is that the contingent fee must be included in the client's gross income, under the assignment of income doctrine (i.e., taxpayers cannot escape taxation by assigning income to which they are entitled)—but the fee operates as a miscellaneous itemized deduction.[9]

In contrast, the Fifth Circuit upheld tax penalties imposed on a person who settled a defamation action and did not include the proceeds in income, because reliance on the advice of an attorney and CPA about the tax consequences of the settlement was not reasonable (the attorney said he was not a tax lawyer and recommended getting tax advice). However, the part of the settlement that represented the attorney's contingent fee was not gross income for tax purposes.[10]

[¶4130] [NEW] Capital Gains Tax

During the supplement period, the special extra-low capital gains rates under TRA '97 took effect. For assets purchased after 12/31/00 and held for at least five years, capital gains will be taxed at only 18% (or 8% for low-bracket taxpayers).

In October 2000, the IRS proposed Regs explaining some issues about the IRC §121 exclusion of capital gains on the sale of the taxpayer's principal residence.[11] Under the proposal, where the debtor-taxpayer satisfies the ownership and use tests, the Chapter 7 or Chapter 11 bankruptcy estate will also qualify for exclusion of gains. Taxpayers can elect to apply §121 to the sale of remainder interest in a principal residence, not just sale of the entire property. The exclusion can be taken in part if the taxpayer does not satisfy the durational requirements, if the taxpayer has to leave the principal residence for health reasons, or if the taxpayer has to relocate for work.

Furthermore, for a taxpayer who resides on two properties, the one that is used more is the "principal residence." For properties partially used as a residence and partially for business (e.g., a property containing a home office or a property encompassing both personal residence and rental apartment(s)), only gain relative to the residential portion is excludable, and depreciation adjustments taken after May 6, 1997 also affect the calculation.

A Tax Court memorandum decision from early 2001 holds that a divorced taxpayer is not responsible for tax on his share of capital gains on a former marital home that was allotted to him in the divorce decree, because the property was titled in his wife's name, not in his or in joint name. Therefore, he was not liable for penalties for substantial underpayment either. The court concluded that the husband did not have an ownership interest in the property, even though it was "marital property" in that it was purchased by one spouse during the marriage, and he was allocated half of the sale proceeds as part of the divorce process.[12]

[¶4150] Deductions

Under T.D. 8864, 2000-7 IRB 614, a receipt or other documentation is not required to substantiate a travel and expense deduction for an item other than lodging, and that does not exceed $75 (the prior limit was $25). All lodging expenditures for trips away from home must be documented. For the year 2000, the mileage allowance for business use of a personal automobile (whether owned or leased by the taxpayer) is 32.5 cents per mile.

Notice 99-59, 1999-52 IRB 761 warns taxpayers and their representatives about disallowance of losses on abusive tax shelters, such as partnerships that contribute cash to foreign corporations in exchange for their common stock, followed by transactions that reduce the value of the common stock to $0.

[¶4150.2] Classes of Itemized Deductions

An independent contractor insurance agent's relationship with an insurance company was terminated. He was awarded punitive damages against the insurer with respect to unpaid commissions. The IRS characterized his litigation costs as Schedule A miscellaneous itemized deductions, subject to a floor of 2% of AGI. But, because of the nexus with the taxpayer's business, the Tax Court treated it as a Schedule C deduction,[13] and drew no distinction between compensatory and punitive damages. However, the Tax Court held that the IRS position would have been correct in the case of an employee, because then the expense would have been an unreimbursed business expense relating to the performance of services as an employee.

[¶4150.4.1] Home Office Deduction

Although the bedroom in a floor covering contractor's home was used exclusively and regularly for business purposes, it nevertheless failed to qualify for the home office deduction, because the floor covering services were performed at various job sites, which precluded the home office from operating as his principal place of business.[14]

No home office deduction was available for a truck driver; although he used part of his home to do paperwork, nevertheless his principal place of business was the truck itself, not the space asserted as a home office.[15]

[¶4195] [NEW] Tax Issues in Bankruptcy

Under Bankruptcy Code §523(a)(1)(A), income taxes for which a return was due in the three years before the filing of the petition are not dischargeable, but other taxes are dischargeable. According to the Sixth Circuit, a prior Chapter 13 petition does not automatically toll the three-year period for a taxpayer now in Chapter 7. However, the federal government is entitled to seek tolling on the basis of misconduct or manipulation of the bankruptcy system by the debtor.[16]

According to the First Circuit—although other Circuits disagree—interest on post-petition tax obligations in a Chapter 7 case takes fifth priority; it is not a first-priority administration expense.[17]

The taxpayer's IRC §172 election to waive NOL carryovers is irrevocable—that is, the taxpayer cannot revoke it; but if the election has the effect of a Bankruptcy Code §548 fraudulent transfer, the trustee can avoid the election.[18]

ENDNOTES

1. *Merkel v CIR*, 192 F.3d 844(9th Cir. 1999).
2. *Czepiel v. CIR*, TC Memo 1999-289 (1999). Similarly, *Jones v. Comm'r*, TC Memo 2000-219 (7/20/00), requires a divorcing husband to include in income the $68,000 that resulted when he cashed out his IRA and paid the money to his wife, based on a divorce-related agreement to transfer the IRA interest to her. But because of the cash-out, and because the wife did not place the funds into another IRA, the entire amount was not merely income for the husband but a premature distribution subject to the 10% penalty.
3. *Layman II v. CIR*, TC Memo 1999-218 (1999).
4. *Sherman v. CIR*, TC Memo 1999-202 (1999).
5. *Henry v. CIR*, TC Memo 1999-205 (1999).
6. *Reisman v. Comm'r*, TC Memo 2000-173 (5/25/00).
7. *Estate of Schoeneman*, TC Memo 2000-161 (5/18/00).
8. *Hukkanen-Campbell v. Commissioner*, TC Memo 2000-180 (6/12/00). A similar analysis about the attorney's lien resulted in inclusion of the contingent fee in the client's taxable income in *Coady v. CIR*, 2000-1 USTC ¶50,528 (9th Cir. 6/14/00).
9. *Kenseth v. Comm'r*, 114 TC No. 26 (5/24/00).
10. *Srivastava v. Comm'r*, 220 F.3d 353 (5th Cir. 7/21/00).
11. REG-105235-99, 65 FR 60,136 (10/10/00).
12. *Suhr v. CIR*, TC Memo 2001-28 (2/8/01).
13. *Guill v. CIR*, 112 TC No. 22 (1999).
14. *Cole v. CIR*, TC Memo 1999-207 (1999).
15. *Duncan v. Comm'r*, TC Memo 2000-269 (8/24/00).
16. *Palmer v. U.S.*, 219 F.3d 580 (6th Cir. 2000).
17. *U.S. v. Yellin*, 251 B.R. 174 (1st Cir. 2000).
18. *U.S. v. Sims*, 218 F.3d 948 (9th Cir. 2000).

Tax Enforcement

[¶4310.3] IRS Summonses

Taxpayers are not entitled to notice when the IRS issues a summons to a bank in an effort to collect taxes (even if other purposes are also present). Nor do the taxpayers have a right to petition to quash the summons.[1]

The general rule under Code §7609(a)(1) is that the IRS has to notify anyone whose financial records are sought under a third-party summons, and the recipients of the notice have the right to ask the District Court to quash the summons. However, §7609(c)(2)(D) provides an exception where the summons aims at collecting an assessment or judgment. In this case, the taxpayers alleged that the summons was investigative, not merely aimed at collection.

But the Seventh Circuit, like the Tenth, applies the §7609(c)(2)(D) exception to all collection summonses, even if they also have additional purposes. The taxpayers contended that the exception should not be applied to them because the underlying tax assessment was made against a partnership, not the taxpayers as individuals, but in the Seventh Circuit view, the exception is applicable to any assessed tax liability, without limitation to cases in which the third-party summons targets the taxpayer subject to the assessment.

Under T.D. 8939, 2001-12 IRB 899, the taxpayer's "last known address" for mailing notices is generally the address given on the taxpayer's most recently filed and properly processed federal tax return—unless the taxpayer gives the IRS clear and concise notification of a different address. Revenue Procedure 2001-18, 2001-8 IRB 708 says that a taxpayer wishing to indicate a change of address should send the notification to the IRS Service Center for the old address or to the Customer Service Division in the local area office. IRS Form 8822 operates as an acceptable clear and concise notification of the address change.

[¶4330.5] [NEW] Compromises Between Taxpayer and IRS

T.D. 8922, 2001-6 IRB 508 contains Temporary and Proposed Regulations as to when a taxpayer who settles an IRS case by making a qualified offer is a "prevailing party" entitled to recover reasonable administrative and litigation costs from the federal government.

The taxpayer prevails if the offer lowers the taxpayer's liability (as compared with the last qualified offer). The taxpayer must exhaust administrative remedies; must satisfy the Code §7430(c)(4)(A)(ii) net worth requirements; and must not have prolonged the litigation unreasonably. The award is limited to reasonable costs incurred on or after the date of the last qualified offer, with respect to adjustments included in the last qualified offer and litigated to a judicial determination.

[¶4350] The Collection Process

As a result of the automatic stay in bankruptcy, a tax lien can't attach to an asset that a debtor inherits in the course of the proceeding, although a tax lien that is perfected pre-petition usually attaches to after-acquired assets by operation of law. The bankruptcy trustee cited Bankruptcy Code §362(a)(5) automatically staying any "act" to perfect liens against a debtor's property, to the extent that they secure pre-filing claims. The IRS said that its lien attached to the property by operation of law, so no "act" was performed, but the Fourth Circuit disagreed.[2]

When a bankruptcy reorganization plan fails to be confirmed, and if the IRS imposes a proper levy, then the money that the debtors deposited into the reorganization plan goes directly to the IRS instead of being returned to the debtors.[3] In other words, the IRS levy provisions (Code §6331) outweigh the Bankruptcy Code provisions (at §1326(a)(2)). The Ninth Circuit also ruled that it was appropriate for the IRS to serve notice of levy on the bankruptcy trustee instead of the debtors, because service is proper on any third party who has possession of the debtor's property or has a duty to the debtor.

Taxpayers received a timely notice of deficiency that did not have a date stamped in the "Last Day to File a Petition with the U.S. Tax Court" box. The taxpayers nevertheless filed a timely tax court petition. They claimed that the notice was invalid because of the omission of this date.

They therefore claimed that the statute of limitations for collection was not tolled, and the IRS was too late to collect the taxes. However, the Tax Court said that the formally defective notice was nevertheless timely, and the taxpayers were not prejudiced by the omission of the date; therefore, the statute of limitations was tolled and the deficiency could be collected.[4]

The Ninth Circuit required the IRS to do an employee-by-employee audit of a restaurant to determine liability for unreported tip income; it is not acceptable to calculate the liability by extrapolating the rate of tips on credit cards to the restaurant's gross receipts.[5]

The IRS could collect estate tax liability from a transferee of estate assets, on the basis of a notice of deficiency sent to the estate 26 days before the statute of limitations ran on the assessment. The estate filed a Tax Court petition; therefore, under Code §6503(a)(1), the limitations period was suspended from the mailing of the notice of deficiency until 60 days after the Tax Court decision became final. Subsequently, because the notice of transferee liability satisfied the one-year limitations period of Code §6901(c), the transferee was liable for the tax, since he had unclean hands and was on notice of the estate tax liability when he received the property.[6]

A criminal fine imposed by a District Court for tax evasion is not credited against the civil fraud penalty imposed by the IRS.[7] Although the IRS reduces civil deficiencies to account for restitution, this criminal fine was punitive, not restitutionary, in nature. Because the criminal and civil penalties serve different purposes, they can't be offset.

[¶4350.2] [NEW] Collection by Levy

The IRS notified a taxpayer of intention to levy with respect to income taxes for the years 1991-1993. The taxpayer's IRS appeal was unsuccessful. The Tax Court says that, unless irregularities in the assessment are shown, the Appeals Officer can properly rely on Form 4346 (Certificate of Assessments and Payments) to determine what taxes were assessed. The taxpayer is not entitled to subpoena and examine witnesses during the IRS Appeals Office hearing.[8]

In a Third Circuit case from 2000, an employer corporation claimed that the taxpayer defrauded the corporation (and failed as well to pay his taxes). The corporation brought a wrongful levy action against the IRS, claiming that the levied funds (the employee's pension) should be paid to the corporation as restitution. But the statute of limitations on third-party wrongful levy actions is jurisdictional and is not subject to equitable tolling, because the IRS should be kept free of belated actions filed by creditors of taxpayers.[9]

[¶4350.4] [NEW] [Bankruptcy Issues]

There is a circuit split as to whether the three-year statute of limitations (tax claims are not dischargeable if the return was due during the three years pre-petition) is automatically tolled in a second bankruptcy proceeding to account for the prior bankruptcy proceeding. No circuit rules out tolling entirely; the question is whether, as the First, Third, Seventh, Eight, Ninth, and Tenth Circuits say, tolling is automatic, or whether it can be granted on equitable grounds on a case-by-case basis.[10]

The Western District of Texas held in 2000 that the government could not confirm a real estate foreclosure that was ordered to satisfy tax liens arising out of a default judgment, because the taxpayer filed a bankruptcy petition on the morning of the foreclosure sale itself. In this reading, Texas requires a valid foreclosure sale to divest the owner's interest in the property; an order of foreclosure is not enough. Because the taxpayer still owned the property when the bankruptcy petition was filed, the foreclosure could not be confirmed. However, the District Court remanded the case to see if the automatic stay should be lifted on the basis of the taxpayer's bad-faith bankruptcy conduct.[11]

According to the Ninth Circuit, the IRS could levy on all of a husband's pension benefits, irrespective of the bankruptcy debtor-wife's community property interest in the benefits. In this reading, the husband is liable for tax debts plus interests in all community property adequate to support a tax levy.[12]

When a partner files for bankruptcy, the way that the partner's distributive share is allocated between the partner and the bankruptcy estate is not a partnership item under IRC §6231(a)(3). Therefore, it is not necessary that the allocation be resolved in a partnership-level proceeding (IRC §§6221-6234). If the estate retains beneficial ownership of a partnership share at the close of the partnership tax year, the partner's distributive share for the entire partnership tax year is reportable by the bankruptcy estate.[13]

[¶4360] Tax Litigation

The Eleventh Circuit denied a bankruptcy discharge for $2 million in tax liability, because the debtor had transferred assets to his wife as a tax avoidance measure. Bankruptcy Code §523(a)(1)(C) forbids discharge of taxes that the debtor willfully attempted, in any manner, to evade or defeat.

The two-year statute of limitations for the government to get back an erroneous tax refund starts when the refund check clears the Federal Reserve Bank and the Treasury Department authorizes payment—not when the taxpayer receives the check.[14]

An IRS Notice of Determination with respect to the classification of workers in an air conditioning business demanded additional employment taxes. The taxpayer's argument was that the Code §6501(a) three-year statute of limitations had expired. The IRS claimed an indefinite extension of the statute of limitations because of the taxpayer's fraud in the filing of the employment tax returns. But, in February 2001, the Tax Court ruled that the taxpayer was not guilty of fraud. His credible testimony, as corroborated by his office manager and accountant, was that he believed that the proper payments were made. He acted without intention to conceal, mislead, or otherwise prevent collections, so the Tax Court held that the collection effort was time-barred.[15]

[¶4370] Innocent Spouse Relief

On January 31, 2000, the IRS published a detailed explanation, in Revenue Procedure 2000-15, 2000-5 IRB 447, of how an innocent "requesting spouse" can obtain equitable relief from federal tax liability that was, in effect, created by the other spouse, but where relief is unavailable under Code §6013, the general provision for innocent spouse relief. For instance, equitable relief may be available to protect against the consequences of liabilities that were properly reported but never paid, whereas §6013 is inapplicable in this situation.

The application for equitable relief must be made within two years of the IRS's initial collection activity. Equitable relief will be denied if there were interspousal transfers of assets designed to defeat tax collection, or if the tax return was filed with fraudulent intent. Furthermore, the spouses must be divorced or separated for equitable relief to be available, and the innocent spouse must be at risk of economic hardship if relief is denied.

Code §6015(f), granting relief of tax liability that is not available under §6015(b) or (c), if it would not be equitable to hold the taxpayer liable under all the facts and circumstances of the case, gives the Tax Court jurisdiction to review denial of innocent spouse relief.[16]

A person who signs a joint return is not an "innocent spouse" if he or she knows that income was received but not reported, even if the spouse relies on the non-innocent spouse's representations about the tax status of the item.[17]

If the IRS decides to grant innocent spouse relief, the other spouse has a right to litigate this decision—because its result will be to increase the non-electing spouse's tax liability.[18]

Regulations were proposed on January 17, 2001 (66 FR 3888). Under these proposals, an "erroneous item" that gives rise to potential liability is any item that causes tax liability to be reduced because of its omission or misstatement. The spouse merely needs to be aware of the existence of the item, not necessarily its proper tax treatment, to lose innocent spouse characterization. A facts and circumstances test is applied to determine actual knowledge—for instance, did the spouse claiming innocence have an interest in the property creating the tax item? Did the spouse avoid inquiring into the couple's financial status? Did the other spouse transfer assets to the spouse asserting innocence? Under the proposal, a return signed under duress is not a real joint return, and therefore cannot give rise to joint and several liability.

[¶4380] Treatment of Overpayments

In February, 2000, the Supreme Court ruled that, to calculate the three-year look-back period under Code §6511(b)(2)(A) [amount of credit or refund on overpayment of tax], the salient date is the due date of the tax return rather than the date the tax liability is assessed.[19] (The taxpayer got an extension, but missed the extended deadline too and filed late.) The look-back period is three years plus the four-month extension.

Remittances of estimated tax or withholding are paid on the due date of the return, so they were deemed paid on April 15, making the taxpayer too late and relieving the IRS of the obligation to credit his account because he missed the three-year-plus-four-month deadline.

If a taxpayer reports an overpayment for a particular tax year and gets a refund or credit, and the IRS later determines a deficiency for that tax year, interest runs on the part of the deficiency in excess of the overpayment as of the date of the refund or the date the amount was applied toward estimated tax for the following tax year.[20]

Taxpayers who send a payment to the IRS without indicating toward which liabilities it should be applied cannot later call for allocation to a particular tax year, nor can they protest when the IRS allocates the payment so as to create an overpayment in one year and a deficiency in another.[21]

[¶4400] Taxpayer Rights and Advocacy

Announcement 2000-4, 2000-3 IRB 317, sets up a two-year test period (starting 1/1/00), during which a taxpayer and the IRS Appeals Office can jointly request binding arbitration of unsettled factual issues within the Appeals administrative procedure, when negotiations for settlement have failed. The arbitrator's decision is not appealable.

IR-1999-76, from October 4, 1999, discusses a new kind of offer in compromise, available to taxpayers facing severe or unusual economic hardship. Under this procedure, an offer in compromise can be accepted even if the collectability of the debt is not actually in doubt.

Application is made on the new Form 656-A, which is filed in addition to (and does not replace) the standard Form 656, the application to have the IRS accept an offer in compromise. First, the IRS determines whether the regular offer in compromise procedure applies; then the applicability of the new program (which is limited to taxpayers in very severe financial trouble) is considered. The new program is not to be used merely as a planning device to avoid taxes.

Also see T.D. 8829, 1999-32 IRB 235, publishing Temporary Regulations (effective 7/21/99) and Proposed Regulations for the offer in compromise program. The IRS will consider hardship and equity factors, not just the former test (doubt as to collectability of the tax liability).

Hardship, in this context, means illness or disability preventing the taxpayer from earning a living. This is in conjunction with medical bills that will exhaust the taxpayer's resources, to the point that the taxpayer would not be able to pay living expenses if the assets were liquidated and applied toward the tax liability. Hardship also means that the taxpayer can't borrow against his or her assets, and a property seizure would have adverse consequences.

However, an offer in compromise will not be accepted if it would undermine the IRS's compliance efforts—for instance, if the taxpayer had a history of noncompliance or deliberately avoided paying tax liabilities.

The IRS has a commitment to develop tables of living allowances to standardize determinations as to ability to pay, and will develop additional guidelines about offers in compromise made by low-income taxpayers. The statute of limitations is suspended during the period of the taxpayer's disability and inability to manage financial affairs.[22]

Revenue Procedure 99-28, 1999-29 IRB describes an optional new procedure that taxpayers can request to speed up referral of unresolved examination or collection issues to the IRS Office of Appeals. An issue is suitable if referral is likely to speed up resolution of the entire case, the issues are fully developed, and the IRS District Office agrees with the taxpayer that early referral to Appeals is appropriate. However, issues can't be referred if the IRS Office of Chief Counsel intends to litigate them, or once the 30-day letter has already been issued.

Notice 99-50, 1999-40 IRB 444 (10/4/99), proposes a Revenue Procedure under which appeals officers are not allowed to communicate ex parte with other IRS employees. The proposal implements the IRSRRA '98 mandate to the IRS to eliminate ex parte communications in the interest of preserving the independence of appeals officers. In the past, the public perceived appeals officers as subject to undue influence from tax collection and examination employees.

Appeals officers are still permitted to make general inquiries about a case or ask if information has been requested or received—but an appeals officer is not permitted to discuss the substance of the taxpayer's case with other IRS staffers without disclosure to the taxpayer. The taxpayer (or representative) is entitled to participate in the intra-agency discussion, which must be scheduled to reasonably accommodate the taxpayer's convenience.

ENDNOTES

1. *Barmes v. U.S.,* 199 F.3d 386 (7th Cir. 1999).
2. *U.S. v. Gold,* 178 F.3d 718 (4th Cir. 1999).
3. *Beam v. CIR,* 192 F.3d 941 (9th Cir. 1999).
4. *Smith v. CIR,* 114 TC No. 29 (6/8/00).
5. *Fior d'Italia Inc. v. U.S.,* 69 LW 1557 (9th Cir. 3/7/01).
6. *E. Fridovich v. Comm'r,* TC Memo 2001-32 (2/12/01).
7. *Schachter,* 113 TC No. 14 (1999).
8. *Davis v. Comm'r,* 115 TC No. 4 (7/31/00).
9. *Becton Dickinson & Co. v. Wolckenhauer,* 215 F.3d 340 (3rd Cir. 2000).

10. Compare *Young v. U.S.*, 233 F.3d 56 (1st Cir. 2000) with *Palmer v. U.S.*, 219 F.3d 580 (6th Cir. 2000).
11. *U.S. v. Bishop*, 2000-2 USTC ¶50,740 (W.D. Tex. 8/18/00).
12. *In re McIntyre v. U.S.*, 222 F.3d 655 (9th Cir. 7/13/00).
13. *Katz v. Comm'r*, 116 TC No. 2 (1/21/01).
14. *U.S. v. Commonwealth Energy System*, 235 F.3d 11 (1st Cir. 2000).
15. *Neely v. Comm'r*, 116 TC No. 8 (2/13/01).
16. *Fernandez v. Comm'r*, 114 TC No. 21 (5/10/00), acq.; *Charlton v. Comm'r*, 114 TC No. 22 (5/16/00).
17. *Cheshire v. Comm'r*, 115 TC No. 15 (12/21/00).
18. *Corson v. Comm'r*, 114 TC No. 24 (5/18/00).
19. *Baral v. U.S.*, 528 U.S. 431 (Sup.Ct. 2000).
20. Rev.Rul. 99-40, 1999-40 IRB 441. Also see Rev.Proc. 2000-43, 2000-43 IRB 404, which also deals with ex parte communications between appeals officers and other IRS staffers.
21. *Pace v. CIR*, TC Memo 2000-300 (9/25/00).
22. Code §6511(h)(2)(A); see Revenue Procedure 99-21, 1999-17 IRB 18 for rules of proof on this issue.

¶5000

Federal Civil Procedure

[¶5001]

In May, 2000, the Supreme Court decided a somewhat atypical civil procedure case,[1] striking down the Violence Against Women Act, 42 USC §13981, which provided a federal civil cause of action to the victims of gender-related violence. In the Supreme Court's view, Congress was unjustified in passing this legislation, because neither the Commerce Clause §5 nor the Fourteenth Amendment (cited by Congress as authority) provides appropriate authority for the legislation.

The Eighth Circuit declared that one of its own rules, 28A(i) [unpublished opinions are not precedent and should not be cited], violates Article III of the Constitution and is thus invalid. The theory is that allowing a court to avoid the precedent-setting effect of its own decisions gives federal judges too much power, because Article III implies that judges must cope with consequences of all their decisions, whether or not published.[2]

In May, 2001, the Ninth Circuit (one of the seven circuits that limit or reject citation of unpublished opinions) refused to impose sanctions on a lawyer for citing an unpublished opinion in a brief. In the Ninth Circuit, an unpublished opinion can be cited for factual purposes but not to establish a point of law.[3]

[¶5010] The Federal Court System

On April 17, 2000, the Supreme Court approved several Federal Rules amendments, to take effect December 1, 2000, Congress did not take steps to prevent effectiveness of the rules: see 69 LW 2279 (11/14/00).[4] Changes were made in the FRCP as follows:

- Rule 4(l): When a federal employee is sued in his or her individual capacity for acts connected to the performance of duties on behalf of the United States, service must be made on the United States. The amendment also allows reasonable time to cure a failure to serve all required parties in suits against a federal agency, officer, or employee.

- Rule 12(a)(3): A federal officer or employee sued in individual capacity has 60 days to file an answer.

Various changes have been made to the discovery rules:

- Rule 5(d): Discovery materials can't be filed until they have been used in a proceeding.
- Rule 26(a): Parties' initial disclosure obligation is extended to cover information that the disclosing party may use to support claims or defenses, other than solely for impeachment. Eight categories of proceedings are exempt from initial disclosure.
- Rule 26(b)(1): Party-controlled discovery is limited to nonprivileged matter relevant to a claim or defense of any party. For good cause, the court can order discovery of any matter relevant to subject matter of the action. In other words, the rule change gives the court a more active role in limiting discovery to relevant materials and issues.
- Rule 26(b)(2): District Courts are not permitted to impose local rules that change the presumptive national limits on numbers of depositions and interrogatories under Rules 30, 31, 33 or the Rule 30(d)(2) limit on length of depositions. But modifications by court order or agreement are still possible.

[¶5020] Jurisdiction

On April 3, 2000, the Supreme Court affirmed without opinion a Fifth Circuit holding that 26 USC §1367 gives the District Court supplemental jurisdiction over unnamed class members who do not meet the amount-in-controversy requirement for diversity jurisdiction.[5]

Bank shareholders can go to the Federal Circuit to sue the United States, in order to get damages against the FDIC for breach of a contract involving a bank's capital requirements.[6] Neither the Tucker Act nor case law rules out derivative suits by a shareholder of a federal contractor when the agency that is allegedly in breach has a conflict of interest as to the contractor's operations.

Although ERISA authorizes nationwide service of process, that doesn't automatically give a federal court personal jurisdiction over every entity that has minimum contacts with the United States; personal jurisdiction can still be exercised only where it is fair and reasonable.[7] The case involves an employee benefits plan participant's attempt to get managed care coverage of a relative's psychiatric treatment. The plan made the certification decision in Utah; the employee and the patient lived in Tennessee; the employer was headquartered in Georgia, and the plan was administered in Alabama.

In the Tenth Circuit reading, personal jurisdiction requires forum contacts. However, Utah was an appropriate venue, because making decisions about care was a contact, and the defendant would have free access to Utah attorneys for representation.

It was proper for a District of Columbia trial court to exercise personal jurisdiction over a Maryland grocery store where a District resident slipped and fell.[8] Advertisements by the grocery chain (including the theme "no matter where you live it's worth the drive") constituted purposeful business activity that would bring the store within the D.C. long-arm statute's reach. The court treated the metropolitan D.C. region as a unified commercial community. The court was willing to see nexus between the ads and the slip-and-fall claim, because it was reasonably foreseeable that District residents would shop at the stores, and sooner or later one of them was going to fall. But the court insisted its analysis was fact-driven: An employee who slipped in a Maryland warehouse wouldn't be able to sue in the District of Columbia, because the ads didn't target such workers.

A Pennsylvania resident's negligence and strict liability products claims against an out-of-state cigarette manufacturer and a local cigarette retailer (Rite Aid) could not be brought in federal court, according to the Eastern District of Pennsylvania.[9] The plaintiff alleged the wrongful death of the plaintiff's decedent because of cigarettes made by Philip Morris and sold by Rite Aid. Philip Morris got the case removed to federal court, arguing that diversity was still present because the plaintiff had fraudulently joined the local defendant solely to defeat diversity.

However, in the Eastern District view, as long as local law provided a colorable cause of action against the local defendant, joinder was not fraudulent. In this analysis, the plaintiff need not present a winnable case, only one that cannot be characterized as wholly insubstantial and frivolous.

The plaintiff's allegation that the design of the cigarettes failed to reduce carcinogens was an allegation of a specific defect, not just inherent dangers of tobacco, and thus was colorable in Pennsylvania. The plaintiff also charged Rite Aid with negligence (the breach of an asserted duty not to sell products that are not reasonably safe), which is not a mere failure-to-warn claim subject to preemption by the Federal Cigarette Labeling and Advertising Act.

In 1999, the Eleventh Circuit struck down a state (Florida) statute that requires leave of court before requesting punitive damages in any pleading,[10] on the grounds that it conflicts with the FRCP 8(a)(3) requirement that pleadings include a demand for the relief sought. In this analysis, the plaintiff is not precluded from using her demand for $10 million in punitive damages (without leave of court) to satisfy the minimum diversity jurisdictional amount.

At that time, the Eleventh Circuit held that, in a class action, punitive damages can be aggregated if the award reflects the wrongfulness of the conduct rather than a particular person's damages. The question is not whether the state law is procedural (i.e., federal law governs) or substantive (state law governs) but whether the state procedural requirement contradicts federal procedure. If it does, the federal rule has to apply unless the federal rule itself either violates the Rules Enabling Act or is unconstitutional.

However, the Eleventh Circuit reheard the case and reversed itself[11] and now takes the position that neither punitive damages nor attorneys' fees can be aggregated toward the $75,000 minimum in a class action under Florida's deceptive advertising statute. Instead, the amount in controversy depends on pro rata allocation of the claimed punitive damages and attorneys' fees.   Furthermore, where the relevant statute gives class members a separate and distinct right to recover attorneys' fees, and the statutory attorneys' fees compensate class members for their injuries, the fees cannot be aggregated toward the jurisdictional minimum.

Another unsuccessful argument by the plaintiff was that the desired injunctive relief was worth more than $75,000. However, the Eleventh Circuit, on rehearing, noted that the defendant could satisfy any such injunction by raising its store prices rather than lowering its catalogue prices, which would not help the plaintiffs. There were too many speculative ways in which Office Depot could change its pricing behavior, or class members could change their purchasing behavior, for this to satisfy the amount in controversy requirement.

[¶5050] Statute of Limitations

The Supreme Court dealt with the statute of limitations for civil RICO cases in early 2000.[12] The statute of limitations is clearly four years; the problem is when the cause of action accrues. The Supreme Court refused to accept the "injury and pattern" discovery rule preferred by some Circuits (although it did not express clearly what the appropriate accrual rule would be).

Injury discovery means that the cause of action accrues when the plaintiff knows or should have known that injury occurred. Injury and pattern discovery defers accrual until the plaintiff knows or should have known not only that injury occurred, but also that there was a pattern of racketeering injury.

Another possibility was the "last predicate act" rule. This calls for accrual at the time the plaintiff knows or should have known of the injury and its part in a pattern of racketeering injury, restarted with each new predicate act within the same pattern of injury. This test was rejected by the Supreme Court in 1997[13] because it could have the effect of extending the statute of limitations far beyond the Congressional intent. The Supreme Court also noted that civil RICO is patterned after the Clayton Act, and Clayton Act causes of action generally accrue upon commission of an act of injury to the plaintiff's business.

The Court rejected the injury and pattern rule because it would allow proof of acts that are really too remote in time to be cognizable. Because the RICO definition of pattern requires at least two acts in 10 years, with a four-year limitation period, 14 years can be compassed, so further extension might frustrate the purpose of a statute of limitations (preventing stale claims from being litigated).

Disagreeing with most commentators, the Florida Court of Appeals decided late in 2000 that 28 USC §1367(d) [tolling of the statute of limitations on state claims while the claims are pending in federal court] also applies to state claims over which the federal court has supplemental jurisdiction but which are voluntarily dismissed with the intention of refiling in state court.[14]

Florida's 20-year statute of limitations for actions to enforce in-state judgments has been held also to apply to registration and enforcement under the Uniform Foreign Money Judgments Recognition Act (UFMJRA). The Florida Court of Appeals decided[15] that the policy underlying the statute would be better served by using the local statute of limitations rather than Florida's five-year statutory statute of limitations for enforcement of foreign judgments. The purpose of the statute was to make U.S. judgments enforceable in foreign courts by giving foreign countries reason to believe their judgments would be enforced in the United States.

Pre-UFMJRA law required a judgment creditor to sue in Florida on the foreign judgment, prove it was valid and entitled to enforcement, and get a Florida judgment on the basis of the foreign one.

UFMJRA says that judgments of foreign countries for recovery of a sum of money can be recognized and made entitled to enforcement by filing an authenticated copy of a final and conclusive judgment that could be enforced by the foreign court. The judgment party files an authenticated copy of the judgment with the clerk of the court and records it in the public records where enforcement is sought. The court clerk has to send notice to the judgment debtor at the address provided by the judgment creditor.

The debtor has 30 days to file objections to recognition of the judgment; if none are filed, then the clerk records a certificate. Either side can get a hearing in which the court orders the judgment to be granted or denied recognition. The judgment becomes enforceable after issuance of the certificate or order.

Minnesota says that the Eleventh Amendment does not permit tolling of the statute of limitations on state-court claims against the state itself if the state defendant has not consented. Therefore, an age discrimination suit against a state employer that was dismissed on Eleventh Amendment grounds in federal court was time-barred in the state court.[16]

[¶5070] Removal

Early in 2001, the Supreme Court tackled some complex removal issues.[17] The petitioner initially brought suit in California state court for breach of contract and various business torts. The respondent removed the case to federal court, then had it dismissed as time-barred under the two-year California statute of limitations. The respondent is a Maryland corporation, and the suit was still timely under Maryland state law (where a three-year statute of limitations prevailed), so the petitioner re-filed the suit there. The respondent got the case dismissed again, this time as res judicata.

In the Supreme Court view, the appropriate claim preclusion rule is the rule of the state in which the federal court sits. The Maryland court was wrong to say that the dismissal in the California federal court (although on the merits) necessarily precluded a Maryland state case. Uniformity is served—and undesirable forum shopping discouraged—by applying the state rule.

The Seventh Circuit permits removal of a case from state to federal court, even if the case has made more than one round trip already;[18] 28

USC §1446(b) doesn't rule out sequential petitions for removal. In this case, first the defendants asserted diversity to remove the tort suit from the state to the federal system. The District Court sent the case back to the state system on the grounds that the amount in controversy was under $75,000.

In state court, the plaintiffs admitted that the damages sought were over $75,000, and the defendants asked for the case once again to return to the federal courts, but the District Court said that successive removals are forbidden. In the Seventh Circuit reading, paragraph 2 of §1446(b) deals with notice of removal when a case that was not originally removable becomes so, and thus an unsuccessful earlier attempt at removal is not dispositive. Furthermore, plaintiffs should not be able to derive benefit from manipulating damage claims.

A late-2000 Sixth Circuit case made a similar pilgrimage. A trip-and-fall case against Wal-Mart was instituted in state court and removed to federal court. After removal, the plaintiff stipulated that damages did not exceed $75,000. The Sixth Circuit held that the stipulation does not divest the federal court of jurisdiction, on the theory that plaintiffs could be given too much power. The Sixth Circuit held that removal was proper when it was made, based on the allegations in the complaint at that time.[19]

The Eleventh Circuit view is that, when considering the appropriateness of the removal of a diversity case, the District Court can properly consider evidence submitted after the filing of the removal petition, as long as the evidence reflects events as of the time of removal. Eleventh Circuit precedent is that when the ad damnum falls below the federal jurisdictional minimum, the defendant is placed in the odd position of having to prove that the plaintiff's victory will result in higher damages than the plaintiff actually claimed.[20]

State courts retain the power to bill plaintiffs for court costs after their cases are removed.[21] The federal removal statute says a state court "shall proceed no further" after removal, but state courts are permitted to undertake ministerial tasks, such as disposing of obsolete files and assessing costs—as long as the assessment and billing of the costs is supported by a rational basis. The plaintiffs could not convince the Sixth Circuit that they had due process and equal protection claims based on being treated differently from prevailing plaintiffs whose cases were not removed. The Sixth Circuit didn't think they were really similarly situated, in that the state wouldn't have any other way of recouping expenses related to removed cases, because it can't pursue losing defendants.

[¶5080.5] Class Actions

Unless there has been a demonstration of fraud, court approval is not needed for side settlements that resolve peripheral disputes in a class action whose settlement has already been approved.[22] Absent class members have no right to get the courts involved, because the main settlement is unaffected. Rule 23(e) governs court approval of dismissal or compromise of an entire class action, not side settlements.

In many instances, certification has been denied to class action applicants, or certification has been revoked in mass tort cases.

For instance, the Eleventh Circuit did not permit class action plaintiffs to aggregate their claims (compensatory and punitive damages and attorneys' fees) to reach the $75,000 jurisdictional minimum. In this interpretation, each plaintiff alleges the breach of his or her own insurance policy contract, and thus the compensatory damage claims are all separate and distinct. According to the Eleventh Circuit, there was no single title or right that the entire class was attempting to uphold.[23]

To expedite settlement of a tobacco case, the Eastern District of New York denied class certification of consolidated personal injury suits that would have allowed plaintiffs to opt out with respect to punitive damages. The court held that it was better to have a broader class with respect to all compensatory and punitive damages, allowing class members to opt out with respect to individual compensatory damages but not as to punitive damages.[24]

Certification of a Rule 23(b)(3) class was denied in a suit brought by three Florida corporations on behalf of state residents, alleging that insurance companies unlawfully inflated the premiums for commercial insurance coverage. Certification was denied because the class was not identifiable, and the criteria of predominance and superiority were not met. Furthermore, each of the 40,000 class members would have to prove reliance on the insurer's misrepresentation, plus damages.[25]

The Sixth Circuit invalidated a limited fund class action settlement of a heart pacemaker case, because a Rule 23(b)(1)(B) "fixed fund" is a finite resource such as a bank account, not a variable fund whose size is determined by negotiation.[26]

But this is not to say that all class actions have been ruled out in all circumstances. The New Jersey Superior Court did certify a class of people who bought "vanishing premium" life insurance between 1985 and 1989, under the state's Consumer Fraud Act and common law fraud theory. While recognizing that most states would deny the class action, the New Jersey court cited the state's liberal class action practice for common grievances where individual suits are not feasible.[27]

The order naming the lead plaintiff in a securities fraud litigation case is not a collateral order that can be immediately appealed by other would-be potential lead plaintiffs, because the order does not conclusively determine a question or resolve an important issue that is separate from the merits of the case. Furthermore, the order can be reviewed on appeal from the final judgment.[28]

[¶5110] Res Judicata

Certification of a class in federal court prevents investors angered at the outcome of a condominium project from relitigating their contract claims, although they could bring fraud claims in state court.[29]

The plaintiff group that opted out or reserved the right to object to the proposed settlement was not in control of the earlier litigation. Therefore they are not bound to a judgment that was rendered after they opted out, the settlement collapsed, and they went to state court. There were two groups of plaintiffs who invested. In 1991, a class including both groups was certified, but only as to two contract claims. The class won. In 1992, another (b)(3) class including both groups was certified, to approve a settlement of remaining claims. But enough people opted out to impair the class certification.

That raises the question of whether the state court action is between the same parties, or parties in privity with those parties, so that res judicata is present. Privity could exist in two situations: when nonparties who control litigation are bound by the results, and when nonparties are bound because they are adequately represented by a party. In this case, the plaintiffs didn't have enough control to trigger privity and there wasn't enough accountability either on the basis of financial relationship or acquiescence in representation.

[¶5210] Federal Pleadings

An April, 2000 Supreme Court case[30] arose out of a patent infringement dispute between Ohio Cellular Products Corp. (OCP) and Adams USA. The District Court dismissed the case and ordered OCP to pay Adams' attorneys' fees and costs. The District Court decided that Nelson, who was OCP's president and sole shareholder, had deceived the Patent and Trademark Office about its patents, and that OCP was chargeable for this.

Adams didn't think OCP would be able to pay the judgment, so it moved under FRCP 15 to amend its pleadings and add Nelson as an individual as a party from whom fees could be collected. OCP also applied under Rule 59(e) to have the judgment amended to make Nelson liable for the fee award immediately.

The District Court granted both motions, and the Federal Circuit affirmed, even though it's uncommon to add a party after entry of judgment. However, the Federal Circuit didn't think there was prejudice to Adams, because he didn't show that he could have done anything else to stave off judgment if he'd been named from the initiation of litigation.

The Supreme Court held that it was an error to amend the judgment immediately after allowing the pleading to be amended. Rules 12 and 15 notions of due process require Nelson to have a chance to contest personal liability after becoming a party and before entry of judgment. He was never given a chance to contest the issue of personal liability. Also, Rule 15(a) allots 10 days to plead to parties who are added after the time to respond to original pleading, whereas Adams was subjected to personal liability without even getting an amended pleading.

[¶5310] Provisional Remedies

A District Court can't freeze defendants' assets when general creditors ask only for a money judgment,[31] on the basis that federal courts' general equitable powers do not extend to issuing preliminary injunctions in cases that are pure actions at law. But this principle does not apply when equitable remedies are also in the picture, according to the Fourth Circuit.[32]

In this Medicare fraud case, treble damages were potentially available. The government also wanted remedies for unjust enrichment, wanted to reverse fraudulent transfers, sought to impose a constructive trust to be imposed on the defendants' assets, and sought an injunction to freeze defendants' assets to prevent their transfer outside the United States. The Fourth Circuit found adequate nexus between the assets to be frozen and the relief the suit was designed to obtain.

Under this reading, FRCP 64 incorporates all state law remedies calling for seizure of person or property to satisfy the judgment sought by the action, interpreted here to mean all state procedures that authorize meaningful interference with property in order to safeguard the potential satisfaction of the judgment—including state authorization of injunctions. The state here (Maryland) did provide for injunctions.

The Third Circuit vacated (except as to two retirees) a preliminary injunction requiring the defendant to maintain full funding of health benefits for 136 retirees, pending trial of ERISA claims.[33] The other plaintiffs didn't provide enough evidence to support a conclusion of irreparable harm.

The plaintiffs alleged breach of fiduciary duty by misrepresenting and omitting facts about retiree health benefits, with the result that deceived employees elected early retirement because they believed the benefits would continue for life. After their retirement, the company switched from a self-insured plan with low premiums to multiple insured plans, most of which had meaningful copayment requirements.

The Third Circuit accepted the likelihood of success on the merits as to breach of fiduciary duty, but did not see proof of irreparable harm (i.e., harm that could not be redressed later via compensatory damages). Only the two retirees as to whom the injunction was not lifted testified that they would have to choose between necessaries and health insurance premiums; their testimony was not enough to draw an inference that all the plaintiffs confronted the same choice. Irreparable harm cannot be inferred from a small amount of individualized testimony from individuals who are not necessarily representative of the entire group. Simple affidavits showing risk of irreparable harm to all plaintiffs would have been sufficient, but they were not provided.

[¶5340] [NEW] Settlement

Although other mass-tort settlements involving tobacco and asbestos failed to achieve court approval, the Eastern District of Pennsylvania did approve the settlement of a class action about the diet drugs Pondimin and Redux in August, 2000. The class comprised plaintiffs who have developed or are at risk of developing damaged heart values because they used the drugs. The agreement called for two funds: $1 billion for medical monitoring and $2.55 billion to compensate plaintiffs at between $7,389 and $1.5 million apiece, depending on their age, extent of injury, and duration of drug use. The court found that the class is cohesive enough, only one manufacturer rather than an entire industry was sued, and objective criteria were provided for allocating damages to plaintiffs.[34]

[¶5400.6] Dismissal of Actions

The plaintiff has an absolute right under FRCP 41(a)(1)(i) to dismiss the action before the defendant answers or files a motion for summary judgment—no matter how far the case has progressed otherwise.[35] The court has no discretion to mandate continuation of the action once voluntary dismissal is demanded, even if discovery has consumed a great deal of time and effort.

The District Court does not have jurisdiction to review the terms and conditions of a Rule 41(a)(1) voluntary dismissal, says the Ninth Circuit.[36] Once a notice of voluntary dismissal is filed, a Rule 59(e) motion to alter or amend the judgment cannot be used to determine whether the dismissal was with or without prejudice. That can only be done if another action is filed. The dismissal is effective on filing, and no court order is required, so the defendant has no remedy and there's nothing that the District Court can do; the parties are restored to *status quo ante*.

[¶5500] Evidence

In addition to the F.R.C.P. rule changes noted above, changes were also made by the Supreme Court affecting the F.R.E.:

- Rule 103 has been amended to provide that a claim of error as to a pre-trial ruling can be preserved even if the objection or offer of proof is not renewed.
- Rule 404(a) now permits an alleged victim to introduce evidence attacking the defendant's character, to rebut imputations about the same trait in the alleged victim.
- Rule 701 allows scientific and technical testimony to be reviewed under the rules for expert testimony—this was done to prevent circumvention of *Daubert* and *Kumho Tire* by introducing testimony by experts while calling them lay witnesses.
- Rule 702 has been redrafted in light of those two decisions, to assist the court in its role of determining whether expert testimony is admissible based on its reliability and potential to assist the jury.
- The Rule 703 amendment limits admission of information that is used by experts to form the opinion as to which they testify.

- Rules 803(6), 902(11), and 902(12) as amended make it easier to introduce evidence of activities that are conducted on a regular basis without live witness testimony to set the foundation.

A cause of action for negligence is available[37] to litigants who say they were harmed when a third party negligently destroyed evidence critical to their suit. (Here, the plaintiff's insurance company took possession of the van involved in a fatal accident, claiming that it would be kept at the company's storage facility for inspections relative to a products liability suit against the manufacturer, but the van was destroyed before the tests were performed.) However, there is no independent cause of action for mere spoliation of evidence.

The Alabama court imposed a three-part test for the prima facie case. The third party alleged to have erred must have had actual knowledge of pending or potential litigation (because constructive knowledge is not enough to impose a duty to preserve evidence); must have volunteered or have been asked to undertake a duty; and the missing evidence must really have been vital to the case. Furthermore, breach of the duty to preserve has to be the proximate cause of the plaintiff's inability to bring suit or prevail in a suit already instituted.

Once the plaintiff has made out this prima facie case, the defendant can overcome the presumption by showing that, even if the evidence had been available, the plaintiff would have lost the case anyway.

Damages for the prevailing plaintiff equal the compensatory damages that would have been awarded on the underlying cause of action, but punitive damages are available only if the evidence was willfully or wantonly destroyed.

Arkansas has similarly refused to recognize a separate tort cause of action for spoliation of evidence, although the cause of action is recognized in Alaska, Florida, New Jersey, New Mexico, and Ohio. California initially accepted the cause of action, but that decision was overruled in light of other available remedies.[38]

[¶5500.7.2] Opinion Evidence

Polygraph evidence is not reliable enough to qualify as Rule 702 scientific evidence, because the error rate in live tests is not known; the scientific community doesn't accept it to demonstrate facts that will be presented in court; and there aren't accepted reliable standards for quality control.[39]

In a February, 2000 case, the Eastern District of New York certified a rather large class—four million retailers!—in an antitrust suit alleging that the issuers of Visa and MasterCard illegally used their market domination to force stores that accepted their credit cards also to accept the issuers' debit cards[40] (with much larger fees than the issuer collected on credit cards), thus constituting an illegal tying action.

The court adopted a modified *Daubert* test for admission of expert testimony in the context of class certification. A report that is not admissible at trial might be admitted on the issue of whether or not the plaintiffs satisfied Rule 23's prerequisites for class certification. Because in this context the judge, not the jury, sees the evidence, the risk of misinformation is much lower. The plaintiffs wanted to use expert testimony from an economist to prove that their allegations that illegal tying led to economic injury could be resolved on a classwide basis.

The class was certified based on showing that common proof can show injury in fact, and that substantive claims and market power can be resolved class-wide; decertification can always be done if the individual damages later are found to outbalance the common questions.

Of course, *Kumho Tire,* extending the *Daubert* standard to engineering and other technical evidence, applies in Kentucky. The standard for reviewing trial court decisions about admissibility is abuse of discretion. Therefore, a mechanical engineer's testimony about design defects in a wheel rim should have been excluded.[41] A 1999 Second Circuit case brought under Lanham Act §43(a)(2) by one pharmaceutical company against a competitor involves allegedly false promotional pitches made by sales representatives to doctors.

The Eleventh Circuit says that the trial court has flexibility in serving as the *Daubert* gatekeeper for expert testimony. But when an opponent objects to the admission of testimony, the District Court abuses its discretion by failing to make a complete record of its rationale. The appellate court must be able to determine if the relevant law was applied properly. [42]

It was held[43] that scientifically conducted surveys of doctors' impressions of what the sales representatives said are admissible at various stages of the case, involving several hearsay exceptions. FRE 803(3) [present state of mind] allows admission for the limited purpose of establishing a pattern of implied falsehood (i.e., the survey expresses the declarant's state of mind at the time of utterance).

Rule 807, the residual hearsay rule, may also justify admission of memory surveys to prove the facts remembered, and therefore prove that statements (about the sedative effects of the product) are literally false. Although the District Court refused to admit the surveys, the Second Circuit said it should not have decided without analyzing the strength or weakness of the survey methodology.

A police officer's testimony that the voice of someone he heard but didn't see sounded like a black male was admissible. It was within the scope of lay opinion.[44] He could certainly testify whether it was a man or a woman, and someone who is reasonably familiar with and has a rational basis for perception can testify about the race/nationality of the person uttering spoken words.

[¶5500.9] Hearsay and Hearsay Exceptions

A video created in order to teach an OB/GYN procedure to doctors can be introduced in a medical malpractice case as an FRE 803(18) "learned treatise." A treatise is not necessarily printed on paper, and the Second Circuit considered videotape merely a "contemporary variant" of a print treatise.[45]

The Second is the first Circuit to take up this issue. In the state courts, Texas and Arizona have admitted videotapes on this basis, but Massachusetts and North Carolina have declined to do so.

However, the closing credits for the video included a statement, "This video does not define a standard of care," which should have been redacted under FRE 403 as unduly prejudicial, because it tends to suggest that litigation about particular birth injuries is inappropriate. A new trial was not required for this failure to redact, because the trial judge made sure that evidence was properly focused.

In a medical malpractice case, the Physician's Drug Reference (PDR), taken by itself, does not prove the standard of care for doctors in prescribing and monitoring drugs. PDR excerpts, offered in isolation, are hearsay.[46] They might be admissible to supplement expert testimony about the degree of risk of the drug in the context of the plaintiff's condition. (She became quadriplegic after a severe stroke when she was taking birth control pills.)

PDR excerpts are necessarily hearsay when offered to prove the truth of the stroke risks of estrogen, but the plaintiff's position was that the PDR is generally recognized by doctors as setting the standard of care for prescribing. The PDR has been accepted as prima facie evidence of the standard of care in Illinois and Minnesota, but in this case, New York joins New Jersey, Hawaii, and Utah in treating the PDR as only some evidence that the fact-finder can choose to consider in the context of other standard-of-care testimony.

According to the New York court, the standard of care for any profession is set by the best practices of the profession itself. The PDR comprises information provided by drug manufacturers, essentially to improve their own liability position by disclosing risks. It serves purposes other than diagnosis and treatment. Nor does the learned intermediary doctrine create a hearsay exception for the PDR, because a learned intermediary's warning is evaluated by the fact-finder for accuracy, clarity, and relative consistency rather than for its truth.

Florida passed a law (Stats. §90.803(24)) providing a special hearsay exception for certain out-of-court statements by the elderly and disabled. The statute was struck down in 1999[47] as an unconstitutional violation of the Sixth Amendment right of confrontation. (However, a somewhat similar provision on out-of-court statements of child victims of sex crimes was upheld.)

The case arose when the prosecution wanted to introduce two statements (one sworn, one unsworn) made to the police by an 84-year-old robbery victim. The victim died before the trial, and had not been deposed.

The statute permitted admission of an out-of-court statement of an elderly or disabled person (one aged 60 or older, suffering from infirmities of aging to the point that the capacity for self-protection is impaired), where there was no indication of lack of trustworthiness, based on a trial-court finding that the statement's reliability was adequately safeguarded. The declarant must either testify or be unavailable in a situation in which there is corroboration of the offense.

Although firmly rooted hearsay exceptions can oust the confrontation clause, the Florida court did not deem this unique and new exception to qualify. The exception for child victims of sex crimes was sustainable because it was narrower and imposed tests for the reliability of the statements.

[¶5500.11] Privilege

The psychotherapist–patient privilege, like the attorney–client privilege, is subject to the crime-fraud exception. In the First Circuit view, the societal interest in encouraging candor in treatment has to be subordinated to the prevention of future crime and fraud, e.g., in health insurance and personal injury claims.[48] However, the Sixth Circuit refuses to make an exception to the therapist-patient privilege even for dangerous patients who make threats to others.[49]

According to a recent Connecticut decision,[50] the "crime/fraud exception" is broad enough to remove protection from communications with an attorney that were intended to further a civil fraud; the exception is not narrowly limited to communications in pursuit of criminal fraud.

Even if the corporation itself refuses to waive the attorney-client and work-product privileges, a corporate officer testifying before the Grand Jury can waive the privileges.[51] The Second Circuit remanded the matter to consider issues of when implied waiver will be considered fair and when an officer can speak on behalf of the corporation. When a waiver of the privileges is found, fairness demands that it be tailored narrowly to the degree of prejudice suffered by the government from non-production of the documents in question.

According to the Federal Circuit, an opinion of counsel as to the tax consequences of a proposed merger, printed in the proxy statement soliciting support for the transaction, waived attorney-client privilege in all documents involved in giving the tax advice—but privilege was not waived with respect to other legal issues raised by the merger.[52]

Documents exchanged between a law firm and a PR firm hired in anticipation of a lawsuit are not covered by the attorney-client privilege, because they do not contain confidential communications made in order to obtain legal advice.[53] Furthermore, disclosure to the PR firm would destroy privilege in any case. The material is not work product as defined by FRCP 26(b)(3) because that is limited to material relating to strategies for the conduct of litigation, not the effect of litigation on public perception of the litigants.

[¶5600] Appeals

An early 2000 Supreme Court case[54] resolves a circuit split and permits an appellate court to direct entry of judgment as a matter of law when it finds that some evidence was erroneously admitted at trial—and the remaining evidence won't support the verdict. FRCP 50(d) doesn't require a remand to the District Court to determine whether to enter judgment for the defendant or have a new trial; the Court of Appeals can resolve the question.

Rule 50(d) says that if an appellate court reverses the judgment when the losing party appeals from a trial court denial of motion for JMOL (judgment as matter of law), the court is not precluded from determining that the appellee is entitled to a new trial. The appellate court can direct the trial court to decide the availability of a new trial. However, this rule doesn't specifically allow the Court of Appeals to direct entry of JMOL.

The Supreme Court ruled that it shouldn't really matter whether the appellate rationale was that the winning party failed to present sufficient evidence, or whether the inadmissible evidence in the record was crucial to the determination at trial. Either way, the party whose verdict is set aside has notice of the alleged deficiency in the evidence, and can argue for supporting the jury verdict or for a new trial.

The Supreme Court rejected the argument that it's unfair to allow JMOL at appellate level, because the plaintiffs, confronted with that possibility, would have submitted more evidence. But in the post-*Daubert* atmosphere, plaintiffs know that expert testimony (the kind at issue in this case) is a perilous foundation for a case.

When a District Court dismisses one count of a civil case and transfers the remaining counts to a different district, the dismissal is only an appealable final decision if it is certified under FRCP 54(b) for immediate appeal.[55] If this is not done, the dismissed count accompanies the others, and must be appealed in the transferee court.

A bankruptcy court's denial of a claim of exemption is a 28 USC §158(a)(1) "final order." Therefore, as the Ninth Circuit made explicit what was implied by earlier decisions, not only is immediate appeal available—it is mandatory if the point is to be appealed at all.[56]

[¶5630] [NEW] Interest and Costs

The Third Circuit set guidelines for awarding costs to a prevailing defendant under FRCP 54(d)(1) in *In re Paoli Railroad Yard PCB Litigation.*[57] The Third Circuit ruled that the District Court can reduce the award made by the clerk for, e.g., the prevailing party's unclean hands, dilatory tactics, noncompliance with process, or the losing party's inability to pay. But costs should not be reduced because the loser acted in good faith, because the case was complex or involved close issues, or because of the parties' relative financial status. The District Court reviews the clerk's award of costs de novo; when the District Court itself sets the costs, review is for abuse of discretion only.

Post-judgment interest on an attorney's fee award runs from the date the District Court renders a money judgment as defined by 28 USC

§1961(a), not from the point at which the District Court declares that the prevailing party should receive a fee award.[58]

[¶5670] Arbitration and ADR

NCCUSL issued a Revised Uniform Arbitration Act (RUAA), substantially revising the original Uniform Arbitration Act, which dates back to 1955. In particular, §10 permits consolidation of arbitration proceedings on the motion of a party, as long as the same parties are involved (or the same parties plus a third party), the claims arise out of the same or related transactions, and there are common issues of law or fact justifying the consolidation. See http://www.law.upenn/edu/bll/ulc/ulc_frame.htm for the text of the RUAA.

There were numerous cases in 2000 involving arbitration clauses in consumer credit agreements. In 1999, Alabama ruled that the Magnuson-Moss Act invalidates arbitration provisions within written warranties, but that decision was reversed in 2000.[59]

The Supreme Court heard a consumer credit arbitration case and ruled that the consumer borrower could not invalidate the arbitration clause merely because it was silent as to allocation of arbitration costs.[60] The court did not accept the borrower's argument that such silence put her at risk of prohibitive costs if she exercised her arbitration remedy. The party who seeks to invalidate the arbitration agreement has the burden of producing evidence on the cost issue, which the consumer failed to do.

A New York trial court permitted a payday loan borrower to get discovery from the lender bank in a credit discrimination suit in the New York State court system, notwithstanding an arbitration clause. In this reading, the FAA allows arbitration agreements to be set aside for good cause, including unconscionability. In this case, the plaintiff alleges unconscionable lending practices, and at any rate, the defendant can renew its motion to compel arbitration after completion of discovery.[61]

An Arkansas court refused to enforce the arbitration clause in a payday loan agreement because of the lack of mutuality: borrowers were required to arbitrate, whereas the lender could sue to collect the loan. The court treats arbitrability as purely a matter of contract construction, and found the contract presumptively unenforceable because of its one-sidedness.[62]

Although the Truth in Lending Act and the Electronic Funds Transfer Act refer to class actions, the Third Circuit has ruled that it does not conflict with the statutory purpose to enforce an arbitration clause in a loan agreement. In other words, it is not unlawful for consumers to agree to by-pass litigation even in an area where class actions are recognized.[63]

A Supreme Court decision from March, 2000[64] permits a motion to confirm, vacate, or modify an FAA arbitration award to be brought either where it was made or in any district that would be proper under the general venue statute (28 USC §1391(a)(2)), because FAA venue is permissive.

FAA §9 governs venue for confirmation of an award; this section lays venue in the district where the award was made unless the arbitration agreement specifies a different one. But venue is proper (under the general venue provision) in the district in which a contract is performed.

The FAA was enacted in 1925, when venue concepts were far more restrictive than they are now; FAA was intended to liberalize the then-prevailing concepts.

An FRCP 27 motion for emergency discovery is proper to preserve evidence for later transmission under seal to an arbitrator.[65] (In this case, the plaintiff wanted to prevent a shipowner from repairing an engine, because the repairs would obscure the condition of the engine, which is what the arbitrator was supposed to decide.)

The basic arbitration rule is that District Courts should not intervene in arbitral discovery unless special circumstances are present—as, in the Fourth Circuit's view, they were present in this case. The District Court has jurisdiction even though there is no federal litigation underway, because a federal-court motion might be brought to compel arbitration, seek security, or enforce the eventual arbitration award.[66]

The U-4, the securities industry arbitration agreement, has given rise to a good deal of controversy both with respect to claims from brokerage clients and securities industry employees. On November 3, 1999, the SEC published an order approving the NASD's proposed changes to arbitration of employment discrimination claims under the U-4. The intent is to strengthen the arbitration process and provide predictable methods for resolving claims that could either be arbitrated or litigated.

Claims of up to $100,000 can be heard by one arbitrator, rather than by a panel. All employment discrimination claims must go to qualified, nonindustry arbitrators. The arbitrator can award reasonable attorneys' fees. Employers can avoid bifurcation of claims (especially claims joined with claims not involving discrimination) between litigation and arbitration.

In a securities arbitration case, a good-faith allegation that the arbitrator manifestly disregarded federal law is enough to give the federal court system jurisdiction over a motion to vacate the award, because manifest disregard of federal law does raise a substantial federal question.[67]

With respect to labor arbitration, another well-established subject for arbitration, the Tenth Circuit ruled that instead of submitting a case about job reductions to arbitration, the District Court should first have rendered a decision as to whether the matter was arbitrable at all. In this view, the question of whether a Collective Bargaining Agreement obligates parties to arbitrate a particular grievance is one for the court, not an arbitrator to decide—unless the CBA clearly and unequivocally demands arbitration.[68]

The Fourth Circuit held in early 2001 that an arbitration agreement dividing fees and costs between the employer and employee is not per se unenforceable. A case-by-case analysis should be made, involving the employee's ability to pay and whether the costs are likely to be substantial enough to deter employees from pursuing worthwhile claims.[69]

The Supreme Court decided in March, 2001 that the Federal Arbitration Act applies in general to employment contracts; the FAA's exception for "contracts of employment of seamen, railroad employees, or any other class of workers engaged in foreign or interstate commerce" refers only to transportation workers, not any workers involved in interstate commerce. Therefore, pre-dispute arbitration clauses are not necessarily unenforceable merely on the grounds that they involve workers in interstate commerce.[70] An article by Michael Delikat and Rene Kathawala, "Enforcing Pre-Dispute Arbitration Agreement," *N.Y.L.J.* 5/1/01, available through law.com, cites several recent cases permitting enforcement of pre-dispute arbitration requirements, e.g., *Chanchani v. Salomon/Smith Barney, Inc.*, 2001 WL 204214 (S.D.N.Y. 3/1/01) [enforcing arbitration policy in employee handbook]; *Wright v. SFX Entertainment Inc.*, 2001 WL 103433 (S.D.N.Y. 2/7/01) [written employment agreement with arbitration clause]; *Marcus v. Masucci*, 118 F.Supp.2d 453 (S.D.N.Y. 2000) [U-4 arbitration clause].

The District Court for the District of Kansas held that a computer dealer's standard contract terms—including an arbitration agreement—that were packed in the box with the computer constituted "proposed alterations to the sales agreement" (UCC 2-207). Therefore, they were enforceable only if the customer assented to them.[71] However, several courts have held "shrinkwrap" and "clickwrap" agreements enforceable even though the customer does not consent to them in advance.

ENDNOTES

1. *U.S. v. Morrison,* 529 U.S. 598 (Sup.Ct. 2000).
2. *Anastoff v. U.S.,* 223 F.3d 898 (8th Cir. 2000). An en banc rehearing on December 18, 2000 declared the underlying case moot, because the IRS agreed to grant the taxpayer the requested refund, but did not reach the question of what precedential effect, if any, should be given to un-published opinions: *Anastoff v. U.S.,* No. 99-3917 EM, 69 LW 2424.
3. *Sorchini v. City of Covina,* 01 C.D.O.S. 3514, 5/4/01), discussed in Jason Hoppin, "9th Circuit Takes Soft Line on No-Cite Rule," *The Recorder,* 5/7/01, available on law.com.
4. See *http://www.uscourts.gov/about.html.*
5. *Free v. Abbott Laboratories Inc.,* 529 U.S. 333 (Sup.Ct. 2000).
6. *First Hartford Corporation Pension Plan & Trust v. U.S.,* 194 F.3d 1379 (Fed.Cir. 1999).
7. *Peay v. Bellsouth Medical Assistance Plan,* 205 F.3d 1206 (10th Cir. 2000).
8. *Shoppers Food Warehouse v. Moreno,* 68 LW 1502 (D.C. 2/17/00).
9. *Carter v. Philip Morris Corp.,* 68 LW 1524 (E.D. Pa. 2/23/00).
10. *Cohen v. Office Depot,* 184 F.3d 1292 (11th Cir. 1999).
11. *Cohen v. Office Depot,* 68 LW 1532 (11th Cir. 2/24/00).
12. *Rotella v. Wood,* 528 U.S. 549 (Sup.Ct. 2000).
13. *Klehr v. A.O. Smith Corp.,* 521 U.S. 179 (Sup.Ct. 1997).
14. *Blinn v. Fla. Dep't of Transportation,* 69 LW 1407 (Fla.App. 12/29/00).
15. *Le Credit Lyonnais S.A. v. Nadd,* 741 So.2d 1165 (Fla.App. 1999).
16. *Regents of U. of Minnesota v. Raygor,* 620 N.W.2d 680 (Minn. 2001).
17. *Semtek Int'l Inc. v. Lockheed Martin Corp.,* #99-1551, 69 LW 4147 (Sup.Ct. 2/27/01).
18. *Benson v. SI Handling Systems,* 188 F.3d 780 (7th Cir. 1999).
19. *Rogers v. Wal-Mart Stores,* 230 F.3d 868 (6th Cir. 2000).
20. *Sierminski v. Transouth Financial Corp.,* 216 F.3d 945 (11th Cir. 2000).
21. *Lawrence v. Chancery Court of Tennessee,* 188 F.3d 687 (6th Cir. 1999).
22. *Duhaime v. John Hancock Mutual Life Insurance Co.,* 183 F.3d 1 (1st Cir. 1999).
23. *Morrison v. Allstate Indemnity Co.,* 228 F.3d 1255 (11th Cir. 2000). The court relied on *Cohen v. Office Depot Inc.,* 204 F.3d 1069 (11th

Cir. 2000) for the proposition that, when the amount in controversy is being determined, punitive damages are divided equally among all the class members, and attorneys' fee claims cannot be aggregated if the right to recover them in separate and distinct and state law treats the fee award as compensation for the underlying injuries.

24. *Simon v. Philip Morris Inc.*, 69 LW 1319 (E.D.N.Y. 11/6/00).
25. *Gibbs Properties Corp. v. Cigna Corp.*, 69 LW 1015 (M.D. Fla. 6/16/00).
26. *In re Telectronic Pacing Systems Inc.*, 221 F.3d 870 (6th Cir. 2000).
27. *Varacallo v. Massachusetts Mutual Life Ins. Co.*, 752 F.3d 807 (N.J. Super. 2000).
28. *Z-Seven Fund Inc. v. Ehrlich*, 69 LW 1254 (9th Cir. 10/18/00).
29. *Becherer v. Merrill Lynch*, 193 F.3d 413 (6th Cir. 1999).
30. *Nelson v. Adams USA Inc.*, 529 U.S. 460 (Sup.Ct. 2000).
31. *Grupo Mexicano de Desarollo SA v. Alliance Bond Bund Inc.*, 527 U.S. 308 (Sup.Ct. 1999).
32. *U.S. ex rel Rahman v. Oncology Associates PC*, 198 F.3d 489 (4th Cir. 1999).
33. *Adams v. Freedom Forge Corp.*, 204 F.3d 475 (3rd Cir. 2000).
34. *In re Diet Drugs Products Liability Litigation*, 69 LW 1136 (E.D. Pa. 8/28/00).
35. *American Soccer Co. v. Score First Enterprises*, 187 F.3d 1108 (9th Cir. 1999).
36. *Commercial Space Management Co. v. Boeing Co.*, 193 F.3d 1074 (9th Cir. 1999), citing *American Soccer Co., supra.*
37. *Smith v. Atkinson*, 68 LW 1493 (Ala. 2/4/00).
38. *Goff v. Harrold Ivest Trucking Co.*, 27 S.W.3d 387 (Ark. 2000).
39. *U.S. v. Cordoba*, 194 F.3d 1053 (9th Cir. 1999).
40. *In re Visa Check/MasterMoney Antitrust Litigation*, 68 LW 1516 (E.D.N.Y. 2/22/00). Also see *Caridad v. Metro-North Commuter Railroad*, 191 F.3d 283 (2nd Cir. 1999), for the proposition that weighing competing expert evidence is not appropriate at the pure certification stage.
41. *Goodyear Tire and Rubber Co. v. Thompson*, 11 S.W. 3d 575 (Ky. 2000).
42. *Goebel v. Denver & Rio Grande Western RR Co.*, 68 LW 1775 (10th Cir. 6/12/00).
43. *Schering Corp v. Pfizer Inc.*, 189 F.3d 218 (2nd Cir. 1999).
44. *Clifford v. Commonwealth*, 7 S.W.3d 371 (Ky. 1999).
45. *Costantino v. Herzog*, 203 F.3d 164 (2nd Cir. 2000).

46. *Spensieri v. Lasky,* 723 N.E.2d 544 (N.Y. 12/2/99).
47. *Conner v. State,* 68 LW 1183 (Fla. 9/16/99).
48. *In re Grand Jury Proceedings (Violette),* 183 F.3d 71 (1st Cir. 1999).
49. *U.S. v. Hayes,* 227 F.3d 578 (6th Cir. 2000).
50. *Olson v. Accessory Controls & Equipment,* 757 A.2d 14 (Conn. 2000).
51. *In re Grand Jury Proceedings,* 219 F.3d 175 (2nd Cir. 2000).
52. *In re Pioneer Hi-Bred Int'l Inc.,* 69 LW 1544 (Fed.Cir. 2/5/01).
53. *Calvin Klein Trademark Trust v. Wachner,* 69 LW 1371 (S.D.N.Y. 12/5/00).
54. *Weisgram v. Marley Co.,* 528 U.S. 440 (Sup.Ct. 2000).
55. *Hill v. Henderson,* 195 F.3d 671 (D.C. Cir. 1999).
56. *Preblich v. Battley,* 181 F.3d 1048 (9th Cir. 1999).
57. 221 F.3d 449 (3rd Cir. 2000).
58. *Eaves v. Cape May County, NJ,* 239 F.3d 527 (3rd Cir. 2001).
59. *Southern Energy Homes Inc. v. Ard,* 68 LW 1784 (Ala. 6/2/00), reversing *Southern Energy Homes v. Lee,* 732 So.2d 994 (Ala. 1999).
60. *Green Tree Financial Corp.- Alabama v. Randolph,* #99-1235, 69 LW 4022 (Sup.Ct. 12/11/00). See Jacqueline E. Mottek, "The Impact of Mandatory Arbitration Clauses on Class Certification," 69 LW 2307 (11/28/00) for an excellent review of some highly complex procedural issues.
61. *Hayes v. County Bank,* 69 LW 1159 (N.Y.Sup. 8/14/00).
62. *Showmethemoney Check Cashiers Inc. v. Williams,* 27 S.W.3d 361 (Ark. 2000); semble, *Ramirez v. Circuit City Stores Inc.,* 90 Cal.Rptr. 2d 916 (Cal.App. 1999).
63. *Johnson v. West Suburban Bank,* 225 F.3d 366 (3rd Cir. 2000).
64. *Cortez Byrd Chips Inc. v. Bill Harbert Construction Co.,* 529 U.S. 193 (Sup.Ct. 2000).
65. *In re Application of Deiulemar Compagnia di Navigazione SPA for the Perpetuation of Certain Evidence,* 198 F.3d 473 (4th Cir. 1999).
66. 64 FR 2288.
67. *Greenberg v. Bear, Stearns & Co.,* 220 F.3d 22 (2nd Cir. 2000).
68. *Oil, Chemical & Atomic Workers Int'l Union v. Conoco Inc.,* 69 LW 1553 (10th Cir. 3/7/01).
69. *Bradford v. Rockwell Semiconductor Systems,* 69 LW 1480 (4th Cir. 1/22/01).
70. *Circuit City Stores, Inc. v. Adams,* #99-1379, 2001 WL 273205 (Sup. Ct. 3/21/01).
71. *Klocek v. Gateway Inc.,* 104 F.Supp.2d 1332 (D.Kan. 2000).

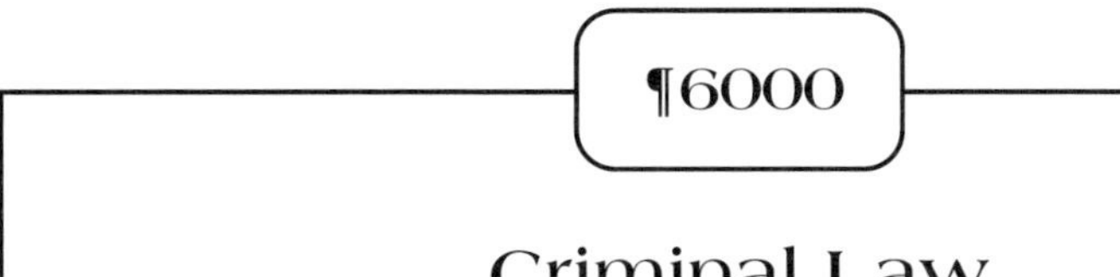

¶6000

Criminal Law

[¶6001]

As ever, criminal cases represented a very large part of the Supreme Court docket, and occupied much time for lower courts. And, as usual, the predominant issues were search and seizure and the death penalty. Many cases continue to explore and amplify the meaning of AEDPA.

A police officer guilty of false arrest is liable for punitive damages in the arrestee's §1983 civil rights action if and only if the police officer had either an evil motive or subjective awareness that probable cause to arrest was lacking.[1] The jury has discretion to award punitive damages based on the plaintiff's showing of the defendant's evil motive or intent, or reckless or callous indifference to the federal rights of others (a perceived risk that the defendant's actions would violate federal law). Egregious or outrageous acts could support an inference of evil motive, but are not necessarily determinative of the punitive damage issue.

In this case, the plaintiff was arguably disruptive when filming local government meetings for his cable TV show, and was arrested for disorderly conduct when he refused to turn off the camera. Qualified immunity was not available to the police officer, because the state Open Meeting Law gave the plaintiff the right to film the meeting, and a reasonable official would have understood that.

The state of mind to prove a §1983 claim is not the same as for punitive damages, in that it requires only intent to perform the arrest, not intent to violate civil rights. Although the arrest was wrongful, punitive damages were inappropriate because there was no evidence of malice or reckless indifference to Constitutional rights.

As usual, Federal Rules amendments were promulgated and approved by the Supreme Court, this time on April 17, 2000, effective December 1, 2000 unless Congress makes changes.[2]

Amended F.R.E. 404(a) deals with proof of character via introduction of evidence of reputation or opinion; the alleged victim of a crime can attack any trait in the defendant that the defendant has asserted to show the alleged victim's poor reputation or poor opinion about him or her.

243

Perhaps the most important change in the F.R.Crim.P. was the new Rule 32.2, dealing with forfeiture, especially the jury's role and the ability of third parties to challenge forfeiture. Amended Rule 7(c)(2) requires the charging instrument to give notice that the defendant owns potentially forfeitable property.

[¶6002] Substantive Criminal Law

The Third Circuit has upheld[3] 18 USC §2252 (ban on intrastate possession of child pornography, where material was produced using items that have traveled in interstate commerce) as against a Commerce Clause challenge. The Commerce Clause allows regulation of an intrastate activity if regulation is an essential part of controlling a broader interstate market. It was reasonable for Congress to believe that intrastate possession of child pornography stimulates greater demand for interstate trafficking.

Downloading child pornography from the Net to a computer isn't the kind of "transporting or shipping" envisioned by 18 USC §2252(a)(1);[4] Congress enacted separate provisions for receiving–distributing and transporting–shipping. Downloading images supplied by somebody else is a simple possession offense violating §2252(a)(2), but is not tantamount to the more serious transporting offense.

A June, 2000 decision of the Texas Court of Appeals invalidates the state's Penal Code section prohibiting deviate sexual intercourse with another individual of the same sex. The court concluded that the provision violates the Texas Constitution's Equal Rights Act, not because the ERA protects homosexual conduct, but because limiting the offense to same-sex couples is subject to strict scrutiny.[5]

Computer crime was one focus of attention in 2000. The Internet False Identification Prevention Act of 2000, P.L. 106-578 (12/28/00) directs the U.S. Attorney General and the Secretary of the Treasury to collaborate for two years on a coordinating committee to promote the investigation and prosecution of offenses under 18 USC §1028(d)(3): "creation and distribution of false identification documents." P.L. 106-578 makes it clear that transferring identification documents by electronic means can be illegal. In this context, a false identification document is one that appears to be government-issued but is not. The crime includes making either false documents, or software tools to create them, available online.

The Computer Crime Enforcement Act, P.L. 106-572 (12/28/00) creates a federal grant program so that states and local law-enforcement jurisdictions can combat computer crime and educate consumers in how to protect themselves against it. The statute appropriates $25 million each for fiscal years 2001, 2002, 2003, and 2004.

According to the Ninth Circuit, the Computer Fraud and Abuse Act, 18 USC §1030(e)(8)(A), definition of "damage" as conduct causing loss to "one or more individuals" applies to damages to a corporation.[6] Nor is the CFAA's coverage limited to outsider hackers—it is triggered, for instance, by an employee's use of the employer's computer to transmit the employer's trade secrets to a competitor. Furthermore, any kind of wrongdoing is considered "fraud" for this purpose; proof of common-law fraud is not required, and loss of proprietary information is cognizable damage.[7]

The Department of Justice manual for prosecuting intellectual property crimes (e.g., fraud committed with computers; cyberstalking; child pornography; identity theft) can be found at http://www.cybercrime.gov/crimes.html.

The District Court for the District of New Jersey invalidated the state system for regulating dissemination of information about sex offenders under "Megan's Law," finding it Constitutionally inadequate. Enforcement of the notification provisions was enjoined until the state develops a notification system with better protection for privacy of registrants: a uniform method of distributing notices to ensure that all counties will distribute the information only to authorized recipients.[8]

The plaintiffs are individuals required to make disclosures in intermediate and high risk groups. The District Court agreed with the plaintiffs that the state doesn't adequately prevent disclosure of registrants' home addresses to unauthorized persons. There has to be a uniform method of distribution so that notices will be distributed in all counties to, and only to, those who are supposed to get them.

21 USC §848(b), the Continuing Criminal Enterprise (CCE) statute requiring life sentences for principals in drug dealing conspiracy, sets out sentencing factors, not substantive elements of an aggravated offense, in the view of the Seventh Circuit.[9] A footnote in *Jones v. U.S.*[10] implies that the (b) circumstances are aggravating elements of the CCE offense, and therefore have to be charged in the indictment and then proved beyond a reasonable doubt. Since then, there have been many challenges by defen-

dants who claim that language in statutes that is assumed to constitute sentencing factors actually spells out elements of the crime.

The Seventh Circuit interpretation is that most Circuits don't go so far as to read *Jones* to make any fact (other than prior conviction) that increases the maximum penalty, an element that must be charged and proved at trial, because that would make trials even more cumbersome than they are now, and the Supreme Court would not announce a major new principle in a footnote in a comparatively minor case.

The Seventh Circuit reads §848(b) to comprise sentencing factors, as indicated by the section's title ("life imprisonment for engaging in CCE") which sounds like sentencing factors. The actual definition of CCE is deferred to (c), where the elements are located; and the phrase "shall be imprisoned" divides the elements of the crime from the sentencing factors.

Also see ¶6080 for discussion of post-*Jones* sentencing issues.

Commerce Clause challenges to the Child Support Recovery Act (CSRA) have been overwhelmingly unsuccessful[11], However, in 2000, the Sixth Circuit held that Congress exceeded its power by enacting this statute, which makes it a crime to fail to make support payments for a child who lives in another state.[12] Although the Second is one of the Circuits that has approved the CSRA, the Southern District of New York held in early 2001 that this analysis of Congressional power is outmoded in light of *U.S. v. Morrison*, 529 U.S. 598 (Sup.Ct. 2000), the case that struck down the Violence Against Women Act.[13]

[¶6003] Capacity Issues

Given the present state of medical and legal knowledge, evidence about the defendant's alleged "multiple personality disorder" is inadmissible on the issues of sanity and diminished capacity.[14] Although the syndrome is generally accepted by mental health professionals, there is no way to decide if someone with MPD is legally insane. Thus, the evidence is inadmissible.

An expert witness can testify as to whether a defendant who pleaded insanity did or did not suffer from severe mental disease as defined by 18 USC §17, even though FRE 704(b) prohibits testimony on ultimate issues in insanity cases.[15] The true ultimate issue for an insanity defense is the defendant's capacity to understand the nature, quality, and wrongfulness of acts at the time of their commission. The Fifth Circuit also requires the defendant to demonstrate insanity by convincing clarity as a prerequisite for the issuing going to the jury.

[¶6005] [NEW] Defenses

In a mid-2000 Eighth Circuit case, an informer sold heroin to the defendant, then coerced the defendant to re-sell the heroin to a police officer by threatening to terminate his drug supply. The Eighth Circuit treated this as entrapment as a matter of law, in that no reasonable jury could consider the defendant pre-disposed to commit the offense of drug trafficking.[16]

[¶6010] Multi-Party Offenses

Due process prevents a state from offering irreconcilable descriptions of events in sequential prosecutions of two defendants for same crime.[17] At the petitioner's trial, the prosecution relied on out-of-court statements that made the accomplice the actual killer, making the petitioner liable for felony murder. At another trial, the prosecution used the theory that someone else did the killing before the petitioner and his accomplice even arrived at the scene. The Eighth Circuit says that trials that involve manipulation of evidence are inherently unfair—but because this is a new rule, it can't be used retroactively in habeas cases.

Early in 2001, the California Supreme Court eliminated the common-law "rule of consistency," which had required that if all the other co-conspirators have been acquitted, the last alleged co-conspirator to be tried must be acquitted because there is no one left for him to have conspired with. The rationale is that a person who is guilty beyond a reasonable doubt should be convicted irrespective of the fates of the alleged co-conspirators.[18]

[¶6020] Elements of Offenses

A state statute that reduces the amount of evidence needed for a conviction, by knocking out the corroboration requirement for certain types of evidence (here, sex abuse of a minor), is ex post facto and can't be used to obtain a conviction of an offense prior to the enactment of the statute.[19]

A California statute has been upheld[20] which allows an otherwise time-barred prosecution for sexual abuse of a child to be brought at any time within one year of the victim's complaint that is corroborated by independent evidence.

The court didn't think that extending the statute of limitations violated Due Process or operated ex post facto. An ex post facto law makes an act criminal even though it was permitted when it was done; increases punishment after the crime was committed; or removes a defense that was available when the crime was committed. But the defenses in question are those involving the elements of the crime or justification or excuse for the crime—not mere timing. Ex post facto ensures that people can assess the consequences of a course of conduct before committing it. (Arguably, however, statutes of limitations fall into the same category.) Due process isn't involved, because there are crimes for which there is no statute of limitations.

[¶6020.3] [NEW] Sex Offenses

Early in 2001, the Supreme Court considered the case[21] of an individual confined under the Washington State Community Protection Act of 1990 as a sexually violent predator, i.e., a person with a mental abnormality or personality disorder that makes it likely that he will continue to engage in predatory acts of sexual violence. The Kansas statute, which is quite similar, has already been upheld by the Supreme Court in *Kansas v. Hendricks*, 521 U.S. 346 (Sup.Ct. 1997) on the grounds that it is non-punitive and satisfies substantive due process. The 2001 case asserts that the actual conditions of confinement make the statute, even if facially acceptable, unacceptably punitive as applied. But the Supreme Court ruled that a civil statute cannot be punitive as individually applied; the court must look to the face of the statute.

[¶6020.8] [NEW] Larceny and Fraud Offenses

In the Fourth Circuit's view, the SEC did not have the power to seek remedies under the Securities Act and Exchange Act against a broker who had been convicted of 13 counts of wire fraud for converting funds belonging to a mentally disabled client. Even though the conversion involved a brokerage account, it did not occur in connection with a securities transaction—not every theft from a brokerage account triggers SEC anti-fraud enforcement.[22]

[¶6020.10] RICO

A RICO civil conspiracy plaintiff has to allege that the overt act in furtherance of the conspiracy that injured the plaintiff was either an act of racketeering under 18 USC §1961(1), or at least otherwise wrongful under

RICO.[23] In this case, the plaintiff claimed to have been fired for refusing to participate in unlawful conduct.

The Eleventh Circuit, affirmed by the Supreme Court, said that he had no RICO case because RICO does not provide standing to sue for termination or any other act that is not an act of racketeering or otherwise is brought under RICO. At common law, suit for civil conspiracy requires injury by an act that is otherwise tortious.

[¶6030] Fourth Amendment Issues

[¶6030.1] [NEW] Introduction

In its 5-4 decision of April 24, 2001, *Atwater v. City of Lago Vista*, #99-1408, 121 S.Ct. 1536, the Supreme Court ruled that it does not constitute a search and seizure in violation of the Fourth Amendment to arrest an individual for violating a misdemeanor or lesser offense (in this case, a mandatory seatbelt law) that is punishable only by a fine and not by incarceration.

The Fourth Amendment is violated by a hospital's policy of performing warrantless drug testing, without consent, on pregnant women who show signs of drug addiction, and then reporting the test results to the police. The Supreme Court refused to extend the "special needs" exception for searches that can be done without individualized suspicion because they are done for reasons other than law enforcement.[24]

The Second Circuit held that staging a "perp walk"— parading an arrestee outside a police precinct house solely so that the news media can film him there—violates the Fourth Amendment, because the manner and scope of searches must be reasonable. Decision was reserved as to the propriety of informing the media when a prisoner will be transported for legitimate law enforcement purposes. However, although the practice was deemed not to serve any legitimate law enforcement purposes, the detectives conducting the "perp walk" were entitled to qualified immunity.[25]

In 2000, Iowa joined about a dozen other states that refuse to enact a good-faith exception to the exclusionary rule, on the grounds that admitting illegally obtained evidence would serve as judicial condonation of the illegality.[26]

[¶6030.4] What is a Search?

In a Supreme Court case decided early in 2001,[26A] the police had probable cause to believe that the defendant had marijuana in his house. They refused to let him enter his house unaccompanied by a police officer for a period of about two hours while they sought a search warrant. The Supreme Court refused to suppress the marijuana found pursuant to the warrant, because the restraint was reasonable and tailored to the law enforcement need to prevent the defendant from destroying evidence, and the minimal intrusion on his privacy was reasonable on balance.

A Second Circuit drug case from late 2000 involved an apartment in which the police reasonably believed quantities of cocaine were present. (Through work with an informant, the police observed someone leaving the apartment with a kilo of cocaine.) The police feared that the surveillance would be compromised, so they followed a food delivery person. When the defendant opened the apartment door to receive the food delivery, the police ordered everyone out of the apartment for a stop and frisk. This action was upheld by the Second Circuit, on the grounds that there is no legitimate privacy interest in whatever is knowingly exposed to the public—including sights that are visible through the open door when a delivery is received.[27]

Yet a rather similar fact pattern led to the opposite result in California.[28] The police got the defendant out of his house by telling him (untruthfully) that a plainclothes police car had collided with his car. The California Court of Appeals said that even his later consent would not justify searching his person. In this analysis, police trickery is not acceptable if the ruse is not related to the criminal activity but plays on a common vulnerability. (Even law-abiding citizens would want to investigate an alleged accident involving their cars.)

For Fourth Amendment purposes, the Supreme Court ruled in April, 2000[29] that a search occurs when a police officer manipulates (before opening) a piece of soft luggage that a bus passenger put in the overhead compartment. Placing luggage where other passengers could touch and handle it does not constitute a surrender of the expectation of privacy. In this case, an agent got on the bus to check the immigration status of passengers. When he squeezed the luggage in the bins, he found a brick-like object in the defendant's bag, which turned out to be a large quantity of amphetamines.

Rejecting the prosecution contention that the luggage in the bin was "exposed to the public," the Supreme Court differentiated between patting luggage and performing a visual inspection of objects out in the open.

Tactile examination of luggage is the equivalent of a *Terry* pat-down. People use carry-on luggage for items they want to keep close at hand. The Fourth Amendment is implicated because the expectation is that another passenger, or a bus employee, may handle the luggage, but not to investigate it.

Nebraska defines[30] a canine sniff outside a dwelling in search of illegal drugs as an "investigative tool" which can be used to develop probable cause to issue a search warrant, if there was reasonable suspicion to bring the dog in the first place. In contrast, however, the District of Nebraska says[31] that a canine sniff is not even a search, and finds no expectation of privacy in the hallway outside one's apartment.

A thermal scan of the outside of a defendant's home (looking for hot spots that show high heat levels consistent with indoor marijuana cultivation) is not a search, and thus does not require a warrant.[32] There was no actual intrusion (although intrusion might evolve as technology becomes more sophisticated), and there is no subjective expectation of privacy in the heat emissions from one's home. The defendant did nothing to dissipate the waste heat, so could not have been trying to conceal it and asserting a privacy interest. Nor would a subjective expectation have been reasonable, because nothing objective was revealed, only amorphous hot spots in the roof and walls.

The Ninth Circuit did not require a warrant to place a magnetized tracking device on the undercarriage of a car which U.S. Forest Service Agents had already seen in a surveillance video of a marijuana patch in a national forest.[33] The Fourth Amendment was not involved because there was neither a search nor a seizure.

The agents got the defendant's address by tracing the license plate and then placed two tracking devices on his car when it was parked in a driveway (not within the curtilage). One transmitter failed, the other one signaled the police when he went to harvest marijuana plants from the patch.

The court said that the devices weren't placed in a hidden or enclosed area, and the defendant didn't assert an expectation of privacy in the undercarriage of his vehicle. Property is only seized when there is a meaningful interference with the owner's possessory interest. Here, all that occurred was a minimal technical trespass; the owner could still exercise dominion and control over the vehicle.

Property moved by one police officer during a lawful search can be in the "plain view" of another officer, thus justifying a warrantless seizure by the second officer.[34] In this case, a purse and ID card, evidence of an armed robbery, were removed from the glove compartment and placed on the front seat of a car during a valid protective search.

An exception to the exclusionary rule is sometimes recognized for "plain touch" or "plain feel" as well as "plain sight"—for instance, when a patdown reveals the unmistakable silhouette of a gun. However, an Alabama case refuses to apply this principle when a police officer frisking a suspect finds a Tic-Tacs container—which he knows is commonly used to hold drugs—and orders the suspect to open it. The rationale is that the feel of a closed container, unlike the feel of contraband itself, is not sufficiently incriminating to provide probable cause.[35]

It is permissible to detain and frisk a visitor who appears just after a house has been searched pursuant to a warrant, if the police have a reasonable suspicion that the visitor is armed and dangerous.[36]

[¶6030.4.1] Reasonable Expectation of Privacy

A guest visiting a friend during the day has a Fourth Amendment expectation of privacy,[37] because nearly all social guests do have such an expectation; a commercial justification for presence on the property is not required.

The defendant had a reasonable expectation of privacy within his home, requiring suppression of evidence when the police made a warrantless entry into the side yard of the house and observed through an uncurtained window (not visible from the sidewalk, only from the yard) that the defendant was packaging drugs.[38]

The Ninth Circuit treated a garage whose door was open exactly like any other part of a house where work is done and possessions are stored; hence, a warrant was required to arrest the defendant.[39]

Even if the bags are within the curtilage, the Fourth Amendment is not violated by a warrantless search or seizure of garbage bags put out for collection, because the expectation of privacy has been surrendered by discarding the materials.[40]

[¶6030.5] Search Warrants

The Seventh Circuit declined to apply the exclusionary rule in a case[41] in which the search warrant lacked particularity, but the search in effect was done the same way it would have been if the warrant had been properly drafted. In this view, exclusion is too severe a sanction for the gravity of the violation.

At the beginning of 2000, the Sixth Circuit declined to recognize[42] a proposed exception to the exclusionary rule, one that would permit admission of evidence seized under a residential search warrant even though the police failed to wait long enough before making a forcible entrance onto the premises. Evidence should be excluded if the knock-and-announce part of the reasonableness requirement is violated. The proposed independent source doctrine applies only if there have been two searches, with the proper one independent of the defective one; the warrant can't provide an independent source for the evidence.

In mid-2000, the Ninth Circuit articulated[43] a three-part test for valid, warrantless entry into a home under the emergency doctrine:

- The police have reasonable grounds to believe that an emergency exists and their assistance is needed immediately to protect life or property.
- The primary intent of the search is NOT to make an arrest or seize evidence.
- There is reasonable basis (equivalent to probable cause) to associate the emergency with the place that is searched.

Because of the special needs of the parole system, justifying departures from conventional Fourth Amendment principles, Colorado does not require reasonable grounds for believing that parole was violated as a prerequisite for a warrantless parole search. A valid parole search must take place pursuant to a statute, in furtherance of the rehabilitative and supervisory purposes of the parole system and must not be arbitrary, capricious, or harassing.[44]

[¶6030.7] Vehicle Searches

Arresting a driver does not authorize a warrantless search of closed containers in the vehicle that the police know or should know belong to passengers who have not been arrested. A full search is not permissible under the Washington State Constitution, even if the police reasonably perceive a threat.[45]

The South Dakota rule permits warrantless search of the purse of a passenger, given probable cause, when the driver of the car is arrested.[46]

The Massachusetts Constitution does not authorize the police to make passengers get out of the vehicle during a routine traffic stop, because the intrusion on privacy is more than minimal.[47]

The Tenth Circuit refused to enunciate a bright-line test under which the police would always be allowed to ask lawfully detained motorists if they were carrying weapons. (It is not a subject on which candor can be expected.) The Tenth Circuit required that questions asked during a traffic stop, even one that is not prolonged past a reasonable duration, must be related to the original purpose of the stop. The results of unduly broad questioning must be suppressed.[48]

In mid-1999, Washington State also applied its own Constitution to demand more than the Supreme Court precedent requires. In this reading, the state constitution forbids traffic stops made because the police wanted to investigate criminal activity for which they lacked reasonable suspicion for a normal investigation.[49]

In 1999, several cases arose involving police programs of surveillance of taxicabs. Cab drivers are always at high risk of robbery and other violence from passengers, but the surveillance is controversial because of its potential restrictions on the freedom of cab drivers and passengers and the potential for uncovering evidence of crime unrelated to violence against the drivers.

The New York case[50] says that the Fourth Amendment is violated by the police program of doing suspicionless safety checks on taxicabs, because *Brown v. Texas*[51] requires suspicionless stops to come under a plan with explicit, neutral limitations on the discretion of police officers. In the cases at bar, the police stopped taxis, gave out safety pamphlets, and asked about safety practices—and also ordered passengers out of the taxi. A couple of suspicious-looking passengers turned out to be holding crack.

In this reading, the reasonableness of a vehicle stop depends on the gravity of the public concerns involved; the extent to which seizures under the plan advance public interests; and the extent of interference with individual liberty. Preventing holdups of cab drivers is a worthwhile objective, but the state did not prove that these patrol stops were any more effective than fixed checkpoint stops performed by uniformed officers in police cars. Drivers should have been assured that they were stopped based on a uniform system and were not subjected to unfair police discretion.

In contrast, the First Circuit case[52] from early 2000 holds that the rights of passengers (including the defendant, arrested on gun charges during a stop) are not violated by a taxi driver vehicle protection program that the taxi owner consented to. The cab displayed a decal saying that it was subject to visual inspection by the police.

In this reading, the owner's consent also operated as consent by the taxi driver, because the consent was for the benefit of the driver rather than an attempt to detect wrongdoing by the driver.[53] Under *Sitz,* an operator's consent is reasonable justification for a stop, and under this program, police discretion is not unfettered—stops are only done to check driver safety. The First Circuit held these stops to be brief, imposing only a minor limitation on passengers' liberty.

Substituted consent was authorized by the Fifth Circuit in mid-2000, when it ruled that the Border Patrol did not violate the Fourth Amendment by relying on consent from the operators of the bus company to detain a commercial bus. The court's interpretation was that bus passengers always take the risk that the person controlling the area will give consent to detention. The court also deemed the passengers' knowledge that the bus stops frequently to pick up passengers as assumption of risk that the bus might make additional, unplanned stops for Border Patrol agents to enter the bus.[54]

Late in 2000, the Supreme Court affirmed the Seventh Circuit, ruling that vehicle checkpoints for drug interdiction violate the Fourth Amendment. In this analysis, checkpoints are permissible to satisfy purposes closely related to vehicles, such as drunk driving and patrolling the borders—but not for generalized law enforcement purposes. The severity of the drug problem does not justify checkpoints that operate without individualized suspicion.[55] Although the Supreme Court finds drunk driving checkpoints acceptable under the U.S. Constitution, some states find them unacceptable.[56]

The Fifth Circuit held[57] that a lawful traffic stop turned into a Fourth Amendment violation when the police, without justification, detained the defendant for a ten- to fifteen-minute period to have a drug-sniffing dog inspect his car. The case arose when a rental car was stopped for tailgating. (The car had not been reported stolen.) The driver and passenger gave conflicting stories about who rented the car. The drug-sniffing canine indicated the driver's seat, where the police found cocaine carried by the driver. The court said that there was reasonable suspicion that the car was stolen, but not that drug trafficking was going on. Detention should have ended as soon as the license plate check turned up negative.

[¶6030.8] Stops and Pat-Downs

The defendant fled after seeing a number of police cars converge on an area of known narcotics traffic. Based on its expectations that weapons are very often found near narcotics transactions, the police caught up with the defendant and patted him down. In early 2000, the Supreme Court found that the circumstances justified a *Terry* stop.[58]

Although mere presence in a high-crime area is not enough to justify a stop, the Supreme Court reviewed state cases as to whether unprovoked flight is grounds for reasonable suspicion. The characteristics of an area are relevant in determining whether the police have grounds for further investigation. Nervous, evasive behavior is a factor. The court says unprovoked flight is the opposite of the kind of "going about one's business" that Constitutional sanctions are intended to protect. In this reading, flight is not necessarily an indication of criminal activity, but it's good enough to justify the limited intrusion of a *Terry* stop.

Miami police received an anonymous call that a young black man in a plaid shirt, standing at a particular bus stop, had a gun. A March, 2000 Supreme Court case[59] holds that it violates the Fourth Amendment for the police to stop and frisk someone on the basis of such an anonymous tip; anonymous tips cannot be reviewed under a special, more relaxed standard merely because it is claimed that the subject of the tip has a gun. Although *Alabama v. White*[60] allows a stop on reasonable suspicion, based on an anonymous tip from a known reliable informant (and some courts have allowed firearm exceptions even if the tip isn't good enough by *White* standards), the Supreme Court found this tip to be insufficient to support a stop. A tip is not reliable merely because the tipper knew that the tippee was present at a bus stop, because this does not demonstrate that the tipper had reliable information about the presence of a gun. Relaxed standards for gun tips could easily lead to relaxed standards for drug tips, making it easy for malicious people to cause trouble with unfounded anonymous tips.

In a high-crime area, an anonymous tipster flagged down police officers. The tipster said that he had just seen two men, whom he described, one of whom had a gun. The police saw the men and accosted them. One suspect fled and was caught by the police in possession of a loaded gun. The Third Circuit found the gun to be admissible. Subsequent flight was part of the res gestae creating reasonable suspicion under *Hodari D.* and *Wardlow.* Furthermore, the police had reasonable suspicion for a stop, based on the tipster's report of an event he had just witnessed.[61]

The District of Columbia Court of Appeals said that individuals who identify themselves to the police in the course of a tip are presumed reliable, whereas an anonymous phone tip corroborated only by innocent details is not. The court placed the fact pattern of this case[62] somewhere in the middle. An anonymous tipster approached a police officer. He refused to give his name but told the officer that a black man in a wheelchair on a nearby corner was selling crack that he kept in plastic bags in his right boot. The officer saw that the defendant, in his wheelchair and wearing unlaced boots, was at the described location. The court accepted the tip as reasonable, because it is easier to fabricate a tip for malicious reasons by telephone than in person, and because wearing unlaced boots is unusual behavior.

The Fourth Amendment was not violated by stopping a car described in an anonymous tip about erratic driving; the possible risk caused by a drunk driver justifies the stop even though it would not be an adequate basis for stopping the car to search for weapons.[63]

The Ninth Circuit said that reasonable suspicion must be particularized, not based on a characteristic that is widely shared in the area. Thus, in a county that was 73% Hispanic, a person's Hispanic appearance could not justify a stop to check for illegal aliens,[64] and that in fact yielded contraband (drugs and guns). However, the stop was held to be justified by other factors, including defendants in separate cars making U-turns to avoid the checkpoint.

[¶6035] Fifth Amendment Issues

Although the Supreme Court hinted that it might have decided *Miranda* differently if presented with the case today, the Court chose to uphold *Miranda* on stare decisis grounds in its mid-2000 decision, *Dickerson v. U.S.*, 530 U.S. 428 (Sup.Ct. 2000).

Despite some indications that the Supreme Court was dissatisfied with *Miranda*, the Court voted 7-2 to retain the requirement of a pre-interrogation warning, finding it to have become a part of the culture of law enforcement and not unduly burdensome to enforcement.

The Supreme Court tackled another Fifth Amendment issue in *United States v. Hubbell,* #99-166 (6/5/00), 68 LW 4449. As part of the Whitewater investigation, the respondent, who entered into a plea agreement, agreed to provide information. The respondent was subpoenaed to produce documents for the Arkansas Grand Jury. He refused to produce the documents, or even state whether he had them, on Fifth Amendment grounds. He was then offered immunity and, in return, produced extensive documents. The respondent was indicted subsequent to an investigation based on those documents.

The Supreme Court required dismissal of the indictment, because the Fifth Amendment forbids compelled testimony, and producing documents in response to a subpoena can be both testimonial and compelled. Furthermore, the Fifth Amendment can protect even information that is not itself inculpatory if its effect is to lead to the discovery of incriminating evidence.

Where, as here, the producer of documents is granted immunity, the prosecution has a duty to show an independent source for incriminating information, separate and apart from the compelled testimonial production of documents.

Waiver of the right to silence can be knowing (and hence valid) as long as the defendant understands the *Miranda* warning, even if the defendant fails to understand the consequences of making an inculpatory statement. Thus, statements made by a defendant who knew that the police would use those statements against him, but who also believed that God would set him free from prison if he confessed, did not have to be suppressed.[65]

Nor did the Ninth Circuit require suppression of statements made by a capital murder suspect during a three-day delay in arraignment (arraignment was required within 48 hours under California law). The defendant's warrantless arrest occurred inside a house where he committed felony murder. He said that he wanted to give statements about crimes in Utah, so the police detained him for two days without arraigning him so that a Utah detective could question him. The Ninth Circuit treats suppression as the preferred but not the only remedy for delays in arraignment, and the confessions to the Utah crimes were freely volunteered and were not the product of law enforcement delay.[66]

A police officer executing a no-knock, nighttime warrant for evidence of drug dealing did not violate *Miranda* by asking "Is there anything else we need to be aware of?" To the Eighth Circuit,[67] the query arose out of concern for police safety, so it fell under the *Quarles*[68] exception to *Miranda*. *Quarles* allows omission of Miranda warnings when public safety is threatened and spontaneous inquiry is necessary. In this case, the police knew the suspect had been involved in unlawful use of a weapon. They handcuffed him. When asked if there was anything else the police needed to know, he told them there was a loaded handgun in the closet.

A deputy sheriff did not violate a suspect's *Miranda* rights by saying "Sure" when a suspect who had invoked the right to silence said, "Can I be up front with you?"[69] because the deputy's answer did not elicit an incriminating response. (The next thing the suspect said was "I didn't intentionally kill her" and "It was an accident.") A response that doesn't prevent a suspect from making an incriminating statement is not tantamount to police interrogation.

If an interrogatee asks a clear question about *Miranda* rights, the interrogator has a duty to stop asking questions and answer the question (or at least make a good-faith attempt to do so).[70] Therefore, the police did have an obligation to answer a murder suspect who waived *Miranda* and inculpated himself, was asked if he wanted to speak without presence of counsel, and asked what good a lawyer would do.

Former employees of a corporation (who resigned after the corporation responded to subpoenas) can assert Fifth Amendment privilege to avoid producing corporate documents that would incriminate them.[71]

Because they're no longer current employees, they don't hold the documents in a representative capacity, so the "collective entity" rule (that a custodian produces the documents as a corporate, not a personal, act) doesn't apply.

The Sixth Circuit decided in early 2000 that the prosecution case in chief cannot (consistent with the Fifth Amendment) use the accused's pre-arrest, *pre-Miranda* silence.[72] (Six other Circuits—splitting three and three—have ruled on this issue.) This habeas case based on ineffective assistance of counsel involves a defendant who alleges that his lawyer should have raised the issue. The prosecutor's closing argument used the fact that the defendant (who had been observed shooting his girlfriend and her mother) didn't say anything except "talk to my lawyer" as evidence that he was not too intoxicated to have formed an intent to kill, because the statement showed consciousness of the seriousness of his situation.

References made at trial to the defendant's nationality that are not directly related to identification or another relevant issue (here, references to a drug defendant as a Cuban) violate the Fifth Amendment requirement of a fair trial and could impel reversal of the conviction, even if it is supported by ample untainted evidence.[73]

[¶6040] Sixth Amendment Issues

According to the Supreme Court,[74] a prosecutor did not violate the Sixth Amendment by pointing out to the jury that, because a testifying defendant was present for the whole trial, he had the opportunity to tailor his testimony to conform to witness statements. Because there was no Sixth Amendment violation, the Court of Appeals should not have granted habeas relief.

This sex-crime case involved conflicting testimony between the defendant and the alleged victim. The defense counsel accused the prosecution witnesses of lying, and the prosecutor responded with comments about the defendant's ability to tailor his testimony. In the Supreme Court view, this is not the same as commenting on failure to testify, which impermissibly asks jurors to use silence as evidence of guilt.

According to a 2001 Supreme Court decision,[75] the right to counsel attaches with respect to related offenses only if the offenses are the "same" under the *Blockburger* test (see main volume), that is, if proving the second offense does not require proof of any facts not required to prove the first offense. The fact pattern of this case is that, when the defendant was arrested for another crime, he confessed to a burglary but said he didn't know anything about the disappearance of two people from the house he burglarized. Later, he confessed to his father that he had killed those two people. His father contacted the police, and he confessed to the murders and was sentenced to death. The Texas Court of Criminal Appeals ruled that the right to counsel had already attached in connection with the offense for which he was originally arrested, but the Supreme Court disagreed, thus finding his custodial interrogation to be proper and his confession to be admissible.

The confrontation guarantee of the Sixth Amendment precludes crucial prosecution witnesses from testifying anonymously at trial. Concerns for the witnesses' safety can justify non-disclosure of their identity before trial, but they must be identified at trial.[76]

There was a lack of effective assistance of counsel (and thus a Sixth Amendment violation) when a conspiracy defendant's lawyer was absent (because of illness) when the government presented evidence against 17 jointly-tried drug co-conspirators. Even though the prosecutors did follow the court order telling them not to present evidence directly implicating this defendant while his lawyer was gone,[77] the Fifth Circuit says that the trial court should have informed the defendant of his rights and asked him what he wanted done while his lawyer was gone. The court treated it as a situation in which the defendant neither had counsel during the period of absence nor waived it. In a conspiracy case, it's difficult to distinguish directly from indirectly inculpatory testimony. Any evidence about the conspiracy tends to at least implicate all its members, and the attorney's presence is useful for cross-examination to limit this inculpatory effect.

The Confrontation Clause is violated by admitting statements made in custody by nontestifying co-defendants who hope for leniency for themselves.[78] Following *Lilly* (main volume), the statements did not qualify for any firmly rooted hearsay exception, nor did they have sufficient indicia of reliability to rehabilitate them. The statements were not against the interest of the declarants (they tended to equalize the distribution of blame), and *Lilly* may make it irrelevant whether or not the declarations were against interest or not.

Whether or not the defense can show prejudice, a prosecutor acts inappropriately by eavesdropping on a conversation between a defendant and the defendant's attorney. Therefore, the prosecutor's office has to be disqualified, and the conviction has to be reversed.[79] (The defendant and his lawyer met in the sheriff's office polygraph room after the defendant turned himself in for murder; police and a prosecutor listened to and recorded their conversation.) The prosecutor in question also participated in the trial and gave the closing argument, which resulted in a death sentence. South Carolina's position is that the defendant needs to show either prejudice or deliberate prosecutorial misconduct to make out a Sixth Amendment case; he or she is not required to show both.

[¶6040.6] Forfeiture and the Right to Counsel

The federal government's interest in forfeiture of tainted property prevails over an innocent divorcing spouse's interest in the same property as awarded by a state court divorce decree. The question is whether the federal government could have executed on its interest when it sought to do so, not at the point in time that the court divided the property.[80]

A third party bona fide purchaser, or a person who had a vested right in the property before the criminal act was committed, can petition under

21 USC §853(n)(6)(A) for relief from forfeiture. However, an innocent wife's community property interests in the profits of drug trafficking could not be deemed to have vested before the commission of the acts. Therefore, in the Ninth Circuit view,[81] relief from forfeiture was not appropriate. Furthermore, the intention of the provision was to exempt innocent instrumentalities of crime (e.g., a family car used to perpetrate a robbery) but not proceeds of the crime.

The Fourth Amendment entitles anyone who has a privacy interest in property seized by law enforcement officials to receive notice and an opportunity to challenge the administrative subpoena for the property. The seizure of the property doesn't extinguish the Fourth Amendment limits on the subpoena.

In this case,[82] local officers investigating a robbery and murder had a warrant to search the Hell's Angels clubhouse. They seized numerous documents which they put into the county storage facility. Later, an FBI agent with an administrative subpoena got some of the documents for use in a drug investigation. None of the seized property was used in the robbery/murder prosecution.

In the Northern District of California view, law enforcement officials are limited in their right to transfer seized property to third parties. Special procedures are needed to protect Fourth Amendment rights when documents are in the hands of a subpoenaing party whose interests are adverse to those of the owners of the documents.

Subpoenas served on law enforcement officials become self-executing, which violates the basic principle that subpoenas are subject to challenge. If the subpoena had been served directly on the Hell's Angels, they could have received hearings on various issues; but the subpoenas were served on the local officials who had already seized the materials for other purposes.

See the Civil Asset Forfeiture Reform Act of 2000, P.L. 106-185 (4/25/00) for the amended text of 18 USC §983, giving general rules for civil forfeiture proceedings; warrant requirements for seizures; the innocent owner defense; motions to set aside forfeitures, etc.

[¶6055] Pretrial Discovery

Brady requires the state prosecutor to tell the defense that the attorney for a so-called eyewitness who testified in exchange for leniency as to drug offenses originally told the lawyer that he hadn't seen anything that day.

Impeachment material is just as subject to *Brady* as directly exculpatory evidence.[83]

[¶6060] Plea Bargaining

The Constitution requires that plea bargains be knowing and voluntary. Therefore, according to the Ninth Circuit, it is improper for prosecutors to make defendants waive their rights under *Brady v. Maryland* [disclosure of exculpatory material in the prosecution's control] in order to participate in a fast-track plea bargaining program that reduces the sentences by two levels. The Ninth Circuit ruling is that defendants cannot make an informed decision about whether or not to go to trial without access to the *Brady* material.[84]

The defendant in a Third Circuit case[85] admitted to another, and more serious, offense during a guilty plea colloquy. Without a formal agreement that makes statements part of the plea bargain, this does not operate as a "stipulation" to the more serious offense that can justify a more serious Guideline under Guidelines 1B1.2(a). However, Circuits other than the Third have defined a broader range of utterances as stipulations.

The First Circuit permitted prosecution of a long-time supplier of information about organized crime, despite FBI agents' promises that they would not use the information against the informant—FBI agents don't have the authority to confer use immunity.[86]

[¶6065] Juries and Jury Trials

In a fraud trial, 21 counts went to the jury. The jury said one of the jurors couldn't concentrate or remember what had happened, and wouldn't discuss the case with the other jurors, which they construed as inability to deliberate. The trial judge dismissed that juror, seated an alternate, and the defendant was convicted on some counts.

The Ninth Circuit reads F.R.Crim.P. 23(b) to provide that just cause for dismissal includes inability to deliberate impartially[87] but it's improper to grant jurors' request to dismiss a juror if the request arises out of a disagreement about the merits of the case.

Courts aren't supposed to interfere with the secrecy of jury deliberations, but on the other hand, they have to figure out whether a dismissal request can be granted. If the record generates any reasonable possibility that dismissal was sought because of a juror's unpopular view on the merits of the case, the court can't dismiss the juror. The only options are to instruct the jury to overcome differences and deliberate, or declare a mistrial. "Any reasonable possibility" doesn't mean "any" possibility; the court doesn't have to be "firmly convinced" of the rationale to deny the request. Here, the evidence seemed to show they were angry about her opinion, so the juror should have been retained.

Maryland law allows any defendant, regardless of race or the nature of the case, to have the voir dire include probes of racial, ethnic, and cultural bias held by potential jurors,[88] a broader range of inquiry than Supreme Court precedent demands.[89] According to the Maryland court, a defendant can either get a racial bias voir dire question that does not classify him/her as a member of a particular race, or can self-classify self and define the question in accordance with that classification. The defendant must self-identify to get questions on cultural or ethnic bias.

As prescribed by the Federal Rules of Criminal Procedure, a defendant was given 10 peremptories to pick 12 jurors, plus one more to pick the alternate. The defendant challenged a prospective juror for cause because he said that he would favor the prosecution. The District Court refused to excuse him. The defendant objected unsuccessfully and finally used a peremptory to get rid of him. The defendant was convicted on all charges.

The Ninth Circuit ruling was that, although it was an error not to remove that particular juror for cause, the Sixth Amendment was not violated because he did not sit on the jury and the defendant received a jury whose impartiality was not challenged.

On reviewing the case, the Supreme Court[90] refused to adopt the government position that the defendant must use a peremptory challenge to strike a juror removable for cause, in order to preserve the claim of denial of fair trial. However, the Supreme Court held that this case did not violate Rule 24(b). The defendant was merely entitled to 11 peremptory challenges—not the right to use them in situations of his own choosing. He could, after all, have left the allegedly prejudiced individual on the jury and appealed; he chose instead to exercise the peremptory. In other words, having only a bad choice does not equal no choice.

In the post-*Martinez-Salazar* environment, it is no longer appropriate automatically to reverse a conviction because of procedures that hamper the defendant's strategic exercise of peremptory challenges. Instead, the proper standard of review is harmless error.[91]

Gay men and lesbians are a cognizable group, so excluding them from juries purely on the basis of sexual orientation violates the state (California) constitution right to a representative jury.[92] (Peremptories were exercised against two lesbians who worked for the same gay and lesbian foundation.) The rationale here is the Sixth Amendment guarantee of a venire that fairly represents the community.

A group is cognizable if its members have a common perspective that derives from their life experience as group members. This court says gay people, like blacks and women, have a history of common oppression, which certainly doesn't mean that they all think alike. Lack of recognizability doesn't alter the situation, because ethnicity can be as difficult to detect as sexual orientation. Although sexual orientation is not supposed to be an outright inquiry at voir dire, if orientation becomes known, it cannot be the sole ground for excluding a juror.

Batson (main volume) says that an allegation of discriminatory use of peremptories requires establishment of a prima facie case of discrimination (proof of facts and circumstances that raise an inference of discrimination). Next, the party asserting the peremptory rebuts with a race-neutral reason for the challenge. The California cases require the attacker of the peremptory to show a strong likelihood of discrimination—language that does not appear in *Batson*.

Lately, California courts have been applying a lower standard of scrutiny to peremptories than the federal Constitution permits, by requiring a strong likelihood, not just raising the inference. However, the peremptory at issue in a recent Ninth Circuit case[93] seemed appropriate. She was the first person of her race to be questioned. The prosecutor struck her and one more person of the same race from the jury, but allowed a third of that race to be seated. The second strike had plausible reasons, and the juror who was accepted was once a defense witness in a criminal case, so there didn't seem to be any racial animus.

Even without a specific showing of prejudice, the Colorado rule is that a court's erroneous dismissal for cause of a potential juror must result in reversal if it has the effect of giving the prosecution an additional peremptory challenge. The extra challenge gives an advantage by making it easier to select a jury likely to accept the party's arguments.[94]

A 1999 case[95] forbids Connecticut courts to give the traditional "missing witness" instruction: such an instruction permits the jury to infer that if a party fails to produce an available witness whose testimony in the case seems obviously relevant, the testimony—if given—would be unfavorable to the party. The court based its decision on changes in the discovery rules, and the possibility that an expected witness might not be called for reasons other than unfavorable testimony. However, it is permissible to raise an argument that not calling a particular witness is a sign of weakness in the case that should have called him or her.

In September, 1999, the Central District of California decided a habeas case turning on an apparent issue of first impression.[96] The holding is that ex parte communication by a judge to deliberating jurors about a question of substantive law is a structural error, whose impact on jury functions cannot be reviewed, and harmlessness analysis doesn't apply.

In this case, before the second day of deliberations, the judge met with jurors (outside the presence of lawyers) to warn jurors that the fire alarm was going to be tested. One juror asked a question about admissibility of prior bad-acts evidence, which the judge answered. The defendant moved for a mistrial on the grounds that the ex parte communication led jurors to speculate that there might have been relevant evidence excluded for this reason. (This case arose before AEDPA's changes in habeas standards.)

Naturally, this was an error—but was it harmless? Relief was granted because it could have been structural or trial error, and at least there was grave doubt as to harmlessness.

Even though the court admits it was "indecorous," reversal is not required based on an ex parte warning from a government agent to a defense witness, delivered during trial, that the witness might be prosecuted for perjury. (The witness responded by withdrawing exculpatory testimony about the defendant.) But lack of decorum is not lack of Due Process, so the trial result could stand.[97]

The prosecutor violated the defendant's right to present a defense by, in effect, driving a defense witness off the stand by adding to the trial court's advice about the privilege against self-incrimination and possibly threatening to reinstitute dropped charges against the witness if she testified.[98] The court agreed that other interpretations could be put on it, but it was heavy-handed enough to meet the defense burden of showing that the witness was coerced not to testify.

[¶6067] Mistrial

The Hawaii's state constitution's definition of double jeopardy bars a second prosecution after a mistrial or reversal on appeal that stemmed from prosecutorial misconduct that was so egregious that it satisfied an objective test that the defendant was denied a fair trial.[99]

The prosecutorial conduct in question was a prosecutor's rebuttal statement, in a black soldier's trial for molesting a 12-year-old girl, that every mother's nightmare is "finding some black, military guy on top of your daughter." Defense counsel objected to this as an appeal to racism, but the objection was overruled and mistrial was denied.

The Hawaii appeals court agreed that "black, military guy" is a clearly inflammatory statement in a case where there was no identification issue and thus race was irrelevant to guilt or innocence. "Every mother's nightmare" is an improper plea for sympathy and demand for jury identification. So the error in this case was not harmless; the sole question was the availability of retrial.

The test, according to this court, is not the prosecutor's subjective intent but whether the defendant was deprived of a fair trial. Because the prosecution itself created the risk of double jeopardy, it was not permitted to retry the defendant.

[¶6075] Evidence

Post-*Kumho,* there are greater problems in introducing special-skill evidence, so part of an expert witness's testimony was excluded because empirical verification of validity of handwriting comparison evidence was lacking. However, the defense expert witness's testimony on eyewitness identification was admissible.[100]

California Evidence Code §1108, which permits introduction of evidence of other sex crimes to show the defendant's propensity to commit such crimes, survived a Due Process challenge.[101]

The statute was held acceptable because admission of other acts is not unrestricted, and there is a balancing test to avoid unduly prejudicial admissions. Acts are admitted only if: they are relevant, similar in nature, and not too remote in time; there is no doubt that the defendant committed those acts; admission is not likely to prevent jurors from deliberating fairly; the burden on the defendant and prejudicial effect are not excessive. The court is obligated to consider less prejudicial alternatives, such as admitting only some other acts or keeping out inflammatory details of a particular offense.

Tennessee applied a three-pronged analysis as to whether a fair trial can be conducted despite missing (and allegedly exculpatory) evidence that has been lost or destroyed by the state.[102] The questions are: How much negligence was involved in losing the material? What is the significance of the missing material, in light of the reliability and probative value of whatever substitute or secondary evidence remains available? Was there sufficient other evidence to support a conviction?

The ban imposed by 18 USC §201(c)(2) on promising anything of value for a witness's testimony doesn't preclude prosecutors from offering the testimony of an informer who is paid for truthful testimony.[103] This decision extends *Richardson*[104] which allows admission of testimony obtained by government promise of leniency.

The District Court for the District of New Jersey refused to admit testimony by an FBI agent about "forensic stylistics" (whether, on the basis of materials the defendant is known to have written, he also wrote the threatening letters), as to the authorship of the letters.[105] But, based on his experience, the agent can testify about "markers" (patterns in the writings) that he finds significant to the authorship question. Forensic stylistics doesn't qualify as an accepted scientific technique—there's only one article in the literature, there are no professional academic degrees granted in the discipline, and its scientific reliability has not been demonstrated. However, by analogy with handwriting analysis, the agent can testify as an expert on comparison of markers between known and disputed samples. He can assist the jury by testifying about comparison of the documents and commonness or rarity of the alleged markers.

New Jersey doesn't admit expert testimony on "linkage analysis" (whether the defendant actually committed this crime, based on its similarities to other crimes known to be committed by the defendant).[106] But the expert can testify about similarities between the crimes even though no conclusions can be drawn by the expert about the defendant's guilt.

In this case, the expert testified on the distinction between modus operandi (which a perpetrator can change consciously) and ritualistic elements (which are less controlled because they reflect underlying motivations). The court likened this to evidence about psychological profiles of rapists, which are similarly inadmissible, because the court did not believe that a particular psychological profile is typical. The testimony was precluded by the limited number of linkage analysts and the absence of peer review. However, the witness's testimony as an expert on criminal investigation techniques was admissible.

Washington still follows *Frye*, even after *Daubert*, so the question is whether novel scientific principles are accepted by the relevant scientific community. Testimony as to a drug recognition protocol used by specially trained police officers to determine impairment by seven classes of drugs is admissible, because the scientific community accepts the protocol and its illustration chart.[107]

North Carolina permits a hearsay exception for out-of-court statements made for the purposes of medical diagnosis and treatment. The critical issue is the actions of the declarant in seeking medical treatment, not the medical personnel. Therefore, the exception was not available with respect to a psychologist's examination of a four-year-old rape victim, because the child had no conception of seeking medical treatment.[108]

It was not an abuse of discretion under FRE 403 for a trial court to permit the prosecution to present evidence of a plea agreement and guilty plea made by an accomplice testifying in a Medicare fraud case—even if the defense has promised not to challenge the credibility of the witness.[109] The credibility of someone who admits participation in a crime is always at issue, and introducing a guilty plea is probative of issues other than mere credibility.

The Third Circuit held that there are three reasons why the guilty plea of accomplice-witness can be probative: (1) letting the jury assess the witness's credibility; (2) preventing jurors from suspecting that the current defendant is a victim of selective prosecution; (3) clarifying why the witness has first-hand knowledge of the crime.

The defendants' promise not to challenge the accomplice's credibility didn't remove credibility as an issue in the case; jurors are always required to assess the credibility of all witnesses.

Absent exceptional circumstances, a prosecution witness cannot be impeached with evidence that, after a *Miranda* warning, the witness terminated an interview with a law enforcement agent, because such evidence strongly tends to be more prejudicial than probative.[110]

[¶6080] Sentencing

A March, 2000 Supreme Court holding[111] is that it was not an impermissible ex post facto action for the Georgia parole board to amend its rules, making it possible to hold parole reconsideration hearings every eight years instead of every three. At the time the prisoner committed the crime that resulted in his imprisonment, parole board rules required lifers who had not been given parole at their first hearing to get a reconsideration every three years.

Later, invoking statutory discretion, the board changed its rules to call for reconsideration at least every eight years, and to perform review after three years unless it seemed unreasonable to expect that parole would be granted.

To the Eleventh Circuit, the extension subjected the prisoner to a risk of increased punishment, and thus was ex post facto. The Supreme Court disagreed. The state parole board is entitled to significant discretion in granting parole. The amendment doesn't necessarily increase the period of incarceration (the affected prisoners have already received life sentences), and the parole board also has a policy allowing early reconsideration based on changed circumstances or new information.

The supervised release period under 18 USC §3264(e) begins on the day of the prisoner's actual release, even if he or she should have been released earlier.

A March, 2000 Supreme Court case[112] involves a defendant imprisoned on multiple convictions. Some of the convictions were overturned, by which time the defendant had already been imprisoned for two and a half years longer than the remaining convictions would warrant. He was also sentenced to a period of supervised release. There are statutory situations under which supervised release can run concurrent with other sanctions, but the statute does not mention this situation, so the period of supervised release cannot be reduced by the excess time in prison.

Another Supreme Court case with a similar caption, but involving a different prisoner,[113] construes the 1994 amendments to 18 USC §3583(e)(3) [revocation of supervised release]. Prior to the amendments, the District Court could impose a second supervised release term after revoking the first one and reimprisoning the defendant.

The 1994 amendment, adding §3583(h), expressly authorizing a second term of supervised release, does not apply retroactively, so there is no ex post facto problem.

The Supreme Court returned to sentencing issues yet again in March, 2001. The Sentencing Guidelines treat a "career offender" as one with two or more prior felony convictions for violent or drug-related crimes. The sentencing judge must treat "related" convictions as a single prior conviction. Convictions that are consolidated for sentencing are deemed related—but consolidation can be functional as well as formal. Because the District Court is closer to the fact situation, the Supreme Court requires a deferential standard of review when an appeals court reviews the trial court's determination about consolidation.[114]

Under the federal "three strikes" provision (18 USC §3559(c)), it is an affirmative defense that a prior conviction should be disqualified from the calculation. This provision has been upheld by the Sixth Circuit[115] which did not find any due process problems with the requirement that the defendant prove disqualification of the conviction by clear and convincing evidence.

"Grouping" of offenses under the Guidelines results in a shorter sentence. Late in 2000, the Ninth Circuit ruled that convictions for mail and wire fraud and money laundering should not have been grouped; the laundering conviction should not be grouped with crimes yielding proceeds that were subsequently laundered.[116]

In mid-2000, Virginia altered its previous rule (that the jury should not be instructed as to the availability of parole) in light of statutory changes. Therefore, the new rule is that the jury should be informed that Virginia has abolished parole. The jury should also be informed if the defendant will become mathematically eligible for geriatric release, but items such as good-time credits and executive clemency are too speculative to become the subject of instructions.[117]

It is presumed improper to give the findings of a criminal sentencing proceeding preclusive effect in a civil action. Preclusive effect might be proper in a limited range of circumstances. The Second Circuit forbade[118] the SEC from offensive collateral estoppel in a civil case to prevent the defendant from relitigating issues that resulted in a criminal sentence. The court ruled that preclusion would be unfair, because the findings were not necessary to the ultimate sentence; were not fully litigated; and preclusion wouldn't promote judicial economy in the civil suit.

The defendant was convicted of conspiracy to obstruct justice with respect to an alleged fraud, but was acquitted of RICO charges with securities fraud predicate felonies. The court asserted that its findings were at least a preponderance of the evidence that the defendant had committed securities fraud, and enhanced the sentence in response to Guidelines on interference with the administration of justice. The civil suit for disgorgement and injunctive relief was stayed pending the criminal proceedings; afterwards, the SEC moved for summary judgment, saying that the criminal sentence estopped the defendant from denying that he had committed securities fraud.

The court wasn't convinced. The balance between efficiency and fairness requires four criteria for offensive collateral estoppel:

- Issues are identical in both proceedings.
- The issue in prior proceedings must have been actually litigated and decided.
- The prior proceeding gave full and fair opportunity for litigating the issue.

- The previously litigated issue must have been essential to arriving at a valid and final judgment on the merits.

The court points out that the defendant's opportunity to get discovery or present evidence in a sentencing proceeding is fairly limited, and defendants have a motive not to anger anyone during sentencing. Anyway, granting preclusive effect would contribute to making sentencing proceedings more complex—and wouldn't necessarily do all that much to make civil litigation simpler. Preclusion is certainly not available in this case. Securities fraud is not causally related to sentence enhancement for interfering with the administration of justice, and elements of obstruction of justice are not the same as those for securities fraud.

Because the right to remain silent includes the right not to cooperate with the authorities, it is improper to increase a sentence within the guidelines range based on the defendant's failure to cooperate after conviction. However, *Roberts v. U.S.*, 445 U.S. 552 (Sup.Ct. 1980) does allow failure to cooperate to be considered by the sentencing court, and *U.S. v. Klotz*, 943 F.2d 707 (7th Cir. 1991), a post-guidelines case, says that the line between sentencing rewards and punishments is now easy to see. The benchmark is the guidelines range, so noncooperation is a valid decisional factor within the guidelines range.

It constitutes impermissible double-counting to enhance an assault sentence by assessing it as aggravated (i.e., with an elevated base offense level) and also applying an offense-level increase for using a dangerous weapon. (The defendant was convicted of trying to run down two INS agents with his car.[119]) Courts are split as to whether the guideline phrase "otherwise used" means that the item used as a weapon is inherently so dangerous that merely having it during the crime is an aggravating element, or whether it can be applied to an ordinary object that is in fact deployed as a weapon.

If the court believes that the defendant was the victim of selective prosecution, this can justify a downward departure from the guidelines.[120] *Koon v. U.S.*[121] won't let the sentencing court categorically exclude any factor that is not specifically barred by the guidelines, so there is a potentially unlimited number of factors that could be relevant.

According to the Seventh Circuit,[122] a District Court's determination whether the defendant's prior offenses were "consolidated" under the career offender provision is a fact issue, and thus the appeals court should be deferential in its review. This decision resolves a conflict within the Seventh Circuit, but exacerbates the conflict among the Circuits on this point.

The Tenth Circuit struck down the Bureau of Prisons' regulation governing the use of sentence reduction to reward prisoners convicted of nonviolent offenses for completing drug treatment programs.[123] In this view, the Bureau of Prisons can't deny eligibility to prisoners whose sentences for nonviolent crimes were enhanced for carrying, possession, or use of firearms. In contrast, however, the Ninth Circuit considers it a reasonable extension of the BOP's discretion to deny sentence reduction for drug treatment if the prisoner's offense involved firearms.[124]

[¶6080.3] [NEW] *Apprendi* Issues

The Supreme Court decided an extremely significant case on sentencing issues in late June, 2000. *Apprendi v. New Jersey*[125] builds on the earlier case of *Jones v. U.S.*[126] *Jones* requires that, in federal court, any fact other than prior conviction that increases the maximum penalty for a crime must be charged in the indictment, submitted to the jury, and proved beyond a reasonable doubt. *Apprendi* extends the jury consideration and proof beyond reasonable doubt criteria to state courts.

Even post-*Apprendi*, however, the Second Circuit permits a District Court to impose consecutive rather than concurrent sentences based on facts that the court itself (not the jury) finds by a preponderance of the evidence (not beyond a reasonable doubt), in that there is no Constitutional right to concurrent rather than consecutive sentencing. This case[127] also permits the District Court to consider conduct outside the time covered by the indictment in imposing consecutive or concurrent penalties.

According to the Fourth, Fifth, Sixth, and Ninth Circuits,[128] 21 USC §841(b) [increased maximum sentence based on the quantity of drugs] creates a new offense. The quantity of drugs becomes a fact that the jury must find beyond a reasonable doubt, not a fact that the court can determine by a preponderance of the evidence.

However, according to the Seventh Circuit,[129] leadership in a continuing criminal enterprise, as a factor in imposing a life sentence, is not a separate offense that requires proof beyond a reasonable doubt. In this analysis, the *Apprendi* defendant was at risk of a much higher sentence, whereas 21 USC §848(b) imposes a life sentence on all principal administrators and organizers of CCEs.

(¶6085) Capital Punishment

After hearing testimony on aggravating and mitigating factors, members of a capital jury asked the judge if they could sentence the defendant either to life or to death, or whether they had to impose the death penalty. The judge responded by reminding them of a paragraph in the jury instructions (whose adequacy had already been upheld for providing adequate consideration of mitigating factors), explaining their sentencing options. Based on the testimony on aggravation, the jury imposed the death penalty.

The Supreme Court found[130] that there was no Constitutional violation when the judge directed the jury's attention to the instructions. The defense closing argument had already pointed out that they could vote for a life sentence even if aggravating factors were present. There might be a slight possibility that jurors were deterred from voting for life imprisonment, but that's not enough to prove a Constitutional violation, which requires a reasonable likelihood of deterrence.

Under the South Carolina capital sentencing scheme, the jury sentences the convicted person (the only options are death or life without parole) if the jury is unanimous as to the presence of one or more aggravating factors. If the jury is not unanimous on this point, the judge renders sentence of either life imprisonment or a mandatory 30-year minimum. In March, 2001, the Supreme Court ruled that the jury must be informed that the defendant cannot be paroled, even though the judge rather than the jury may have to render the actual sentence.[131]

Even if the sentence is not predicated on a finding of future dangerousness, a capital murder defendant is entitled to a jury instruction that life imprisonment means life without the possibility of parole.[132] During deliberations, this jury asked the judge if "life" meant a mere term of years or whether the defendant would indeed be confined for life. The judge told the jury that state law required them to return the appropriate sentence without concerning themselves about post-sentence matters. The jury sentenced the defendant to death.

Since juries are not supposed to speculate to the defendant's detriment because of penal policies, they should be informed of policies that prevent the defendant from being released. Otherwise, juries might vote for death as the perceived only means of preventing the defendant's release, even though they would prefer the defendant to receive a true life sentence without possibility of parole.

Two cases from 2000 reach differing conclusions on the impact of religious concepts on sentencing. In the Georgia case[133] it was held that a murder defendant was denied Due Process at the sentencing phase of his trial because the prosecutor referred to biblical authority for the death penalty. The passages quoted suggested that a higher law calls for the death penalty, thus potentially overbearing the discretion that state law gives to the jury.

In contrast, the Ohio case[134] holds that neither Due Process nor Ohio sentencing law is violated by a judge consulting a religious text (a Bible verse about children) while pondering what sentence to impose (the effect of the victim's age as a sentencing factor in a rape case), or quoting that text during the sentencing proceeding, as long as the judge complies with the law and the proceedings remain fundamentally fair.

Later in 2000, the Ninth Circuit granted habeas relief with respect to a death sentence rendered after the prosecutor told the jury that the death sentence vindicates divine authority and gives the executed person a chance of atoning and being redeemed. The Ninth Circuit used Eighth Amendment analysis to require the death sentence to derive from the specific statutory factors —which do not include religious concepts.[135]

Another Ninth Circuit decision, rendered a day later, denies the defense access to prosecution memoranda and death penalty evaluation forms (used by prosecutors to decide whether or not to seek a capital sentence), on the grounds that these documents are privileged and the Sixth Circuit does not mandate access.[136]

A mid-2000 Arizona case permits the defense to question potential jurors about the depth of their feelings when they say they are unable to set aside their moral objections to the death penalty if they are required to assess the defendant's guilt. In this reading, harmless error analysis is not appropriate if the trial court dismisses jurors before the defense has a chance to rehabilitate them.[137]

Arkansas courts would not admit testimony from a murder victim's widow that she forgave the murderer and does not think he should be executed. The statement was deemed to qualify neither as a mitigating circumstance nor as victim impact testimony, which is limited to material that counteracts mitigating factors.[138]

[¶6087] Post-Conviction Remedies

Faretta v. California, 422 U.S. 806 (Sup.Ct. 1975) does indicate that there may be a right for criminal defendants to represent themselves at the trial level, after making a knowing and intelligent waiver of counsel. However, that does not obligate states to allow convicted persons to represent themselves on direct appeal.

A January, 2000 Supreme Court decision says that not all of the *Faretta* reasoning is applicable to appeals.[139] Historically, the right of self-representation derives from a time when lawyers were scarce, and the Sixth Amendment deals strictly with trials, not appeals. English precedent provides little useful guidance, because that system did not allow criminal appeals until 1907.

In that the Sixth Amendment doesn't apply at the appellate level, any right to self-representation must be Due Process-based. States have discretion to decide that the need for professional representation outweighs the interest in self-representation (although state constitutions can also recognize a self-representation right).

In April, 2000, the Supreme Court decided two related cases. In the first, #98-8384, the court held that the AEDPA limits on federal habeas for state-court claims require upholding the judgment if the state court applies the correct federal standard in a reasonable way, even if it conflicts with a federal court's interpretation of the law.[140] The limits on habeas review imposed by 28 USC §2254(d)(1) are more than just a codification of *Teague v. Lane.*[141] Section 2254(d)(1) rules out habeas unless the state court "resulted in a decision that was contrary to, or involved an unreasonable application of, clearly established Federal law, as determined by the Supreme Court of the United States."

A state decision is contrary to Supreme Court precedent if the state court's conclusion is the opposite of the one the Supreme Court reached on a question of law, or if it reaches the opposite conclusion from the Supreme Court on facts that are materially indistinguishable from the ones the Court ruled on. But this is not true of the ordinary state court decision, applying an existing legal standard to the facts of the prisoner's case.

Pre-AEDPA, federal habeas courts used a plenary or de novo standard. *Teague* limited this, making it exceptional for a federal court to grant habeas relief on the basis of a rule of law that was not established when the state court made direct review of the prisoner's conviction. Under *Teague,* state court resolution of a mixed question is reviewed de novo. But §2254(d)(1) says it's not enough to justify habeas relief if the state court applied federal law erroneously or incorrectly; relief is justified only if the state court acted unreasonably.

The second case, #99-6615, holds that §2254(e)(2) doesn't apply unless the petitioner or counsel has been at fault, which is defined as displaying a lack of diligence or even worse conduct. In this case, a prisoner sentenced to death failed on direct appeal and in state habeas proceedings, then tried to obtain federal habeas on various grounds.

The District Court wanted to have an evidentiary hearing on some of the claims. The Fourth Circuit said that §2254(e)(2) ruled out an evidentiary hearing. Section 2254(e)(2) says that the availability of an evidentiary hearing is limited if the defendant "failed" to develop the factual basis of the claim in state proceedings.

The Supreme Court refused to accept a no-fault reading of the provision. To the High Court, to fail means not developing the factual basis because of lack of diligence or greater fault. Diligence means the prisoner's reasonable attempt, based on information available at the time, to investigate and pursue claims in state court (whether or not they could have been successful). In the case at bar, the petitioner was not to blame for underdevelopment of the factual basis of claim on alleged juror bias and prosecutorial misconduct, so the case was remanded for further proceedings.

In April, 2000, the Supreme Court held[142] that the 28 USC §2253(c) requirements for certificate of appealability apply to the appeal of a denial of habeas filed after the AEDPA effective date, irrespective of the filing date for the habeas petition itself. If the District Court denies the petition on procedural grounds without reaching Constitutional issues, certiorari should issue whenever the petitioner shows that reasonable judges would at least find it debatable whether there was a valid Constitutional claim and whether the District Court was correct in its procedural ruling.

If the initial petition was dismissed other than on its merits, e.g., for failure to exhaust state remedies, the next petition is not a second or successive petition as defined by AEDPA. The petition can properly include claims that were not in the original petition.

The counsel appointed for a convicted murderer's appeal decided that appeal would be frivolous. California procedure nevertheless requires the attorney to include in the brief anything on the record that might arguably support the appeal. In an early 2000 Supreme Court case,[143] the defendant asserted ineffective assistance of counsel as grounds for habeas relief. The District Court and Ninth Circuit agreed that prejudice could be presumed because counsel omitted at least two issues from the brief.

The Supreme Court view is that states can adopt any procedure that adequately safeguards the right to appellate counsel. An attorney who believes that appeal would be frivolous can request the court to let him withdraw or dispose of the case without filing briefs on the merits. The case was remanded for further consideration of the ineffective assistance claim. The test is whether the lawyer was objectively unreasonable in failing to find appealable issues, and whether the defendant can demonstrate prejudice. It is presumed that the state procedure is reliable; the defendant must overcome the presumption.

Two defendants were convicted of operating a hazardous waste facility without a permit. Each one appealed to a different intermediate state court. One defendant's conviction was affirmed, but the other conviction was reversed. The petitioner's conviction became final when the Pennsylvania Supreme Court denied further review of his case. The other defendant's case was reviewed, and it was held that the state law didn't apply to individuals who did have a permit even though they grossly failed to abide by its terms.

The defendant asked the Pennsylvania court system to reconsider his identical conviction, but the application was denied. He asserted entitlement to federal habeas relief based on the other case, about his own co-defendant.

In late 1999, the Supreme Court returned the case to Pennsylvania for consideration of whether the co-defendant's case articulated a new principle or merely explicated existing state environmental law.[144]

It constitutes ineffective assistance for counsel to fail to consult with a defendant (who has not given clear instructions to appeal or refrain from appealing) about the potential for appeal if, based on information the attorney knew or should have known, a rational defendant would want to appeal, or the defendant reasonably showed interest in appealing. To prevail on such a claim, the defendant must also show a reasonable probability that, with appropriate consultation, he would have filed a timely appeal.[145]

See *Edwards v. Carpenter*[146] on the standards for bringing habeas corpus claims based on ineffective assistance of counsel. The attorney's ineffectiveness in not preserving a claim for state-court review could be adequate grounds for habeas relief, but only if the ineffectiveness was severe enough to achieve independent Constitutional status.

An Iowa case from 1999 holds that lawyers were not culpable in providing ineffective assistance of counsel when they talked a client, who admitted to them where he hid a murder weapon, into telling a medical expert where it was.[147] Lawyers aren't allowed to interfere with the investigation by hiding the incriminating evidence themselves, but they don't have to disclose to the prosecution if they have information from the client about evidence that is left undisturbed. There was no ineffective assistance because the defendant never denied that he killed his wife or hid the weapon, but only claimed self-defense.

The limitations period for filing a federal habeas petition (28 USC §2244(d)(2)) is still tolled when a properly filed application for state collateral review (including post-conviction) is pending, even if it is possible that there is a procedural bar to the state claim.[146] In the Second Circuit view, "properly filed" merely means filed in conformity with procedural requirements such as notice and place of filing. However, the "broader" interpretation is that a petition can't be properly filed under state law if it is procedurally barred.[149]

Apparently, a District Court staff failed to keep the court's electronic "docket sheet" up to date. Shortly after the Southern District of Florida denied the petitioner's habeas petition, a final order was entered on the official docket record, but not the Public Access to Court Electronic Records (PACER) system. The petitioner's lawyer kept checking PACER, but didn't see the final order there—or get a copy of the order by mail. He only found out about the order over a year after the 30-day filing deadline for appeal had run, and only as part of a conversation with a court employee.

In the view of the Eleventh Circuit,[150] that excuses a habeas petitioner's failure to meet the deadline for appealing the denial of relief.

The court "officially invited" reliance on the electronic system, and the petitioner reasonably relied on it. Therefore, even though in general there is no jurisdiction over an untimely appeal, this unique circumstance does justify relief.

The Eleventh Circuit view is that an untimely appeal can be forgiven because of reasonable and good faith reliance on judicial action that lulls the appellant into inactivity. Electronic dockets are supposed to benefit everybody via greater efficiency, so reliance is not inappropriate.

The District Court and its own home page describe PACER as official, and the District Court is not relieved of responsibility merely because apparently the mistake was made by the court clerk's office, not the court itself.

[¶6087.2.3] [NEW] Ineffective Assistance of Counsel

Early in 2001, the Supreme Court ruled that an allegation of ineffective assistance of counsel, with respect to grouping of offenses, cannot be denied merely because the sentence was "only" enhanced by 6-21 months. Any extra duration of imprisonment may constitute prejudice under *Strickland v. Washington*, 466 U.S. 668 (Sup.Ct. 1984).[151]

Somewhat surprisingly, the Fifth Circuit held in late 2000 that it is not necessarily prejudicial under the Sixth Amendment if the defense counsel falls asleep during a capital trial—if the defendant can't prove what was going on during the part of the trial the attorney slept through. The Fifth Circuit held that even if prejudice could be presumed, the defendant would not benefit because it would be a "new rule" for purposes of *Teague v. Lane*, 489 U.S. 288 (Sup.Ct. 1989) and therefore not available for habeas review.[152]

[¶6090] [NEW] Prison Litigation

According to the Supreme Court's 2000 decision[153] upholding 18 USC §3626 [defendant prison officials are entitled to an automatic stay of injunctions granted to prisoner litigants if the court fails to make the required statutory findings], courts do not have the equitable power to enjoin the automatic stay—it must be permitted to take effect.

Although 42 USC §1997e(a) requires dismissal of a Prison Litigation Reform Act (PLRA) case if the prisoner fails to exhaust administrative remedies before bringing suit, the administrative grievance need not name everyone who was later made a defendant in the federal suit. The prisoner merely has to include all the information in his possession at the time of filing the grievance.[154]

The PLRA's cap on legal fees for prisoner's rights cases [42 USC §1997e(d) (3)] was upheld by the Sixth Circuit, in that capping fees serves a rational state purpose by limiting frivolous litigation.

However, the Western District of Wisconsin reached the opposite conclusion, finding that the cap does violate Equal Protection because the government interests, although legitimate, are not rationally related to the fee cap because there is no reason to differentiate prisoners from nonprisoners. Furthermore, the Western District did not believe that prisoners think about the size of the fee award when deciding whether to pursue a grievance in federal court.[155]

ENDNOTES

1. *Iacobucci v. Boulter,* 193 F.3d 14 (1st Cir. 1999).
2. See 68 LW 2637.
3. *U.S. v. Rodia,* 194 F.3d 465 (3rd Cir. 10/20/99).
4. *U.S. v. Mohrbacher,* 182 F.3d 1041 (9th Cir. 1999).

5. *Lawrence v. State*, 69 LW 1004 (Tex.App. 6/8/00).
6. *U.S. v. Middleton*, 231 F.3d 1207 (9th Cir. 2000).
7. *Shurgard Storage Centers Inc. v. Safeguard Self Storage Inc.*, 119 F.Supp.2d 1121 (W.D. Wash. 2000).
8. *Paul P. v. Farmer*, 92 F. Supp.2d 410 (D.N.J. 2000).
9. *U.S. v. Hardin*, 68 LW 1613 (7th Cir. 3/30/00).
10. 526 U.S. 227 (Sup.Ct. 1999).
11. See, e.g., *U.S. v. Bongiorno*, 106 F.3d 1027 (1st Cir. 1997); *U.S. v. Sage*, 92 F.3d 101 (2nd Cir. 1996).
12. *U.S. v. Faasse*, 227 F.3d 660 (6th Cir. 2000).
13. *U.S. v. King*, 69 LW 1544 (S.D.N.Y. 2/8/01).
14. *State v. Greene*, 984 P.2d 1024 (Wash. 1999).
15. *U.S. v Dixon*, 185 F.3d 393 (5th Cir. 1999).
16. *U.S. v. Brooks*, 215 F.3d 842 (8th Cir. 2000).
17. *Smith v. Groose*, 205 F. 3d 1045 (8th Cir. 2000).
18. *People v. Palmer*, 69 LW 1463 (Cal. 1/18/01).
19. *Carmell v. Texas*, 529 U.S. 513 (Sup.Ct. 2000).
20. *People v. Frazer*, 88 Cal.Rptr.2d 312 (Cal. 1999).
21. *Seling v. Young*, #99-1183, 69 LW 4073 (Sup.Ct. 1/17/01).
22. *SEC v. Zandford*, 238 F.3d 559 (4th Cir. 2001).
23. *Beck v. Prupis*, 529 U.S. 494 (Sup.Ct. 2000).
24. *Ferguson v. Charleston, S.C.*, #99-936, 69 LW 4184 (Sup.Ct. 3/21/01).
25. *Lauro v. Charles*, 219 F.3d 202 (2nd Cir. 2000).
26. *Iowa v. Cline*, 617 N.W.2d 277 (Ia. 2000).
26A. *Illinois v. McArthur*, #99-1132, 69 LW 4096 (Sup.Ct. 2/20/01)
27. *U.S. v. Gori*, 230 F.3d 44 (2nd Cir. 2000).
28. *People v. Reyes*, 69 LW 1159 (Cal. 8/17/00).
29. *Bond v. U.S.*, 529 U.S. 334 (Sup.Ct. 2000).
30. *State v. Ortiz*, 600 N.W.2d 805 (Neb. 1999).
31. *U.S. v. Langarcia-Ambrosia*, 68 LW 1239 (D. Neb. 9/9/99).
32. *U.S. v. Kyllo*, 190 F.3d 1041 (9th Cir. 1999).
33. *U.S. v. McIver*, 186 F.3d 1119 (9th Cir. 1999).
34. *Maddox v. U.S.*, 68 LW 1511 (D.C. 2/4/00).
35. *Ex Parte Warren*, 69 LW 1208 (Ala. 9/8/00).
36. *U.S. v. Bohannon*, 225 F.3d 615 (6th Cir. 2000).
37. *Morton v. U.S.*, 68 LW 1119 (D.C. App 8/12/99).
38. *People v. Camacho*, 69 LW 1086 (Cal. 7/27/00).
39. *U.S. v. Oaxaca*, 233 F.3d 1154 (9th Cir. 2000).

40. *State v. Sampson*, 765 A.2d 629 (Md. 2001).
41. *U.S. v. Stefonek*, 179 F.3d 1030 (7th Cir. 1999).
42. *U.S. v. Dice*, 200 F.3d 978 (6th Cir. 2000).
43. *U.S. v. Cervantes*, 219 F.3d 882 (9th Cir. 2000).
44. *People v. McCullough*, 69 LW 1080 (Colo. 7/3/00).
45. *State v. Parker*, 987 P.2d 73 (Wash. 11/4/99).
46. *State v. Steele*, 69 LW 1064 (S.D. 6/14/00).
47. *Commonwealth v. Gonsalves*, 711 N.E.2d 108 (Mass. 6/14/99).
48. *U.S. v. Holt*, 229 F.3d 931 (10th Cir. 2000).
49. *State v. Ladson*, 979 P.2d 833 (Wash. 1999).
50. *In re Muhammad F.*, 700 N.Y.S.2d 77 (N.Y. 1999).
51. 443 U.S. 47 (Sup.Ct. 1979).
52. *U.S. v. Woodrum*, 68 LW 1455 (1st Cir. 1/20/00).
53. *U.S. v. Matlock*, 415 U.S. 164 (Sup.Ct. 1974) lets a third party with legitimate joint access and control consent to the search of an area.
54. *U.S. v. Hernandez*, 215 F.3d 483 (5th Cir. 2000).
55. *Indianapolis v. Edmond*, 520 U.S. 651 (Sup.Ct. 2000).
56. See, e.g., *State v. Gerschoffer*, 738 N.W.2d 713 (Ind.App. 2000), on the grounds that stops are made without probable cause or individualized suspicion of the driver.
57. *U.S. v. Dortch*, 199 F.3d 193 (5th Cir. 1999).
58. *Illinois v. Wardlow*, 528 U.S. 119 (Sup.Ct. 2000).
59. *Florida v. J.L.*, 529 U.S. 266 (Sup.Ct. 2000).
60. 496 U.S. 325 (Sup.Ct. 1990).
61. *U.S. v. Valentine*, 232 F.3d 350 (3rd Cir. 2000).
62. *Davis v. U.S.*, 759 A.2d 665 (D.C. App. 2000).
63. *State v. Boyea*, 69 LW 1383 (Vt. 12/1/00).
64. *U.S. v. Montero-Camargo*, 208 F.3d 1122 (9th Cir. 2000).
65. *People v. Daoud*, 614 N.W.2d 152 (Mich. 2000).
66. *Anderson v. Calderon*, 232 F.3d 1053 (9th Cir. 2000).
67. *U.S. v. Williams*, 181 F.3d 845 (8th Cir. 1999).
68. *N.Y. v. Quarles*, 467 U.S. 649 (Sup.Ct. 1984).
69. *People v. Gonzalez*, 987 P.2d 239 (Colo. 1999).
70. *Almeida v. State*, 737 So.2d 520 (Fla. 1999).
71. *In re Three Grand Jury Subpoenas Duces Tecum*, 191 F.3d 173 (2nd Cir. 1999).
72. *Combs v. Coyle*, 205 F.3d 269 (6th Cir. 2000).
73. *U.S. v. Cabrera*, 222 F.3d 590 (9th Cir. 2000).
74. *Portuondo v. Agard*, 529 U.S. 61 (Sup.Ct. 2000).

75. *Texas v. Cobb*, #99-1702, 69 LW 4213 (Sup.Ct. 4/2/01).

76. *Alvarado v. Superior Court*, 11 Cal.Rptr.2d 149 (Cal. 8/17/00).

77. *U.S. v. Russell*, 68 LW 1552 (5th Cir. 3/1/00).

78. *U.S. v. Gomez*, 191 F.3d 1214 (10th Cir. 1999).

79. *State v. Quattlebaum*, 68 LW 1470 (S.C. 1/26/00).

80. *U.S. v. Kennedy*, 201 F.3d 1324 (11th Cir. 2000).

81. *U.S. v. Hooper*, 229 F.3d 818 (9th Cir. 2000).

82. *Hell's Angels Motorcycle Corp. v. Monterey County*, 89 F.Supp.2d 1144 (N.D. Cal. 2000).

83. *Spicer v. Roxbury Correctional Institute*, 194 F.3d 547 (4th Cir. 1999).

84. *U.S. v. Ruiz*, 69 LW 1549 (9th Cir. 3/5/01).

85. *U.S. v. Nathan*, 188 F.3d 190 (3rd Cir. 1999).

86. *U.S. v. Flemmi*, 225 F.3d 78 (1st Cir. 2000).

87. *U.S. v. Symington*, 68 LW 1023 (9th Cir. 6/22/99).

88. *Hernandez v. State*, 742 A.2d 952 (Md. 1999).

89. See, e.g., *Ristaino v. Ross*, 424 U.S. 598 (Sup.Ct. 1976) [voir dire on racial bias is appropriate only in cases in which racial issues are an inextricable part of conduct of the trial]; *Ham v. South Carolina*, 409 U.S. 524 (Sup.Ct. 1973) [allegation by black defendant that drug charges were motivated by his civil rights work]; *Rosales-Lopez v. U.S.*, 451 U.S. 182 (Sup.Ct. 1981) [asserting a general but nonconstitutional right to have questions to discover prejudice included in voir dire where there is a reasonable possibility that jurors will be influenced by racial prejudice.

90. *U.S. v. Martinez-Salazar*, 528 U.S. 304 (Sup.Ct. 2000).

91. *U.S. v. Patterson*, 68 LW 1758 (7th Cir. 6/1/00).

92. *People v. Garcia*, 92 Cal. Rptr.2d 339 (Cal. App. 2000).

93. *Wade v. Terhune*, 202 F.3d 1190 (9th Cir. 2000).

94. *People v. Lefebre*, 5 P.3d 295 (Colo. 2000).

95. *Connecticut v. Malave*, 737 A.2d 442 (Conn. 1999).

96. *Delgado v. Rice*, 67 F.Supp.2d 1148 (C.D. Cal. 1999).

97. *U.S. v. Williams*, 205 F.3d 23 (2nd Cir. 2000).

98. *Kansas v. Finley*, 68 LW 1559 (Kan. 2/25/00).

99. *Hawaii v. Rogan*, 984 P.2d 1231 (Hawaii 10/5/99). This is broader than *Oregon v. Kennedy*, 456 U.S. 667 (Sup.Ct. 1982), in which double jeopardy only bars retrial after mistrial due to prosecution error if the prosecution acted with the specific intent of forcing the defendant to move that a mistrial be declared.

100. *U.S. v. Hines,* 68 LW 1016 (D. Mass. 6/11/99).
101. *People v. Falsetta,* 89 Cal.Rptr.2d 847 (Cal. 1999).
102. *State v. Ferguson,* 2 S.W.3d 912 (Tenn. 1999).
103. *U.S. v. Anty,* 203 F.3d 305 (4th Cir. 2000).
104. *U.S. v. Richardson,* 195 F.3d 192 (4th Cir. 1999).
105. *U.S. v. Van Wyk,* 68 LW 1518 (D.N.J. 2/8/00).
106. *State v. Fortin,* 745 A.2d 509 (N.J. 2000).
107. *State v. Baity,* 991 P.2d 1151 (Wash. 2000).
108. *State v. Hinnant,* 523 S.E.2d 663 (N.C. 2000).
109. *U.S. v. Universal Rehabilitation Services Inc.,* 205 F.3d 657 (3rd Cir. 2000).
110. *U.S. v. Zaccaria,* 69 LW 1560 (1st Cir. 2/14/01).
111. *Garner v. Jones,* 529 U.S. 244 (Sup.Ct. 2000).
112. *U.S. v. Johnson,* 529 U.S. 53 (Sup.Ct. 2000).
113. *Johnson v. U.S.,* 529 U.S. 694 (Sup.Ct. 2000).
114. *Buford v. U.S.,* #99-9073, 69 LW 4182 (Sup.Ct. 3/20/01).
115. *U.S. v. Gatewood,* 230 F.3d 186 (6th Cir. 2000).
116. *U.S. v. Syrax,* 69 LW 1390 (9th Cir. 12/13/00). Earlier, *U.S. v. Green,* 225 F.3d 955 (8th Cir. 2000), held that grouping is improper because money laundering does not have the same victims as the underlying crimes. However, *U.S. v. Emerson,* 128 F.3d 557 (7th Cir. 1997), actually directs grouping in this situation.
117. *Fishback v. Commonwealth,* 69 LW 1016 (Va. 6/9/00).
118. *U.S. v. Rivera (Walden),* 196 F.3d 144 (2nd Cir. 1999).
119. *U.S. v. Farrow,* 198 F.3d 179 (6th Cir. 1999).
120. *U.S. v. Coleman,* 188 F.3d 354 (6th Cir. 1999).
121. 518 U.S. 81 (Sup.Ct. 1996).
122. *U.S. v. Buford,* 201 F.3d 937 (7th Cir. 2000).
123. *Ward v. Booker,* 203 F.3d 1249 (10th Cir. 2000).
124. *Bowen v. Hood,* 202 F.3d 1211 (9th Cir. 2000).
125. 530 U.S. 466 (Sup.Ct. 2000).
126. 526 U.S. 227 (Sup.Ct. 1999).
127. *U.S. v. White,* 69 LW 1517 (2nd Cir. 2/13/01).
128. *U.S. v. Rebmann,* 69 LW 1148 (6th Cr. 2000); *U.S. v. Rogers,* 228 F.3d 1318 (5th Cir. 2000); *U.S. v. Nordby,* 225 F.3d 1053 (9th Cir. 2000); *U.S. v. Doggett,* 230 F.3d 160 (5th Cir. 2000); *U.S. v. Angle,* 230 F.3d 113 (4th Cir. 2000).
129. *U.S. v. Smith,* 223 F.3d 554 (7th Cir. 2000).
130. *Weeks v. Angelone,* 528 U.S. 225 (Sup. Ct. 2000).

131. *Shafter v. South Carolina*, #00-5250, 69 LW 4175 (Sup.Ct. 3/20/01), applying *Simmons v. South Carolina*, 512 U.S. 154 (Sup. Ct. 1994) even where the potential for judicial sentencing is present..

132. *Yarbrough v. Commonwealth*, 519 S.E.2d 602 (Va. 1999).

133. *Carruthers v. State*, 68 LW 1591 (Ga. 3/6/00).

134. *State v. Arnett*, 724 N.E.2d 793 (Ohio 2000).

135. *Sandoval v. Calderon*, 231 F.3d 1140 (9th Cir. 2000).

136. *U.S. v. Fernandez*, 231 F.3d 1240 (9th Cir. 2000).

137. *State v. Anderson*, 4 P.3d 369 (Ariz. 2000).

138. *Greene v. State*, 69 LW 1488 (Ark. 2/1/01).

139. *Martinez v. California Court of Appeal*, 528 U.S. 152 (Sup.Ct. 2000).

140. *Williams v. Taylor*, 529 U.S. 420 (Sup.Ct. 2000).

141. 489 U.S. 288 (Sup.Ct. 1989).

142. *Slack v. McDaniel*, 529 U.S. 473 (Sup.Ct. 2000).

143. *Smith v. Robbins*, 528 U.S. 259 (Sup.Ct. 2000).

144. *Fiore v. White*, 528 U.S. 23 (Sup.Ct. 1999).

145. *Roe v. Flores-Ortega*, 528 U.S. 470 (Sup.Ct. 2000).

146. 529 U.S. 446 (Sup.Ct. 2000).

147. *Wemark v. State*, 602 N.W.2d 810 (Iowa 1999).

148. *Bennett v. Artuz*, 199 F.3d 116 (2nd Cir. 1999).

149. See, e.g., *Dictado v. Ducharme*, 189 F.3d 889 (9th Cir. 1999); *Tinker v. Hanks*, 172 F.3d 990 (7th Cir. 1999)

150. *Hollins v. Dept of Corrections*, 191 F.3d 1324 (11th Cir. 1999).

151. *Glover v. U.S.*, #99-8576, 69 LW 4058 (Sup.Ct. 1/9/01).

152. *Burdine v. Johnson*, 69 LW 1304 (5th Cir. 10/27/00).

153. *Miller v. French*, 530 U.S. 327 (Sup.Ct. 2000).

154. *Brown v. Sikes*, 212 F.3d 1205 (11th Cir. 5/25/00).

155. Compare *Hadix v. Johnson*, 230 F.3d 840 (6th Cir. 2000) with *Johnson v. Daley*, 117 F.Supp.2d 889 (W.D.Wis. 2000).

¶7000

Regulation of the Practice of Law

[¶7001]

The First Circuit directed the District Court for the District of Puerto Rico to enjoin the bar association from compelling its members to pay for group life insurance until the Puerto Rico Supreme Court clarified the status of the requirement under local law.[1]

However, the First Circuit decided not to remand the matter to the District Court to decide the relevancy of using dues to establish an insurance program to the mission of a bar association. The First Circuit view is that there can be important Constitutional issues even when the dues are not used for ideological purpose.

First Amendment associational rights are involved in compelled financial support for a program that is distasteful to the payor, even on non-ideological grounds. In the union context, it might be justified to use members' funds in a way they dislike, because of the unions' need to maintain countervailing power against the employers. But lawyers don't need an integrated bar to have the power to compete in the marketplace—and even states that do not have an integrated bar manage to have practicing lawyers!

Generally, corporations can't conspire with their agents, so a lawyer and a client can't be held liable for conspiracy that allegedly occurred during an attorney–client relationship when the lawyer offered advice in an official rather than a personal capacity[2]—whether or not the lawyer had a personal motivation for the actual advice.

An attorney defending a corporate client charged with intellectual property infringement has no duty to investigate whether the client's CGI policy might provide indemnification or defense costs. There are situations (e.g., an automotive personal injury case) in which a lawyer might have to raise the insurance issue, but in a business case, there is no duty to inquire into the availability of insurance for the client.[3]

[¶7010.2] Rule 1.2 Scope of Representation

Where the defendant has not given clear instructions to appeal or to waive appeal, it constitutes ineffective assistance for counsel for the attorney to fail to consult with the defendant about taking an appeal. The test is whether, based on the information the attorney knew or should have known, a rational defendant would want to appeal. The alternate test is whether the defendant reasonably showed an interest in pursuing an appeal. To prevail on such a claim, the defendant must also show a reasonable probability that, with appropriate consultation, he would have filed a timely appeal.[4]

[¶7010.4] Rule 1.4 Communication

When a lawyer leaves a firm, both the lawyer and the ex-firm have a duty to protect client interests and vindicate the client's right to choose own representation. Model Rule 1.4 requires[5] disclosure of the scheduled departure of a lawyer who is responsible for representing the client, or who is a principal in the firm's delivery of services to the client.

The lawyer, the firm's responsible members, or both can perform notification; if feasible, joint notice is preferable. An attorney who thinks the firm will not give notice should give the notice personally, making written memoranda of conversations.

In fact, lawyers can inform their clients of impending departure even before they have formally resigned. It is not a violation of Rule 7.3 (solicitation) to tell a client in person or over the phone that the lawyer will be leaving, and written contact after leaving is also acceptable. But pre-resignation notice should only go to current clients, and clients should be made aware that they decide who will complete their matter.

On request by the client, a departing lawyer should provide enough information about his or her new affiliation for the client to make an informed decision about staying with the original firm or transferring representation to the lawyer's new affiliation.

There are fiduciary and unfair competition issues involved, for instance as to what information a departing lawyer can take. It is acceptable to take research memos, pleadings, and forms to the extent they're public domain or are considered the lawyer's own property. Taking copies of documents created for general use in the practice could be acceptable, but taking materials reasonably regarded by the firm as proprietary is problematic. Clients determine the disposition of their own files. It is permissible to keep copies of documents dealing with representation of ex-clients, as long as confidentiality is preserved.

¶7010.6] Rule 1.6 Attorney–Client Confidences

The attorney-client privilege is subject to the so-called "crime-fraud" exception. According to a recent Connecticut decision,[6] this is broad enough to remove protection from communications with an attorney that were intended to further a civil fraud as well as communications in pursuit of criminal fraud.

According to the Third Circuit, when the government seeks to assert the crime-fraud exception, it is not required to prove that subpoenaing the defendant's attorney is the only way to get the information in question.[7]

Furthermore, because a Grand Jury is considered investigatory rather than adversarial, a grand jury target whose attorney is subpoenaed is not entitled to review the ex parte documents that the government uses to assert the crime-fraud exception.[8] The Third Circuit reached this result because the documents sought by the target included Grand Jury secrets entitled to protection; ex parte affidavits are sufficient to establish the crime-fraud exception.

In-house counsel is not an "innocent attorney" who can invoke the work product privilege to prevent disclosure under the crime-fraud exception. The Fifth Circuit's theory is that the in-house counsel's interest in the confidentiality of the documents (as distinct from the corporation's interest) is not legally cognizable. In any event, the privilege belongs to the client, not the attorney.[9]

Attorney-client privilege applies to communications between co-defendants and their shared attorney as to issues affecting their joint defense.[10]

The Tenth Circuit has held[11] that federal prosecutors can be required to comply with a Colorado rule of professional conduct that imposes conditions before a lawyer can be subpoenaed to gain information about a current or former client. The requirement doesn't violate the Supremacy Clause. The state rule imposes a requirement that the prosecutor have a reasonable belief that the information sought is essential to the success of an ongoing prosecution or investigation; is not privileged; and is not otherwise available. The District Court found the rule unconstitutional to the extent that it regulated federal prosecutors and Grand Juries. The state didn't appeal that part of the ruling. The federal government appealed the District Court's holding that the rule was valid and bound federal attorneys in other kinds of criminal proceedings.

While appeal was pending, Congress passed the McDade Act, 28 USC §530B, which requires federal attorneys to comply with state laws and rules of attorney conduct, so the Tenth Circuit framed the question as whether the rule is an ethical rule covered by the McDade Act or a substantive or procedural rule that conflicts with federal law.

Factors in distinguishing between ethical and substantive/procedural rules include the principle that ethics rules control behavior that the legal profession recognizes as inappropriate, and such rules—unlike substantive and procedural rules—deal with morals and principles.

They are directed at attorneys themselves—i.e., the attorney is personally responsible; substantive and procedural rules tend to go to the success of the claim. The court decided that the rule in question was an ethics rule because it goes to the consensus about the nature of the attorney–client relationship; has the vague sweeping character of a moral pronouncement; and governs the prosecutor's behavior rather than the progress of the case.

The Tenth Circuit also rejected the argument that the rule is inconsistent with subpoena rules of F.R.Crim.P. 17, and thus fails under the Supremacy Clause— the court says that the federal rule just explains how to issue a proper subpoena, and doesn't remove the court's power to require proper behavior by federal prosecutors.

According to the Tenth Circuit,[12] a bankruptcy trustee does not automatically maintain control over the attorney–client privilege or its waiver with respect to pre-petition, good-faith, affirmative civil claims against third persons with whom the debtor did business. The court should review each case in camera to decide if the trustee has the right to control assertion or waiver.

The Southern District of New York held[13] that work product protection is broader than attorney–client privilege protection (with respect to discovery of notes made by a director's assistant at a board meeting).

The corporation waived attorney–client privilege with respect to discussions about counsel's legal advice at board meetings, because the assistant was allowed to attend. But the notes became work product because they summarized confidential legal advice rendered in contemplation of litigation.

Even if the corporation itself refuses to waive the attorney-client and work-product privileges, a corporate officer testifying before the Grand Jury can waive the privileges.[14] The Second Circuit remanded the matter to consider issues of when implied waiver will be considered fair and when an officer can speak on behalf of the corporation. When a waiver of the privileges is found, fairness demands that it be tailored narrowly to the degree of prejudice suffered by the government from non-production of the documents in question.

A Texas case sets a new standard for when an attorney can obtain work product from the client's former attorney (disqualified on the basis of conflicts). There is a rebuttable presumption that work product contains confidential information—but the client has the right to rebut the presumption. The client is not required to prove that confidential material is contained in the work product.[15]

According to the Federal Circuit, an opinion of counsel as to the tax consequences of a proposed merger, printed in the proxy statement soliciting support for the transaction, waived attorney-client privilege in all documents involved in giving the tax advice—but privilege was not waived with respect to other legal issues raised by the merger.[16]

Documents exchanged between a law firm and a PR firm hired in anticipation of a lawsuit are not covered by the attorney-client privilege, because they do not contain confidential communications made in order to obtain legal advice.[17] Furthermore, disclosure to the PR firm would destroy privilege in any case. The material is not work product as defined by FRCP 26(b)(3) because that is limited to material relating to strategies for the conduct of litigation, not the effect of litigation on public perception of the litigants.

Unlike some other states, California deems the attorney–client privilege to outweigh a trustee's duty to report to trust beneficiaries, so communications between trustee and counsel, dealing with trust administration, are privileged, and there's no duty to share the information with beneficiaries.[18]

It doesn't violate Pennsylvania's Rule of Professional Conduct 1.6(c)(3) for a former in-house counsel to reveal confidential information about the ex-employer in connection with pursuing a wrongful termination claim.[19] However, the attorney must give advance warning to the ex-employer; must restrict the use of the information as much as possible; and must take reasonable steps to preserve confidentiality, such as depositing information in court under seal, producing it in camera, and entering into confidentiality agreements.

Before it claims attorney-client privilege, a corporation must determine that a staff member of its in-house legal department actually is an attorney. If the corporation hires a person who only purports to be an attorney (in this case, someone who had passed a bar exam but had not been admitted), it cannot claim the privilege.[20]

Whether it's permissible to consult another lawyer, revealing client confidences, without the consent of the client, depends on the reason for seeking consultation with another lawyer or bar counsel, according to a Maine opinion dating to the end of 1999.[21]

Consultation is improper with any attorney who represents an adverse party in a substantially related matter (or whose firm does). Otherwise, if the consultation is for the benefit of the client, the consulted lawyer becomes the client's attorney, at least for limited purposes. If no attorney–client relationship is created, then privileged information (confidences) cannot be disclosed, but secrets can be divulged based on the consulted attorney's representation that they will not be further communicated.

On the other hand, if the consultation is for the benefit of the consulting lawyer, the consulted lawyer can enter into an attorney–client relationship with the consulting lawyer—and the consulting lawyer must be careful to avoid violating the attorney–client privilege of the underlying client without that party's consent.

Consultation with bar counsel is permissible to avoid ethical violations or to defend a lawyer against accusations of unethical conduct, but the propriety of a consultation doesn't provide implied authority to disclose client secrets or confidences, and the bar counsel does not enter into an attorney–client relationship with the client.

[¶7010.7] Rule 1.7 Conflict of Interests

A law firm must be disqualified if it hires a lawyer who previously performed significant work for the opponent in the same litigation; screening measures are inadequate. A Chinese Wall is acceptable only if the new firm can rebut that the lawyer obtained material client confidences in the course of past representation.[22]

A law firm isn't disqualified from representing a corporation in a lawsuit just because that client, with different counsel, brought similar claims against another one of the firm's corporate clients in separate but contemporary litigation.[23] The situation didn't put the law firm in the position of having to establish wrongdoing by a current client, nor was it seeking a judgment that would have a direct adverse impact on a current client, and the client was a very large financial institution that had relationships with many law firms.

When a corporate in-house lawyer is hired by a law firm, the law firm can represent new clients with interests materially adverse to a corporate ex-employer, without prior consent of the ex-employer, but not if the lawyer in question personally represented the corporate ex-employer in the same or a substantially related matter, or where the protected information relevant to current matter emerged.[24]

Mere past employment in a corporate legal department does not always disqualify the attorney, if there was no personal direct involvement or supervision that gave the attorney access to protected information.

In effect, the relevant Rule is 1.9(a) on material adverse interest, not 1.13 on representing an organization. Although consent by the old client can resolve some problems, the new client may have to consent, too. And if the lawyer does become disqualified, Rule 1.10(a) may require disqualification of the entire firm.

When a lawyer leaves one firm for another, what information can the new firm ask for—and the new employee give—about past clients and representation, so the new firm can do conflict checks? (Since 1996, New York firms have been subject to an explicit obligation to maintain formal systems to find conflicts.)

A 1999 New York ethics opinion[25] says that the new firm is required to collect information about the clients of the prior firm, especially the identity of clients the lawyer did work for and the nature of the work. The extent of required information depends, e.g., on the nature of the firm's practice; the size of the former firm; and how long the attorney spent there.

Although detailed requirements for conflicts checks have not been published in New York, the rule does require the firm's system to be effective. Long-range research is not necessary, only information about matters that are likely to relate to new or ongoing representation. For a small firm, a list of all clients might be reasonable; for a large firm, probably only a list of the lawyer's own clients is required.

[¶7010.8] [NEW] Rule 1.8 Prohibited Transactions

A practice much more common during the dot.com boom than it is today was for attorneys to accept part or all of their compensation for representing start-up companies in the form of stock in those companies. A Formal Opinion of the ABA Standing Committee on Ethics and Professional Responsibility[26] states that it is permissible for a lawyer or law firm to take an ownership interest in a client, either instead of cash or as an investment opportunity that arises in conjunction with representation. The Opinion says that Rule 1.8 must be read in conjunction with Rule 1.5 (fees must be reasonable) and Rule 2.1 (the client must get the independent professional judgment of the attorney at all times).

The Association of the Bar for the City of New York's counterpart opinion[27] rejects any per se prohibition on a lawyer's taking securities (including stock options) as a fee, as long as the client is aware of the ethics rules about doing business with clients; the client's interests are not adversely affected; and the fee is not excessive as of the time that the deal was made.

[¶7010.9] Rule 1.9 Representation Against Former Clients

With respect to a disqualification motion, there is an attorney–client relationship between an insurer and the law firm it hires to represent an insured. Therefore, when the insurance company is sued by that law firm, the insurer is the attorney's client for conflicts purposes.[28]

A lawyer who changes firms is not automatically barred from litigating against a client represented by other attorneys in the former firm— as long as the attorney in question did not represent the client and did not have access to confidential information about that client.[29]

[¶7010.15] Rule 1.15 Overseer of Client's Property

Because the IOLTA system has been held not to be a "taking" in violation of the Fifth Amendment, clients who object to the interest being used for legal services programs aren't entitled to just compensation. There's no link between the clients and the programs, so the Western District of Texas decided early in 2000 that they are not forced to engage in First Amendment "compelled speech."[30]

The 2000 case is the remand of *Phillips v. Washington Legal Foundation.*[31] Because of the absence of a taking, and the limited period of time involved, the use of the interest to fund legal services was upheld. The client had no economic loss because, absent IOLTA, the bank would keep the interest; the client didn't have an investment expectation, because the funds would not have earned net interest; and they were not unfairly singled out because the plaintiffs were not burdened at all.

But the Ninth Circuit disagreed early in 2001.[32] The Ninth Circuit noted that the Washington IOLTA law also applies to non-lawyer "closing officers," who were the plaintiffs in this case.

Issues of stewardship of the client's property also arise in connection with settlements. According to the Los Angeles County Bar Association Ethics Committee,[33] it is ethical for an attorney/physician who formed an organization to advocate for HMO patients to draft retainer agreements stating that the attorney will accept smaller settlements in HMO cases in return for publicizing the settlement (that is, the attorney will not accede to a gag clause in order to get a larger settlement for the client). The attorney's viewpoint is that HMO misconduct should not be concealed. In the Bar Association view, as long as the client retains control over settlement decisions—and as long as the attorney is willing to accept a smaller fee because of the smaller settlement—this practice is ethical.

The New York State Bar Association's take on gag clauses[34] is that settlement agreements should not be drafted to require secrecy with respect to matters that are not otherwise protectable. For example, the settlement terms in an employment discrimination case can properly be kept confidential, but the agreement should not suppress all information about the defendant's business operations. An excessively broad gag clause has the effect of restricting the lawyer's right to practice law, and thus is unethical. Nor may an attorney properly agree not to represent other employees on discrimination claims against the same employer.

According to South Carolina, the doctrine of champerty, which forbids third parties to finance lawsuits in return for a share of the eventual recovery, is "dated," and will not prevent enforcement of a financing contract. In this reading[35] the financing contract is enforceable unless it is unreasonable or involves overreaching by the financing party. The court declined to decide whether a lawyer can ethically finance a suit he or she is not involved in litigating; it is generally improper for a litigator to provide funding for one of his or her own cases.

[¶7010.16] [NEW] Rule 1.16 Decline, Withdrawal, Termination of Representation

According to Utah ethics regulators,[36] when a lawyer hears the client lie to a judge, it is insufficient to remain silent and continue to represent the client. The lawyer has a duty to try to get the client to "correct" the statement. If the client refuses, the lawyer should seek permission to withdraw from representation. If withdrawal is denied, the lawyer has an obligation to inform the court that it has been misinformed. In this reading, there is no Constitutional right to lie to the court, and silence on the part of the attorney would help the client to lie.

[¶7010.23] [NEW] Rule 3.3 Candor

The Arizona State Bar Commission on the Rules of Professional Conduct deems protection of a criminal defense client to outweigh the duty of candor.[37] Therefore, the defense attorney is not required to reveal the client's intent to lie during a plea bargaining colloquy (e.g., a repeat offender represents himself as a first-time offender). However, the attorney is not permitted to make affirmative material misrepresentations or certify that misrepresentations made by the client are true.

[¶7010.26] Rule 3.6 Trial Publicity

The absolute privilege that lawyers have in judicial proceedings doesn't insulate them against defamation liability with respect to communications with news media about a pending case.[38] The purpose of the privilege is encouraging zealous advocacy, a value that is not served by unrestricted contact with the press. In fact, a lawyer can be sued for defamation based on communications that more or less restate the allegations of the client's pleading.

But see a contemporary Ohio case[39] granting absolute privilege to defamatory comments made by a lawyer about a third party in a letter sent to the adversary's counsel even before suit was filed. The Ohio rationale is that the attorney's privilege/duty to represent the client zealously begins before the trial, extending to communications to the opposing attorney that are reasonably related to the case.

[¶7010.28] Rule 3.8 Prosecutor Responsibilities

The Sixth Amendment is violated when a prosecutor deliberately eavesdrops on a conversation between a criminal defendant and his attorney, whether or not the defense can show that prejudice resulted—and even if the conversation occurred before the defendant was charged. (In this case, the lawyer interviewed the client in a sheriff's office polygraph room that had a video camera).[40]

[¶7010.34] Rule 5.1 Responsibilities of Firm Partners/Supervisors

Not only is a law firm vicariously liable for fraud committed by its associate, but the Minnesota Court of Appeals found a firm subject to treble damages under an antifraud statute.[41] If the lawyer committed fraud in the firm's offices, during office hours, while performing normal services for clients, the firm is liable, because not only should firms be encouraged to supervise their associates, but defrauded clients should have a deeper pocket to recover from than that of a disbarred lawyer.

Once a former shareholder departs and practices law somewhere else, a professional corporation is no longer permitted to keep using that lawyer's last name.[42] Retaining the name is not misleading if the attorney continues to be a shareholder in the firm (although a disclaimer should be used to avoid deception of the public), but it violates Rules 7.11 and 7.5 (misleading name or letterhead) if there is no ongoing proprietary relationship. The departed attorney cannot be referred to as a partner emeritus if the firm is not, in fact, a partnership.

In general, a firm can have a relationship with an independent contractor attorney who works solely for the firm, as long as confidentiality and conflict of interest rules are satisfied. If the requirements for that relationship are met, either a part-time or full-time attorney can be described as "of counsel" to the firm.[43]

If the lawyer is of counsel, or gets direct supervision, clients generally don't have to be informed of the independent contractor arrangement. The payment arrangement between the firm and the lawyer need not be disclosed to clients if the services are billed as reasonable charges for professional services, not as disbursements.

An of-counsel attorney is permitted to have direct contact with firm clients, as long as the client gets full disclosure—but the attorney should not be held out as a partner or associate of the firm. It is permissible for an attorney not designated of counsel to provide legal services for clients, with or without direct client contact. The firm adopts the attorney's work product as its own even if it doesn't directly supervise the independent contractor attorney.

If the independent contractor attorney's services are treated as a disbursement, the firm has to charge the client what it actually pays. A markup is permitted only if the actual compensation is disclosed and the client consents. It is also permissible to bill a reasonable amount without disclosure, based on the lawyer's qualifications, just as the firm would do for its own associates.

Disclosure of the arrangement is not required if the attorney acts under the direct supervision of the firm's attorneys. Absent such supervision, the client must be informed of, and must consent to, having the independent contractor work on his or her case.

[¶7010.37] [NEW] Rule 5.4 Attorney Independence

After two years of study, the ABA came out against multidisciplinary practice (MDP).[44]

The organization did not recommend any changes in its rules against sharing fees with non-lawyers—even other professionals such as CPAs. The ABA believes that there is a public interest in preserving the "core values" of the legal profession, including complete control of law firms by lawyers and bans on sharing fees with non-attorneys.

[¶7010.39] Rule 5.6 Restrictions on Practice

A law firm's shareholder agreement is permitted to restrict the lawyer's right to engage in private practice after leaving the firm, as a condition of receiving benefits paid under a bona fide retirement plan.[44A] The canonical exception for retirement benefits is not limited to the situation in which a firm member stops practicing law entirely.

Connecticut's ethics rules and public policy are not violated by a law firm partnership's noncompete clause that rules out retirement benefits for partners who resign and compete with the firm.[45] Although restrictions on the right to practice law are discouraged, they are balanced against the law firm's legitimate interest in preserving its own sources of income.

A firm's informal relationship with a major client is not a business opportunity that a former partner can be held liable for misappropriating. The Georgia Court of Appeals indicated that it might have reached a different result if the law firm had operated under a retainer agreement with the business client, or if all of the business' legal work had been directed to the firm.[46]

[¶7010.40] Rule 5.7 Law-Related Services

A California ethics opinion from 1999[47] says that lawyers who engage in activities (like real estate brokerage or investment advice) that overlap with the practice of law are still subject to legal ethics rules (e.g., confidentiality, conflict of interest). This is particularly necessary if the recipient of the cognate services knows that the service provider is a lawyer. Special care is required for marketing materials that refer to the service provider as an attorney; the requirements for attorney advertising are triggered if the client might reasonably conclude that legal services are being contracted for.

The general rule is that when a lawyer provides both legal and nonlegal services to a client, all services are considered legal for compliance purposes. In this analysis (although some states disagree), getting a fee from a portfolio manager for referring clients doesn't count as impermissible fee splitting, but it is a business transaction with a client and therefore disclosure and consent obligations are triggered.

Several opinions have been handed down dealing with the extent to which it is proper for attorneys to pay financial advisers for client referrals, and vice versa. The Ohio view is[48] that lawyers can never get fees for referring clients to financial services firms, because the potential conflicts are irreconcilable.

The proposal about which advice was sought called for an investment services group to pay lawyers for referring clients who needed services. The fee would be negotiated in advance of the referral, and products would only be offered to clients after prior suitability review by the referring attorney.

Ohio's disciplinary board said that a lawyer is obligated to be an objective fiduciary when recommending a financial service provider. The lawyer's duty of loyalty to the client demands making a referral free of conflict, not a referral to whoever pays the largest fee. Although Connecticut, Missouri, and Rhode Island take the position that the client can cure the potential conflict by informed consent, Ohio says that even full disclosure and consent can't cure the conflict.

The Michigan opinion says that, as long as the client gives written consent after the lawyer discloses his or her interest, and as long as the client is advised of the possibility of getting independent advice of counsel or consulting a different financial adviser, it is not unethical for a lawyer to receive a referral fee (usually a percentage of the client's ongoing fees paid to the adviser).[49] The theory is that clients expect, and even want, referrals to other professionals.

When the traffic flows in the other direction, Utah has ruled[50] that it's not per se unethical for a lawyer to take a percentage of the financial adviser's commission from the client as a referral fee.

However, the lawyer can only do it after an objective determination that there is no conflict of interest in the particular client situation, and that the client is likely to benefit from the arrangement. The client is entitled to written disclosure that the attorney receives a fee from the adviser. On the other hand, Arizona, Kentucky, Nevada, and New York say that such payments are per se unethical, irrespective of disclosure.

A related question is the "captive law firm," a firm that is made up of full-time salaried employees of insurance companies whose professional time is devoted to defending those insurance companies. In West Virginia, attorneys in those firms are permitted to represent customers of the insurer, as long as confidentiality is maintained. Florida, Georgia, Missouri, and Tennessee have also allowed captive firms to defend insureds, but North Carolina and Kentucky have disapproved the practice.[51]

Ohio allows[52] lawyers to refer clients to a company that will buy a partial interest in their judgment pending appeal, but such a company is not permitted to interfere with the attorney–client relationship or try to influence the outcome of the litigation. Lawyers can't sell an interest in their expected share of the judgment, because that would be a prohibited business transaction and would also give the third party too much influence over litigation.

The company's business model is to decide if the offered judgment is likely to be upheld on appeal. If so, it buys a minority interest, taking the risk of reversal, in that neither the lawyer nor the client is required to make repayment after a reversal.

The general disciplinary rule is that lawyers are not allowed to acquire a proprietary interest in a case, and are prevented from assisting a client financially other than by advancing or guaranteeing litigation expenses. However, a 1999 amendment permits a lawyer to accept the risk of loss on litigation expenses.

The Ohio ruling permits a lawyer to refer clients to this company, but only after deciding that the referral is in the client's best interests, based on the lawyer's assessment of the client's actual need for funds. Lawyers are forbidden to accept fees for such referrals, because that would give them an incentive to mishandle cases in the interests of future appeals and referral fees.

An agreement between a lawyer and a nonprofit referral service run by a bar group, calling for the lawyer to give the group a percentage of fees from the referred client (on a sliding scale, going up to 25%), is ethical and enforceable.[53] Illinois Rule of Professional Conduct 7.2(b) allows lawyers to pay the usual charges of a not-for-profit referral service; it doesn't violate the policy concerns implicated in the ban on splitting fees with nonlawyers.

In fact, under this analysis, public policy favors funding bar groups with referral fees so they can carry out their public functions. There's no Illinois caselaw on the issue of the reasonableness of the 25% figure.

A bar association referral service is not liable to a client for making a referral without checking whether the lawyer had malpractice insurance, or whether the lawyer would perform competently.[54] The court's view was that referral services perform a valuable function for both the public and the bar, and imposing liability for nonsupervision would impair this useful function.

[¶7010.41] Rule 6.1 Pro Bono

Louisiana Supreme Court restrictions on the types of indigent clients that law students can represent in clinical programs were upheld as constitutional in 1999.[55] The restrictions don't violate any constitutionally protected interests of students, faculty, or potential clients. In this reading, future lawyers don't have a constitutional right to represent clients in court; potential clients have no right to representation in civil cases; and the clinic funders' injury is too theoretical to give them standing.

[¶7010.45] Rule 7.1 Communication

An attorney has a First Amendment right to make a truthful representation that he or she has Martindale-Hubbell's highest (AV) rating.[56] It is not necessary, the Eleventh Circuit says, to disclose that the ratings are based on subjective data whose sources are confidential, despite the ABA's concern that unsophisticated potential clients might be confused about the value of the rating.

Ethical rules against misrepresentation, and governing communication with an adversary without notice to opposing counsel, do not apply to a situation in which a lawyer uses undercover investigators who pose as consumers in order to document unfair business practices such as trademark infringement.[57]

[¶7010.47] Rule 7.3 Contacting Prospective Clients

It is improper for lawyers to pass out brochures at events (e.g., a county fair) or even hire someone else to do it for them, because this constitutes a forbidden in-person solicitation.[58] Nevertheless, brochures are a permissible advertising method, which can be mailed to the general public; included in a direct mail solicitation; displayed on a counter at an event where it would be improper for the lawyer to hand them out; displayed at a business or professional office; given in person to a client or anyone who asks for one; or disseminated through legal service or referral organizations.

The District of Columbia Bar has ruled[59] that it is ethically permissible for lawyers to use on-line exchanges where corporations post Requests for Proposals for their legal work—provided that the lawyers' responses to the RFPs are not false or misleading. It is also permissible to pay to participate in Web-based bidding services as long as the payments are disclosed to potential clients (so they will be aware of the need to recoup the payments as an element of the fee). The Web can also be used to recruit class action plaintiffs, once again as long as the notice is not false or misleading, and proper financial disclosures are made.

[¶7010.50] [NEW] Admission to the Bar

A lawyer who has been admitted pro haec vice in a case is entitled to notice and hearing before revocation of that admission.[59A]

Late in 2000, the Ninth Circuit upheld California Court Rule 983, which permits only a non-resident attorney to seek pro haec vice admission and excludes California residents from this process[59B] In this reading, there is no protectable property interest in pro haec vice admission and no Constitutional right for attorneys to avoid taking their state's bar examination. Furthermore, states can permissibly hold their own lawyers to a higher standard than outsiders.

According to the Colorado Court of Appeals, a lawyer who is admitted in Wisconsin but not in Colorado must refund to the client all fees paid for pre-litigation legal services in Colorado, because Colorado law permits recoupment of all fees paid to "unlicensed persons." Subsequent pro haec vice federal admission does not entitle the attorney to payment under state law for previous work.[60]

On the other hand, an Illinois attorney who is admitted before the District of Arizona but not in the Arizona state courts is permitted to practice—and receive a fee!—for work done in the Bankruptcy Court of the District of Arizona. The Ninth Circuit says that federal and state bar admissions are completely separate.[61]

[¶7010.54] Rule 8.5 Discipline Authority

The Ninth Circuit ruled in 1999 that the District Court violated a lawyer's right to Due Process by disbarring him in federal court (based on disbarrment in state court) without first issuing an Order to Show Cause or otherwise reviewing the state proceeding.[62] Although the federal court can impose reciprocal discipline, it must do more than rubber-stamp the state proceeding. At a minimum, it must examine the record to ascertain the fairness of the state proceeding.

A disbarred lawyer seeking reinstatement is entitled to review and rebut the Character Committee report prepared in connection with his reinstatement request before a decision is made. The lawyer is entitled to a copy of the report (whether positive or negative) to correct errors and respond to concerns raised in the report.[63]

When patent lawyers are doing patent work, they are nonetheless subject to state professional conduct rules, including disciplinary investigations. Even though federal courts have exclusive original jurisdiction over patent actions, and the PTO has power to regulate patent attorneys, nevertheless Congress did not intend to preempt state law disciplinary powers over patent attorneys.[64]

State bar officials retain the power to conduct disciplinary proceedings against a lawyer who was acquitted of criminal charges arising out of the conduct involved in the proceeding.[65] Conviction precludes relitigation (in disciplinary proceeding) of facts conclusively determined in the criminal trial, but does not have comparable effect after acquittal. The transcripts from the criminal trial can be used for disciplinary purposes in lieu of live testimony, where testimony was consistent and a live witness corroborates the narrative.

An Indiana decision from mid-2000[66] upholds a public reprimand to an attorney for pursuing an appeal without disclosing authoritative case law (in a case that the attorney litigated himself!) that was contrary to the client's position and not cited by the opposing attorney. In this view, the attorney should have discussed this precedent with the client when the client was deciding whether or not to pursue an appeal in a drunk driving case. As the attorney was aware from the earlier case, the Indiana law is that viewing the standard video on the rights of a DUI arrestee constitutes adequate information for the arrestee to make a knowing and voluntary guilty plea, and therefore will not later be permitted to withdraw the plea.

A $350 sanction was proper against an attorney who was late when the verdict was rendered after she had been ordered to remain available. In the Second Circuit's view[67], an attorney is an officer of the court and therefore the federal court system has inherent authority to impose sanctions even if there has been no finding of bad faith by the attorney. A bad-faith finding is required to impose sanctions for misconduct that is part of representation of the client but not for misconduct that interferes with the judge's ability to manage the courtroom.

A lawyer's obligation to report misconduct to disciplinary authorities is absolute, and is stronger than the policy against disclosing confidential materials surrendered during discovery.[68] Therefore, a lawyer who suspects unethical conduct by a former colleague, who sues the first attorney, can include information uncovered during this litigation in an unsealed counterclaim, despite the protective order protecting the materials.

[¶7020] Attorney Malpractice

Surviving children of a deceased divorce litigant do not have a cause of action against their mother's divorce lawyer for malpractice (failing to resolve her divorce case while she was still alive, so that the children's inheritance would not be lost). In this reading, a lawyer has no duty to children of his or her clients.[69]

Many courts have taken up the question of contribution and indemnity in legal malpractice cases. Recently, Maryland joined Illinois, Massachusetts, New York, Washington, and Wisconsin in allowing such a defendant to seek contribution or indemnity from successor attorneys, including replacement attorneys negligent in settling the client's case.[70]

Under Michigan's tort reform statute, however, joint and several liability is eliminated, and the defendant is liable only on the basis of pro rata share of fault. Therefore, a law firm sued for malpractice is not entitled to contribution from the malpractice plaintiff's successor attorneys.[71] California will not permit an attorney paid by a client's insurer and then sued by the insurer for malpractice to seek indemnification from the attorneys also hired by the insurer as "monitoring counsel".[72] California recognizes a public policy against cross complaints in malpractice actions, on the grounds that the availability of such a cause of action discourages successor attorneys from doing a rigorous job.

The judgment and the underlying findings of fact in an attorney disciplinary proceeding are relevant and admissible in a malpractice suit against the same attorney. Although the ethics rules don't determine civil liability, they are evidence of the standard of care.[73]

A lawyer who fails to obtain a procedural entitlement (e.g., jury trial) for a client is guilty of malpractice if it wasn't a mere nuisance suit and the client encountered ascertainable damages from the failure. Even the loss of a procedure advantage that was not essential to preserve substantive rights can be malpractice.[74]

A lawyer who asserts the one-year period for filing malpractice claims as an affirmative defense has the burden of proving the client's actual or constructive discovery of the alleged malpractice within the one-year frame.[75]

[¶7030] Other Laws Affecting the Practice of Law

An attorney or law firm "regularly" collects debts if it does so as a matter of course for its clients; for certain clients; or if debt collection is a substantial (whether or not it is a principal) part of the practice. The firm involved in a 1999 Sixth Circuit case[76] did 50-75 collections a year, representing about 2% of its practice, and didn't have any dedicated staff or software for collections, so collection was not "regular" and the Fair Debt Collection Practices Act (FDCPA) was not triggered.

[¶7040.1] Sanctions Outside Rule 11

The Bankruptcy Code does not preempt state-court sanctions imposed for filing a bankruptcy petition in bad faith for the purpose of delaying state court proceeding.[77] *Koffman*[78] says that the Bankruptcy Code preempts state-law counterclaims for abuse of process and malicious prosecution, because the risk of incurring heavy state-court damages could discourage bankruptcy filings. The *Koffman* opinion acknowledges that FRBP 9011 sanctions for abuse of process aren't strong enough to imply Congressional intent to preempt.

The *Prince* court cites this and also distinguishes between tort causes of action and ethical sanctions. Sanctions don't bear the potential for substantial damages, so impose less of a chilling effect. Furthermore, there is no particular bankruptcy connection for sanctions, which can be imposed on anyone who interferes with trial court proceedings. In this case, the bankruptcy petition had already been dismissed, so the state court was not usurping Bankruptcy Court authority.

[¶7050.1] [NEW] Law Firm Partnerships

The New York rule permits non-lawyer employees to participate in a firm's profit-sharing plan that is based on the revenues of the entire firm— but it is not permissible to pay non-lawyers a bonus calculated as a percentage of the fee paid by a client brought in by the non-lawyer.[79]

[¶7050.1.2] [NEW] Compensation of Partners

When a law firm makes a year-end profit distribution to a partner who has filed for bankruptcy protection, the firm must turn over to the trustee all funds attributable either to legal work done by the partner during that year before the petition, or to the partner's capital contribution. In this case[80] the law firm did not wind up its affairs, although the partner's bankruptcy technically resulted in the dissolution of the firm.

Under Bankruptcy Code 541(s), the partner's interest in the law firm is property of the bankruptcy estate. Under the relevant state law (Virginia), continuance of the firm despite its formal dissolution means that title to the firm's assets vested in the continued partnership. Although the bankruptcy trustee does not have the power to force the winding up of the partnership, the other partners must account to the trustee for the value of the bankrupt partner's interest.

[¶7060] Attorneys' Fees

A federal District Court has not only the power but the obligation to review the fairness of the attorneys' fee provision of a class action settlement— even if none of the class members have an objection (or even have standing to raise one). In the Ninth Circuit view,[81] the court's equitable jurisdiction to decide ancillary matters even post-settlement is not dependent on the presence of a complaining party with standing. (In this securities fraud case, there were objections, but the objector lacked standing, because the settlement didn't directly compensate the plaintiffs.)

A class action can't be a common fund case if there is no cash award; and here, the defendant paid the attorneys' fees.The defendant corporation agreed to declare future dividends according to a formula, but not to pay plaintiffs for past conduct. The plaintiffs' counsel negotiated with the defendant for a fee of close to $3 million. The District court, affirmed by the Ninth Circuit, reduced the fee to $1.15 million and awarded almost $50,000 for the challenge to the objecting party.

Considerations of fairness and efficiency favor letting unnamed, non-intervening class members appeal the fee award to the class counsel (as distinguished from the settlement itself). The Ninth Circuit vacated an award of 30% to the class counsel because the District Court did not provide an adequate explanation of why it exceeded the 25% benchmark for percentage awards.[82]

If a fee award is otherwise proper, it is not forfeited by the use of salaried in-house counsel, in which case the award will depend on a "cost-plus" analysis of the attorney's salary and overhead, not the market rates charged by law firms.[83]

Pennsylvania permits a nonrefundable fee agreement in a general retainer.[84] The arrangement was set up by a bankrupt asbestos company (i.e., a sophisticated corporation, not a vulnerable individual) in order to keep qualified counsel available for an indeterminate number of asbestos-related suits. (The company's bankruptcy rendered concerns about payment rational.) The agreement called for a one-time nonrefundable payment of $1 million, fixed-fee quarterly payments, and payments according to a fee schedule for trial.

Ten weeks after signing the agreement, the company fired the law firm for dilatory performance, and sued for return of the $1 million. The Third Circuit held the contract to be reasonable and enforceable both when made and when terminated. It was a general retainer in return for guaranteed availability of the attorney; it was not a specific retainer (advance against services), which would be at least partially refundable. The court didn't believe the argument that nonrefundable retainers lock in clients with attorneys whom they no longer want to represent them; in this case, the defendant felt comfortable dismissing the firm (although they might not have done so if they had believed that the retainer would genuinely be forfeit).

Under New York law, when a law firm breaks up and a lawyer leaves with a contingent fee case, the case is an asset of the firm unless it was agreed to the contrary. Therefore, when the departed lawyer gets paid after the conclusion of the case, the lawyer must remit to the firm the value of the case as of the time of the dissolution of the firm—not just a quantum meruit amount representing the value of the services performed by the firm prior to its dissolution.[85]

A late-2000 Colorado case says that an attorney discharged from a contingent fee case can seek a quantum meruit payment only if the retainer agreement explicitly places the client on notice that this is a potential consequence of discharging the attorney. The agreement in question said that the attorney could collect an "hourly" rate if terminated before the case was concluded, and therefore the attorney could not recover in quantum meruit.[86]

Whether one divorcing spouse must pay the other's attorney's fees is a perpetual debate. A Missouri case from 2001 holds that it was not an abuse of discretion for the trial court to order the husband to pay the wife's fees for the divorce case and the appeal on the fee issue, because of the husband's greater earnings and earning potential and his grossly improper conduct during the marriage, including spousal abuse. In contrast, a North Dakota case does not consider general fault during the marriage to justify a fee award on behalf of the better-behaved but higher-earning spouse. In this analysis, improper litigation conduct would justify a fee award, but improper marital conduct would not.[87]

Unless the agreement specifies to the contrary, a contingent fee agreement giving the attorney a percentage of "any amount received" via a settlement or judgment must be interpreted to mean the net amount (minus counterclaims, for example) and not the gross.[88]

A party does not have "response costs" under CERCLA §107 merely because the party's attorney has advanced preparatory expenses such as soil testing, and the party would have to reimburse the attorney if and when it succeeds in the CERCLA case.[89]

Post-judgment interest on an attorney's fee award runs from the date the District Court renders a "money judgment" (28 U.S.C. §1961(a)), not the earlier point at which the District Court indicates that the prevailing party should receive a fee award.[90]

[¶7060.1] [NEW] Prevailing Party

A defendant won an environmental law case by showing that the plaintiff lacked standing. In the Seventh Circuit's view, the prevailing defendant encountered injuries (in the form of legal fees), and therefore was not debarred from recovering attorneys' fees even though the federal court lacked jurisdiction over the case. However, a fee award was not made in this particular case, because the plaintiffs' suit, although unsuccessful, was neither frivolous nor groundless.[91]

A Tenth Circuit case from mid-2000[92] holds that a prevailing defendant in a Lanham Act case was properly denied attorneys' fees, because the proper test is not only whether the plaintiff's suit had objective foundation, but whether the plaintiff acted in subjective good or bad faith.

A roughly contemporary Third Circuit case looks at the Lanham Act §35(a) grant of fee awards in exceptional cases from another perspective.[93] In this reading, fee awards are not limited to cases of willful infringement. Vexatious litigation conduct (here, bad faith negotiations with the objective of destroying a weaker competitor) is also relevant.

[¶7060.3] Fee Calculations and the Lodestar

Special expertise in tax law and Texas community property and insurance law, claimed by an attorney, did not constitute a "special factor" that would justify raising the fee award over the Code §7430 amount. Nor does egregious conduct on the part of the government constitute a special factor.[94]

In an ERISA case that provides a common fund (the employer seized $12.5 million in surplus pension assets that should have been distributed to retirees), the District Court has discretion to award either the lodestar or a percentage of the recovery under the common fund doctrine.[95]

Using the lodestar was not an abuse of discretion, because counsel was reasonably compensated and there was no unjust enrichment. The plaintiffs' attorneys stipulated that a $460,000 fee was reasonable under the ERISA fee provision, 29 USC §1132(g)(1), allowing reasonable fees to either side.

The attorneys also sought 20-30% of the common fund. The attorneys claimed that the District Court erred as a matter of law by saying that ERISA fee provision bars common-fund award, but the Third Circuit reading is that the District Court did not preclude common fund awards in general, merely found it unfair in the particular case. Thus, the standard of review was abuse of discretion.

The plaintiffs' attorneys say they shouldn't be penalized for taking the case to judgment (and getting a statutory fee) rather than settling (and getting a common fund fee). Such a penalty would create a risk of conflict of interest, if they had a motive to force clients into an unfavorable settlement to raise their own fee.

However, the Third Circuit position is that percentage fees should be cross-checked against the lodestar anyway, to prevent grants of excessive fees. A common fund award could also be proper even in a case that goes to judgment, e.g., where the defendant is bankrupt or otherwise unable to cover the fees, or where there was no other way to get competent counsel.

A Second Circuit case from March, 2000 says that although the District Court has discretion in a common fund case to use either the lodestar or the percentage-of-fund method, the lodestar cannot simply be disregarded.[96]

The total plaintiff class recovery from Drexel Burnham's bankruptcy case and settlements with other defendants exceeded $54 million. Class counsel sought 25% of the common fund—i.e., $13 million, whereas the lodestar amount was $2.1 million. The Second Circuit, while admitting that some courts treat 25% as a benchmark in common fund cases, refused to apply a multiplier to the lodestar amount, viewing the starting point for the analysis as the fee that would prevail, in an efficient legal market.

An attorney who has a contingent fee agreement can collect a percentage of court-awarded fees as long as the agreement unambiguously authorizes this.[97] If the agreement is silent or ambiguous, the percentage is calculated based on the total recovery minus the court-awarded fee. The lawyer gets only the larger of the two.

The catalyst theory (covering a plaintiff who doesn't get a judgment or a formal settlement, but whose suit is a substantial factor in changing the defendant's conduct) is still viable in §1988 cases (award of fees to civil rights prevailing party), according to the Eleventh[98] and eight other circuits. The Fourth Circuit, however, says that *Farrar v. Hobby*[99] eliminates the catalyst theory. The other nine Circuits treat the viability of catalyst theory as limited, but not entirely absent.

Farrar says that a civil rights plaintiff doesn't "prevail" without getting at least some relief on the merits of the claim (an enforceable judgment against the defendant, or comparable relief through a settlement or consent decree; the relief must directly benefit the plaintiff as of the time of the judgment or settlement). The Eleventh Circuit is willing to apply the catalyst theory if, and only if, there is no formal judgment, consent decree, or settlement. Thus, a §1988 fee award is possible even without formal relief, if the defendant's voluntary action is sufficient to redress the plaintiff's grievances.

Attorneys' fees are not included in determining the minimum amount in controversy required by 27 USC §1332(a) (even though the fees might be deducted from the common fund).

The Eleventh Circuit disapproved[100] the tactics of attorneys who file nationwide class actions in states that have made very big punitive damage awards in the past, while keeping the complaint's ad damnum below the minimum for federal diversity jurisdiction, waiting until the one-year period for removal to federal court has expired, then amending the complaint seeking punitive damages. The common fund attorneys' fee is not part of the matter in controversy, because the fee isn't a "single title or right" of the plaintiff.

Employees who prevail by settling their employment discrimination claims at the administrative level do not have the right to bring a separate Title VII action in District Court to recover their attorneys' fees. The Eastern District of Virginia decided in 1999 that there is no federal jurisdiction over such claims.[101]

The agreement provided that if the parties couldn't agree on the fee question, the defendant agency would pay fees as provided under 29 CFR §1614.501(e), which allows the agency to set the fee amount, subject to a right of appeal to the EEOC. The employee wanted $310/hour, the CIA offered $250, the EEOC called for $275, so the employee sued for the difference between the $310 and $275 hourly rates.

Of course, the District Court has jurisdiction over actions brought under Title VII, but the Eastern District of Virginia had to decide if an independent action for attorneys' fees falls into this category. The District Court held that "actions under this subchapter" means proceedings to enforce substantive employment rights; fee awards are only discretionary and ancillary to these proceedings. The statutory use of "action" refers to a substantive one and not a suit solely for collateral or ancillary relief.

In late 2000, the Sixth Circuit ruled that the Prison Litigation Reform Act (PLRA; see ¶6090) fee cap serves a rational purpose in limiting frivolous litigation, and therefore does not deny equal protection to prisoners. But a District Court case two days later takes the opposite position: that although the government interests are legitimate, they are not rationally related to the fee cap, which does violate equal protection by treating prisoners differently from non-prisoners. In this analysis, prisoners are not influenced by the potential size of a hypothetical attorneys' fee award when deciding whether or not to litigate about prison conditions.[102]

As a general rule, an attorney who has a contingent fee agreement is not permitted to charge the client extra for collecting the judgment or settlement proceeds, in that collecting a judgment is the normal objective of litigation. The Third Circuit permits[103] an exception in a case where collection efforts go far beyond what the parties contemplated when they made the agreement. If you're that worried, you should specify in the original agreement what constitutes normal collection efforts and how much you can get paid for the abnormal ones.

A law firm cannot withdraw from a contingent fee case because it thinks it won't earn enough, and then demand a quantum meruit award for work already done; withdrawal without good cause means that the attorney is not entitled to payment.[104]

A clause in a retainer agreement requiring the client to reimburse the attorney for the reasonable fees and costs of collecting unpaid bills is unenforceable[105] because it prevents clients from making valid objections to their bills. Such a clause might even violate the ethical rule against representation that is limited by the attorney's own interests.

If it is clear that a lawyer has seriously violated fiduciary duty to a client, forfeiture of the lawyer's fee can be ordered as an equitable remedy even if the client can't show actual damages. However, the appropriate degree of forfeiture varies with circumstances. The extent of forfeiture is a question of law, and therefore goes to the judge, not the jury.[106]

The Minnesota state statute regulating the availability and amount of fees that can be awarded to Worker's Compensation claimants has been held unconstitutional,[107] on the grounds that it interferes with the inherent judicial power to regulate fees. Although statutes can offer guidelines, the final decision on fee awards rests with the judge.

The 35 USC §285 attorneys' fee award to reimburse the prevailing party can exceed the amount actually paid by the named injured party. In early 2000, the Federal Circuit affirmed an award that included fees paid by the parent corporation of the parent of the prevailing party (a defendant in a patent infringement action). Section 285 is supposed to discourage worthless suits and compensate prevailing parties; it's not relevant who actually ended up paying the fees.[108]

[¶7060.4] [NEW] Tax Deductibility of Fees

Antitrust litigation over American Stores Co.'s acquisition of Lucky Stores was prolonged, and went all the way to the Supreme Court. American

Stores deducted its legal fees from this process as ordinary and necessary business expenses. However, in mid-2000, the Tax Court agreed with the IRS view: that the fees were encountered because of the acquisition of Lucky Stores, and therefore must be capitalized rather than currently deducted.[109]

[¶7060.5] [NEW] Attorneys' Fees and Bankruptcy

The question of attorneys' fees is always a complex one (after all, the bankruptcy debtor is at least theoretically in financial trouble). In the current climate, where the number of bankruptcy filings will increase, but there is a real possibility that drastic bankruptcy reform legislation will be passed, the issues will become even more complex.

Although Bankruptcy Code §330(a) has been amended to remove the phrase "or the debtor's attorney" from the list of people eligible to receive fees for post-petition services, the Ninth Circuit treats the removal as a scrivener's error, saying that the deletion was inadvertent and makes the statutory language ambiguous[110], and the Third Circuit agrees.

There is a split in authority: the Fifth Circuit and some Bankruptcy Courts say that the language is not ambiguous, and thus precludes the fee award, but the Second Circuit and a second group of Bankruptcy Courts disagree.

In the Ninth Circuit view, prior to 1994, it was clear that Chapter 7 attorneys could collect fees for post-petition services. After the amendment, the categories of persons eligible for "reasonable compensation" is different from the categories to whom the court "may award" payment, and the statutory text is grammatically incorrect.

If an attorney receives unearned fees, and does not return the fees in compliance with a judge's declaration that the fee agreement is invalid, the fees become a debt that is not dischargeable in bankruptcy, because a severe violation of the fiduciary relationship with the client constitutes "defalcation" as defined by the Bankruptcy Code.[111]

In this case, New York's Surrogate's Court declared the lawyer's agreement with Andy Warhol's estate was invalid because it called for payment of a percentage of the estate, with no limiting factor. The attorney had already received $4.85 million by the time the court ordered the fee reduced to $3.5 million.

The position of the Bankruptcy Court, as affirmed by the District Court, is that the lawyer thereby incurred a $1.35 million debt, but not in a fiduciary capacity, because Bankruptcy Code §523(a)(4) is limited to trustees of express or technical trusts, not constructive or implied trusts. But the Second Circuit disagreed, applying the defalcation provision to constructive trusts, and even regular commercial debts.

In this view, the attorney–client relationship is always fiduciary, and fee arrangements are part of the attorney–client relationship. A fiduciary commits defalcation when the accounts fail to balance, even if there has been no wrongful intent. The lawyer should have restricted the fee to the value of his services (rather than the value of artworks in a rapidly rising market) or, at a minimum, obtained advance court approval for the unusual and questionable fee agreement.

Failure to get approval of an attorney's fees as required by Bankruptcy Code §329 and local rules resulted in disgorgement of the fees (even though they were reasonable in amount) because of the attorney's deliberate noncompliance with the rules.[112]

Bankruptcy Code §328(a) [dealing with retainers, hourly rates, and contingent fees], and not the lodestar, should be used to review a special counsel's application for legal fees submitted to the Chapter 11 trustee, because the court order appointing the special counsel specified a part-hourly, part-contingent system of compensation, thus making the lodestar irrelevant.[113]

The Eighth Circuit denied fees entirely to an attorney who delegated too much of the bankruptcy-related work to a paralegal, because excessive delegation meant that the lawyer did not properly represent the clients.[114] In fact, the attorney was ordered to disgorge fees already received, plus the U.S. Trustee's investigative costs for the matter.

The automatic stay is not violated when an attorney charges a client in Chapter 7 a fee for post-petition services that the bankruptcy court later found to be unreasonable, in that the attorney had no reason to believe that the services were unreasonable at the time of rendition.[115]

However, in the Ninth Circuit view, the automatic stay does not apply to attorneys' fees awarded as a sanction for frivolous litigation (in this case, a frivolous appeal as defined by F.R.A.P. 38), because the sanction is imposed to carry out government policy, not to protect either private rights or the government's pecuniary interest in the sanctioned lawyer's property. Therefore, Bankruptcy Code §362(b)(4) governs making the automatic stay inapplicable to actions by a governmental unit to enforce the police or regulatory power.[116] Subsequently, the attorney and Chapter 11 filer must pay the sanctions.

[¶7070] Law Practice in the Internet Era

Apparently, a District Court staff failed to keep the court's electronic "docket sheet" up to date. Shortly after the Southern District of Florida denied the petitioner's habeas petition, a final order was entered on the official docket record, but not the Public Access to Court Electronic Records (PACER) system. The petitioner's lawyer kept checking PACER, but didn't see the final order there—or get a copy of the order by mail. He only found out about the order over a year after the 30-day filing deadline for appeal had run, and only as part of a conversation with a court employee.

In the view of the Eleventh Circuit,[117] that excuses a habeas petitioner's failure to meet the deadline for appealing the denial of relief.

The court "officially invited" reliance on the electronic system, and the petitioner reasonably relied on it. Therefore, even though in general there is no jurisdiction over an untimely appeal, this unique circumstance does justify relief.

The Eleventh Circuit view is that an untimely appeal can be forgiven because of reasonable and good faith reliance on judicial action that lulls the appellant into inactivity. Electronic dockets are supposed to benefit everybody via greater efficiency, so reliance is not inappropriate. The District Court and its own home page describe PACER as official, and the District Court is not relieved of responsibility merely because apparently the mistake was made by the court clerk's office, not the court itself.

Ohio permits[118] attorneys to give legal advice online for a fee, subject to the same ethical constraints as offering legal advice in any other setting (e.g., over the telephone). The legal advice is required to be competent; trade names for the online service are barred, as are joint ventures between attorneys and nonattorneys; advice should not be given outside Ohio unless that is permissible under the rules of the receiving state; and a lawyer should not recommend employment of him- or herself or another lawyer in the firm unless the client asked for advice about employment of an attorney.

It's permissible to put an intake form on a Web site, so potential clients can e-mail questions to the site and agree to pay for an e-mail response. The lawyer has an ethical duty to inform the potential client if the lawyer does not think an e-mail response will be sufficient. The intake form must call for sufficient information for a conflict check. The e-mail response must include a statement that the answer to the query was researched under Ohio law and answered by an Ohio-licensed attorney.

Florida has a new rule on Internet advertising by Florida attorneys, setting a standard for computer-accessed communications.[119] Lawyer and law firm Web sites are information provided at a prospective client's request, so they are subject to the separate rule governing that situation (but not to the requirement that lawyer advertisements be filed with the disciplinary authorities).

Firm sites must disclose all jurisdictions in which members are licensed, and must give at least one bona fide office location. Rule 4-7.6(c) says that unsolicited e-mail to potential clients is direct mail, so it has to conform to the direct mail rule, must have "legal advertisement" in the subject line, and must disclose at least one bona fide office location. Other computer-accessed communications dealing with the services of a lawyer or law firm are treated as lawyer advertising.

A Nassau County (New York) ethics opinion permits lawyers to pay to be listed as sponsors on banner ads on Web sites that give information about particular fields of law.[120] However, disclaimers are required to conform to New York advertising requirements. (The site charges an additional fee for a link to the advertising attorney's own Web site.)

The service also maintains lists of attorneys in particular fields of law by geographic area, in alphabetical order, but "Lead Counsel" who pay more are listed first. The ethics committee considers the banner ads acceptable, because it's clear that viewers are seeing a paid advertisement rather than a neutral recommendation. However, to prevent confusion to the public, sponsorships should be sold for comparatively brief periods and not restricted to one attorney.

The service is also required to post a disclaimer that it is not a referral service, doesn't endorse or recommend any attorney, and the information on the site doesn't come from the sponsors. But the lead counsel identification is unacceptable, because it implies special skill rather than payment of a greater-than-usual fee.

Sale of links is not unethical, as long as there is no direct communication with the actual lawyer or real-time dialogue with the office. Because directories are allowed to refer to an attorney's concentration in a particular practice area, the (functionally similar) sponsor label is also permitted. Of course, Web sites can reach outside New York State, but this is permissible as long as the advertisement identifies the jurisdictions in which each attorney is licensed.

The opinion treats the site and its advertisements as closer to print or broadcast ads than private written solicitations, so advance filing with the committee is not required. The service stores hard copies of sponsor advertisements, which are given to the advertising attorneys so they can satisfy the requirement that copies of broadcast ads be kept for at least a year.

ENDNOTES

1. *Romero v. Colegio de Abogados de Puerto Rico,* 204 F.3d 291 (1st Cir. 2000).
2. *Heffernan v. Hunter,* 189 F.3d 405 (3rd Cir. 1999).
3. *Darby & Darby PC v. VSI International Inc.,* 69 LW 1260 (N.Y. 10/24/00).
4. *Roe v. Flores-Ortega,* 528 U.S. 470 (Sup.Ct. 2000).
5. ABA Standing Comm. on Ethics & Professional Resp., Formal Op. 99-414, 68 LW 2597 (9/8/99).
6. *Olson v. Accessory Controls & Equipment,* 757 A.2d 14 (Conn. 2000).
7. *In re Grand Jury,* 69 LW 1532 (3rd Cir. 2/20/01).
8. *In re Grand Jury Subpoena,* 69 LW 1103 (3rd Cir. 8/4/00).
9. *In re Grand Jury Subpoena,* 220 F.3d 406 (5th Cir. 2000).
10. *Gordon v. Boyles,* 9 P.3d 1106 (Colo. 9/11/00).
11. *U.S. v. Colorado Supreme Court,* 68 LW 1147 (10th Cir. 9/1/99).
12. *Foster v. Hill,* 188 F.3d 1259 (10th Cir. 1999).
13. *National Education Training Group Inc. v. SkillSoft Corp.,* 68 LW 1031 (S.D.N.Y. 6/10/99).
14. *In re Grand Jury Proceedings,* 219 F.3d 175 (2nd Cir. 2000).
15. *In re George,* 69 LW 1051 (Tex. 7/6/00).
16. *In re Pioneer Hi-Bred Int'l Inc.,* 69 LW 1544 (Fed.Cir. 2/5/01).
17. *Calvin Klein Trademark Trust v. Wachner,* 69 LW 1371 (S.D.N.Y. 12/5/00).
18. *Wells Fargo Bank NS v. Superior Court,* 68 LW 1495 (Cal. 1/13/00).
19. Philadelphia Bar Association Professional Guidance Comm., Op. 99-6, 68 LW 2133 (August, 1999).
20. *Financial Technologies v. Smith,* 69 LW 1431 (S.D.N.Y. 12/19/00).
21. Maine Board of Bar Oversees Professional Ethics Comm., Op. 171, 68 LW 2451 (12/24/99).
22. *Kassis v. Teacher's Insurance and Annuity Ass'n,* 68 LW 1063 (N.Y. 7/1/99).
23. *Sumitomo Corp. v. JP Morgan & Co.,* 68 LW 1543 (S.D.N.Y. 2/8/00).

24. ABA Standing Comm. on Ethics & Prof'l Resp., Formal Opinion 99-415, 68 LW 2598 (9/8/99).
25. New York State Bar Ass'n Comm. on Prof'l Ethics, Op. 720, 68 LW 2227 (8/27/99).
26. Formal Op. 00-418 (7/7/00); see 69 LW 2067-8.
27. Committee on Professional and Judicial Ethics Formal Op. 2000-3; see 69 LW 2120.
28. *State Farm v. Federal Ins. Co.*, 86 Cal Rptr.2d 20 (Cal. App. 1999).
29. *Adams v. Aerojet-General Corp.*, 69 LW 1511 (Cal.App. 2/7/01).
30. *Washington Legal Foundation v. Texas Equal Access to Justice Foundation*, 86 F.Supp.2d 624 (W.D. Tex. 2000).
31. 524 U.S. 156 (Sup.Ct. 1998).
32. *Washington Legal Foundation v. Legal Foundation of Washington*, 236 F.3d 1097 (9th Cir. 2001).
33. Formal Op. 505 (8/21/00); see 69 LW 2215.
34. NYSBA Comm. on Prof'l Ethics Op. 730 (7/27/00), 69 LW 2102.
35. *Osprey Inc. v. Cabana Limited Partnership*, 68 LW 1767 (S.C. 2000).
36. Utah State Bar Ethics Advisory Op. Comm. Op. 00-06 (9/29/00); see 69 LW 2246.
37. Op. 2000-02, March 2000; 69 LW 2035.
38. *Kennedy v. Zimmerman*, 601 N.W.2d 61 (Iowa 1999).
39. *Krakora v. Gold*, 68 LW 1255 (Ohio App. 9/28/99).
40. *State v. Quattlebaum*, 68 LW 1470 (S.C. 1/26/00).
41. *Baker v. Ploetz*, 597 N.W.2d 347 (Minn.App. 1999).
42. Maryland State Bar Ass'n Comm. on Ethics, Op. 00-03, 68 LW 2339 (10/4/99).
43. Virginia State Bar Standing Comm. on Legal Ethics, Op. 1735, 68 LW 2357 (10/20/99).
44. See 69 LW 2042-5.
44A. *Donnelly v. Brown, Winick, Graves, Gross, Baskerville, Schoenebaum and Walker PLC*, 599 N.W.2d 677 (Iowa 1999).
45. *Schoonmaker v. Cummings and Lockwood of Connecticut PC*, 747 A.2d 1017 1608 (Conn. 2000).
46. *Jenkins v. Smith*, 69 LW 1079 (Ga.App. 6/7/00).
47. California State Bar Standing Comm. on Prof'l Responsibility and Conduct, Formal Op. 1999-154, 68 LW 2166 (8/27/99).
48. Ohio Supreme Court Board of Commissioners on Grievances and Discipline, Op. 2000-1, 68 LW 2549 (2/11/00). See 68 LW 2631 (4/25/00) for a summary of the ethics pronouncements on this issue.

49. Michigan State Bar Comm. on Professional and Judicial Ethics, Informal Op. RI-317 (2/14/00).

50. Utah State Bar Ethics Advisory Opinion Comm., Op. 99-07 (12/3/99).

51. West Virginia State Bar Lawyer Disciplinary Board, Op. 99-01, 7/9/99, discussed at 68 LW 2198.

52. Ohio Sup. Ct. Board of Commissioners on Grievance and Discipline, Op. 99-6, 68 LW 2483 (12/2/99).

53. *Richards v. SSM Health Care Inc.*, 68 LW 1467 (Ill. App. 1/26/00).

54. *Bourke v. Kazaras*, 746 A.2d 642 (Pa.Super. 2000).

55. *Southern Christian Leadership Conference v. Louisiana Supreme Court*, 61 F.Supp.2d 499 (E.D. La. 1999).

56. *Mason v. Florida Bar*, 208 F.3d 952 (11th Cir. 2000).

57. *Gidatex S.r.L. v. Campaniello Imports Ltd.*, 68 LW 1239 (S.D.N.Y. 1999).

58. Ohio Sup. Ct. Bd. of Comm'rs on Grievances and Discipline, Op. 99-5, 68 LW 2294 (10/8/99).

59. D.C. Bar Legal Ethics Comm. Op. 302 (11/21/00), 69 LW 2515.

59A. *Jensen v. Wisconsin Patient Compensation Fund*, 69 LW 1499 (Wis. 2/13/01).

59B. *Paciulan v. George*, 69 LW 1243 (9th Cir.10/17/00).

60. *Koscove v. Bolt*, 69 LW 1559 (Colo. App. 2/15/01).

61. *Brown v. Smith*, 222 F.3d 618 (9th Cir. 2000).

62. *In re Kramer*, 193 F.3d 1131 (9th Cir. 1999).

63. *In re Citrin*, 706 N.Y.S.2d 72 (N.Y. 2000).

64. *Schindler v. Finnerty*, 74 F.Supp.2d 253 (E.D.N.Y. 1999).

65. *In re Segal*, 719 N.E.2d 480 (Mass. 1999).

66. *In re Thonert*, 69 LW 2150 (Ind. 8/22/00).

67. *U.S. v. Rosario (Seltzer)* , 69 LW 1195 (2nd Cir. 9/25/00).

68. *Skolnick v. Altheimer & Gray*, 68 LW 1623 (Ill. 3/23/00).

69. *Strait v. Kennedy*, 13 P.3d 671 (Wash.App. 2000).

70. *Parler & Wobber v. Miles & Stockbridge PC*, 756 A.2d 526 (Md. 2000).

71. *Kokx v. Bylenga*, 69 LW 1127 (Mich.App. 7/11/00).

72. *Shaffery v. Wilson, Elser, Moskowitz, Edelman & Dickel*, 98 Cal.Rptr.2d 419 (Cal.App. 2000).

73. *Roy v. Diamond*, 68 LW 1319 (Tenn.App. 10/30/99).

74. *Jones Motor Co. v. Holtkamp, Liese, Beckemeir & Childress PC*, 197 F.3d 1190 (7th Cir. 1999).

75. *Samuels v. Mix*, 91 Cal.Rptr.2d 273 (Cal. 12/30/99).

76. *Schroyer v. Frankel*, 197 F.3d 1170 (6th Cir. 1999).

77. *Prince v. MacDonald*, 68 LW 1116 (Mich.App. 8/13/99).

78. *Koffman v. Osteoimplant Technology*, 182 B.R. 115 (Bank. Md. 1995).

79. New York State Bar Ass'n Comm. on Professional Ethics Op. 733, 10/5/00; see 69 LW 2537.

80. *Beaman v. Shearin*, 224 F.3d 346 and *Beaman & Vandeventer Black LLP*, 224 F.3d 353, both 4th Cir. 2000.

81. *Zucker v. Occidental Petroleum Corp.*, 192 F.3d 1323 (9th Cir. 1999).

82. *Powers v. Eichen*, 229 F.3d 1249 (9th Cir. 2000).

83. *Soft Solutions Inc. v. Brigham Young University*, 68 LW 1793 (Utah 5/19/00).

84. *Ryan v. Butera, Beausang, Cohen & Brennan*, 193 F.3d 210 (3rd Cir. 1999).

85. *Santalucia v. Sebright Transp. Inc.*, 69 LW 1335 (2nd Cir. 11/9/00).

86. *Dudding v. Norton Frickey & Associates*, 69 LW 2263 (Colo. 10/10/00).

87. Compare *Brady v. Brady*, 27 Family Law Reporter 1237 (Mo.App. 3/20/01) with *Reiser v. Reiser*, 27 FLR 1153 (N.D. 1/31/01).

88. *Levine v. Bayne, Snell & Krause Ltd.* , 69 LW 1483 (Tex. 2/1/01).

89. *Trimble v. Asarco Inc.*, 232 F.3d 946 (8th Cir. 2000).

90. *Eaves v. Cape May County, New Jersey*, 239 F.3d 527 (3rd Cir. 2001).

91. *Citizens for a Better Environment v. Steel Co.*, 230 F.3d 923 (7th Cir. 2000).

92. *Nat'l Ass'n of Professional Baseball Leagues Inc. v. Very Minor Leagues Inc.*, 223 F.3d 1143 (10th Cir. 2000).

93. *Secura Comm Consulting Inc. v. Secura-Com Inc.*, 224 F.3d 273 (3rd Cir. 2000).

94. *A. Cervin Estate*, 2000-1 USTC ¶60,367 (5th Cir. 2000).

95. *Brytus v. Spang & Co.*, 203 F.3d 238 (3rd Cir. 2000).

96. *Goldberger v. Integrated Resources Inc.*, 68 LW 1611 (2nd Cir. 3/28/00).

97. *Cambridge Trust Co. v. Hanify and King PC*, 721 N.E.2d 1 (Mass. 1999).

98. *Morris v. West Palm Beach, Fla.*, 194 F.3d 1203 (11th Cir. 1999).

99. 506 U.S. 103 (Sup.Ct. 1992).

100. *Davis v. Carl Cannon Chevrolet-Olds Inc.,* 182 F.3d 792 (11th Cir. 1999).
101. *Chris v. Tenet,* 68 LW 1087 (E.D.Va. 7/28/99). The employer in this case, by the way, was the Central Intelligence Agency.
102. Compare *Hadix v. Johnson,* 230 F.3d 840 (6th Cir. 2000) with *Johnson v. Daley,* 117 F.Supp.2d 889 (W.D. Wis. 2000).
103. *Dardovitch v. Holtzman,* 190 F.3d 125 (3rd Cir. 1999).
104. *Bell & Marra PLLC v. Sullivan,* 6 P.3d 965 (Mont. 2000).
105. *Lustig v. Horn,* 732 N.E.2d 613 (Ill.App. 2000).
106. *Burrow v. Arce,* 68 LW 1063 (Texas 7/1/99).
107. *Irwin v. Surdyk's Liquor,* 599 N.W.2d 132 (Minn. 1999).
108. *Automated Business Companies Inc. v. NEC America Inc.,* 202 F.3d 1353 (Fed.Cir. 2000).
109. *American Stores Co. v. Comm'r,* 114 TC No. 27 (7/26/00).
110. *U.S. Trustee v. Garvey, Schubert & Barer,* 195 F.3d 1053 (9th Cir. 1999), Semble *In re Top Grade Sausage,* 227 F.3d 123 (3rd Cir. 2000), whereas *Inglesby, Falligant, Horne, Covington & Nash PC v. Moore,* 197 F.3d 1354 (11th Cir. 1999) and *Andrews & Kurth LLP v. Family   Snacks Inc.,* 157 F.3d 414 (5th Cir. 1998) hold that the plain language of the statute precludes a fee award.
111. *Andy Warhol Foundation for Visual Arts Inc. v. Hayes,* 183 F.3d 162 (2nd Cir. 1999).
112. *In re Redding,* 251 B.R. 547 (W.D. Mo. 2000).
113. *Peele v. Cunningham,* 218 F.3d 443 (5th Cir. 2000).
114. *Walton v. LaBarge,* 223 F.3d 859 (8th Cir. 2000).
115. *Sanchez v. Gordon,* 69 LW 1532 (9th Cir. 3/5/01).
116. *Berg v. Good Samaritan Hospital,* 230 F.3d 1165 (9th Cir. 10/23/00).
117. *Hollins v. Dept of Corrections,* 191 F.3d 1324 (11th Cir. 1999).
118. Ohio Supreme Court Board of Commissioners on Grievances and Discipline, Op. 99-9, 68 LW 2388 (12/2/99).
119. 68 LW 2387 Amendments to Rules Regulating the Florida Bar—Advertising Rules Fla. No. 92,297 (12/17/99), 68 LW 2387. This document also provides that out-of-state attorneys are not subject to Florida's amended advertising rules, because such conduct is already forbidden as unauthorized practice of law.
120. Nassau County Bar Ass'n Comm. on Professional Ethics, Op. 99-3, 68 LW 2245 (9/29/99).

¶7500

Computers and the Law

[¶7501]

In August, 1999, the Ninth Circuit vacated[1] the preliminary injunction that Sun had obtained against Microsoft for breach of its license to use Java, and remanded the case. If the allegedly breached items in a copyright license were limitations on the scope of the license (not covenants of independent contractors), then irreparable harm can be presumed from the breach. However, the existence (or otherwise) of a breach is a question to be decided under state copyright law.

The Department of Justice's Computer Crimes and Intellectual Property section published a manual on prosecuting computer crimes, e.g., the use of computers in perpetrating fraud, identity theft, gambling, cyberstalking, child pornography, and unauthorized sale of prescription drugs. See http://www.cybercrime.gov/crimes.html.

The Computer Fraud and Abuse Act (18 USC §1030)is triggered when a computer is used in interstate or international commerce or communications. It is not limited to outsider hackers; it is implicated, for instance, when an employee uses the employer's computer to transmit trade secrets of the employer to a competitor. The court used the term "fraud" quite broadly for all forms of wrongdoing, without limitation to common-law fraud.[2]

The CFA was also violated when a former employee maliciously changed passwords and deleted a company's billing system and two of its databases, because a corporation is considered an "individual" under the CFA ban on conduct that causes loss to "one or more individuals."[3]

[¶7510.2] [NEW] Typical Law Office Applications

Recent ethics opinions have permitted attorneys to affiliate with Web sites that list attorneys for potential clients, and also to use online exchanges where corporations post Requests for Proposals for legal representation.[4]

[¶7515] Legal Implications of Computer Code and Software

It is permissible for the Digital Millennium Copyright Act's amendments to Copyright Act §117, allowing software to be loaded into computer memory for repair purposes, to have retroactive effect.[5] Retroactivity is permissible because the amendments do not impose any new duties and tend to reduce rather than increase liability.

Intermediate copying of a game system's basic input/output system (BIOS) was fair use, according to the Ninth Circuit in early 2000,[6] because it was done for reverse engineering purposes (i.e., to make a game console that could play Sony PlayStation games). The functional elements in the software are entitled only to low-level copyright protection; the defendant carried out transformative use; and the reverse-engineered product didn't supersede the copyrighted product, so the use was fair. In the Ninth Circuit analysis, disassembling a program can be fair use if it is necessary to gain access to the functional elements of the software.

In February, 2000, the Southern District of New York granted a preliminary injunction against the distribution of DeCSS, a computer program used to circumvent the Content Scramble System of encryption for DVDs[7] in order to make digital copies of movies in the DVD format. Injunction was granted based on the likelihood that a violation of 17 USC §1201(a)(2), the DMCA anti-circumvention provision, would be found. The DMCA provisions have survived a First Amendment challenge based on restrictions on distribution of the program to the public.

DeCSS was made available on the Internet. The MPAA and its members moved under DMCA to have it taken off the servers. The Southern District agreed with them that DeCSS conforms to the DMCA definition, and it has no commercially significant purpose other than accessing copyright materials without consent of the copyright proprietors. (The Second Circuit heard arguments in the appeal early in 2001; at press time for the 2002 Supplement, it had not rendered its decision.)

The program is not entitled to a reverse engineering defense, because that relates to copyrighted computer programs, not "technological copyright protection schemes" within the meaning of the Act. The DMCA does provide exemptions for encryption research and security testing, but both require the consent of the copyright holder, which was signally lacking in this case.

The Southern District also rejected First Amendment-based arguments, because the First Amendment doesn't protect infringement, and the government interest in protecting copyrighted works is greater than the burden on DeCSS imposed by restricting its online distribution.

The Sixth Circuit has held computer source code to be an expression for exchanging programming information and concepts, which is therefore entitled to First Amendment protection as speech.[8] The court drew an analogy to a musical score, which can be read by people with specialized knowledge, even though it does not communicate to the general public.

In this case, the District Court had upheld the Export Administration Regulations, 15 CFR Part 730-74, against a First Amendment challenge, saying that encryption source code is inherently functional and therefore not protected as speech. (The current regulations as amended now allow export of most off-the-shelf encryption software.[9]) Although national security can outweigh speech protection, the record was not complete enough to indicate whether it should do so in this case.

On September 16, 1999, the Clinton administration eliminated most of the remaining rules that had served to prevent U.S. firms from selling strong encryption software outside the United States, although the Department of Commerce is still required to give its consent for exporting such software.[10]

Software was introduced to make the Torah (Jewish scriptures) searchable by computer. Michael Drosnin used this software to produce what he asserts are prophetic messages encoded within the Torah. Mr. Drosnin wrote a successful book, "The Bible Code," about these messages. The publisher of the software sued Drosnin for copyright infringement. However, the Southern District of New York held that searchable matrices of Torah text produced using the software are not protected by copyright, even though the software itself is copyrightable.[11]

[¶7520] E-Commerce

In July, 1999, the National Conference of Commissioners on Uniform State Laws approved the Uniform Electronic Transactions Act (UETA) and the Uniform Computer Information Transaction Act (UCITA), paving the way for adoption by state legislatures.[12] UETA adoption was unanimous; the vote on UCITA, described as "a model law that provides rules for licensing contracts between users and software vendors or vendors of information in electronic form" was 43 in favor, 6 opposed, 2 abstentions.

UETA is not substantive, merely a procedural or enabling law so electronic transactions can be effectuated. Under UETA, contracts entered into online, like electronic documents, records, and signatures, are presumed valid; there is no presumption of invalidity based on the digital nature of the communications.

An electronic signature is a sound, symbol, or process attached to or logically associated with a process and executed or adopted with the intent to sign. Therefore, an encrypted digital signature would count; so would a name at the end of an e-mail message if intended as a signature; so would a click-through that identifies its sender. However, certain documents and transactions are excluded from the reach of UETA: UCC transaction and wills, codicils, and testamentary trusts.

UCITA covers many areas: It endorses shrinkwrap licenses; subjects software licenses to the warranty rules current for goods; requires conspicuous disclaimers of warranties; permits customers to reject the Terms of Service under the license and get a full refund; allows recovery of all types of damages, including damages for injury caused by software defects; and approves choice of law clauses (the law of the forum in which the retailer is located, unless a different forum is specified). UCITA allows a licensor of software to disable the software once a license is canceled. It covers electronically transmitted information, but excludes other types of information licensing, such as those relating to print media and motion pictures. In the 1999-2000 legislative session, UCITA was introduced in the Hawaii, Illinois, New Jersey, and Oklahoma legislatures, but did not pass.[13]

In December, 1999, Pennsylvania became the first state to adopt UETA,[14] through legislation (SD 555) recognizing electronic documents and signatures used in online commercial transactions. (California already had a UETA-inspired law, but one that did not entirely follow the language proposed by the Commissioners. Therefore, effective January 15, 2000, electronic records, signatures, and writings are legal unless a notarized signature is needed [e.g., wills or trusts].) In case of dispute, the party asserting invalidity of the contract must prove it; the proponent does not have to prove the validity of the contract.

In general, any kind of e-signature can be used for any kind of e-transaction. However, in the Pennsylvania version of the law, in transactions between businesses or business and government, the business must agree at the outset of the transaction which protocol or security procedure will be used. In case of dispute, the complaining party has to prove that the contract is invalid; the other party doesn't have to prove that it's valid.

The federal act P.L. 106-229, the "Electronic Signatures in Global and National Commerce Act" (nicknamed eSign), was passed on June 30,

2000. Broadly speaking, it makes it possible to sign contracts and enter into transactions with the same legal force and effect whether consent of the parties is indicated by written signatures or electronic "signatures." Under this statute, too, an electronic signature is a "sound, symbol, or process, attached to or logically associated with a contract or other record and executed or adopted by a person with the intent to sign the record."

Documents can be acknowledged or notarized with the digital "signature" of the person making the acknowledgment or the notary. Furthermore, statutory and regulatory record retention requirements can be satisfied with digital files. However, consumers are entitled to demand hard copy instead of or as a means of memorializing an electronic agreement. Moreover, eSign does not apply to wills, codicils, testamentary trusts, or family law documents, and it applies only to Articles 2, 2A and part of Article 1 of the UCC.

States are allowed to modify, limit, or supersede eSign by adopting UETA, or by being consistent with eSign, referring to eSign itself, and by being technology-neutral rather than favoring a specific technology.

The Northern District of Illinois ruled that a pop-up license agreement displayed by a Web browser is a "writing" under the Federal Arbitration Act, even though the options for saving and printing the document were not conspicuous. Because users could create a hard copy, the arbitration agreement could be enforced.[15]

[¶7520.3] Taxation of E-Commerce

The news about the National Tax Association's two-year study of state and local taxation of e-commerce is that, in September 1999, the deliberative body surrendered, admitting its inability to reach consensus.[16]

In the same month, the Advisory Commission on Electronic Commerce (which was set up under the Internet Tax Freedom Act, main volume) solicited governors and tax experts for their suggestions about applying existing laws to the problem of Internet taxation. The Commission noted that any collection formula that is adopted must simplify the existing sales tax system; avoid imposing new taxes; not burden sellers; and protect customers' privacy.

The initial written proposal was submitted by Dean Andal, vice chair of the California State Board of Equalization; see *http://www.boe.ca.gov/members/dandal/eleccomm/eleccomm.htm.*

The tax administrators of thirty states joined in the Streamlined Sales Tax Project (SSTP), which issued model legislation under which sales tax could be collected and administered efficiently for Internet sales. The federal moratorium on "new" taxes on Internet sales is scheduled to expire in October, 2001, so it is likely that Congress will take action either to extend it or create a uniform system of sales tax administration.[17]

[¶7530] Jurisdiction in Cyberspace

The Northern District of Georgia has issued a pioneering order,[18] permitting attorneys in a bankruptcy case to serve process by e-mail—possibly the first e-mail service in North America, although e-mail service made its British debut in 1996. It is possible that the e-mail service was allowed precisely because the defendant was a foreign corporation; the court system is less likely to bypass the conventional methods of service on domestic defendants. (The Northern District of Georgia is one of nine courts in the Electronic Case File project of the Administrative Office of the U.S. Courts.) A default order was issued on August 24, after the defendant failed to respond to e-mail service on June 25.

The New York Supreme Court granted the state Attorney General an injunction to prevent an online gambling company based in Antigua (where online gambling is legal) from accepting bets placed by New York residents.[19] The court treated placing bets and using the Internet to transmit information as "gambling activity" within New York State. The casino was guilty of fraud under New York State law and also violated the federal Wire Act, Travel Act, and Interstate Transportation of Wagering Paraphernalia Act.

Early in 2000, the D.C. Circuit joined[20] the Second, Fifth, Sixth, and Ninth Circuits in holding that the mere fact that a site is accessible to residents within a forum will not support personal jurisdiction over site owners who are outside the forum. Under this analysis, Web access is like a telephone call; there's no persistent course of conduct by the site owner. Furthermore, given the very large number of Web sites, allowing jurisdiction purely on that basis would swamp conventional concepts of jurisdiction.

A Vermont company whose Web site includes an e-mail address for contacting the site owners, but does not allow online ordering (orders are supposed to be placed by mail or fax), is not subject to jurisdiction in Texas, because the Fifth Circuit ruled[21] that the site is purely passive, and the e-mail address does not offer true interaction with residents of the forum state.

In contrast, according to the Northern District of Texas, a Minnesota corporation that owns a site over which it regularly does business with Texas residents is subject to the personal jurisdiction of the federal court in Texas, in that the defendant purposefully directed contacts at Texas and sought the benefits of commercial activity within the state.[22]

A Fifth Amendment challenge to 15 USC §1125(d)(2) Anticybersquatting Consumer Protection Act failed, when the Eastern District of Virginia[23] upheld the provision that allows a trademark owner to bring an in rem proceeding against the domain name itself when personal jurisdiction against the registrant or other potential defendant is unavailable. Such an in rem proceeding can be brought in the judicial district where the registrar, registry, or other domain name authority is located, but only if the court finds that the plaintiff can't get personal jurisdiction, or despite due diligence can't locate an appropriate potential defendant.

The Eastern District did not accept the defense contention that in rem jurisdiction is constitutional only if the res has minimum contacts with the jurisdiction sufficient to support personal jurisdiction.

Where the alleged infringement consists of registration of a domain name, and an attempt to sell that name to the trademark owner, the tort of trademark infringement occurred (if at all) in the forum that is the residence of the trademark owner—even if the defendant conducted no other business activity in that forum.[24]

[¶7530.1] [NEW] ISP Safe Harbor

Communications Decency Act immunity for service providers extends to eBay, not merely to providers of bulletin-board-type services (e.g., AOL). Therefore, eBay cannot be sued in state court because of content placed on eBay by third parties, relating to the sale of pirated sound recordings.[25]

[¶7540] Domain Names

Network Solutions Inc. (NSI) is no longer the sole entity permitted to register domain names; since June, 1999, this has been a space in which competition is permitted. However, in September, 1999, NSI and the Internet Corporation for Assigned Names and Numbers (ICANN) entered into an agreement under which NSI will retain the ability to register domain names and will keep up a database of registered names for at least four years.[26]

On November 16, 2000, the Internet Corporation for Assigned Names and Numbers (ICANN) approved seven new gTLDs (classes of top-level domain name) out of 44 submitted for approval. The new gTLDs are .museum, .aero, .biz, .info, .name, .pro, and .coop. The .biz and .info domains are general commercial domains. The .aero domain is restricted to air transport services. Individuals can register .name domains for their personal use, and .pro domains will initially be issued to members of the professionals of law, medicine, and accounting; perhaps other professions will be registered later.[27]

For purposes of the federal law against the dilution of a famous trademark, a mark is only protected if it was famous when the defendant first used the allegedly diluting mark in commerce.[28] A contrary result would permit plaintiffs to delay litigation until they could establish the "fame" of their trademark.

The name tnn.com (for a computer networking firm) was held not to infringe TNN (a country music TV station), since the services identified by the marks were completely different.

A firearm manufacturer's use of "gunsareus.com" was held by the Southern District of New York not to infringe the ToysRUs trademark[29] in that the marks are not excessively similar, and toys and guns do not represent the same market. (Well, let's hope not.) Internet users are able to distinguish between such dissimilar designations. With no likelihood of confusion, a dilution action could not be maintained.

In February, 2000, the Second Circuit handed down the first appellate ruling on 15 USC §1125(d), which was enacted by the 1999 Anticybersquatting Consumer Protection Act,[30] but the holding is limited to its somewhat unusual facts and thus is not dispositive of the issue in general.

It was a trademark violation for a Christmas tree farm to use a URL confusingly similar to the logo of a well-known mail order company. Sportsman's Market has been using "Sporty's" at least since 1985, when it registered its logo as a trademark. The defendant, Omega, knew about this when it registered "sportys.com" with Network Solutions Inc. Nine months later, in 1996, Omega formed the Sporty's Farm subsidiary to grow and sell Christmas trees. Sporty's Farm brought a declaratory judgment action to be allowed to keep using sportys.com; Sportsman's counterclaimed and named Omega as third-party defendant for, inter alia, trademark dilution.

At the District Court level, it was held that "sporty's" was a famous mark entitled to protection, and was diluted by Omega and Sporty's Farm.

However, an injunction was the only relief ordered. The anticybersquatting law was enacted when the court was under appeal. The ACP was applied on appeal, because the law was enacted to assist courts in this situation.

The Second Circuit held "sporty's" to be a distinctive mark (not necessarily a "famous" one), and held "sportys.com" to be close enough to be confusingly similar.

Furthermore, there was ample evidence in the record as to bad faith. Omega didn't have any intellectual property rights in "sportys.com" when it registered the URL; the company's legal name is Omega and not Sporty's; and it didn't actually sell any Christmas trees until after the litigation began. Furthermore, Omega was planning to compete directly with Sportsman's in the aviation market, and Omega knew "sporty's" was famous within that market. The Second Circuit affirmed the injunction but also declined to award damages, because willfulness as defined by the Famous Trademark Dilution Act was not found.

This case was followed by many other cybersquatting rulings. The Eastern District of Virginia treats the two types of actions (in rem and in personam) as mutually exclusive. A plaintiff cannot sue an allegedly infringing domain name registrant in personam and simultaneously proceed in rem against the domain name itself. Furthermore, in rem jurisdiction is available only if the alleged infringer cannot be sued in personam.[31] The same court requires bad faith to be pleaded as an element of the in rem action, despite the fact that the statutory language mentions bad faith only in connection with the in personam cause of action.[32]

The domain name epix.com, registered in good faith for a site promoting video image processing and software design services in Oregon, does not infringe the trademark Epix used by an Illinois company for image processing products and services, because the two companies' businesses are not in the same market or channels of commerce.[33]

The Fourth Circuit ruled that a company called Virtual Works Inc. knew that its vw.net domain name would cause confusion with the Volkswagen trademark. Because vw.net's owners sought to obtain financial benefit from the confusion (by selling vw.net to Volkswagen), they were not acting in good faith. Virtual Works was ordered to transfer the vw.net domain name, but no money damages were ordered, because they had registered the domain name before the ACPA took effect.[34]

According to the Southern District of New York, use of someone else's trademark in metatags (indexing information used to identify Web sites) but not in the domain name is not a violation of the ACPA, because the fair use doctrine protects the use of the trademark in metatags. Because the metatags are not easily viewed by site users, they are not likely to cause confusion with the trademark, and hence there was no Lanham Act §43(a) violation.[35]

Maximum statutory damages, plus an attorney's fee award of over $30,000, were imposed in a cybersquatting case that rules that the ACPA is violated by registering domain names that are deliberate misspellings of a plaintiff's famous and distinctive domain name. This was intended to lure Web users who are then required to view 10-15 advertisements for which the infringing registrant gets paid.[36]

Even if the services are not identical, the use of remarkably similar trademarks on Web services creates a likelihood of confusion. Therefore, the Ninth Circuit enjoined Walt Disney's use of a Go Net logo that was confusingly similar to GoTo.com's logo.[37]

At the beginning of 2000, the Southern District of New York granted a preliminary injunction[38] to a wholesaler against a retail jewelry Web site with a domain name similar to the wholesaler's trademark, because the retail site could confuse the wholesaler's customers into thinking it was competing against them.

The Eastern District of Virginia declined to decide[39] whether a domain name registration constitutes "property" on which a lien can be placed, because the judgment creditor can use self-help remedies to satisfy a default judgment against an infringer. In other words, the plaintiff was required to go through the domain name dispute policy before trying to enforce the default judgment in court.

The Eastern District of Virginia deemed having the NSI cancel the infringer's domain name registration to be a superior remedy to enforcement of a personal property lien. (In an earlier ruling in the case, statutory damages of $5,000 were awarded, and the defendant was permanently enjoined against further infringing use of the mark. When the defendant failed to pay the judgment, the plaintiff sought a writ to satisfy the judgment out of the judgment debtor's personal property, i.e., the infringing domain name.)

The domain name registrar NSI is not liable for contributory trademark infringement when a third party registers a domain name that infringes an existing service mark.[40] NSI provides a service (analogous to postal service) and not a product. It doesn't control the means of infringement to an extent that would permit it to be held contributorily liable, because NSI merely registers names on request and doesn't determine the right to use the name. Therefore, although, for example, a flea market operator can be liable for contributory infringement because it supplies a marketplace for the sale of infringing goods, NSI does not exercise sufficient control over the third party's means of infringement to be liable.

The Second Circuit held that NSI did not commit any antitrust violations by refusing to adopt new generic top-level domains (gTLDs) to supplement the existing .com, .org, .edu, .gov, .net, and .mil.[41]

Although the District Court immunized NSI from antitrust liability (treating it as a federal instrumentality), the Second declined to impose a status-based analysis immunizing all government contractors from antitrust liability. But in this case, the challenged conduct was compelled by the terms of its cooperative agreement with the federal government and government policies about operating the domain name system. NSI couldn't have granted the plaintiff's request for new TLDs even if it had wanted to.

The plaintiff's (unsuccessful) contention was that domain names protected expressive speech. Although the court agreed that the existing gTLDs are communicative and theoretically protected by the First Amendment, its conclusion was that they are mere three-letter acronyms without expressive content, and any prior restraint is minimal enough to be ignored.

Merely registering a domain name with Virginia-based NSI is not an adequate minimum contact to give rise to in personam jurisdiction in Virginia, so the proceeding will have to be brought in rem, and the plaintiff will have the burden of proving lack of personal jurisdiction.[42]

A parody site that made fun of a local newspaper, using the paper's name as its URL, engaged in the "use in commerce" required by the Lanham Act.[43] The site was linked to another site used for commercial purposes, and using the paper's trademark in this way affected the paper's ability to offer its own services in commerce. The large disclaimer on the site didn't prevent initial confusion when users first got to the parody site.

At least some courts recognize a privilege of using similar domain names for comment or criticism of the registrant of the underlying name. The District Court for the District of Minnesota held that the non-commercial use in a domain name of a string of characters identical to the plaintiff's trademark was not an infringement, where the purpose was criticism of the insurer. First Amendment considerations were deemed to outweigh any initial confusion. The ACPA was not violated because the defendant did not act in bad faith.[44]

A January, 2001 WIPO case, using the UDRP procedure, holds that a domain name in the form "[Trademark]sucks.com" or that otherwise indicates a lack of affiliation with the trademark, can be maintained even over the trademark holder's objection, because the domain name is not confusingly similar to the trademark.[45]

[¶7542] Domain Name Disputes

One of the crucial characteristics of the Internet is that URLs must be unique: Only one site can have a particular URL (although the sheer volume of sites demands that many sites will have URLs that are quite similar).

In August, 1999, ICANN adopted an advisory committee recommendation that there be a mandatory ADR policy for cybersquatting allegations for .com, .org, and .net domains.[46] On October 24, 1999, ICANN approved the Uniform Domain Name Dispute Resolution Policy (UDRP), and by May, 2000, 120 decisions had already been issued.[47]

The World Intellectual Property Organization (WIPO) issued a report in April, 1999 listing factors in the determination of whether or not adoption of a URL was done in good faith in the trademark context.

For instance, it's evidence of bad faith to offer to sell, rent, or transfer the domain name back to the trademark holder for money; to attempt to confuse Web users for financial gain by using a deceptive name; to prevent the trademark owner from using the mark; or to register a domain name to interfere with a competitor's business. Factors militating against bad faith: The domain holder has legitimate fair or noncommercial use of the mark, with no intent to mislead consumers; the domain name holder is commonly known by the name (even if it doesn't have trademark rights); and there was a request for money, but only to the extent of cost reimbursement.

Reverse domain name hijacking should also be prevented: This is the situation in which a large, powerful company threatens a suit against an individual or small company that has a legitimate interest in the name.

The proposed ADR policy would mandate ADR if a third party complains of bad-faith registration, as evidenced by:

- Use of a name identical or misleadingly similar to a trademark in which the complainant has rights.
- The registrant doesn't have rights or legitimate interests in the name.
- The name has been registered and used in bad faith.

The sole remedy available is cancellation of the domain name or transfer of name to the successful complainant.

Under this proposal, domain names can't be transferred while ADR is pending, or for 15 days after the conclusion of the proceeding. Transfer during litigation or arbitration is also prohibited, unless the transferee agrees in writing to be bound by the decision.

The National Arbitration Forum Web site, *http://www.arbforum.com,* contains the reports of several domain name arbitrations. ICANN has accredited the National Arbitration Forum to carry out the Uniform Dispute Resolution policy. A February, 2000 decision, for instance, holds that a Canadian company acted in bad faith by registering a .net URL when it knew that another company had already registered its nearly identical trademark as a .com.[48] The .net registration was canceled.

The PTO issued an examination guide in September, 1999,[49] explaining that in applications for trademarks, the com, .org, and .net TLDs will be treated like (800) numbers (i.e., as essential functional prefixes and suffixes with no specific meaning), rather than as indications of the source of goods.

A domain name mark can be registered as a trademark if, but only if, it functions as a source identifier. That is, potential purchasers must perceive it as a source indication, not just an informational indication of the URL. An application to use *www.whatzis.com,* and a specimen of use in the form of an ad "visit us at *www.whatzis.com*" won't show use as a service mark.

If a business creates a site only to advertise its own products or services, the domain name can't be registered as a trademark. Nor will the PTO register a mark consisting of a surname plus a TLD, or a generic name (e.g., bank.com, chicken.com) or a purely descriptive geographic term (e.g., Boston.com).

[¶7550] Pornography

In the Ninth Circuit view, the Child Pornography Protection Act (CPPA) violates the First Amendment if it prohibits a visual depiction that appears to be or conveys the impression of a minor involved in sexual activities, because such a prohibition is a content-based restriction on speech which lacks compelling governmental interest.[50] Not only is the statutory language vague and overbroad, but it lacks the interest that would be present in protecting real children from being depicted in pornography.

In the Third Circuit view[51], preliminary injunction against enforcement of this statute is justified because it is probably overbroad and violates the First Amendment, in that it subjects publishers to the standards of all sorts of communities, even though they are unable to prevent access in communities with stricter standards as to which materials pander to the prurient interests in minors.

But the First Circuit upheld the CPPA,[52] finding that CPPA's definition of child pornography satisfies Constitutional scrutiny.

The New York state law, Penal Law §235.22, survived a Constitutional challenge in April, 2000.[53] The law penalized the combination of the transmission of sexually explicit material and an attempt to entice a minor into sexual conduct. It was sustainable because it banned a combination of speech and illegal activity, not pure speech.

California's Court of Appeals upheld a ban on knowing Internet transmission of material that is harmful to minors in conjunction with an attempt to engage a minor in sexual conduct.[54] The legislation was deemed proper under the First Amendment and the Commerce Clause. There's no undue burden on interstate commerce, because the offense requires at least an attempt at illegal conduct within California, and the law aims to deter harmful sexual conduct, not speech.

According to the Ninth Circuit,[55] downloading child pornography from the Internet to a personal computer isn't the kind of "transporting or shipping" visualized by 18 USC §2252(a)(1) when Congress enacted separate provisions for receiving–distributing and transporting–shipping child pornography. Downloading images supplied by somebody else is only a possession offense violating §2252(a)(2).

According to the District Court for the District of New Hampshire, domain name registrar NSI is not a state actor. Therefore, it did not violate the First Amendment by refusing to register sexually-oriented phrases as domain names. Even if the NSI had been a state actor, in this reading domain names are purely functional and not a forum for Constitutionally protected debate.[56]

[¶7560] Privacy Issues

The Children's Online Privacy Protection Act, P.L. 105-277, became effective during the Supplement period. On October 20, 1999, the FTC issued a final rule about the collection and use of information about child (i.e., under-13) visitors to commercial Web sites, implementing the Children's Online Privacy Protection Act, P.L. 105-277.[57]

Under the Final Rule, the operators of commercial sites targeting children must:

- Put a notice on the site as to what information is collected about child users, and how the information is used.
- Get "verifiable consent" of a parent before collecting/using/disclosing such information.
- Give parents a reasonable means to review information collected from their children.
- Give parents the ability to refuse the use of the information, and to make the site owner delete the information.
- Gather only as much information from a child as is necessary to participate in a game, win a prize, etc.
- Have procedures to protect the security, integrity, and confidentiality of personal information collected from children.

A site can legitimately provide information requested by children (rather than collecting information from them), but notice to the parent is nonetheless required. A safe harbor is provided for a one-time request by a child for help with homework. It's also permissible to enter a child in a contest or send a child an online newsletter, as long as the parent is notified and given a chance to restrict use of personal information about the child.

Verifiable consent is any reasonable effort (reasonable in light of the state of technology) to make sure parents know the site operators' practices for collection, use and disclosure of personal information, and that they authorize the information collection. For two years, a nonsecure method of obtaining consent (for instance, e-mail) can be used to get consent, but only for internal use of the information (e.g., site owner's own marketing campaign). The theory is that it's too easy for kids to pose as their parents via e-mail.

For information that will be disclosed to third parties (including visitors to chat rooms), the method of obtaining consent must be secure—for instance, a credit card, digital signature, or passworded e-mail. The FTC will reassess the security issues after two years.

For policy guidelines for safeguarding confidential information, see the Online Privacy Alliance site:

http://www.privacyalliance.org/resources/ppguidelines.shtml

and the Better Business Bureau's BBBOnline:

http://www.bbbonline.org/businesses/privacy/sample.html

An airline pilot set up a password-protected Web site to protest the airline's labor policies. He did not give access to either management or union representatives. He alleged that another pilot gave the password to an airline vice president, who was greatly angered by the content of the site. The pilot sued for violation of 18 USC §2511 (the wiretap law) and 18 USC §2701 (the Stored Communications Act, which bans unauthorized access to a facility that provides electronic communications services). Although the two federal statutes are similar, the wiretap statute permits higher civil damages. The Ninth Circuit ruled that the contents of a secure site are indeed electronic communications, and unauthorized interception of them is a wiretap.[58]

According to the Southern District of New York, it was a violation of the posted Terms of Service, and therefore a breach of contract, for an Internet service provider to extract information from a registrar's Who Is database (information about persons and companies that had registered domain names) for use in marketing.[59]

[¶7570] Linking and Framing

Deep linking (placing hyperlinks to interior pages of a site rather than to the home page) is neither a per se violation of the Copyright Act nor unfair competition—it's merely the functional equivalent of using a library card catalog to find a specific item.[60] Hyperlinking isn't copying, and it's not copyright infringement to use facts taken from publicly available Web pages.

A defendant who created links to sites containing copyrighted expression, and encouraged others to view and copy the copyrighted materials without the consent of the copyright holder, committed active encouragement of infringement and probably contributory infringement.

According to the District Court for the District of Utah,[61] browsing creates a "copy" for Copyright Act purposes, but the court wouldn't go so far as to say that mere linking generates liability for contributory copyright infringement. However, the plaintiff got a preliminary injunction barring the defendant from posting URLs that the defendant knew or had reason to know contained material infringing the plaintiff's copyrights.

ENDNOTES

1. *Sun Microsystems Inc. v. Microsoft Corp.*, 188 F.3d 1115 (9th Cir. 1999).

2. *Shurgard Storage Centers Inc. v. Safeguard Self Storage Inc.*, 119 F.Supp.2d 1121 (W.D. Wash. 2000).

3. *U.S. v. Middleton*, 231 F.3d 1207 (9th Cir. 2000).

4. D.C. Bar Legal Ethics Committee Op. 302, 11/21/00 (see 69 LW 2515); Nassau County Bar Ass'n Comm. on Prof'l Ethics Op. 01-4 (2/6/01) (see 69 LW 2541).

5. *Telecomm Technical Services Inc. v. Siemens Rolm Communications Inc.*, 68 LW 1080 (N.D. Ga. 7/6/99).

6. *Sony Computer Entertainment Inc. v. Connectix Corp.*, 203 F.3d 596 (9th Cir. 2000).

7. *Universal City Studios Inc. v. Reimerdes,* 82 F.Supp.2d 211 (S.D.N.Y. 2000). Also see Mark Hamblett, "2nd Circuit Weighs DVD Copying," *N.Y.L.J.* 5/2/01, available on law.com, for a discussion of the argument before the Second Circuit in the appeal of this case. The main issues were whether the DMCA is unconstitutional on First Amendment grounds versus the entertainment industry's argument that publishing DeCSS code on the Internet is the equivalent of publicizing the combination of a bank safe or interfering with the operation of smoke detectors.

8. *Junger v. Daley,* 68 LW 1602 (6th Cir. 4/4/00).

9. *Bernstein v. DOJ,* 176 F.3d 1132 (9th Cir. 1999) held the export regulations to be an unconstitutional prior restraint on speech, but the decision was withdrawn, 192 F.3d 1308 (also 9th Cir. 1999) when the Ninth Circuit decided the case en banc, and then remanded it to the three-judge appellate panel after the regulations were amended.

10. See 68 LW 2186.

11. *Torah Soft Ltd. v. Drosnin*, 00 Civ. 5650 (SAS), discussed in Michael A. Ricca, "Copyright Infringement Charges Dismissed Against 'Bible Code' Author," *N.Y.L.J.* 4/3/01, available on law.com.

12. See 68 LW 2069.

13. See "Uniform Software Law Headed for Nearly a Dozen States, Battles Looming All Around," (no by-line), 69 LW 2182 (10/3/00).

14. *http://www.legis.state.pa.us/wu01/li/bi/bt/1999/0/sb0555p1555.htm;* discussed at 68 LW 2358.

15. *In re Real Networks Inc. Privacy Litigation*, 68 LW 1767 (N.D. Ill. 5/8/00).

16. See 68 LW 2158.

17. The model state law can be found at http://www.streamlinedsalestax.org. See "State and Federal Officials Attempt to Resolve Internet Tax Dilemma," (no by-line), 69 LW 2510 (2/27/01).

18. *International Telemedia Assn. Inc. v. Diaz;* see 68 LW 2167.

19. *New York v. World Interactive Gaming Corp.*, 68 LW 1112 (N.Y. Sup. 7/22/99).

20. *GTE New Media Services Inc. v. BellSouth Corp.*, 201 F.3d 168 (D.C. Cir. 2000).

21. *Mink v. AAAA Development*, 190 F.3d 333 (5th Cir. 1999). Also see *Telebyte Inc. v. Kendaco Inc.*, 105 F.Supp.2d 231 (E.D.N.Y. 2000): New York court does not have jurisdiction over a trademark infringement suit merely because New Yorkers could access the Washington-based Web site that allegedly infringed the plaintiff's trademark.

22. *American Eyewear Inc. v. Peeper's Sunglasses and Accessories Inc.*, 68 LW 1767 (N.D. Tex. 5/16/00).

23. *Caesars World Inc. v. Caesars-Palace.com*, 68 LW 1558 (E.D. Va. 3/3/00).

24. *McRae's Inc. v. Hussain*, 105 F.Supp.2d 594 (S.D. Miss. 2000).

25. *Stoner v. EBay Inc.*, 69 LW 1320 (Cal.Super. 11/7/00).

26. Text of the agreement: *http://www.icann.org*, discussed at 68 LW 2187.

27. See "ICANN Approves Seven Top-Level Domains; Winners Continue to Negotiate Fine Print" (no by-line), 69 LW 2329 (12/5/00).

28. *The Network Network [sic] v. CBS Inc.*, 68 LW 1592 (C.D. Cal. 1/18/00).

29. *Toys "R" Us Inc. v. Feinberg*, 26 F.Supp.2d 639 (S.D.N.Y. 10/28/99).

30. *Sporty's Farm LLC v. Sportsman's Market Inc.*, 202 F.3d 489 (2nd Cir. 2000).

31. *Alitalia Linee Aree Italianee SpA v. Casinoalitalia.com*, 128 F.Supp.2d 340 (E.D. Va. 2001).

32. *Harrods Ltd. v. Sixty Internet Domain Names*, 110 F.Supp.2d 420 (E.D. Va. 2000).

33. *Interstellar Starship Services Inc. v. Epix Inc.*, 69 LW 1432 (D. Ore. 1/3/01).

34. *Virtual Works Inc. v. Volkswagen of America Inc.*, 238 F.3d 264 (4th Cir. 2001).

35. *Bihari v. Gross*, 69 LW 1240 (S.D.N.Y. 9/25/00).

36. *Electronics Boutique Holdings Corp. v. Zaccarini*, 69 LW 1286 (E.D. Pa. 10/30/00).

37. *GoTo.com Inc. v. Walt Disney Co.*, 202 F.3d 1199 (9th Cir. 2000).

38. *First Jewellery [sic] Company of Canada Inc. v. Internet Shopping*, 68 LW 1512 (S.D.N.Y. 1/31/00).

39. *Dorer v. Arel*, 60 F.Supp.2d 558 (E.D. Va. 9/3/99).

40. *Lockheed Martin Corp. v. Network Solutions Inc.*, 177 F.3d 1310 (9th Cir. 1999) and 194 F.3d 980 (9th Cir. 1999), followed in *Bird v. Parsons*, 127 F.Supp.2d 885 (S.D. Oh. 11/27/00).

41. *Name.Space Inc. v. NSI*, 202 F.3d 573 (2nd Cir. 2000).

42. *AOL v. Huang*, 106 F.Supp.2d 848 (E.D. Va. 2000); *Heathmount A.E. Corp. v. Technodome.com*, 106 F.Supp.2d 860 (E.D. Va. 2000).

43. *OBH Inc. v. Spotlight Magazine Inc.*, 86 F. Supp.2d 176 (W.D.N.Y. 2000).

44. *Northland Ins. Cos. v. Blaylock*, 115 F.Supp.2d 1108 (D.Minn. 2000).

45. *Lockheed Martin Corp. v. Parisi*, http://arbiter.wipo.int/domains/decisions/html/2000/d2000-1015.html; there is no www in this domain name. Also see *Bally Total Fitness v. Faber*, 29 F.Supp.2d 1161 (C.D. Cal. 1998), dismissing a complaint because Bally would not be able to prove confusion from the use of ballysucks.com as a domain name.

46. See 68 LW 2139. The WIPO final report can be accessed at *http://wipo2.wipo.int/process/eng/processhome.html*, and the Model Domain Name Dispute Resolution Policy at *http://www.icann.org/santiago/registrar-dispute-policy.htm*

47. The UDRP text is posted at *http://www.icann.org/udrp.* and discussed at, e.g., John Caher, "New Domain Arbitration Rules Get Results," *N.Y.L.J.* 3/14/2000, available through *http://www.law.com;* Amy Benjamin, "Proceedings Under UDRP Are Off and Running," *Nat.L.J.* 5100 p. C1.

48. *Fiber-Shield Industries Inc. v. Fiber Shield Ltd.*, 2/29/00, see 68 LW 2558.

49. Examination Guide No. 2-99, 299, *http://www.uspto.gov/web/offices/tac/notices/guide299.htm.*

50. *Free Speech Coalition v. Reno*, 198 F.3d 1083 (9th Cir. 1999).

51. *ACLU v. Reno*, 217 F.3d 162 (3rd Cir. 2000).

52. *U.S. v. Hilton,* 167 F.3d 61 (1st Cir. 1999).

53. *People v. Foley,* (N.Y. 4/11/00), discussed in John Caher, "NYS Internet Porn Law Upheld," *N.Y.L.J.* 4/12/00, available at *http://www.law.com.*

54. *Hatch v. Superior Court of San Diego County,* 68 LW 1640 (Cal. App. 3/31/00).

55. *U.S. v. Mohrbacher,* 182 F.3d 1041 (9th Cir. 1999).

56. *National A-1 Advertising Inc. v. Network Solutions Inc.,* 69 LW 1224 (D.N.H. 9/28/00); semble *Island Online Inc. v. NSI,* 119 F.Supp.2d 289 (E.D.N.Y. 2000).

57. See *http://www.ftc.gov/os/1999/9910/childrensprivacy.pdf,* discussed by Doug Brown, "The COPPA Is Now Patrolling the Net," *Inter@ctive Week* 3/13/00. The FTC's proposed guidelines for industry self-regulation under the COPPA safe harbor provision appear at 16 CFR §312.10(a).

58. *Konop v. Hawaiian Airlines Inc.,* 236 F.3d 1035 (9th Cir. 2001).

59. *Register.Com Inc. v. Verio Inc.,* 69 LW 1400 (S.D.N.Y. 12/8/00).

60. *Ticketmaster Corp. v. Tickets.com Inc.,* 68 LW 1624 (C.D. Cal. 3/27/00). See Richard Raysman and Peter Brown, "Recent Linking Issues," *N.Y.L.J.* 2/8/00 p. 3, including suggested drafting points for linking agreements.

61. *Intellectual Reserve Inc. v. Utah Lighthouse Ministry Co.,* 75 F.Supp.2d 1290 (D. Utah 1999).

THE 33 BEST WEB SITES FOR LEGAL PROFESSIONALS

The Internet and the legal profession are a perfect match for each other. The growth of data storage technologies and the popularization of Internet tools have opened a vast range of new data to the legal community. The ability to search through cases, laws, precedents, and opinions on a vast and varied array of topics is an invaluable research tool, as well as a great time-saver.

Navigating the online legal world, however, can be a challenging task. The Internet can be simultaneously a richly rewarding and a frustrating source of legal information. You can waste hours searching through a maze of diverse topics for the specific answers you need, or you can click on well-constructed sites that offer useful information, advice, and direct links to even more information.

What are the best legal Web sites—the ones that every legal professional should know about? We present 33 valuable legal Web sites that will give you immediate access to the information necessary to do your job.

Our purpose is to direct you to the most useful legal Web sites. We have tried to offer a variety, each site with something a little different to offer. Some of these Web sites are maintained by law schools or law libraries, some are provided by law firms, some are government sites, some are even fee-based sites.

A well-designed Web site should clearly identify the resources available when you first arrive at its home page. Look over the Table of Contents or Index for the site or review the list of Frequently Asked Questions (FAQ). Take time to search through the available material in each site. Look for specific information of interest to you. Or search for categories that would help you in your work—court cases, laws and regulations, legal organizations, legal forms, etc.

As you visit each Web site and search it's resources, you'll find the ones that are best suited to your own purposes as an individual or to those of your firm. Those sites should be added to your personal bookmark list. You'll find the Internet is the best legal research tool ever developed.

American Association of Law Libraries

www.aallnet.org

The American Association of Law Libraries (AALL) was founded in 1906 to promote and enhance the value of law libraries to the legal and public communities. This Web site offers links to a wide range of primary and secondary sources on a variety of legal subjects. There is direct access to more than 90 law libraries, all law-related journals on the Internet, federal, state and international laws, and many other sources for legal research. Also worthwhile are clear guidelines and practical advice on understanding and using the Internet to perform legal research.

American Bar Association

www.abanet.org

With more than 400,000 members, the American Bar Association is the world's largest voluntary professional membership organization. The ABA's Web site provides information on educational opportunities, upcoming events, and membership benefits. You can also access legal forums and discussion groups or review the *ABA Journal.* The ABA has access to expert opinions, quality research, and objective, high-quality reports and information. Plus, the ABA offers a national platform to exchange ideas, discuss ethics, and explore important legal issues. All in all, this is a well-outfitted site considered by many to be the key nexus point for legal information on the Web.

The Bankruptcy Lawfinder

www.agin.com/lawfind

Created by the law offices of Warren E. Agin, this is a large collection of sites related to personal or business bankruptcy. Review case law, statutes and regulations, or link to federal government bankruptcy-related resources.

The Center for Corporate Law

www.law.uc.edu/CCL

The Center for Corporate Law site is maintained by the University of Cincinnati College of Law. Here you'll find the full text of federal securities laws and accompanying forms and instructions. For example, click on

The Securities Act of 1933 and find the full hypertext version. Also included are the Rules and Forms promulgated under that Act, Regulation S-K, The Securities Exchange Act of 1934, and the Rules promulgated under that Act.

Chicago-Kent College of Law

www.kentlaw.edu

This Web server is maintained by the Chicago-Kent School of Law's Center for Law and Computers. Scroll down to Legal Resources to find an archive of legal-related mailing lists and discussion groups on the Net. You'll also find an updated library of cases heard by the U.S. Court of Appeals Seventh Circuit. Links to law libraries and law schools appear here as well. Via this site you can also receive updates on the program's Electronic Publishing Initiative and the Illinois Institute of Technology.

Commercial Law League of America

www.clla.org.

This trade organization is composed of attorneys who specialize in commercial law, collections, reorganization, and bankruptcy. Read articles of interest, review membership opportunities, access professional certificate programs, receive updates on changes in national bankruptcy law, or contact other associations and organizations of interest to CLLA members.

Findlaw

www.findlaw.com

FindLaw offers an impressive array of free resources and tools for lawyers and other legal professionals. The site has a comprehensive guide to everything of a legal nature on the Web, including links to resources in over 30 practice areas, case law and codes, legal associations, law schools, law reviews, and legal publishers. FindLaw also offers free federal and state laws and links to courts and other databases on the Internet. There are daily updates of new regulations and laws, the latest legal news updated throughout the day, an extensive legal dictionary and even a small business center, offering step-by-step checklists, model business plans, legal and other business forms, and other business documents.

Georgetown University Law Library

www.ll.georgetown.edu

The Edward Bennett Williams Library of the Georgetown University Law Center has built an extremely valuable online collection of resources by selecting, organizing, and creating information on the Internet. The site offers access to law-related Web sites concerning federal law, state and local law, and foreign law, as well as more than 80 specific topic areas. There are links to legal journals and periodicals and to various legal research tools.

Global Legal Information Network

lcweb2.loc.gov/law/GLINv1

The Global Legal Information Network (GLIN) maintains and provides a database of laws, regulations, and other complementary legal sources. The documents included in the database are contributed by the governments of the member nations from the original official texts, which are deposited, by agreement of the members, in a server initially at The Library of Congress of the United States of America.
The basic elements of this database are:

1. Full texts of the documents in the official language of the country of origin;
2. Summaries or abstracts in English; and
3. Thesauri in English and in as many official languages as are represented in the database. The summaries or abstracts are linked electronically to the corresponding full texts.

Currently, information can be searched in English using the instructions appearing on the screen.

Government Printing Office

www.access.gpo.gov

The United States Government Printing Office is a useful source of an enormous amount of free online legal information available from the federal government. GPO Access is one of the few government Web sites established by law and one of the longest running. It is virtually the only government Web site that provides easy, one-stop, no-fee access to information from all three branches of the government. GPO Access links the public to nearly 105,000 individual titles on GPO's servers and an additional 68,000 titles on other federal Web sites. In 1999, GPO Access was selected as one of the top legal research Web sites by *Law Office Computing* magazine and was named best research site for laws and best government site overall by the newsletter *legal.com.*

Hieros Gamos

www.hg.org

Hieros Gamos is a comprehensive law and government portal with lots of content not found anywhere else on the Internet. The site includes links to information on more than 200 legal topics ranging from Aboriginal Peoples to Worker Compensation. The organization and format of each topic is consistent from supranational to local. Automatic searches of other sites or search engines have been predefined to save time. As a result, virtually everything online is directly accessible. Hieros Gamos also includes an Internet Law Library with a select group of documents that can be accessed directly.

Indiana University Virtual Law Library

www.law.indiana.edu/v-lib

In 1992, Indiana University School of Law–Bloomington was chosen by CERN, originators of the World Wide Web Consortium, to be host of the Virtual Law Library. Material within the Virtual Law Library is arranged by organization type (e.g., U.S. Government Servers) and by legal topic (e.g., Contracts). There is also a list of search tools and other comprehensive sites for law.

Internet Legal Resource Guide

www.ilrg.com

The Internet Legal Resource Guide is a categorized index of more than 400 select Web sites in 238 nations, islands, and territories, as well as more than 850 locally stored web pages and downloadable files. This site was established to serve as a comprehensive resource of the information available on the Internet concerning law and the legal profession, with an emphasis on the United States of America. Designed for everyone, it is quality controlled to include only the most substantive legal resources online. The selection criteria are predicated on two principles: the extent to which the resource is unique, as well as the relative value of the information it provides. This Web site is constantly undergoing enhancements and development. New materials are added regularly.

Jurist

www.jurist.law.pitt.edu

Launched at the University of Pittsburgh School of Law in March 1997, *Jurist: The Legal Education Network* is dedicated to advancing the study and understanding of law by providing an authoritative noncommercial forum in which law professors, students, lawyers, judges, journalists, and citizens can share a wide range of legal information and ideas. Experts review online legal resources in their chosen legal fields, as well as produce and edit material in the specific topic area.

Lawguru

www.lawguru.com

LawGuru offers an interesting array of legal information. There are searchable resources for every state, including cases, court opinions, codes, statutes, and bills. From the Legal Resource page, you have direct access to more than 500 legal search engines and a multiple search tool that allows you to search different legal sources from one search box. There is an Internet Law Library with search capability and extensive information on legal employment. On the lighter side is a section on Weird Laws past and present. You can search over 13,000 previously posted legal questions and answers, or ask your own free questions. (You can also join the Attorney Network for free.)

Law Library Resources Xchange

www.llrx.com

LLRX.com is a free Web journal with a special focus on a range of research and technology-related issues for legal professionals. Continuously published since 1996, the site is updated on the 1st and 15th of each month. *LLRX.com* delivers current information on a broad range of topics, offers new and specialized Web sites for legal researchers, technology training sources, reviews of software and online legal database sources, resources for intranets, books on technology topics, and seminar materials and presentations from leading legal and library-related technology conferences.

Lawlinks

www.lawlinks.com

LawLinks represents a comprehensive accumulation of resources linking the legal community. The site offers links to an extensive variety of information, including legal subjects of all types, court decisions, state codes, courtroom and trial procedure, ethics and professional responsibility, professional development, legal support services, and templates of legal documents.

Lawlinks Index

www.kentlaw.edu/clc/lrs/lawlinks

This is a collection of online legal resources from the Chicago-Kent School of Law. Search for resources by a drop-down menu of topics or run a keyword search using their engine. The hotlists indexed here are organized by legal subject, including law schools, libraries, and specialized areas of law: Computer, Environmental, Intellectual Property, Dispute Resolution, and Taxes.

Law News Network

www.lawnewsnetwork.com

Law News Network claims to be the most current and complete source for legal news anywhere. It is updated every business day and offers all original content. These are not news service stories you've already seen in a dozen other places. Law News Network specializes in news stories that cannot be found elsewhere. As a result, legal professionals are able to stay abreast of the latest legal developments. In addition to news, Law News Network offers an Op-Ed section called Open Court, featuring commentary on a wide range of hot-button issues. There are also legal Practice Centers that bring you all the information you need to stay current in your area of specialty.

Laws.com

www.laws.com

LAWS.com claims that it selects only the best, most useful legal Web sites, rather than linking to every law-related site ever created. The site's law resources are broken into multi-function services, topical directories, link indices, court decisions, miscellaneous legal information, and major law firm libraries.

LawSitus

www.lawsitus.com

LawSitus is an easy-to-use starting point for legal research on the Internet. Updated frequently, LawSitus is organized around a simple and uncluttered user interface, is concise and comprehensive, and is free to all without registration. The LawSitus home page contains a table of colored buttons organized into a rough hierarchy around types of material and their relative legal authority. Red buttons are mostly primary sources, green mostly secondary material, and blue buttons are for other information, such as today's news. Clicking a button on the home page retrieves a list of links to publicly accessible databases on the Internet. When several sources of the same or similar information exist on the Internet, only two or three preferred links are listed. For user convenience, a search interface is also included where possible.

Laws Online

www.lawsonline.com

Laws Online is a straightforward and extensive listing of World Wide Web sites dealing with all aspects of law. In addition to the comprehensive listing of legal sites for research, there are directories for such areas as collection, expert witnesses, investigators, process servers, and information brokers.

Legal Forum

www.compuserve.com

[Keyword: lawsig]

This is Compuserve's forum for attorneys and other legal professionals. The Legal Forum offers a virtual watering hole for lawyers to share cases, research tips, and even briefs, online. Post your query on their moderated message boards to solicit responses from other Forum members and the site's Sysops, or download case studies and court opinions from the Forum Library. There is even an area where you can upload a profile of your practice. New users of the Legal Forum should review the New Members Guide under the Forum Notices. You can use the Notices to scan a list of upcoming virtual conferences hosted on this site. Recommended for practitioners of business law.

Legal Information Institute

www.law.cornell.edu

The Legal Information Institute (LII) is headquartered at the Cornell School of Law. Its server offers Gopher-based and WWW-based access to one of the nation's premier collections of legal research tools. Among the document sets available though LII are hypertext versions of all recent Supreme Court decisions, the full U.S. Code, and archives of the *Cornell Law Review.* The site is indexed by source and legal topics, and offers a refreshed selection of items relevant to current legal news and topics.

First-time visitors to the LII site should begin by reviewing What is LII? and The LII's Evolving WWW Standard. Most researchers will begin at LII's parallel topic and source type main menus. The topic menu includes such topics as Constitutional Law and Copyright Law, while the source type menu itemizes material based on its source (Treaty, Legislation, and so on). Researchers looking for federal court rulings can access a searchable index of all U.S. Circuit Court Decisions. You can even hear a RealAudio archive of Supreme Court oral arguments. Track down the e-mail address of faculty or staff at U.S. law schools through the site's e-mail address directory, or link to indexes of other legal information on the Web. This site is a good reference point for a comprehensive legal research project.

Lexis-Nexis

www.lexis-nexis.com

LEXIS-NEXIS makes a credible claim to be the world's premier provider of online business and legal information. The LEXIS legal database and its companion, the NEXIS news database, contain over 28,000 information sources, and the two services support an estimated 400,000 searches every day. In total, LEXIS-NEXIS offers access to the full text of over 2.5 billion documents online. Users wishing to perform searches have the option of the simple, menu-driven Easy Search, full Boolean searches, or a plain English FREESTYLE search.

Not surprisingly, the extensive services of LEXIS-NEXIS come at a price. Pricing plans for the LEXIS-NEXIS services are customized to accommodate the research needs of each firm, company, and individual. Access to LEXIS-NEXIS via the Internet is available through Telnet only. You can also subscribe to the Eclipse feature, which provides an electronic clipping service that saves your search and updates it with new information every day, week, or month. You can even have the LEXIS-NEXIS staff do your searching for you, at a specific charge per minute of online search time. There is nothing else like LEXIS-NEXIS, but its pricing structure means you can rack up significant charges with even a simple search. For someone with regular legal research needs, LEXIS can be indispensable. But for an individual with only the occasional research task, LEXIS-NEXIS should probably be your last stop after all other (cheaper) resources are exhausted.

Loislaw.com

www.loislaw.com

Loislaw.com is a subscription-based legal research site similar to LEXIS and Westlaw. While it does not offer all of the services provided by the other two subscription-based legal Web sites, Loislaw is sufficient for many legal research purposes without the expense of using LEXIS or Westlaw.

Loislaw has more than 8.8 million documents of official law available. Loislaw publishes case law, statutory law, constitutions, administrative law, court rules, and other authority for all 50 states and Washington, D.C., plus the 18 most important federal law libraries. New case law and legislative acts are typically available electronically within 24 to 72 hours of their receipt from the courts and the legislature or other official source. As a subscriber to Loislaw, you can search through state and federal cases, statutes, and regulations from multiple jurisdictions at the same time, cite-check case law and statutes electronically, save searches for re-use, and activate LOIS LawWatch to automatically notify you whenever a new case or Act that fits your search criteria is published by *Loislaw.com*.

Magagni Research Guide to International Law on the Internet

www.spfo.unibo.it/spolfo/ILGUIDE

This site is useful for anyone searching for international law materials and information on the Internet. The Magagni Research Guide provides a wide range of selected and annotated links. You can research databases in such areas as international criminal law, environmental law, law of the sea, air and space law, international trade law, human rights, and humanitarian laws of armed conflicts, as well as search through the international law library database. While the major focus is international law, many of the links will help you search for material in other legal areas as well.

Megalaw.com

www.megalaw.com

MegaLaw.com provides an easy-to-use Internet site that gives legal professionals quick, comprehensive access to information and products that meet their professional and personal needs. The site has specific legal research at the federal, state and local levels, has valuable information on more than 100 legal topics, and links to many other topical law indexes on the Web. MegaLaw offers legal forms by subject, and links to law schools, legal organizations, experts and consultants, law jobs, and four different legal dictionaries. In addition, there is an extensive guide to Law Practice Management Resources, including law practice management sites, software and technology Web sites, and law practice management services.

The Mining Company—Current Events—Law

law.miningco.com/newissues/law

A part of *About.com*'s wide network of topical areas, this site maintains an interesting assortment of legal links and topics, as well as provides the latest developments in a variety of legal areas. You can read the opinions of others, ask questions, participate in current discussions, and submit your own proposed articles and commentary. There is a local law and government index linking to local and regional legal resources throughout the United States and Canada. Each link takes you to the Legal/Government Resources page of an *About.com* Local Guide.

P-Law Legal Resource Locator

www.perrysklaw.com/plaw

The P-Law Legal Resource Locator is a well-designed menu of legal sites broken down into categories. The focus is on legal research aids for attorneys, paralegals, and even nonlegal professionals. Categories of sites include Legislative and Other Government Information Sites, Multi-Category Reference Sites, Specialized Topic Sites, Statistical Sites, and Miscellaneous Sites. There is also a new section called the New York State and Federal Cases, where you will find links to a number of important outside databases of legal documents and case histories, the most important of which are described on these pages.

Rominger Legal

www.romingerlegal.com

Rominger Legal is a free legal research site designed specifically to meet the online research needs of attorneys and legal professionals. This easy-to-use Web site provides legal research links, case law, statutes, regulations, and other law-related information. There are also professional directories listing consultants, court reporters, document retrievers, expert witnesses, private investigators, and process servers.

Stanford Journal
of Law, Business & Finance

www.stanford.edu/group/sjlbf

The Stanford Journal of Law, Business & Finance provides a place for academics and businesspersons to examine emerging legal issues in business and finance. This high-quality, specialized journal is published by the Stanford Law School. The articles are written by professors, law students, and guest writers from prominent law firms. Each issue also features a set of Case Studies that explore specific business deals and include analysis by real-world practitioners. Topics covered by the biannual journal include regulations of financial derivatives, securities litigation reform, and emerging capital markets. The Journal's Web site provides access to the current issue and an archive of past issues, as well as a preview of what's coming in the future. You can preview specific articles in each issue by reading a provided abstract, and can order the print version of any issue for $20. Subscriptions to the Journal are $36. This site is worth a look by attorneys, law students, and financial management professionals.

Westlaw

www.westlaw.com

Westlaw is a subscription-based legal and business research tool for the Internet. Through Westlaw, subscribers have immediate, 24-hour access to over 13,000 databases (billions of pages of information) at their finger-tips. Westlaw offers an array of powerful research tools customized to meet the subscriber's needs. Subscription rates vary according to legal research needs and the number of individuals who will have access to the service.

Subscribers can conduct complete legal and business research on Westlaw, check citations, customize their intranet or active desktop with links to Westlaw, build a table of authorities, and find citing cases. While Westlaw contains over 13,000 databases of information spanning a variety of jurisdictions, practice areas, and disciplines, it's easy to pinpoint just the information desired. You can access federal and state statutes and court cases, federal regulations, KeyCite citation information, public records and court dockets, Westlaw news and business information, insurance materi-als, securities law information, tax law information, and legal forms. Using Westlaw, you can retrieve a single document, verify cases with an online citator, access just your state-specific documents, or search hundreds of databases at once. You can search for information on Westlaw using either Boolean or plain English search methods.

INDEX

Note: All references are to paragraph numbers, not pages.

A

Administration (of estates), 3170.3, 3180
Adoption, 3060, 3310
Advertising (by attorneys), 7010.47
Age Discrimination in Employment Act
    (ADEA), 353
Alimony, 3020.6
Americans with Disabilities Act (ADA), 354
Antenuptial agreements, 3005
Antitrust, 453, 800-840, 1301, 5050, 7540
Appeals, 801, 2195, 3370.2, 5600, 6087
Arbitration, 315, 601, 2010, 4400, 5670,
    7542
Asylum (immigration), 3301, 3315
At-will employment, 351
Attorneys' fees, 310, 2192, 3020.6, 7060,
    7060.3
Automatic stay, 2160
Automobile insurance, 1440

B

Bad faith (insurance), 1480
Bankruptcy, 310, 2100-2196, 3020.2,
    3020.3, 3030.2, 3240, 4195, 4350,
    4350.4, 4360, 7040.1, 7060.3, 7060.5
Business taxes, 400-458

C

Chapter 7 (bankruptcy), 2110.1, 2160,
    3020.3
Chapter 11 (bankruptcy), 2105, 2170
Chapter 13 (bankruptcy), 2110.1
Checks, 220.4
Child custody, 3030.1
Child support, 2190.1, 3030.2
Civil procedure, 5000-5670
Civil union, 3010
Class actions, 1260, 2001, 3260, 5080.5,
    7060
Clayton Act, 801, 5050
Clean Air Act (CAA), 1230

Clean Water Act (CWA), 1220
Collective bargaining agreements (CBAs),
    310
Commercial transactions, 205-280.3
Community property, 340, 3020.3
Comprehensive Environmental Response,
    Compensation and Liability Act
    (CERCLA), 1210, 1210.1
Computer crime, 6002
Computers and Internet, 7070, 7500-7570
Confidentiality, 7001, 7010.6
Conflict of interest, 7010.7
Contribution, 1210.2
Copyright, 810, 1301, 1310-1310.11,
    7515, 7570
Corporate tax, 450
Credit and collections, 2000-2060
Criminal Law, 6000-6090
    Appeals, 6087
    Capacity, 6003
    Computers, 6002
    Death penalty, 6085
    Defenses, 6005
    Discovery, 6055
    Evidence, 6065
    Forfeiture, 6040.6
    Jury trial, 6065
    Mistrial, 6067
    Offenses, 6002, 6020
    Pleas, 6060
    Prison litigation, 6090
    Privacy, 6030.4.1
    RICO, 6020.10
    Search and seizure, 6030.4, 6030.7,
        6030.8
    Self-incrimination, 6035
    Sentencing, 6080
    Sex offenses, 6020.3
    Sixth Amendment, 6040
    Stops, 6030.8
    Vehicles, 6030.7

D

Death penalty, 6085